Building an
Optimizing Compiler

Digital Press Editorial Board

Samuel Fuller, Chairman

Scott E. Cutler

Donald Z. Harbert

Richard G. Hollingsworth

James E. Kuenzel

William Laing

Richard F. Lary

Alan G. Nemeth

Robert M. Supnik

Building an Optimizing Compiler

Robert Morgan

Butterworth–Heinemann
Boston   Oxford   Johannesburg   Melbourne   New Delhi   Singapore

Digital Press is an imprint of Butterworth-Heinemann

Copyright 1998 by Butterworth-Heinemann

 A member of the Reed Elsevier Group

All rights reserved.

No part of this publication may be reproduced, stored in a retrieval system, or transmitted in any form or by any means, electronic, mechanical, photocopying, recording, or otherwise, without the prior written permission of the publisher.

All trademarks found herein are the property of their respective owners.

 Recognizing the importance of preserving what has been written, Butterworth-Heinemann prints its books on acid-free paper whenever possible.

 Butterworth-Heinemann supports the efforts of American Forests and the Global ReLeaf program in its campaign for the betterment of trees, forests, and our environment.

ISBN 1-55558-179-X

The publisher offers special discounts on bulk orders of this book.
For information, please contact:
Manager of Special Sales
Butterworth-Heinemann
225 Wildwood Avenue
Woburn, MA 01801-2041
Tel: 781-904-2500
Fax: 781-904-2620

For information on all Digital Press books available, contact our World Wide Web home page at: http://www.bh.com/digitalpress

Order number: EY-W907E-DP

10 9 8 7 6 5 4 3 2
Printed in the United States of America

Dedication

*I dedicate this book to some of the people
who have inspired me. My mother and father, Florence
and Charles William Morgan, taught me the concept of work.
Jordan Baruch introduced me to the wonders of Computer
Research. Louis Pitt, Jr., and Bill Clough have been
instrumental in helping me understand life and the spirit.
My wife, Leigh Morgan, has taught me that there is more
than computers and books—there is also life.*

CONTENTS

PREFACE xi

1 OVERVIEW 1
1.1 What Is an Optimizing Compiler? 1
1.2 A Biased History of Optimizing Compilers 2
1.3 What Have We Gained with All of This Technology? 4
1.4 Rules of the Compiler Back-End Game 5
1.5 Benchmarks and Designing a Compiler 6
1.6 Outline of This Book 7
1.7 Using This Book as a Textbook 8
1.8 References 11

2 COMPILER STRUCTURE 12
2.1 Outline of the Compiler Structure 13
2.2 Compiler Front End 21
2.3 Building the Flow Graph 24
2.4 Dominator Optimizations 29
2.5 Interprocedural Analysis 34
2.6 Dependence Optimization 35
2.7 Global Optimization 37
2.8 Limiting Resources 46
2.9 Instruction Scheduling 54
2.10 Register Allocation 58
2.11 Rescheduling 62
2.12 Forming the Object Module 63
2.13 References 63

3 GRAPHS 64
3.1 Directed Graphs 65
3.2 Depth-First Search 67
3.3 Dominator Relation 70
3.4 Postdominators 74
3.5 Dominance Frontier 75

Contents

- 3.6 Control Dependence 77
- 3.7 Loops and the Loop Tree 80
- 3.8 Implementing Sets of Integers 90
- 3.9 References 93

4 FLOW GRAPH 94
- 4.1 How Are Procedures Stored? 94
- 4.2 Should the Representation Be Lowered? 98
- 4.3 Building the Flow Graph 100
- 4.4 Structure of Data 112
- 4.5 Structure of Blocks 112
- 4.6 Structure of Instructions 113
- 4.7 Structure of Program Flow Graph 113
- 4.8 Classifying Temporaries 115
- 4.9 Local Optimization Information 117
- 4.10 Global Anticipated Information 121
- 4.11 Global Partial Redundancy Information 124
- 4.12 Global Available Temporary Information 126
- 4.13 Lifetime Analysis 132
- 4.14 References 136

5 LOCAL OPTIMIZATION 137
- 5.1 Optimizations while Building the Flow Graph 139
- 5.2 How to Encode the Pattern Matching 144
- 5.3 Why Bother with All of These Identities? 145
- 5.4 References 146

6 ALIAS ANALYSIS 147
- 6.1 Level of Alias Analysis 150
- 6.2 Representing the *modifies* Relation 151
- 6.3 Building the Tag Table 154
- 6.4 Two Kinds of Modifications: Direct and Indirect 155
- 6.5 The Modification Information Used in Building the Flow Graph 157
- 6.6 Tags for Heap Allocation Operations 158
- 6.7 More Complete Modification Information 159
- 6.8 Including the Effects of Local Expressions 161
- 6.9 Small Amount of Flow-Sensitive Information by Optimization 162
- 6.10 References 164

7 STATIC SINGLE ASSIGNMENT 165
- 7.1 Creating Static Single Assignment Form 167
- 7.2 Renaming the Temporaries 174
- 7.3 Translating from SSA to Normal Form 176
- 7.4 References 186

8 DOMINATOR-BASED OPTIMIZATION 187
- 8.1 Adding Optimizations to the Renaming Process 189
- 8.2 Storing Information as well as Optimizations 192
- 8.3 Constant Propagation 193
- 8.4 Computing Loop-Invariant Temporaries 204
- 8.5 Computing Induction Variables 208
- 8.6 Reshaping Expressions 212
- 8.7 Strength Reduction 216
- 8.8 Reforming the Expressions of the Flow Graph 218
- 8.9 Dead-Code Elimination 219
- 8.10 Global Value Numbering 222
- 8.11 References 231

9 ADVANCED TECHNIQUES 232
- 9.1 Interprocedural Analysis 232
- 9.2 Inlining Procedures 236
- 9.3 Cloning Procedures 239
- 9.4 Simple Procedure-Level Optimization 239
- 9.5 Dependence Analysis 240
- 9.6 Dependence-Based Transformations 244
- 9.7 Loop Unrolling 246
- 9.8 References 248

10 GLOBAL OPTIMIZATION 249
- 10.1 Main Structure of the Optimization Phase 252
- 10.2 Theory and Algorithms 253
- 10.3 Relation between an Expression and Its Operands 270
- 10.4 Implementing Lazy Code Motion for Temporaries 273
- 10.5 Processing Impossible and Abnormal Edges 276
- 10.6 Moving LOAD Instructions 278
- 10.7 Moving STORE Instructions 281
- 10.8 Moving Copy Operations 288
- 10.9 Strength Reduction by Partial Redundancy Elimination 290
- 10.10 References 295

11 LIMITING RESOURCES 296
- 11.1 Design of LIMIT 298
- 11.2 Peephole Optimization and Local Coalescing 300
- 11.3 Computing the Conflict Graph 306
- 11.4 Combined Register Renaming and Register Coalescing 312
- 11.5 Computing the Register Pressure 316
- 11.6 Reducing Register Pressure 319
- 11.7 Computing the Spill Points 322

11.8 Optimizing the Placement of Spill Instructions 329
11.9 References 333

12 SCHEDULING AND RESCHEDULING 334
12.1 Structure of the Instruction-Scheduling Phase 339
12.2 Phase Order 340
12.3 Example 341
12.4 Computing the Trace 344
12.5 Precomputing the Resource Information 350
12.6 Instruction Interference Graph 356
12.7 Computing the Priority of Instructions 361
12.8 Simulating the Hardware 363
12.9 The Scheduling Algorithm 372
12.10 Software Pipelining 378
12.11 Out-of-Order Execution 386
12.12 References 387

13 REGISTER ALLOCATION 388
13.1 Global Register Allocation 390
13.2 Local Register Allocation 400
13.3 References 411

14 THE OBJECT MODULE 412
14.1 What Is the Object Module? 413
14.2 What Segments Are Created by the Compiler? 416
14.3 Generating the Object File 416
14.4 The Complication: Short versus Long Branches 417
14.5 Generating the Assembly File and Additions to the Listing File 419
14.6 Generating the Error File 420
14.7 References 420

15 COMPLETION AND FUTURES 421
15.1 Target Machine 421
15.2 Host Machine 422
15.3 Source Language 422
15.4 Using Other Technology 423
15.5 The Spike Approach 423

APPENDIX A: PROOF OF THE ANTICIPATION EQUATIONS 425

APPENDIX B: SUPERBLOCK FORMATION 428

BIBLIOGRAPHY 429

INDEX 435

PREFACE

Building compilers has been a challenging activity since the advent of digital computers in the late 1940s and early 1950s. At that time, implementing the concept of automatic translation from a form familiar to mathematicians into computer instructions was a difficult task. One needed to figure out how to translate arithmetic expressions into instructions, how to store data in memory, and how to choose instructions to build procedures and functions. During the late 1950s and 1960s these processes were automated to the extent that simple compilers could be written by most computer science professionals. In fact, the concept of "small languages" with corresponding translators is fundamental in the UNIX community.

From the beginning, there was a need for translators that generated efficient code: The translator must use the computer productively. Originally this constraint was due to computers' small memories and slow speed of execution. During each generation of hardware, new architectural ideas have been added. At each stage the compilers have also needed to be improved to use these new machines more effectively. Curiously, pundits keep predicting that less efficient and less expensive translators will do the job. They argue that as machines keep getting faster and memory keeps expanding, one no longer needs an optimizing compiler. Unfortunately, people who buy bigger and faster machines want to use the proportionate increase in size and speed to handle bigger or more complex problems, so we still have the need for optimizing compilers. In fact, we have an increased need for these compilers because the performance of the newer architectures is sensitive to the quality of the generated code. Small changes in the order and choice of the instructions can have much larger effects on machine performance than similar choices made with the complex instruction set computing (CISC) machines of the 1970s and 1980s.

The interplay between computer architecture and compiler performance has been legitimized with the development of reduced instruction set computing (RISC) architectures. Compilers and computer architecture have a mutually dependent relationship that shares the effort to build fast applications. To this end, hardware has been simplified by exposing some of the details of hardware operation, such as simple load–store instruction sets and instruction scheduling. The compiler is required to deal with these newly exposed details and provide faster execution than possible on CISC processors.

This book describes one design for the optimization and code-generation phases of such a compiler. Many compiler books are available for describing the analysis of programming languages. They emphasize the processes of lexical analysis, parsing, and semantic analysis. Several books are also available for describing compilation processes for vector and parallel processors. This book describes the compilation of efficient programs for a single superscalar RISC processor, including the ordering and structure of algorithms and efficient data structures.

The book is presented as a high-level design document. There are two reasons for this. Initially, I attempted to write a book that presented all possible alternatives so that the reader could make his or her own choices of methods to use. This was too bulky, as the projected size of the volume was several thousand pages—much too large for practical purposes. There are a large number of different algorithms and structures in an optimizing compiler. The choices are interconnected, so an encyclopedic approach to optimizing compilers would not address some of the most difficult problems.

Second, I want to encourage this form of design for large software processes. The government uses a three-level documentation system for describing software projects: The A-level documents are overview documents that describe a project as a whole and list its individual pieces. B-level documents describe the operation of each component in sufficient detail that the reader can understand what each component does and how it does it, whereas the C-level documents are low-level descriptions of each detail.

As a developer I found this structure burdensome because it degenerated into a bureaucratic device involving large amounts of paper and little content. However, the basic idea is sound. This book will describe the optimization and code-generation components of a compiler in sufficient detail that the reader can implement these components if he or she sees fit. Since I will be describing one method for each of the components, the interaction between components can be examined in detail so that all of the design and implementation issues are clear.

Each chapter will include a section describing other possible implementation techniques. This section will include bibliographic information so that the interested reader can find these other techniques.

Philosophy for Choosing Compiler Techniques

Before starting the book, I want to describe my design philosophy. When I first started writing compilers (about 1964), I noticed that much research and development work had been described in the literature. Although each of these projects is based on differing assumptions and needs, the availability of this information makes it easier for those who follow to use previous ideas without reinventing them. I therefore design by observing the literature and other implementations and choosing techniques that meet my needs. What I contribute is the choice of technique, the engineering of the technique to fit with other components, and small improvements that I have observed.

One engineering rule of thumb must be added. It is easy to decide that one will use the latest techniques that have been published. This policy is dangerous. There are secondary effects from the choice of any optimization or code-generation technique that are observed only after the technique has been used for some time. Thus I try to avoid techniques that I have not seen implemented at least twice in prototype or production compilers. I will break this rule once or twice when I am sure that the techniques are sound, but no more frequently.

In the course of writing this book, my view of it has evolved. It started out as a recording of already known information. I have designed and built several compilers using this existing technology. As the book progressed, I have learned much about integrating these algorithms. What started out as a concatenation of independent ideas has thus become melded into a more integrated whole. What began as simple description of engineering choices now contains some newer ideas. This is probably the course of any intellectual effort; however, I have found it refreshing and encouraging.

How to Use This Book

This book is designed to be used for three purposes. The first purpose is to describe the structure of an optimizing compiler so that a reader can implement it or a variation (compiler writers always modify a design). The book's structure reflects this purpose. The initial chapters describe the compilation phases and the interactions among them; later chapters describe the algorithms involved in each compilation phase.

This book can also be used as a textbook on compiler optimization techniques. It takes one example and describes each of the compilation processes using this example. Rather than working small homework problems, students work through alternative examples.

Practically, the largest use for this book will be informing the curious. If you are like me, you pick up books because you want to learn something about the subject. I hope that you will enjoy this book and find what you are looking for. Good reading.

1 OVERVIEW

What is an optimizing compiler? Why do we need them? Where do they come from? These questions are discussed in this chapter, along with how to use the book. Before presenting a detailed design in the body of the book, this introductory chapter provides an informal history of optimizing compiler development and gives a running example for motivating the technology in the compiler and to use throughout the rest of the book.

1.1 What Is an Optimizing Compiler?

How does a programmer get the performance he expects from his application? Initially he writes the program in a straightforward fashion so that the correct execution of the program can be tested or proved. The program is then profiled and measured to see where resources such as time and memory are used, and modified to improve the uses of these resources. After all reasonable programmer modifications have been made, further improvements in performance can come only from how well the programming language is translated into instructions for the target machine.

The goal of an optimizing compiler is to efficiently use all of the resources of the target computer. The compiler translates the source program into machine instructions using all of the different computational elements. The ideal translation is one that keeps each of the computational elements active doing useful (and nonredundant) work during each instruction execution cycle.

Of course, this idealized translation is not usually possible. The source program may not have a balanced set of computational needs. It may do more integer than floating point arithmetic or vice versa, or more load and store operations than arithmetic. In such cases the compiler must use the overstressed computational elements as effectively as possible.

The compiler must try to compensate for unbalanced computer systems. Ideally, the speed of the processor is matched to the speed of the memory system, which are both matched to the speed of the input/output (I/O) system. In modern reduced instruction set computer (RISC) systems this is not true: The processors are much faster than the memory systems. To be able to use the power of the processor, the compiler must generate code that decreases the use of the memory system by either keeping values in registers or organizing the code so that needed data stays in the memory cache.

An added problem is fetching instructions. A significant fraction of the memory references are references to instructions. One hopes that the instructions stay in one of the memory caches; however, this is not always the case. When the instructions do not fit in the cache, the compiler should attempt to generate as few instructions as possible. When the instructions do fit in the cache and there are heavy uses of data, then the compiler is free to add more instructions to decrease the wait for data. Achieving a balance is a difficult catch-22.

In summary, the optimizing compiler attempts to use all of the resources of the processor and memory as effectively as possible in executing the application program. The compiler must transform the program to regain a balanced use of computational elements and memory references. It must choose the instructions well to use as few instructions as possible while obtaining this balance. Of course, all of this is impossible, but the compiler must do as well as it can.

1.2 A Biased History of Optimizing Compilers

Compiler development has a remarkable history, frequently ignored. Significant developments started in the 1950s. Periodically, pundits have decided that all the technology has already been developed. They have always been proven wrong. With the development of new high-speed processors, significant compiler developments are needed today. I list here the compiler development groups that have most inspired and influenced me. There are other groups that have made major contributions to the field, and I do not mean to slight them.

Although there is earlier work on parsing and compilation, the first major compiler was the Fortran compiler (Backus) for the IBM 704/709/7090/7094. This project marked the watershed in compiler development. To be accepted by programmers, it had to generate code similar to that written by machine language programmers, so it was a highly optimizing compiler. It had to compile a full language, although the design of the language was open to the developers. And the technology for the project did not exist; they had to develop it. The team succeeded beautifully, and their creation was one of the best compilers for about ten years. This project developed the idea of compiler passes or phases.

Later, again at IBM, a team developed the Fortran/Level H compilers for the IBM 360/370 series of computers. Again, these were highly optimizing compilers. Their concept of quadruple was similar to the idea of an abstract assembly language used in the design presented in this book. Subsequent improvements to the compilers by Scarborough and Kolsky (1980) kept this type of compiler one of the best for another decade.

During the late 1960s and throughout the 1970s, two research groups continued to develop the ideas that were the basis of these compilers as well as developing new ideas. One group was led by Fran Allen at IBM, the other by Jack Schwartz at New York University (NYU). These groups pioneered the ideas of reaching definitions and bit-vector equations for describing program transformation conditions. Much of their work is in the literature; if you can get a copy of the SETL newsletters (NYU 1973) or the reports associated with the SETL project, you will have a treat.

Other groups were also working on optimization techniques. William Wulf defined a language called Bliss (Wulf et al. 1975). This is a structured programming language for which Wulf and his team at Carnegie Mellon University (CMU) developed optimizing compiler techniques. Some of these techniques were only applicable to structured programs, whereas others have been generalized to any program structure. This project evolved into the Production-Quality Compiler-Compiler (PQCC) project, developing meta-compiler techniques for constructing optimizing compilers (Leverett et al. 1979). These papers and theses are some of the richest and least used sources of compiler development technology.

Other commercial companies were also working on compiler technology. COMPASS developed compiler techniques based on p-graph technology (Karr 1975). This technology was superior to reaching definitions for compiler optimization because the data structures were easily updated; however, the initial computation of p-graphs was much slower than reaching definitions. P-graphs were transformed by Reif (Reif and Lewis 1978) and subsequent developers at IBM Yorktown Heights (Cytron et al. 1989) into the Static Single Assignment Form of the flow graph, one of the current flow graph structures of choice for compiler development.

Ken Kennedy, one of the students at NYU, established a compiler group at Rice University to continue his work in compiler optimization. Initially, the group specialized in vectorization techniques. Vectorization required good scalar optimization, so the group continued work on scalar optimization also. Some of the most effective work analyzing multiple procedures (interprocedural analysis) has been performed at Rice under the group led by Keith Cooper (1988, 1989). This book uses much of the flow graph structure designed by the Massive Scalar Compiler Project, the group led by Cooper.

With the advent of supercomputers and RISC processors in the later 1970s and early 1980s, new compiler technology had to be developed. In particular, instructions were pipelined so that the values were available when needed. The instructions had to be reordered to start a number of other instructions before the result of the first instruction was available. These techniques were first developed by compiler writers for machines such as the Cray-1. An example of such work is Richard Sites' (1978) paper on reordering Cray-1 assembly language. Later work by the IBM 801 (Auslander and Hopkins 1982) project and Gross (1983) at CMU applied these technques to RISC processors. Other work in this area includes the papers describing the RS6000 compilers (Golumbic 1990 and Warren 1990) and research work performed at the University of Wisconsin on instruction scheduling.

In the 1970s and early 1980s, register allocation was a difficult problem: How should the compiler assign the values being computed to the small set of physical registers to minimize the number of times data need to be moved to and from memory? Chaitin (1981, 1982) reformulated the problem as a graph-coloring problem and developed heuristics for coloring the graphs that worked well for programs with complex flows. The PQCC project at Carnegie Mellon developed a formulation as a type of bin-packing problem, which worked best with straight-line or structure procedures. The techniques developed here are a synthesis of these two techniques using some further work by Laurie Hendron at McGill University.

1.3 What Have We Gained with All of This Technology?

Considering this history, all the technology necessary to build a high-performance compiler for modern RISC processors existed by about 1972, certainly by 1980. What is the value of the more recent research? The technology available at those times would do the job, but at a large cost. More recent research in optimizing compilers has led to more effective and more easily implemented techniques for optimization. Two examples will make this clearer. The Fortran/Level H compiler was one of the most effective optimizing compilers of the late 1960s and early 1970s. It used an algorithm to optimize loops based on identifying the nesting of loops. In the late 1970s Etienne Morel developed the technique called Elimination of Partial Redundancies that performed a more effective code motion without computing anything about loops (Morel and Renvoise 1979).

Similarly, the concepts of Static Single Assignment Form have made a number of transformation algorithms similar and more intuitive. Constant propagation, developed by Killdall (1973), seemed complex. Later formulations by Wegman and Zadeck (1985) make the technique seem almost intuitive.

The new technology has made it easier to build optimizing compilers. This is vital! These compilers are large programs, prone to all of the problems that large programs have. When we can simplify a part of the compiler, we speed the development and compilation times and decrease the number of bugs (faults, defects) that occur in the compiler. This makes a cheaper and more reliable product.

1.4 Rules of the Compiler Back-End Game

The compiler back end has three primary functions: to generate a program that faithfully represents the meaning of the source program, to allocate the resources of the machine efficiently, and to recast the program in the most efficient form that the compiler can deduce. An underlying rule for each of these functions is that the source program must be faithfully represented.

Unfortunately, there was a time when compiler writers considered it important to get most programs right but not necessarily *all* programs. When the programmer used some legal features in unusual ways, the compiler might implement an incorrect version of the program. This gave optimizing compilers a bad name.

It is now recognized that the code-generation and optimization components of the compiler must exactly represent the meaning of the program as described in the source program and in the language reference manual for the programming language. This does not mean that the program will give exactly the same results when compiled with optimization turned on and off. There are programs that violate the language definition in ways not identifiable by a compiler. The classic example is the use of a variable before it is given a value. These programs may get different results with optimization turned on and turned off.

Fortunately, standards groups are becoming more aware of the needs of compiler writers when describing the language standards. Each major language standard now describes in some way the limits of compiler optimization. Sometimes this is done by leaving certain aspects of the language as "undefined" or "implementation defined." Such phrases mean that the compiler may do whatever it wishes when it encounters that aspect of the language. However, be cautious—the user community frequently has expectations of what the compiler will do in those cases, and a compiler had better honor those expectations.

What does the compiler do when it encounters a portion of the source program that uses language facilities in a way that the compiler does not expect? It must make a conservative choice to implement that facility, even at the expense of runtime performance for the program. Even when conservative choices are being made, the compiler may be clever. It might, for example, compile the same section of code in two different ways and generate code to check which version of the code is safe to use.

1.5 Benchmarks and Designing a Compiler

Where does the compiler writer find the set of improvements that must be included in an optimizing compiler? How is one variant of a particular optimization chosen over another? The compiler writer uses information about the application area for the target machine, the languages being compiled, and good sense to choose a particular set of optimizations and their organization.

Any application area has a standard set of programs that are important for that area. Sorting and databases are important for commercial applications. Linear algebra and equation solution are important for numeric applications. Other programs will be important for simulation. The compiler writer will investigate these programs and determine what the compiler must do to translate these programs well. While doing this, the compiler writer and his client will extract sample code from these programs. These samples of code become *benchmarks* that are used to measure the success of the compiler.

The source languages to be compiled are also investigated to determine the language features that must be handled. In Fortran, an optimizing compiler needs to do strength reduction since the programmer has no mechanism for simplifying multiplications. In C, strength reduction is less important (although still useful); however, the compiler needs to compile small subroutines well and determine as much information about pointers as possible.

There are standard optimizations that need to be implemented. Eliminating redundant computations and moving code out of loops will be necessary in an optimizing compiler for an imperative language. This is actually a part of the first criterion, since these optimizations are expected by most application programmers.

The compiler writer must be cautious. It is easy to design a compiler that compiles benchmarks well and does not do as well on general programs. The Whetstone benchmark contained a kernel of code that could be optimized by using a trigonometric identity. The SPEC92 benchmarks have a kernel, EQNTOT, that can be optimized by clever vectorization of integer instructions.

Should the compiler writer add special code for dealing with these anomalous benchmarks? Yes and no. One has to add the special code in a competitive world, since the competition is adding it. However, one must realize that one has not really built a better compiler unless there is a larger class of programs that finds the feature useful. One should always look at a benchmark as a source of general comments about programming. Use the benchmark to find general improvements. In summary, the basis for the design of optimizing compilers is as follows:

1. Investigate the important programs in the application areas of interest. Choose compilation techniques that work well for these programs. Choose kernels as benchmarks.

2. Investigate the source languages to be compiled. Identify their weaknesses from a code quality point of view. Add optimizations to compensate for these weaknesses.

3. Make sure that the compiler does well on the standard benchmarks, and do so in a way that generalizes to other programs.

1.6 Outline of This Book

Before developing a compiler design, the writer must know the requirements for the compiler. This is as hard to determine as writing the compiler. The best way that I have found for determining the requirements is to take several typical example programs and compile them by hand, pretending that you are the compiler. No cheating! You cannot do a transformation that cannot be done by some compiler using some optimization technique.

This is what we do in Chapter 2 for one particular example program. It is too repetitious to do this for multiple examples. Instead, we will summarize several other requirements placed on the compiler that occur in other examples.

Then we dig into the design. Each chapter describes a subsequent phase of the compiler, giving the theory involved in the phase and describing the phase in a high-level pseudo-code.

We assume that the reader can develop detailed data structures from the high-level descriptions given here. Probably the most necessary requirement for a compiler writer is to be a "data structure junkie." You have to love complex data structures to enjoy writing compilers.

1.7 Using This Book as a Textbook

This compiler design can be used as a textbook for a second compiler course. The book assumes that the reader is familiar with the construction of compiler front ends and the straightforward code-generation techniques taught in a one-term compiler course. I considered adding sets of exercises to turn the book into a textbook. Instead, another approach is taken that involves the student more directly in the design process.

The example procedure in Figure 1.1 is used throughout the book to motivate the design and demonstrate the details. As such, it will be central to most of the illustrations in the book. Students should use the three examples

Figure 1.1   Running Exercise Throughout Book

```
SUBROUTINE MAXCOL(A,N,LARGE,VALUE)
   DOUBLE PRECISION VALUE(N), A(N,N)
   INTEGER N, LARGE(N)
   INTEGER I, J
   DO I = 1, N
      LARGE(I) = 1
      VALUE(I) = DABS(A(1,I))
      DO J = 2, N
         IF (DABS(A(J,I).GT.VALUE(I)) THEN
            VALUE(I) = DABS(A(J,I))
            LARGE(I) = J
         ENDIF
      ENDDO
   ENDDO
END
```

Figure 1.2 Matrix Multiply Example

```
SUBROUTINE MATMUL(A,B,C,N)
   DOUBLE PRECISION A(N,N), B(N,N), C(N,N)
   INTEGER N, I, J, K
   DO I = 1, N
      DO J = 1, N
         C(I,J) = 0.0
      ENDDO
   ENDDO
   DO I = 1, N
      DO J = 1, N
         DO K = 1, N
            C(I,J) = C(I,J) + A(I,K)*B(K,J)
         ENDDO
      ENDDO
   ENDDO
END
```

in Figures 1.2–1.4 as running illustrations of the compilation process. For each chapter, the student should apply the technology developed therein to the example. The text will also address these examples at times so the student can see how his or her work matches the work from the text.

Figure 1.3 Computing the Maximum Monotone Subsequence

```
INTEGER FUNCTION MONOTONE(A,N)
   DOUBLE PRECISION A(N)
   INTEGER C(N), CMAX
   INTEGER I, J, N
   C(N) = 1
   CMAX = 1
   DO I = N - 1, 1, -1
      C(I) = 1
      DO J = I + 1, N
         IF ((X(I) <= X(J)).AND.(C(I) <= C(J)+1) THEN
            C(I) = C(J)+1
         ENDIF
      ENDDO
      IF (CMAX <= C(I)) THEN
         CMAX = C(I)
      ENDIF
   ENDDO
   MONOTONE = CMAX
END
```

Figure 1.4 Recursive Version of a Binary Search

```
INTEGER FUNCTION BINARYSEARCH(A,N,L,U,KEY)
   DOUBLE PRECISION A(N), KEY
   INTEGER L, U, N
   INTEGER M
   IF (U < L) THEN
      BINARYSEARCH = 0
   ELSE
      M = (L+U)/2
      IF (A(M) = KEY) THEN
         BINARYSEARCH = M
      ELSIF (A(M) < KEY) THEN
         BINARYSEARCH = BINARYSEARCH(A,N,L,M-1,KEY)
      ELSE
         BINARYSEARCH=BINARYSEARCH(A,N,M+1,U,KEY)
      ENDIF
   ENDIF
END
```

Figure 1.2 is a version of the classic matrix multiply algorithm. It involves a large amount of floating point computation together with an unbalanced use of the memory system. As written, the inner loop consists of two floating point operations together with three load operations and one store operation. The problem will be to get good performance from the machine when more memory operations are occurring than computations.

Figure 1.3 computes the length of the longest monotone subsequence of the vector A. The process uses dynamic programming. The array $C(I)$ keeps track of the longest monotone sequence that starts at position I. It computes the next element by looking at all of the previously computed subsequences that can have $X(I)$ added to the front of the sequence computed so far. This example has few floating point operations. However, it does have a number of load and store operations together with a significant amount of conditional branching.

Figure 1.4 is a binary search algorithm written as a recursive procedure. The student may feel free to translate this into a procedure using pointers on a binary tree. The challenge here is to optimize the use of memory and time associated with procedure calls.

I recommend that the major grade in the course be associated with a project that prototypes a number of the optimization algorithms. The implementation should be viewed as a prototype so that it can be implemented quickly. It need not handle the complex memory management problems existing in real optimizing compilers.

1.8 References

Auslander, M., and M. Hopkins. 1982. An overview of the PL.8 compiler. *Proceedings of the ACN SIGPLAN '82 Conference on Programming Language Design and Implementation*, Boston, MA.

Backus, J. W., et al. 1957. The Fortran automatic coding system. *Proceedings of AFIPS 1957 Western Joint Computing Conference (WJCC)*, 188-198.

Chaitin, G. J. 1982. Register allocation and spilling via graph coloring. *Proceedings of the SIGPLAN '82 Symposium on Compiler Construction*, Boston, MA. Published as *SIGPLAN Notices* 17(6): 98-105.

Chaitin, G. J., et al. 1981. Register allocation via coloring. *Computer Languages* 6(1): 47-57.

Cooper, K., and K. Kennedy. 1988. Interprocedural side-effect analysis in linear time. *Proceedings of the SIGPLAN 88 Symposium on Programming Language Design and Implementation*, Altanta, GA. Published as *SIGPLAN Notices* 23(7).

Cytron, R., et al. 1989. An efficient method of computing static single assignment form. *Conference Record of the 16th ACM SIGACT/SIGPLAN Symposium on Programming Languages*, Austin, TX. 25-35.

Gross, T. 1983. Code optimization of pipeline constraints. (Stanford Technical Report CS 83-255.) Stanford University.

Hendron, L. J., G. R. Gao, E. Altman, and C. Mukerji. 1993. A register allocation framework based on hierarchical cyclic interval graphs. (Technical report.) McGill University.

Karr, M. 1975. P-graphs. (Report CA-7501-1511.) Wakefield, MA: Massachusetts Computer Associates.

Kildall, G. A. 1973. A unified approach to global program optimization. *Conference Proceedings of Principles of Programming Languages I*, 194-206.

Leverett, B. W., et al. 1979. An overview of the Production-Quality Compiler-Compiler project. (Technical Report CMU-CS-79-105.) Pittsburgh, PA: Carnegie Mellon University.

Morel, E., and C. Renvoise. 1979. Global optimization by suppression of partial redundancies. *Communications of the ACM* 22(2): 96-103.

New York University Computer Science Department. 1970-1976. *SETL Newsletters*.

Reif, J. H., and H. R. Lewis. 1978. Symbolic program analysis in almost linear time. *Conference Proceedings of Principles of Programming Languages V, Association of Computing Machinery*.

Scarborough, R. G., and H. G. Kolsky. 1980. Improved optimization of Fortran programs. *IBM Journal of Research and Development* 24: 660-676.

Sites, R. 1978. Instruction ordering for the CRAY-1 computer. (Technical Report 78-CS-023.) University of California at San Diego.

Wegman, M. N., and F. K. Zadeck. 1985. Constant propagation with conditional branches. *Conference Proceedings of Principles of Programming Languages XII*, 291-299.

Wulf, W., et al. 1975. *The design of an optimizing compiler.* New York: American Elsevier.

2 COMPILER STRUCTURE

The compiler writer determines the structure of a compiler using information concerning the source languages to be compiled, the required speed of the compiler, the code quality required for the target computer, the user community, and the budget for building the compiler. This chapter is the story of the process the compiler writer must go through to determine the compiler structure.

The best way to use this information to design a compiler is to manually simulate the compilation process using the same programs provided by the user community. For the sake of brevity, one principle example will be used in this book. We will use this example to determine the optimization techniques that are needed, together with the order of the transformations.

For the purpose of exposition this chapter simplifies the process. First we will describe the basic framework, including the major components of the compiler and the structure of the compilation unit within the compiler. Then we will manually simulate an example program.

The example is the Fortran subroutine in Figure 2.1. It finds the largest element in each column of a matrix, saving both the index and the absolute value of the largest element. Although it is written in Fortran, the choice of the source language is not important. The example could be written in any of the usual source languages. Certainly, there are optimizations that are more important in one language than another, but all languages are converging to a common set of features, such as arrays, pointers, exceptions, procedures, that share many characteristics. However, there are special characteristics of each source language that must be compiled well. For example, C has a rich set of constructs involving pointers for indexing

Figure 2.1 Finding Largest Elements in a Column

```
SUBROUTINE MAXCOL(A,N,LARGE,VALUE)
   DOUBLE PRECISION VALUE(N), A(N,N)
   INTEGER N, LARGE(N)
   INTEGER I, J
   DO I = 1, N
      LARGE(I) = 1
      VALUE(I) = DABS(A(1,I))
      DO J = 2, N
         IF (DABS(A(J,I).GT.VALUE(I))
            VALUE(I) = DABS(A(J,I))
            LARGE(I) = J
         ENDIF
      ENDDO
   ENDDO
END
```

arrays or describing dynamic storage, and Fortran has special rules concerning formal parameters that allow increased optimization.

2.1 Outline of the Compiler Structure

This book is a simplification of the design process. To design a compiler from scratch one must iterate the process. First hypothesize a compiler structure. Then simulate the compilation process using this structure. If it works as expected (it won't) then the design is acceptable. In the process of simulating the compilation, one will find changes one wishes to make or will find that the whole framework does not work. So, modify the framework and simulate again,. Repeat the process until a satisfactory framework is found. If it really does not work, scrap the framework and start again.

There are two major decisions to be made concerning the structure: how the program is represented and in what order the transformations are performed. The source program is read by the compiler front end and then later translated into a form, called the intermediate representation (IR), for optimization, code generation, and register allocation. Distinct collections of transformations, called *phases,* are then applied to the IR.

2.1.1 Source Program Representation

The source program must be stored in the computer during the translation process. This form is stored in a data structure called the IR. Past experience has shown that this representation should satisfy three requirements:

1. The intermediate form of the program should be stored in a form close to machine language, with only certain operations kept in high-level form to be "lowered" later. This allows each phase to operate on all instructions in the program. Thus, each optimization algorithm can be applied to all of the instructions. If higher-level operators are kept in the IR, then the subcomponents of these operations cannot be optimized or must be optimized later by specialized optimizers.

2. Each phase of the compiler should retain all information about the program in the IR. There should be no implicit information, that is, information that is known after one phase and not after another. This means that each phase has a simple interface and the output may be tested by a small number of simulators. An implication of this requirement is that no component of the compiler can use information about how another component is implemented. Thus components can be modified or replaced without damage to other components.

3. Each phase of the compiler must be able to be tested in isolation. This means that we must write support routines that read and write examples of the IR. The written representation must be in either a binary or textual representation.

The second requirement circumvents one of the natural tendencies of software development teams. When implementing its component, one team may use the fact that another team has implemented its component in a certain way. This works until some day in the future the first team changes some part of its implementation. Suddenly the second component will no longer work. Even worse problems can occur if the second team has the first team save some information on the side to help their component. Now the interface is no longer the intermediate representation of the program but the intermediate representation plus this other (possibly undocumented) data. The only way to avoid this problem is to require the interfaces to be documented and simple.

Optimizing compilers are complex. After years of development and maintenance, a large fraction of a support team's effort will go to fixing the problems. Little further development can be done because there is no time. This situation happens because most compilers can only be tested as a whole. A test program will be compiled and some phase will have an error (or the program compiles and runs incorrectly). Where is the problem? It is probably not at the point in the compiler where you observe the problem. A pithy phrase developed at COMPASS was "Expletive runs downhill." (The actual expletive was used, of course.) This means that the problem occurs somewhere early in the compiler and goes unnoticed until some later phase, typically the register allocation, or object module formation. Several things can be done to avoid this problem:

- Subroutines must be available to test the validity of the intermediate representation. These routines can be invoked by compile-time switches to check which phases create an inappropriate representation.
- Assertions within the phases must be used frequently to check that situations that are required to be true are in fact true. This is often done in production compilers.
- A test and regression suite must be created for each phase. These tests involve special versions of the IR in which a program that has been compiled up to the point of this phase. This IR is input to the phase and then the output is simulated to see if the resulting program runs correctly.

Having these requirements, how is the program stored? The choice is based on experience and then ratified by the manual simulations discussed earlier. In this compiler, each procedure will be stored internally in a form similar to assembly language for a generic RISC processor.

Experience with the COMPASS Compiler Engine taught that the concept of a value computed by an operator must be general. The value may be a vector, scalar, or structural value. Early in the compilation process, the concept of value must be kept as close to the form in the source program as possible so that the program can be analyzed without losing information.

These observations are almost contradictory. We need to be able to manipulate the smallest pieces of the program while still being able to recover the overall structure present in the source program. This contradiction led to the idea of the gradual lowering of the intermediate representation. At first, LOAD instructions have a complete set of subscript expressions. Later these specialized load instructions are replaced by machine-level load instructions.

What does an assembly language program look like? There is one machine instruction per line. Each instruction contains an operation code, indicating the operation to be performed; a set of operands; and a set of targets to hold the results. The following gives the exact form for the intermediate representation, except that the representation is encoded:

1. The instruction, encoded as a record that is kept in a linked list of instructions.

2. An operation code describing action performed. This is represented as a built-in enumeration of all operations.

3. A set of constant operands. Some instructions may involve constant operands. These are less prone to optimization and so are inserted directly in the instruction. The compiler initially will not use many constant operands because doing so decreases the chances for optimization. Later, many constants will be stored in the instructions rather than using registers.

4. A list of registers representing the inputs to the instruction. For most instructions there is a fixed number of inputs, so they can be represented by a small array. Initially, there is an assumption of an infinite supply of registers called *temporaries*.

5. A target register that is the output of the instruction.

The assembly program also has program labels that represent the places to which the program can branch. To represent this concept, the intermediate representation is divided into *blocks* representing straight-line sequences of instructions. If one instruction in a block is executed, then all instructions are executed. Each block starts with a label (or is preceded by a conditional branching instruction) and ends with a branching instruction. Redundant branches are added to the program to guarantee that there is a branch under every possible condition at the end of the block. In other words, there is no fall-through into the next block.

The number of operation codes is large. There is a distinct operation code for each instruction in the target machine. Initially these are not used; however, the lowering process will translate the set of machine-independent operation codes into the target machine codes as the compilation progresses. There is no need to list all of the operation codes here. Instead the subset of instructions that are used in the examples is listed in Figure 2.2.

Now the source program is modeled as a directed graph, with the nodes being the blocks. There is a directed edge between two blocks if there is a

Figure 2.2 Operation Codes Used in Examples

```
iLDC     c => T              Load constant c into temporary T
i2i      T1 => T2            Copy integer temporary T1 into T2
iSLD     (T1) => T2          Load integer from memory location T1 into T2
iCMPGT   T1,T2 => T3         Place true in T3 if and only if T1 > T2
iBCOND   T,B1,B2             If T is true, branch to block B1; otherwise branch to block B2
iSUB     T1,T2 => T3         integer T3 = T1 - T2
iMUL     T1,T2 => T3         integer T3 = T1 * T2
iADD     T1,T2 => T3         integer T3 = T1 + T2
iSST     (T1),T2             Store value T2 into integer location T1
dSLD     (T1) => SF1         Load double precision value in address T1 into SF1
dSST     (T1),SF1            Store value in double precision temporary SF1 into address T1
dABS     SF1 => SF2          Place absolute value of value in SF1 into SF2
dCMPLE   SF1,SF2 => SF3      Place true in SF3 if and only if SF1 <= SF2
dBCOND   SF1,B1,B2           If SF1 is true, branch to B1; otherwise, branch to block B2
d2d      SF1 => SF2          Copy value in SF1 into SF2
BR       B                   Unconditionally branch to block B
```

possible branch from the first block to the second. A unique node called *Entry* represents the entry point for the source program. The entry node has no predecessors in the graph. Similarly, a unique node called *Exit* represents the exit point for the source program, and that node has no successors. In Figure 2.3 the entry node is node B0, and the exit node is node B5.

Figure 2.3 Example Flow Graph

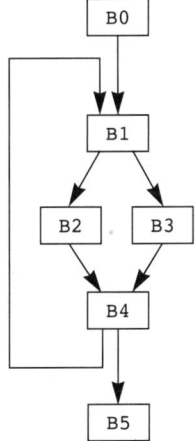

The execution of the source program is modeled by a path through the graph. The path starts at the entry node and terminates at the exit node. The computations within each node in the path are executed in order of the occurrence of nodes on the path. In fact, the computations within the node are used to determine the next node in the path. In Figure 2.3, one possible path is B0, B1, B2, B4, B1, B3, B4, B5. This execution path means that all computations in B0 are executed, then all computations in B1, then B2, and so on. Note that the computations in B1 and B4 are executed twice.

2.1.2 Order of Transformations

Since the compiler structure is hard to describe linearly, the structure is summarized here and then reviewed during the remainder of the chapter. The rest of the book provides the details. The compiler is divided into individual components called phases as shown in Figure 2.4. An overview of each of the phases is presented next.

The compiler front end is language specific. It analyzes the source file being compiled and performs all lexical analysis, parsing, and semantic checks. It builds an abstract syntax tree and symbol table. I will not discuss this part of the compiler, taking it as a given, because most textbooks do an excellent job of describing it. There is a distinct front end for each language, whereas the rest of the compiler can be shared among compilers for different languages as long as the specialized characteristics of each language can be handled.

After the front end has built the abstract syntax tree, the initial optimization phase builds the flow graph, or intermediate representation. Since the intermediate representation looks like an abstract machine language, standard single-pass code-generation techniques, such as used in lcc (Frazer and Hanson 1995), can be used to build the flow graph. Although these pattern-matching techniques can be used, the flow graph is sufficiently simple that a straightforward abstract syntax tree walk generating instructions on the fly is sufficient to build the IR. While building the flow graph some initial optimizations can be performed on instructions within each block.

The Dominator Optimization phase performs the initial global optimizations. It identifies situations where values are constants, where two computations are known to have the same value, and where instructions have no effect on the results of the program. It identifies and eliminates most redundant computations. At the same time it reapplies the optimizations that

Compiler Structure

Figure 2.4 Compiler Structure

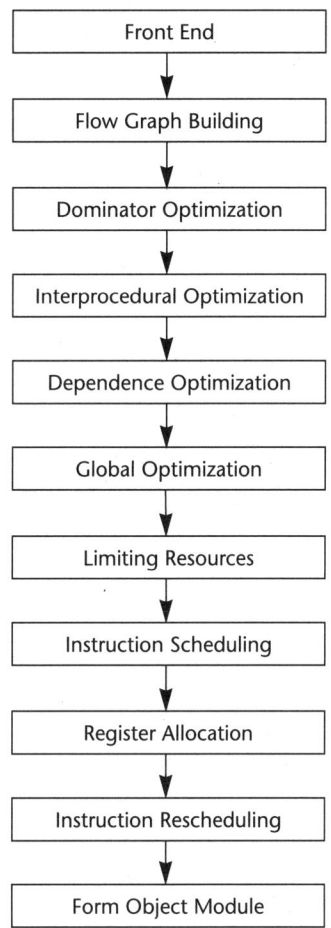

have already occurred within a single block. It does not move instructions from one point of the flow graph to another.

The Interprocedural Optimization phase analyzes the procedure calls within this flow graph and the flow graphs of all of the other procedures within the whole program. It determines which variables might be modified by each procedure call, which variables and expressions might be referencing the same memory location, and which parameters are known to be constants. It stores this information for other phases to use.

The Dependence Optimization phase attempts to optimize the time taken to perform load and store operations. It does this by analyzing array and pointer expressions to see if the flow graph can be transformed to one in which fewer load/stores occur or in which the load and store operations that occur are more likely to be in one of the cache memories for the RISC chip. To do this it might interchange or unroll loops.

The Global Optimization phase lowers the flow graph, eliminating the symbolic references to array expressions and replacing them with linear address expressions. While doing so, it reforms the address expressions so that the operands are ordered in a way that ensures that the parts of the expressions that are dependent on the inner loops are separated from the operands that do not depend on the inner loop. Then it performs a complete list of global optimizations, including code motion, strength reduction, and dead-code elimination.

After global optimization, the exact set of instructions in the flow graph has been found. Now the compiler must allocate registers and reorder the instructions to improve performance. Before this can be done, the flow graph is transformed by the Limiting Resources phase to make these later phases easier. The Limiting Resources phase modifies the flow graph to reduce the number of registers needed to match the set of physical registers available. If the compiler knows that it needs many more registers than are available, it will save some temporaries in memory. It will also eliminate useless copies of temporaries.

Next an initial attempt to schedule the instructions is performed. Register allocation and scheduling conflict, so the compiler attempts to schedule the instructions. It counts on the effects of the Limiting Resources phase to ensure that the register allocation can be performed without further copying of values to memory. The instruction scheduler reorders the instructions in several blocks simultaneously to decrease the time that the most frequently executed blocks require for execution.

After instruction scheduling, the Register Allocation phase replaces temporaries by physical registers. This is a three-step process in which temporaries computed in one block and used in another are assigned first, then temporaries within a block that can share a register with one already assigned, and finally the temporaries assigned and used in a single block. This division counts on the work of the Limiting Resources phase to decrease the likelihood that one assignment will interfere with a later assignment.

Compiler Structure

It is hoped that the Register Allocation phase will not need to insert store and load operations to copy temporaries into memory. If such copies do occur, then the Instruction Scheduling phase is repeated. In this case, the scheduler will only reschedule the blocks that have had the instructions inserted.

Finally, the IR is in the form in which it represents an assembly language procedure. The object module is now written in the form needed by the linker. This is a difficult task because the documentation of the form of object modules is notoriously inaccurate. The major work lies in discovering the true form. After that it is a clerical (but large) task to create the object module.

2.2 Compiler Front End

To understand each of the phases, we simulate a walk-through of our standard example in Figure 2.1 for each phase, starting with the front end. The front end translates the source program into an abstract syntax tree. As noted earlier, I will not discuss the operation of the front end; however, we do need to understand the abstract syntax tree. The abstract syntax tree for the program in Figure 2.1 is given in Figure 2.5.

There is a single tree for each procedure, encoding all of the procedure structure. The tree is represented using indentation; the subtrees of each node are indented an extra level. Thus the type of a node occurs at one indentation and the children are indented slightly more. I am not trying to be precise in describing the abstract syntax tree. The name for the type of each node was chosen to represent the node naturally to the reader. For example, the nodes with type "assign" are assignment nodes.

The "list" node represents a tree node with an arbitrary number of children, used in situations in which there can be an arbitrary number of components, such as blocks of statements. The "symbol" node takes a textual argument indicating the name of the variable; of course, this will actually be represented as a pointer to the symbol table.

The "fetch" node differentiates between addresses and values. This compiler has made a uniform assumption about expressions: Expressions always represent values. Thus the "assign" node takes two expressions as operands—one representing the address of the location for getting the result and the other representing the value of the right side of the assignment. The

Figure 2.5 Abstract Syntax Tree for MAXCOL

```
Procedure
   symbol("MAXCOL")
   list
      symbol("a")
      symbol("n")
      symbol("large")
      symbol("value")
   list
      declare("a",double,array,parameter,bounds=("n","n"))
      declare("n",integer,scalar,parameter)
      declare("large",integer,array,parameter,bounds=("n"))
      declare("value",double,array,parameter,bounds=("n"))
      declare("i",integer,scalar,local)
      declare("j",integer,scalar,local)
   list
      doloop
         symbol("i")
         intconst(1)
         fetch
            symbol("n")
         list
            assign
               subscript
                  symbol("large")
                  list
                     fetch
                        symbol("i")
               intconst(1)
            assign
               subscript
                  symbol("value")
                  list
                     fetch
                        symbol("i")
               absvalue
                  fetch
                     subscript
                        symbol("a")
                        list
                           intconst(1)
                           fetch
                              symbol("i")
            doloop
               symbol("j")
               intconst(2)
               fetch
                  symbol("n")
               list
                  ifthen
                     greater_than
```

Compiler Structure

Figure 2.5 Continued

```
                        absvalue
                           fetch
                              subscript
                                 symbol("a")
                                 list
                                    fetch
                                       symbol("j")
                                    fetch
                                       symbol("i")
                        fetch
                           subscript
                              symbol("value")
                              list
                                 fetch
                                    symbol("i")
             list
                assign
                   subscript
                      symbol("value")
                      list
                         fetch
                            symbol("i")
                   absvalue
                      fetch
                         subscript
                            symbol("a")
                            list
                               fetch
                                  symbol("j")
                               fetch
                                  symbol("i")
                assign
                   subscript
                      symbol("large")
                      list
                         fetch
                            symbol("i")
                   fetch
                      symbol("j")
```

"fetch" node translates between addresses and values. It takes one argument, which is the address of a location. The result of the "fetch" node is the value stored in that location.

Note that this tree structure represents the complete structure of the program, indicating which parts of the subroutine are contained in other parts.

2.3 Building the Flow Graph

The abstract syntax tree is translated into the flow graph using standard code-generation techniques described in introductory compiler books. The translation can be done in two ways. The more advanced method is to use one of the tree-based pattern-matching algorithms on the abstract syntax tree to derive the flow graph. This technique is not recommended here because of the RISC nature assumed for the target machine. Complex instructions will be generated later by pattern matching the flow graph. Instead, the abstract syntax tree should be translated into the simplest atomic instructions possible. This procedure allows more opportunity for optimization.

Thus, the translation should occur as a single walk of the abstract syntax tree. Simple instructions should be generated wherever possible. Normal operations such as addition and multiplication can be lowered to a level in which each entry in the program flow graph represents a single instruction. However, operations that need to be analyzed later (at the equivalent of source program level) are translated into higher-level operations equivalent to the source program construct. These will later be translated into lower-level operations after completion of the phases that need to analyze these operations. The following four classes of operations should be kept in higher-level form:

1. A fetch or store of a subscript variable, $A[i,j,k]$, is kept as a single operation, with operands being the array name and the expressions for the subscripts. Keeping subscripted variables in this form rather than linearizing the subscript expression allows later dependence analysis to solve sets of linear equations and inequalities involving the subscripts.

2. Extra information is kept with normal load and store operations also. This information is needed to determine which store operations can modify locations loaded by load operations. This is particularly important in languages involving pointers. Extra analysis, called *pointer alias analysis*, is needed to determine which storage locations are modified. Loads and stores of automatic variables, that is, variables declared within a routine whose values are lost at the end of the routine, are not generated. Instead these values are handled as if they were temporaries within the program flow graph.

3. Subroutine calls are kept in terms of the expression representing the name of the procedure and the expression representing the arguments.

Compiler Structure

Methods for passing the arguments, such as call-by-value and call-by-reference, are not expanded. This allows more detailed analysis by the interprocedural analysis components later in the compiler.

4. Library routines are handled differently than other procedure calls. If a library procedure is known to be a pure function it is handled as if it were an operator. This allows the use of identities involving the library routines. Other procedure calls may be used in other parts of the analysis of the program, for example, calls on **malloc** are known to return either a null pointer or a pointer to a section of memory unreferenced in other parts of the program.

A straightforward translation will result in the flow graph shown in Figure 2.6. It is shown here to describe the process of translation. It is not actually generated, since certain optimizations will be performed during the translation process. Note that the temporaries are used in two distinct ways. Some temporaries, such as T5, are used just like local variables, holding values that are modified as the program is executed. Other temporaries, such as T7, are pure functions of their arguments. In the case of T7, it always holds the constant 1. For these temporaries the same temporary is always used for the result of the same operation. Thus any load of the constant 1 will always be into T7. The translation process must guarantee that an operand is evaluated before it is used.

To guarantee that the same temporary is used wherever an expression is computed, a separate table called the *formal temporary table* is maintained. It is indexed by the operator and the temporaries of the operands and constants involved in the instruction. The result of a lookup in this table is the name of the temporary for holding the result of the operation. The formal temporary table for the example routine is shown in Figure 2.7. Some entries that will be added later are listed here for future reference.

What is the first thing that we observe about the lengthy list of instructions in Figure 2.6? Consider block B1. The constant 1 is loaded six times and the expression $I - 1$ is evaluated three times. A number of simplifications can be performed as the flow graph is created:

- If there are two instances of the same computation without operations that modify the operands between the two instances, then the second one is redundant and can be eliminated since it will always compute the same value as the first.

Figure 2.6 Initial Program Representation

```
B0:     PROLOG
        iLDC    1               => T7       /constant 1 always in T7
        i2i     T7              => T5       /I = 1, first copy into value
        iSLD    (T2)            => T8       /fetch value of N. T2 address of N
        iCMPGT  T5,T8           => T9       /is I > N
        iBCOND  T9,B5,B1                    /no iterations to execute
B1:     iLDC    1               => T7       /constant 1
        iSUB    T5,T7           => T10      /I - 1
        iLDC    4               => T11      /constant 4
        iMUL    T11,T10         => T12      /4*(i-1)
        iADD    T3,T12          => T13      /address(LARGE(I)), T3 address of LARGE
        iLDC    1               => T7       /constant 1
        i2i     T7              => T14      /put in register for LARGE(I)
        iSST    (T13),T14                   /store the value into LARGE(I)
        iLDC    1               => T7       /constant 1
        iSUB    T5,T7           => T10      /I - 1
        iLDC    8               => T15      /constant 8
        iMUL    T15,T10         => T16      /8*(I-1)
        iADD    T4,T16          => T17      /address(VALUE(I))
        iLDC    1               => T7       /constant 1 - compute address(A(1,I))
        iLDC    1               => T7       /constant 1
        iSUB    T7,T7           => T18      /1 - 1
        iLDC    1               => T7       /constant 1
        iSUB    T5,T7           => T10      /I - 1
        iSLD    (T2)            => T8       /fetch N
        iMUL    T8,T10          => T19      /N*(I-1)
        iADD    T19,T18         => T20      /N*(I-1) + (1-1)
        iLDC    8               => T15      /constant 8
        iMUL    T15,T20         => T21      /8*(N*(I-1) + (1-1))
        iADD    T1,T21          => T22      /address(A(1,I))
        dSLD    (T22)           => SF2      /value A(1,I)
        dABS    SF2             => SF3      /DABS(A(1,I))
        d2d     SF3             => SF1      /copy into value of VALUE(I)
        dSST    (T17),SF1                   /store the value of VALUE(I)
        iLDC    2               => T23      /constant 2 - Initialize index
        i2i     T23             => T6       /setup value of J
        iSLD    (T2)            => T8       /fetch N
        iCMPGT  T6,T8           => T24      /is J > N
        iBCOND  T24,B4,B2                   /yes - no iterations
B2:     iLDC    1               => T7       /1
        iSUB    T6,T7           => T25      /J - 1
        iLDC    1               => T7       /constant 1
        iSUB    T5,T7           => T10      /I - 1
        iSLD    (T2)            => T8       /fetch N
        iMUL    T8,T10          => T19      /N*(I-1)
        iADD    T19,T25         => T26      /N*(I-1) + (J-1)
        iLDC    8               => T15      /constant 8
        iMUL    T15,T26         => T27      /8*(N*(I-1) + (J-1))
        iADD    T1,T27          => T28      /address(A(J,I))
        dSLD    (T28)           => SF4      /value A(J,I)
        dABS    SF4             => SF5      /DABS(A(J,I))
```

Figure 2.6 Continued

```
        iLDC    1              => T7      /constant 1
        iSUB    T5,T7          => T10     /I-1
        iLDC    8              => T15     /constant 8
        iMUL    T15,T10        => T16     /8*(I-1)
        iADD    T4,T16         => T17     /address(VALUE(I))
        dSLD    (T17)          => SF1     /value of VALUE(I)
        dCMPLE  SF5,SF1        => SF6     /comparison
        dBCOND  SF6,B3,B6                 /skip update of variables
B6:     iLDC    1              => T7      /constant 1
        iSUB    T5,T7          => T10     /I-1
        iLDC    8              => T15     /constant 8
        iMUL    T15,T10        => T16     /8*(I-1)
        iADD    T4,T16         => T17     /address(VALUE(I))
        iLDC    1              => T7      /1
        iSUB    T6,T7          => T25     /J-1
        iLDC    1              => T7      /constant 1
        iSUB    T5,T7          => T10     /I-1
        iSLD    (T2)           => T8      /fetch N
        iMUL    T8,T10         => T19     /N*(I-1)
        iADD    T19,T25        => T26     /N*(I-1)+(J-1)
        iLDC    8              => T15     /constant 8
        iMUL    T15,T26        => T27     /8*(N*(I-1)+(J-1))
        iADD    T1,T27         => T28     /address(A(J,I))
        dSLD    (T28)          => SF4     /value A(J,I)
        dABS    SF4            => SF5     /DABS(A(J,I))
        d2d     SF5            => SF1     /update value of VALUE(I)
        dSST    (T17),SF1                 /store it back in memory
        iLDC    1              => T7      /constant 1
        iSUB    T5,T7          => T10     /I-1
        iLDC    4              => T11     /constant 4
        iMUL    T11,T10        => T12     /4*(i-1)
        iADD    T3,T12         => T13     /address(LARGE(I))
        i2i     T6             => T14     /put in register for LARGE(I)
        iSST    (T13),T14                 /store the value into LARGE(I)
        BR      B3
B3:     iLDC    1              => T7      /increment by 1
        iADD    T6,T7          => T29     /J+1
        i2i     T29            => T6      /update value of J
        iSLD    (T2)           => T8      /fetch N
        iCMPGT  T6,T8          => T24     /is J > N
        iBCOND  T24,B4,B2
B4:     iLDC    1              => T7      /constant 1 to increment I
        iADD    T5,T7          => T30     /I+1
        i2i     T30            => T5      /first store into fetch location
        iSLD    (T2)           => T8      /get value of N
        iCMPGT  T5,T8          => T9      /is I > N
        iBCOND  T9,B5,B1                  /more iterations to perform
B5:     EPILOG                            /return from subroutine
```

Figure 2.7 Initial Formal Temporary Table

```
T1    Address(A)                       constant
T2    Address(N)                       constant
T3    Address(LARGE)                   constant
T4    Address(VALUE)                   constant
T5    Value(I)
T6    Value(J)
T7    Constant 1                       constant
T8    Value of N
T9    I > N
T10   I - 1
T11   Constant 4                       constant
T12   4*(I-1)
T13   Address(LARGE(I))
T14   Value(LARGE(I))
T15   Constant 8                       constant
T16   8*(I-1)
T17   Address(VALUE(I))
SF1   Value(VALUE(I))
T18   1 - 1
T19   N*(I-1)
T20   N*(I-1) + (1-1)
T21   8*(N*(I-1) + (1-1))
T22   Address(A(1,I))
SF2   Value(A(1,I))
SF3   DABS(A(1,I))
T23   Constant 2                       constant
T24   J > N
T25   J - 1
T26   N*(I-1) + (J-1)
T27   8*(N*(I-1) + (J-1))
T28   Address(A(J,I))
SF4   Value(A(J,I))
SF5   DABS(A(J,I))
SF6   DABS(A(J,I)) >= VALUE(I)
T29   J + 1
T30   I + 1
T31   0 > N                            added during value numbering
T32   8*N*(I-1)                        added during value numbering
T33   Address(A(1,I)) simplified       added during value numbering
T34   2 > N                            added during value numbering
T35   T28 + 8                          added during strength reduction
T36   T13 + 4                          added during strength reduction
T37   T17 + 8                          added during strength reduction
T38   8*N                              added during strength reduction
T39   T33 + 8*N                        added during strength reduction
```

- *Algebraic identities* can be used to eliminate operations. For example, $A * 0$ can be replaced by 0. This can only occur if the side effects of computing A can be ignored. There is a large collection of algebraic identities that may be applied; however, a small set is always applied with the understanding that new algebraic identities can be added if occasions occur where the identities can improve the program.

- *Constant folding* transforms expressions such as 5 * 7 into the resulting number, 35. This frequently makes other simplifications possible. The arithmetic must be done in a form that exactly mimics the arithmetic of the target machine.

These transformations usually remove about 50 percent of the operations in the procedure. The rest of the analysis in the compiler is therefore faster since about half of the operations that must be scanned during each analysis have been eliminated. The result of these simplifications is given in Figure 2.8.

2.4 Dominator Optimizations

The preliminary optimization phase takes the program represented as a program flow graph as input. It applies global optimization techniques to the program and generates an equivalent program flow graph as the output. These techniques are global in the sense that the transformations take into account possible branching within each procedure.

There are two global optimization phases in this compiler. The initial phase performs as much global optimization as possible without moving computations in the flow graph. After interprocedural analysis and dependence optimization phases have been executed, a more general global optimization phase is applied to clean up and improve the flow graphs further.

The following global optimization transformations are applied.

- If there are two instances of a computation $X * Y$ and the first one occurs on all paths leading from the *Entry* block to the second computation, then the second one can be eliminated. This is a special case of the general elimination of redundant expressions, which will be performed later. This simple case accounts for the largest number of redundant expressions, so much of the work will be done here before the general technique is applied.

- *Copy propagation* or *value propagation* is performed. If an X is a copy of Z, then uses of X can be replaced by uses of Z as long as neither X nor Z changes between the point at which the copy is made and the point of use. This transformation is useful for improving the program flow graph

Figure 2.8 Flow Graph after Simplifications

```
B0:     PROLOG
        iLDC    1               => T7     /constant 1 always in T7
        i2i     T7              => T5     /I = 1, first copy into value
        iSLD    (T2)            => T8     /fetch value of N
        iCMPGT  T7,T8           =>T31     /is I > N
        iBCOND  T31,B5,B1                 /no iterations to execute

B1:     iLDC    1               => T7     /constant 1
        iSUB    T5,T7           => T10    /I - 1
        iLDC    4               => T11    /constant 4
        iMUL    T11,T10         => T12    /4*(i-1)
        iADD    T3,T12          => T13    /address(LARGE(I))
        i2i     T7              => T14    /put in register for LARGE(I)
        iSST    (T13),T14                 /store the value into LARGE(I)
        iLDC    8               => T15    /constant 8
        iMUL    T15,T10         => T16    /8*(I-1)
        iADD    T4,T16          => T17    /address(VALUE(I))
        iSLD    (T2)            => T8     /fetch N
        iMUL    T8,T10          => T19    /N*(I-1)
        iMUL    T15,T19         => T32    /8*N*(I-1)
        iADD    T1,T32          => T33    /address(A(1,I))
        dSLD    (T33)           => SF2    /value A(1,I)
        dABS    SF2             => SF3    /DABS(A(1,I))
        d2d     SF3             => SF1    /copy into value of VALUE(I)
        dSST    (T17),SF1                 /store value into VALUE(I)
        iLDC    2               => T23    /constant 2 - Initialize index
        i2i     T23             => T6     /setup value of J
        iSLD    (T2)            => T8     /fetch N
        iCMPGT  T23,T8          => T34    /is 2 > N
        iBCOND  T34,B4,B2                 /yes - no iterations

B2:     iLDC    1               => T7     /1
        iSUB    T6,T7           => T25    /J - 1
        iSUB    T5,T7           => T10    /I - 1
        iSLD    (T2)            => T8     /fetch N
        iMUL    T8,T10          => T19    /N*(I-1)
        iADD    T19,T25         => T26    /N*(I-1)+(J-1)
        iLDC    8               => T15    /constant 8
        iMUL    T15,T26         => T27    /8*(N*(I-1)+(J-1))
        iADD    T1,T27          => T28    /address(A(J,I))
        dSLD    (T28)           => SF4    /value A(J,I)
        dABS    SF4             => SF5    /DABS(A(J,I))
        iMUL    T15,T10         => T16    /8*(I-1)
        iADD    T4,T16          => T17    /address(VALUE(I))
        dSLD    (T17)           => SF1    /value of VALUE(I)
        dCMPLE  SF5,SF1         => SF6    /comparison
        dBCOND  SF6,B3,B6                 /skip update of variables

B6:     iLDC    1               => T7     /constant 1
        iSUB    T5,T7           => T10    /I - 1
        iLDC    8               => T15    /constant 8
```

Figure 2.8 Continued

```
        iMUL    T15,T10     => T16    /8*(I-1)
        iADD    T4,T16      => T17    /address(VALUE(I))
        iSUB    T6,T7       => T25    /J - 1
        iSLD    (T2)        => T8     /fetch N
        iMUL    T8,T10      => T19    /N*(I-1)
        iADD    T19,T25     => T26    /N*(I-1)+(J-1)
        iMUL    T15,T26     => T27    /8*(N*(I-1)+(J-1))
        iADD    T1,T27      => T28    /address(A(J,I))
        dSLD    (T28)       => SF4    /value A(J,I)
        dABS    SF4         => SF5    /DABS(A(J,I))
        d2d     SF5         => SF1    /update value of VALUE(I)
        dSST    (T17),SF1            /store it back in memory
        iLDC    4           => T11    /constant 4
        iMUL    T11,T10     => T12    /4*(i-1)
        iADD    T3,T12      => T13    /address(LARGE(I))
        i2i     T6          => T14    /put in register for LARGE(I)
        iSST    (T13),T14            /store the value into LARGE(I)
        BR      B3

B3:     iLDC    1           => T7     /increment by 1
        iADD    T6,T7       => T29    /J + 1
        i2i     T29         => T6     /update value of J
        iSLD    (T2)        => T8     /fetch N
        iCMPGT  T6,T8       => T24    /is J > N
        iBCOND  T24,B4,B2

B4:     iLDC    1           => T7     /constant 1 to increment I
        iADD    T5,T7       => T30    /I + 1
        i2i     T30         => T5     /first store into fetch location
        iSLD    (T2)        => T8     /get value of N
        iCMPGT  T5,T8       => T9     /is I > N
        iBCOND  T9,B5,B1            /more iterations to perform

B5:     EPILOG                       /return from subroutine
```

generated by the compiler front end. There are many compiler-generated temporaries such as loop counters or components of array dope information that are really copy operations.

- *Constant propagation* is the replacement of uses of variables that have been assigned a constant value by the constant itself. If a constant is used to determine a conditional branch in the program, the alternative branch is not considered.

- As with local optimization, algebraic identities, peephole optimizations, and constant folding will also be performed as the other optimizations are applied.

The following global optimizations are intentionally *not* applied because they make the task of dependence analysis more difficult later in the compiler.

- *Strength reduction* is not applied. Strength reduction is the transformation of multiplication by constants (or loop invariant expressions) into repeated additions. More precisely, if one has an expression $I * 3$ in a loop and I is incremented by 1 each time through the loop, then the computation of $I * 3$ can be replaced by a temporary variable T that is incremented by 3 each time through the loop.

- *Code motion* is not applied. A computation $X * Y$ can be moved from within a loop to before the loop when it can be shown that the computation is executed each time through the loop and that the operands do not change value within the loop. This transformation inhibits loop interchange, which is performed to improve the use of the data caches, so it is delayed until the later global optimization phase.

Now inspect the flow graph, running your finger along several possible paths through the flow graph from the start block B0 to the exit block B5. The constant 1 is computed repeatedly on each path. More expensive computations are also repeated. Look at blocks B2 and B6. Many of the expressions computed in B6 are also computed in B2. Since B2 occurs on each path leading to B6, the computations in B6 are unnecessary.

What kind of technology can cheaply eliminate these computations? B2 is the dominator of B6 (this will be defined more precisely shortly), meaning that B2 occurs on each path leading from B0 to B6. There is a set of algorithms applied to the Static Single Assignment Form (to be defined shortly) of the flow graph that can eliminate repeated computations of constants and expressions when they already occur in the dominator. Some Static Single Assignment Form algorithms will be in the compiler anyway, so we will use this form to eliminate redundant computations where a copy of the computation already occurs in the dominator. This is an inexpensive generalization of local optimizations used during the construction of the flow graph, giving the results in Figure 2.9.

Repeat the exercise of tracing paths through the flow graph. Now there are few obvious redundant expressions. There are still some, however. Computations performed each time through the loop have not been moved out of the loop. Although they do not occur in this example, there are usually other redundant expressions that are not made redundant by this transformation.

Where are most of the instructions? They are in block B2, computing the addresses used to load array elements. This address expression changes

Figure 2.9 After Dominator Value Numbering

```
B0:     PROLOG
        iLDC     1             => T7      /constant 1 always in T7
        i2i      T7            => T5      /I = 1, first copy into value
        iSLD     (T2)          => T8      /fetch value of N
        iCMPGT   T7,T8         => T31     /is I > N
        iBCOND   T31,B5,B1                /no iterations to execute
B1:     iSUB     T5,T7         => T10     /I - 1
        iLDC     4             => T11     /constant 4
        iMUL     T11,T10       => T12     /4*(i-1)
        iADD     T3,T12        => T13     /address(LARGE(I))
        i2i      T7            => T14     /put in register for LARGE(I)
        iSST     (T13),T14               /store the value into LARGE(I)
        iLDC     8             => T15     /constant 8
        iMUL     T15,T10       => T16     /8*(I-1)
        iADD     T4,T16        => T17     /address(VALUE(I))
        iMUL     T8,T10        => T19     /N*(I-1)
        iMUL     T15,T19       => T32     /8*N*(I-1)
        iADD     T1,T32        => T33     /address(A(1,I))
        dSLD     (T33)         => SF2     /value A(1,I)
        dABS     SF2           => SF3     /DABS(A(1,I))
        d2d      SF3           => SF1     /copy into value of VALUE(I)
        dSST     (T17),SF1               /store value in VALUE(I)
        iLDC     2             => T23     /constant 2 - Initialize index
        i2i      T23           => T6      /setup value of J
        iCMPGT   T23,T8        => T34     /is 2 > N
        iBCOND   T34,B4,B2                /yes - no iterations
B2:     iSUB     T6,T7         => T25     /J - 1
        iADD     T19,T25       => T26     /N*(I-1) + (J-1)
        iMUL     T15,T26       => T27     /8*(N*(I-1) + (J-1))
        iADD     T1,T27        => T28     /address(A(J,I))
        dSLD     (T28)         => SF4     /value A(J,I)
        dABS     SF4           => SF5     /DABS(A(J,I))
        dSLD     (T17)         => SF1     /value of VALUE(I)
        dCMPLE   SF5,SF1       => SF6     /comparison
        dBCOND   SF6,B3,B6                /skip update of variables
B6:     d2d      SF5           => SF1     /update value of VALUE(I)
        dSST     (T17),SF1               /store it back in memory
        i2i      T6            => T14     /put in register for LARGE(I)
        iSST     (T13),T14               /store the value into LARGE(I)
        BR       B3
B3:     iADD     T6,T7         => T29     /J + 1
        i2i      T29           => T6      /update value of J
        iCMPGT   T6,T8         => T24     /is J > N
        iBCOND   T24,B4,B2
B4:     iADD     T5,T7         => T30     /I + 1
        i2i      T30           => T5      /first store into fetch location
        iCMPGT   T5,T8         => T9      /is I > N
        iBCOND   T9,B5,B1                 /more iterations to perform
B5:     EPILOG                            /return from subroutine
```

each time through the loop, so it cannot be moved out of the loop that starts block B2. It changes in a regular fashion, increasing by 8 each time through the loop, so the later global optimization phase will apply strength reduction to eliminate most of these instructions.

2.5 Interprocedural Analysis

All other phases of the compiler handle the program flow graph for one procedure at a time. Each phase accepts as input the program flow graph (or abstract syntax tree) and generates the program flow graph as a result. The interprocedural analysis phase accumulates the program flow graphs for each of the procedures. It analyzes all of them, feeding the program flow graphs for each procedure, one at a time, to the rest of the phases of the compiler. The procedures are not provided in their original order. In the absence of recursion, a procedure is provided to the rest of the compiler before the procedures that call it. Hence more information can be gathered as the compilation process proceeds.

The interprocedural analysis phase computes information about procedure calls for other phases of the compiler. In the local and global optimization phases of the compiler, assumptions must be made about the effects of procedure calls. If the effects of the procedure call are not known, then the optimization phase must assume that all values that are known to that procedure and all procedures that it might call can be changed or referenced by the procedure call. This is an inconvenient assumption in modern languages, which encourage procedures (or member functions) to structure the program.

To avoid these conservative assumptions about procedure calls, this phase computes the following information for each procedure call:

MOD   The set of variables that might be modified by this procedure call.
REF   The set of variables that might be referenced by this procedure call.

Interprocedural analysis also computes information about the relationships and values of the formal parameters of a procedure, including the following information:

Alias   With call-by-reference parameters, one computes which parameters possibly reference the same memory location as another parameter or global variable.

Constant   The parameters that always take the same constant value at all calls of the procedure. This information can be used to improve on the constant propagation that has already occurred.

When array references are involved, the interprocedural analysis phase attempts to determine which part of the array has been modified or referenced. Approximations must be made in storing this information because only certain shapes of storage reference patterns will be stored. When the actual shape does not fit one of the usual reference patterns, a conservative choice will be made to expand the shape to one of the chosen forms.

2.6 Dependence Optimization

The purpose of dependence optimization for a RISC processor is to decrease the number of references to memory and improve the pattern of memory references that do occur.

This goal can be achieved by restructuring loops so that fewer references to memory are made on each iteration. The program is transformed to eliminate references to memory, as in Figure 2.10, in which a transformation called *scalar replacement* is used to hold the value of $A(I)$, which is used on the next iteration of the loop as the value $A(I-1)$. Classic optimization techniques cannot identify this possibility, but the techniques of dependence optimization can. A more complex transformation called *unroll and jam* can be used to eliminate more references to memory for nested loops.

When the references to memory cannot be eliminated completely, dependence-based optimization can be used to improve the likelihood that the values referenced are in the cache, thus providing faster reference to memory. The speed of modern processors exceeds the speed of their memory

Figure 2.10   Example of Scalar Replacement

```
DO I = 2, N                  IF (N > 1) THEN
   A(I) = A(I-1) + A(I)         T = A(1)
ENDDO                           DO I = 2, N
                                   T = T + A(I)
                                   A(I) = T
                                ENDDO
                             ENDIF
```

Figure 2.11 Striding Down the Columns

```
DO I = 1, N                    DO J = 1, N
   DO J = 1, N                    DO I = 1, N
      B(I,J) = A(I,J)*2.0            B(I,J) = A(I,J)*2.0
   ENDDO                          ENDDO
ENDDO                          ENDDO
```

systems. To compensate, one or more cache memory systems have been added to retain the values of recently referenced memory locations. Since recently referenced memory is likely to be referenced again, the hardware can return the value saved in the cache more quickly than if it had to reference the memory location again.

Consider the Fortran fragment in Figure 2.11 for copying array A into B twice. In Fortran, the elements of a column are stored in sequential locations in memory. The hardware will reference a particular element. The whole cache line for the element will be read into the cache (typically 32 bytes to 128 bytes), but the next element will not come from the cache line; instead, the next element is the next element in the row, which may be very far away in memory. By the time the inner loop is completed and the next iteration of the outer loop is executing, the current elements in the cache will likely have been removed.

The dependence-based optimizations will transform Figure 2.11 into the right-hand column. The same computations are performed, but the elements are referenced in a different order. Now the next element from A is the next element in the column, thus using the cache effectively.

The phase will also unroll loops to improve later instruction scheduling, as shown in Figure 2.12. The left column is the original loop; the right col-

Figure 2.12 Original (left) and Unrolled (right) Loop

```
DO I = 1, N                    DO I = 1, N, 4
   B(I) = A(I)                    B(I)   = A(I)
ENDDO                             B(I+1) = A(I+1)
                                  B(I+2) = A(I+2)
                                  B(I+3) = A(I+3)
                               ENDDO
                               DO I = I, N
                                  B(I) = A(I)
                               ENDDO
```

umn is the unrolled loop. In the original loop, the succeeding phases of the compiler would generate instructions that would require that each store to B be executed before each subsequent load from A. With the loop unrolled, the loads from A may be interwoven with the store operations, hiding the time it takes to reference memory. Another optimization called *software pipelining* is performed later, which increases the amount of interweaving even more.

This book will not address the concepts of parallelization and vectorization, although those ideas are directly related to the work here. These concepts are covered in books by Wolfe (1996) and Allen and Kennedy.

2.7 Global Optimization

The global optimization phase cleans up the flow graph transformed by the earlier phases. At this point all global transformations that need source-level information have been applied or the information has been stored with the program flow graph in an encoded form. Before the general algorithm is performed, several transformations need to be performed to simplify the flow graph. These initial transformations are all based on a dominator-based tree walk and the static single assignment method. The optimizations include the original dominator optimizations together with the following.

- *Lowering:* The instructions are lowered so that each operation in the flow graph represents a single instruction in the target machine. Complex instructions, such as subscripted array references, are replaced by the equivalent sequence of elementary machine instructions. Alternatively, multiple instructions may be folded into a single instruction when constants, rather than temporaries holding the constant value, can occur in instructions.

- *Reshaping:* Before the global optimization techniques are applied, the program is transformed to take into account the looping structure of the program. Consider the expression $I * J * K$ occurring inside a loop, with I being the index for the innermost loop, J the index for the next loop, and K the loop invariant. The normal associativity of the program language would evaluate this as $(I*J) * K$ when it would be preferable to compute it as $I * (J*K)$ because the computation of $J * K$ is invariant inside the innermost loop and so can be moved out of the loop. At the same time we perform strength reduction, local redundant expression elimination, and algebraic identities.

- *Strength Reduction:* Consider computations that change by a regular pattern during consecutive iterations of a loop. The major example is multiplication by a value that does not change in the loop, such as *I * J* where *J* does not change and *I* increases by 1. The multiplication can be replaced by a temporary that is increased by *J* each time through the loop.

- *Elimination:* To assist strength reduction and reshaping, the redundant expression elimination algorithm in the dominator optimization phase is repeated.

Consider our sample procedure. The expression *address(A(J,I))* is computed each time through the inner loop. It can be replaced by a temporary that is initialized to *address(A(1,I))* and incremented by 8 each time through the loop.

Strength reduction is performed first on the inner loops, then on the successively outer loops. In this flow graph there are two nested loops. The inner loop consists of the blocks B2, B6, and B3. The variable that changes in an arithmetic progression is *J*, which is represented by the symbolic register T6. The expressions T25, T26, T27, and T28 vary linearly with T6, so they are all candidates for strength reduction; however, T25, T26, and T27 are used to compute T28, so we want to perform strength reduction of T28. T28 is increased by 8 each time through the loop.

To have a place in which to put the code to initialize T28, we insert an empty block between blocks B1 and B2. For mnemonic purposes we will call the block B12, standing for the block between B1 and B2. The compiler puts two computations into the loop (if they are not already available):

1. The expression to initialize the strength-reduced variable, in this case T28. This involves copying all of the expressions involved in computing T28 and inserting them into block B12.

2. The expression for the increment to the strength reduction expression. In this case, it is the constant 8, which is already available.

While inserting these expressions into B12, the compiler will perform redundant expression elimination, constant propagation, and constant folding. In this case, the compiler knows that *J* has value 2 on entry to the loop, so that constant value will be substituted for *J*, that is, for T6.

The code in Figure 2.13 represents the program after strength reduction has been applied to the inner loop. T28 no longer represents a pure expression: It is now a compiler-created local variable. This does not change how the compiler handles the load and store operations involving T28. Since it is

Figure 2.13 Strength-Reduced Inner Loop

```
         ...
         iBCOND    T34,B4,B12               /yes - no iterations
B12:     iSUB      T6,T7        => T25      /J - 1
         iADD      T19,T25      => T26      /N*(I-1) + (J-1)
         iMUL      T15,T26      => T27      /8*(N*(I-1) + (J-1))
         iADD      T1,T27       => T28      /address(A(J,I))
         BR        B2

B2:      dSLD      (T28)        => SF4      /value A(J,I)
         dABS      SF4          => SF5      /DABS(A(J,I))
         dSLD      (T17)        => SF1      /value of VALUE(I)
         dCMPLE    SF5,SF1      => SF6      /comparison
         dBCOND    SF6,B3,B6                /skip update of variables

B6:      d2d       SF5          => SF1      /update value of VALUE(I)
         dSST      (T17),SF1                /store it back in memory
         i2i       T6           => T14      /put in register for LARGE(I)
         iSST      (T13),T14                /store the value into LARGE(I)
         BR        B3

B3:      iADD      T6,T7        => T29      /J + 1
         i2i       T29          => T6       /update value of J
         iADD      T28,T15      => T35      /update value of address(A(J,I))
         i2I       T35          => T28
         iCMPGT    T6,T8        => T24      /is J > N
         iBCOND    T24,B4,B2
```

taking on the same values that it did when it was a pure expression, the side effects of the load and store instructions are the same.

In this rough simulation of the compiler, we see that the compiler needs to perform some level of redundant expression elimination, constant propagation, and folding before strength reduction. We can get that information by performing strength reduction (and expression reshaping) as a part of the dominator-based optimizations discussed earlier.

As a working hypothesis, assume that strength reduction for a single-entry loop is performed after the dominator-based transformations for the loop entry and all of its children in the dominator tree. If we perform strength reduction for a loop at that point, we gain three advantages. First, strength reduction will be applied to inner loops before being applied to outer loops. Second, the loop body will have been already simplified by the dominator-based algorithms. And third, the information concerning available expressions and constants is still available for a block inserted before the entry to the loop.

For the sake of description, the computations in block B3 that are no longer used have been eliminated. In reality they are eliminated later by the dead-code elimination phase. This order makes the implementation of strength reduction easier because the compiler need not worry about whether a computation being eliminated is used someplace else.

Now consider the contents of block B12. We know that the value of *J*, or T6, is 2. So the compiler applies value numbering, constant propagation, and constant folding to this block. One other optimization is needed to obtain good code. The compiler multiplies by 8 after it has performed all additions. The application of distribution of integer multiplication will result in better code since 8 will be added to an already existing value to give the code in Figure 2.14.

We now perform strength reduction on the outer loop. There are three candidates for strength reduction: *address(A(1,I))*, or T33; *address(VALUE(I))*, or T17; and *address(LARGE(I))*, or T13. Again we insert a block B01 between blocks B0 and B1 to hold the initialization values for the loop B1, [B2, B6, B3], B4. The three pointers will be initialized in block B01 and incremented in block B4.

One of the values of this simulation process is to observe situations that you would not have imagined when designing the compiler. There are two such situations with strength reduction:

- The load of the constant 4 into T11 now happens too early. All uses of it have been eliminated, except for updating the pointer at the end of the loop. In this case that is not a problem because the constant will be folded into an immediate field of an instruction later. More complex expressions may be computed much earlier than needed. There is no easy solution to this problem.

- The computation of the constant 8 in block B01 makes the computation in block B1 redundant. Later code-motion algorithms had better identify these cases and eliminate the redundant expressions.

After strength reduction on both loops, the compiler has the flow graph in Figure 2.15.

Figure 2.14 Header Block after Optimization

```
B12:    iADD    T33,T15   => T28    /address(A(2,I)) = address(A(1,I))+8
        BR      B2
```

Figure 2.15 After Strength-Reducing Outer Loop

```
B0:     PROLOG
        iLDC    1               => T7      /constant 1 always in T7
        i2i     T7              => T5      /I = 1, first copy into value
        iSLD    (T2)            => T8      /fetch value of N
        iCMPGT  T7,T8           => T31     /is I > N
        iBCOND  T31,B5,B01                 /no iterations to execute

B01:    i2i     T3              => T13     /address(LARGE(I))
        iLDC    4               => T11     /increment for address(LARGE(I))
        i2i     T4              => T17     /address(VALUE(I))
        iLDC    8               => T15     /increment for address(VALUE(I))
        i2i     T1              => T33     /address(A(1,I))
        iMUL    T15,T8          => T38     /increment for address(A(1,I))
        BR      B1

B1:     iLDC    4               => T11     /constant 4
        i2i     T7              => T14     /put in register for LARGE(I)
        iSST    (T13),T14                  /store the value into LARGE(I)
        iLDC    8               => T15     /constant 8
        dSLD    (T33)           => SF2     /value A(1,I)
        dABS    SF2             => SF3     /DABS(A(1,I))
        d2d     SF3             => SF1     /copy into value of VALUE(I)
        dSST    (T17),SF1                  /store value in VALUE(I)
        iLDC    2               => T23     /constant 2 - Initialize index
        i2i     T23             => T6      /setup value of J
        iCMPGT  T23,T8          => T34     /is 2 > N
        iBCOND  T34,B4,B12                 /yes - no iterations

B12:    iADD    T33,T15         => T28     /address(A(2,I)) = address(A(1,I)) + 8
        BR      B2

B2:     dSLD    (T28)           => SF4     /value A(J,I)
        dABS    SF4             => SF5     /DABS(A(J,I))
        dSLD    (T17)           => SF1     /value of VALUE(I)
        dCMPLE  SF5,SF1         => SF6     /comparison
        dBCOND  SF6,B3,B6                  /skip update of variables

B6:     d2d     SF5             => SF1     /update value of VALUE(I)
        dSST    (T17),SF1                  /store it back in memory
        i2i     T6              => T14     /put in register for LARGE(I)
        iSST    (T13),T14                  /store the value into LARGE(I)
        BR      B3

B3:     iADD    T6,T7           => T29     /J + 1
        i2i     T29             => T6      /update value of J
        iADD    T28,T15         => T35     /update value of address(A(J,I))
        i2I     T35             => T28
        iCMPGT  T6,T8           => T24     /is J > N
        iBCOND  T24,B4,B2
```

Figure 2.15 Continued

```
B4:     iADD    T5,T7       => T30   /I + 1
        i2i     T30         => T5    /first store into fetch location
        iADD    T13,T11     => T36   /increment address(LARGE(I))
        i2i     T36         => T13   /put pointer back in place
        iADD    T17,T15     => T37   /increment address(VALUE(I))
        i2i     T37         => T17   /put pointer back in place
        iADD    T33,T38     => T39   /increment address(A(1,I))
        i2i     T39         => T33   /put pointer back in place
        iCMPGT  T5,T8       => T9    /is I > N
        iBCOND  T9,B5,B1              /more iterations to perform

B5:     EPILOG                        /return from subroutine
```

This is a good point to review. The compiler has created the flow graph, simplified expressions, eliminated most redundant expressions, applied strength reduction, and performed expression reshaping. Except for some specialized code insertions for strength reduction, no expressions have been moved. Code motion will move code out of loops.

The techniques proposed here for code motion are based on a technique called "elimination of partial redundancies" devised by Etienne Morel (Morel and Renvoise, 1979). Abstractly, this technique attempts to insert copies of an expression on some paths through the flow graph to increase the number of redundant expressions. One example of where it works is with loops. Elimination of partial redundancies will insert copies of loop invariant expressions before the loop making the original copies in the loop redundant. Surprisingly, this technique works without knowledge of loops. We combine three other techniques with code motion:

1. A form of strength reduction is included in code motion. The technique is inexpensive to implement and has the advantage that it will apply strength reduction in situations where there are no loops.

2. Load motion is combined with code motion. Moving load operations can be handled as a code motion problem by pretending that any store operation is actually a store operation followed by the corresponding load operation. So a store operation can be viewed as having the same effect on the availability of an expression as a load operation. As will be seen in this example, this will increase the number of load operations that can be moved.

Compiler Structure

3. Store operations can also be moved by looking at the flow graph backward and applying the same algorithms to the reverse graph that we apply for expressions to the normal flow graph. We only look at the reverse graph for store operations.

In this particular example, code motion only removes the redundant loads of the constants 4 and 8. The load of *VALUE(I)* is moved out of the inner loop. It is not a loop-invariant expression since there is a store into *VALUE(I)* in the loop. However, the observation that a store may be viewed as a store followed by a load into the same register means that there is a load of *VALUE(I)* on each path to the use of *VALUE(I)*, making the load within the loop redundant. This gives the code in Figure 2.16.

Figure 2.16   After Code Motion

```
B0:   PROLOG
      iLDC     1              => T7     /constant 1 always in T7
      i2i      T7             => T5     /I = 1, first copy into value
      iSLD     (T2)           => T8     /fetch value of N
      iCMPGT   T7,T8          => T31    /is I > N
      iBCOND   T31,B5,B01               /no iterations to execute

B01:  i2i      T3             => T13    /address(LARGE(I))
      iLDC     4              => T11    /increment for address(LARGE(I))
      i2i      T4             => T17    /address(VALUE(I))
      iLDC     8              => T15    /increment for address(VALUE(I))
      i2i      T1             => T33    /address(A(1,I))
      iMUL     T15,T8         => T38    /increment for address(A(1,I))
      iLDC     2              => T23    /constant 2 - Initialize index
      BR       B1

B1:   i2i      T7             => T14    /put in register for LARGE(I)
      iSST     (T13),T14               /store the value into LARGE(I)
      dSLD     (T33)          => SF2    /value A(1,I)
      dABS     SF2            => SF3    /DABS(A(1,I))
      d2d      SF3            => SF1    /copy into value of VALUE(I)
      dSST     (T17),SF1               /store value into VALUE(I)
      i2i      T23            => T6     /setup value of J
      iCMPGT   T23,T8         => T34    /is 2 > N
      iBCOND   T34,B4,B12              /yes - no iterations

B12:  iADD     T33,T15        => T28    /address(A(2,I)) = address(A(1,I)) + 8
      BR       B2
```

Figure 2.16   Continued

```
B2:    dSLD      (T28)         => SF4      /value A(J,I)
       dABS      SF4           => SF5      /DABS(A(J,I))
       dCMPLE    SF5,SF1       => SF6      /comparison
       dBCOND    SF6,B3,B6                 /skip update of variables

B6:    d2d       SF5           => SF1      /update value of VALUE(I)
       dSST      (T17),SF1                 /store it back in memory
       i2i       T6            => T14      /put in register for LARGE(I)
       iSST      (T13),T14                 /store the value into LARGE(I)
       BR        B3

B3:    iADD      T6,T7         => T29      /J+1
       i2i       T29           => T6       /update value of J
       iADD      T28,T15       => T35      /update value of address(A(J,I))
       i2i       T35           => T28
       iCMPGT    T6,T8         => T24      /is J>N
       iBCOND    T24,B4,B2

B4:    iADD      T5,T7         => T30      /I+1
       i2i       T30           => T5       /first store into fetch location
       iADD      T13,T11       => T36      /increment address(LARGE(I))
       i2i       T36           => T13      /put pointer back in place
       iADD      T17,T15       => T37      /increment address(VALUE(I))
       i2i       T37           => T17      /put pointer back in place
       iADD      T33,T38       => T39      /increment address(A(1,I))
       i2i       T39           => T33      /put pointer back in place
       iCMPGT    T5,T8         => T9       /is I > N
       iBCOND    T9,B5,B1                  /more iterations to perform

B5:    EPILOG                              /return from subroutine
```

Now, we can move the store operations forward using partial redundancy on the reverse program flow graph, as shown in Figure 2.17. The stores into *VALUE(I)* and *LARGE(I)* occurring in the loop can be moved to block B4. Although we think of this as a motion out of the loop, the analysis has nothing to do with the loop. It depends on the occurrence of these store operations on each path to B4 and the repetitive stores that do occur in the loop. Together with dead-code elimination this gives us the final result of the optimization phases.

Compiler Structure

Figure 2.17 After Store Motion

```
B0:    PROLOG
       iLDC    1           => T7      /constant 1 always in T7
       i2i     T7          => T5      /I = 1, first copy into value
       iSLD    (T2)        => T8      /fetch value of N
       iCMPGT  T7,T8       => T31     /is I > N
       iBCOND  T31,B5,B01            /no iterations to execute

B01:   i2i     T3          => T13     /address(LARGE(I))
       iLDC    4           => T11     /increment for address(LARGE(I))
       i2i     T4          => T17     /address(VALUE(I))
       iLDC    8           => T15     /increment for address(VALUE(I))
       i2i     T1          => T33     /address(A(1,I))
       iMUL    T15,T8      => T38     /increment for address(A(1,I))
       iLDC    2           => T23     /constant 2 - Initialize index
       BR      B1

B1:    i2i     T7          => T14     /put in register for LARGE(I)
       dSLD    (T33)       => SF2     /value A(1,I)
       dABS    SF2         => SF3     /DABS(A(1,I))
       d2d     SF3         => SF1     /copy into value of VALUE(I)
       i2i     T23         => T6      /setup value of J
       iCMPGT  T23,T8      => T34     /is 2 > N
       iBCOND  T34,B4,B12            /yes - no iterations

B12:   iADD    T33,T15     => T28     /address(A(2,I)) = address(A(1,I))+8
       BR      B2

B2:    dSLD    (T28)       => SF4     /value A(J,I)
       dABS    SF4         => SF5     /DABS(A(J,I))
       dCMPLE  SF5,SF1     => SF6     /comparison
       dBCOND  SF6,B3,B6             /skip update of variables

B6:    d2d     SF5         => SF1     /update value of VALUE(I)
       i2i     T6          => T14     /put in register for LARGE(I)
       BR      B3

B3:    iADD    T6,T7       => T29     /J + 1
       i2i     T29         => T6      /update value of J
       iADD    T28,T15     => T35     /update value of address(A(J,I))
       i2i     T35         => T28
       iCMPGT  T6,T8       => T24     /is J > N
       iBCOND  T24,B4,B2

B4:    iSST    (T13),T14             /store the value into LARGE(I)
       dSST    (T17),SF1             /store the value into VALUE(I)
       iADD    T5,T7       => T30     /I + 1
       i2i     T30         => T5      /first store into fetch location
       iADD    T13,T11     => T36     /increment address(LARGE(I))
       i2i     T36         => T13     /put pointer back in place
```

Figure 2.17 Continued

```
        iADD    T17,T15     => T37    /increment address(VALUE(I))
        i2i     T37         => T17    /put pointer back in place
        iADD    T33,T38     => T39    /increment address(A(1,I))
        i2i     T39         => T33    /put pointer back in place
        iCMPGT  T5,T8       => T9     /is I > N
        iBCOND  T9,B5,B1               /more iterations to perform

B5:     EPILOG                         /return from subroutine
```

2.8 Limiting Resources

The program flow graph for the procedure has now been transformed into a form suitable for generating instructions for the target machine. There is a one-to-one correspondence between the operations in the program flow graph and instructions for the target machine. There are still three things to determine about the resulting program.

- *Peephole optimization:* Multiple instructions must be combined into single instructions that have the same effect. This includes the classic peephole optimizations together with simplifications involving folding constants into instructions that can use constants.

- *Instruction scheduling:* The order of the instructions must be found. By reordering the instructions, the delays inherent in instructions that take more than one machine cycle can be hidden by the execution of other instructions.

- *Register allocation:* The temporaries used for values in the program flow graph must be replaced by the use of physical registers.

Unfortunately, instruction scheduling and register allocation are interdependent. If the compiler reorders the instructions to decrease execution time, it will increase the number of physical registers needed to hold values. On the other hand, if one allocates the temporaries to physical registers before instruction scheduling, then the amount of instruction reordering is limited. This is known as a *phase-ordering problem*. There is no natural order for performing instruction scheduling and register allocation.

The LIMIT phase performs the first of these three tasks and prepares the code for instruction scheduling and register allocation. It attempts to resolve this problem by performing parts of the register allocation problem before instruction scheduling, then allowing instruction scheduling to occur. Register allocation then follows, plus a possible second round of instruction scheduling if the register allocator generated any instructions itself (spill code).

Before preparing for instruction scheduling and register allocation, the compiler lowers the program representation to the most efficient set of instructions. This is the last of the code-lowering phases.

We begin by modifying the flow graph so that each operation corresponds to an operation in the target machine. Since the instruction description was chosen to be close to a RISC processor, most instructions already correspond to target machine instructions. This step is usually called code generation; however, our view of code generation is more diffuse. We began code generation when we built the flow graph, we progressed further into code generation with each lowering of the flow graph, and we complete it now by guaranteeing the correspondence between instructions in the flow graph and instructions in the target machine.

To illustrate this code lowering, we assume that the target machine contains instructions with small-constant immediate operands. For example, the addition of small constants can be performed with an immediate operand. Or load and store operations can take a constant as an additive part of the address computation. The target machine also has instructions for adding a multiple of 4 or 8 times one register, adding another register, and putting the result in a target register. In other words, we consider a target processor such as the Alpha processor. While performing code lowering, the compiler will also perform the following operations:

- Replacing instructions in the flow graph by equivalent target machine instructions. If the instruction in the flow graph is a target machine instruction, then the compiler leaves it as it is.

- Removing register-to-register copy operations. The compiler no longer honors the convention that a particular expression is computed in a fixed symbolic register. Now all effort is made to eliminate register-to-register copies.

- In the process of code lowering, some blocks will become empty. The compiler deletes them.

The important instructions for the Alpha processor that simplify this particular example are as follows:

- The S4ADDQ instruction computes 4 times one register plus another, simplifying address arithmetic on integer arrays.

- The S8ADDQ instruction computes 8 times one register plus another, simplifying address arithmetic on double-precision arrays.

- The CPYS instruction, which takes two operands, creates a floating point value from the sign of one operand and the absolute value of another. It can be used to compute the absolute value.

The use of these instructions may make other computations unnecessary, such as an instruction that loads a constant, or the multiplication or shift operation (and its target register). These unnecessary computations must be eliminated also. This can be performed partially during the other optimizations or by the execution of the dead-code elimination algorithm.

The compiler also orders the blocks so that the destination pairs in conditional branches can be replaced with fall-through values; however, we do not eliminate the extra part of the branches because register allocation may need to insert blocks and such elimination would change the order of blocks. The code in Figure 2.18 shows the results of code lowering. At this point the restriction that the same expression always be computed in the same register is discarded since this would add unnecessary instructions. Hence the loop variables are incremented by a single iADD instruction. Note that an S8ADDQ instruction is used to increment the pointer referencing the *A* array in the inner loop.

At the same time that the code is being lowered, the LIMIT phase is preparing for instruction scheduling and register allocation by performing the following transformations.

- *Rename:* There are many situations in which the same temporary is used in two independent parts of the procedure. This can happen through the source program using the same automatic variable for two purposes, or through transformations performed by earlier phases of the compiler. One of the sets of uses is now renamed to reference a new temporary. By using independent names, register allocation is more effective. Rename is illustrated in Figure 2.19. In the code on the left, the same index variable is used for two loops. After renaming, two different index variables are used, as seen in the code on the right.

- *Coalesce:* Many register-to-register operations in the program flow graph can be eliminated. In a copy $T1 = T2$, if neither $T1$ nor $T2$ changes on any path from the copy to a use of $T1$, then all references to $T1$ can be replaced by a reference to $T2$, eliminating the copy operation. Eliminating one copy operation can expose the possibility of eliminating more copies. This compiler uses a slightly more general algorithm which eliminates a second temporary if it is known to have the same value as one already computed.

Figure 2.18 After Code Lowering

```
 0   B0:    PROLOG
 1          iLDC     1              => T5     /I = 1
 2          iSLD     (T2)           => T8     /fetch value of N
 3          iBLE     T8,B5,B1                 /no iterations if N <= 0

 4   B1:    iLDC     1              => T14    /LARGE(I) = 1
 5          dSLD     (T1)           => SF2    /value A(1,I)
 6          CPYS     SF2            => SF1    /DABS(A(1,I))
 7          iLDC     2              => T6
 8          iCMPLE   T8,#2          => T34    /is 2 > N
 9          iBCOND   T34,B4,B12               /yes - no iterations

10   B12:   iADD     T1,#8          => T28    /address(A(2,I)) = address(A(1,I))+8
11          BR       B2

12   B2:    dSLD     (T28)          => SF4    /value A(J,I)
13          CPYS     SF4            => SF4    /DABS(A(J,I))
14          dCMPLE   SF4,SF1        => SF6    /comparison
15          dBCOND   SF6,B3,B6                /skip update of variables

16   B6:    d2d      SF4            => SF1    /update value of VALUE(I)
17          i2i      T6             => T14    /put in register for LARGE(I)
18          BR       B3

19   B3:    iADD     T6,#1          => T6     /J + 1
20          iADD     T28,#8         => T28    /update value of address(A(J,I))
21          iCMPGT   T6,T8          => T24    /is J > N
22          iBCOND   T24,B4,B2

23   B4:    iSST     (T3),T14                 /store the value into LARGE(I)
24          dSST     (T4),SF1                 /store the value into VALUE(I)
25          iADD     T5,#1          => T5     /I + 1
26          iADD     T3,#4          => T3     /increment address(LARGE(I))
27          iADD     T4,#8          => T4     /increment address(VALUE(I))
28          S8ADDQ   T8,T1          => T1     /increment address(A(1,N))
29          iCMPGT   T5,T8          => T9     /compare fetch(I) ? fetch(N)
30          iBCOND   T9,B5,B1                 /more iterations to perform

31   B5:    EPILOG                            /return from subroutine
```

- *Pressure:* The register pressure at a point p in the program flow graph is the number of registers needed at p to hold the values that are computed before p and used after p. The maximum register pressure is an estimate of the minimum number of registers needed for allocating registers for the procedure. It is not a precise lower estimate because more registers

Figure 2.19 Computing Right Number of Names

```
DO I = 1, N              DO I1 = 1, N
   A(I) = B(I)              A(I1) = B(I1)
ENDDO                    ENDDO
DO I = 1, M              DO I = 1, M
   C(I) = D(I)              C(I) = D(I)
ENDDO                    ENDDO
```

may be needed due to the interactions of multiple paths through the procedure. However, if the register pressure is higher than the number of available registers, then some temporaries will be stored in memory for part of the procedure. This is called *register spilling*.

- *Spilling:* LIMIT will consider each point where the register pressure exceeds the number of physical registers. It will consider each enclosing loop containing that point and find a temporary that is not used in the loop but which holds a value to be used later (in other words, it is holding a value passing through the loop). It takes the temporary that has that property on the outermost loop, stores it in memory before the loop, and reloads it after the loop (where necessary). This decreases the register pressure by 1 everywhere within the loop. If no loop contains a temporary of this form, a temporary that holds a value but is unused in the block will be chosen. If no such temporary exists, a temporary used or defined within the block will be chosen. This whole process will be repeated until the register pressure has been decreased below the number of available registers everywhere within the procedure.

To compute the register pressure, the compiler needs to know for each point of the flow graph the temporaries that hold a value used later, in other words, the set of temporaries that are live at each point in the program. For illustrative purposes, the set of points where each temporary is live is represented as a set of intervals using the numbers we associated with each instruction in Figure 2.18. If a temporary is live at the beginning of the first instruction of an interval, we will indicate that by using a closed bracket. If it becomes live in the middle of an instruction, we will use an open parenthesis. Figure 2.20 indicates the range of instructions where each register is live.

This information can be used to compute the number of registers needed at each point in the program, otherwise known as the register pressure. If the number of registers needed exceeds the number of physical registers

Compiler Structure

Figure 2.20 Table of Live Ranges

```
T1    [0,30]
T2    [0,2)
T3    [0,30]
T4    [0,30]
T5    (1,30]
T6    (7,22]
T8    (2,30]
T9    (29,30)
T14   (4,15],(17,23)
T24   (21,22)
T28   (10,22]
T34   (8,9)
SF1   (6,15],(16,24)
SF2   (5,6)
SF4   (12,16)
SF6   (14,15)
```

available, then not all temporaries will be able to be assigned to registers. The registers that are live before and after each instruction in the subroutine are shown in Figure 2.21. In this particular case the largest register pressure occurs in the innermost loop. This is frequently true, but is not always the case.

One computes a separate register pressure for each register set: integer and floating point. We have shown the register pressure for integer registers. The register pressure for floating point registers is not shown in Figure 2.21 so as to make the table more understandable; however, there are only three floating registers in the program, so determining the register pressure is straightforward.

Now we compute the register pressure at the beginning of each statement. This is a pair consisting of the number of integer and floating point symbolic or physical registers that are live at the beginning of each instruction. Recall that the formal parameters are live at the beginning of the program (if they are used anywhere in the program), so T1, T2, T3, and T4 are live at the beginning of the subroutine.

As is frequently the case with small flow graphs, there is no register spilling needed. The maximum register pressure is much lower than the number of registers. However, let us pretend that the machine only has eight registers. The register pressure is 9 at the end of the inner loop, so we cannot fit the number of symbolic registers that are live at that point into the available

Figure 2.21   Live Registers and Register Pressure Before Instruction

Inst	Code				Live Registers	Pressure
0	B0:	PROLOG			T1,T2,T3,T4	4
1		iLDC	1	=> T5	T1,T2,T3,T4	4
2		iSLD	(T2)	=> T8	T1,T2,T3,T4,T5	5
3		iBLE	T8,B5,B1		T1,T3,T4,T5,T8	5
					T1,T3,T4,T5,T8	5
4	B1:	iLDC	1	=> T14	T1,T3,T4,T5,T8	5
5		dSLD	(T1)	=> SF2	T1,T3,T4,T5,T8,T14	6
6		CPYS	SF2	=> SF1	T1,T3,T4,T5,T8,T14	6
7		iLDC	2	=> T6	T1,T3,T4,T5,T6,T8,T14	7
8		iCMPLE	T8,#2	=> T34	T1,T3,T4,T5,T6,T8,T14	7
9		iBCOND	T34,B4,B12		T1,T3,T4,T5,T6,T8,T14,T34	8
					T1,T3,T4,T5,T6,T8,T14	7
10	B12:	iADD	T1,#8	=> T28	T1,T3,T4,T5,T6,T8,T14	7
11		BR	B2		T1,T3,T4,T5,T6,T8,T14,T28	8
					T1,T3,T4,T5,T6,T8,T14,T28	8
12	B2:	dSLD	(T28)	=> SF4	T1,T3,T4,T5,T6,T8,T14,T28	8
13		CPYS	SF4	=> SF4	T1,T3,T4,T5,T6,T8,T14,T28	8
14		dCMPLE	SF4,SF1	=> SF6	T1,T3,T4,T5,T6,T8,T14,T28	8
15		dBCOND	SF6,B3,B6		T1,T3,T4,T5,T6,T8,T14,T28	8
					T1,T3,T4,T5,T6,T8,T14,T28	8
16	B6:	d2d	SF4	=> SF1	T1,T3,T4,T5,T6,T8,T28	7
17		i2i	T6	=> T14	T1,T3,T4,T5,T6,T8,T28	7
18		BR	B3		T1,T3,T4,T5,T6,T8,T14,T28	8
					T1,T3,T4,T5,T6,T8,T14,T28	8
19	B3:	iADD	T6,#1	=> T6	T1,T3,T4,T5,T6,T8,T14,T28	8
20		iADD	T28,#8	=> T28	T1,T3,T4,T5,T6,T8,T14,T28	8
21		iCMPGT	T6,T8	=> T24	T1,T3,T4,T5,T6,T8,T14,T28	8
22		iBCOND	T24,B4,B2		T1,T3,T4,T5,T6,T8,T14,T24,T28	9
					T1,T3,T4,T5,T6,T8,T14,T28	8
23	B4:	iSST	(T3),T14		T1,T3,T4,T5,T8,T14	6
24		dSST	(T4),SF1		T1,T3,T4,T5,T8	5
25		iADD	T5,#1	=> T5	T1,T3,T4,T5,T8	5
26		iADD	T3,#4	=> T3	T1,T3,T4,T5,T8	5
27		iADD	T4,#8	=> T4	T1,T3,T4,T5,T8	5
28		S8ADDQ	T8,T1	=> T1	T1,T3,T4,T5,T8	5
29		iCMPGT	T5,T8	=> T9	T1,T3,T4,T5,T8	5
30		iBCOND	T9,B5,B1		T1,T3,T4,T5,T8,T9	6
					T1,T3,T4,T5,T8	5
31	B5:	EPILOG				0

registers. The symbolic registers T1, T3, T4, T5, T6, T8, T14, T24, and T28 are live at the point at which the pressure is 9; however, T1, T3, T4, T5, and T8 are not referenced (defined or used) in the inner loop. Therefore one of them can be spilled before the loop and reloaded after the loop. This will decrease the register pressure by 1 throughout the loop. Ideally, we would

Compiler Structure

choose the register that is referenced in as few nested loops as possible. These temporaries are all referenced in the next loop, however, so we will arbitrarily choose to store T5, which is the temporary representing I.

We use the stack (SP is a dedicated register) to spill registers to memory. Note that the register pressure has peaked at one point, and that by spilling a register we have decreased the register pressure at other points.

The insertion process takes two steps. First insert a store operation at the beginning of the outermost loop where the temporary (T5) is not referenced, and insert load operations at the exits from the loop if the temporary is live on exit. Second, optimize the placement of the loads and stores by moving the loads as far as possible toward the beginning of the program and the stores toward the end of the program. This gives us the code in Figure 2.22.

Figure 2.22 Load and Store Operations for Spilling

Inst	Code				Live Registers	Pressure
0	B0:	PROLOG	(8 byte stack)		T1,T2,T3,T4	4
1		iLDC	1	=> T5	T1,T2,T3,T4	4
		iSST	(SP),T5		T1,T2,T3,T4,T5	5
2		iSLD	(T2)	=> T8	T1,T3,T4	3
3		iBLE	T8,B5,B1		T1,T3,T4,T8	4
					T1,T3,T4,T8	4
4	B1:	iLDC	1	=> T14	T1,T3,T4,T8,T14	5
5		dSLD	(T1)	=> SF2	T1,T3,T4,T8,T14	5
6		CPYS	SF2	=> SF1	T1,T3,T4,T8,T14	5
7		iLDC	2	=> T6	T1,T3,T4,T8,T14	5
8		iCMPLE	T8,#2	=> T34	T1,T3,T4,T6,T8,T14	6
9		iBCOND	T34,B4,B12		T1,T3,T4,T6,T8,T14,T34	7
					T1,T3,T4,T6,T8,T14	6
10	B12:	iADD	T1,#8	=> T28	T1,T3,T4,T6,T8,T14,T28	7
11		BR	B2		T1,T3,T4,T6,T8,T14,T28	7
					T1,T3,T4,T6,T8,T14,T28	7
12	B2:	dSLD	(T28)	=> SF4	T1,T3,T4,T6,T8,T14,T28	7
13		CPYS	SF4	=> SF4	T1,T3,T4,T6,T8,T14,T28	7
14		dCMPLE	SF4,SF1	=> SF6	T1,T3,T4,T6,T8,T14,T28	7
15		dBCOND	SF6,B3,B6		T1,T3,T4,T6,T8,T14,T28	7
					T1,T3,T4,T6,T8,T14,T28	7
16	B6:	d2d	SF4	=> SF1	T1,T3,T4,T6,T8,T28	6
17		i2i	T6	=> T14	T1,T3,T4,T6,T8,T28	6
18		BR	B3		T1,T3,T4,T6,T8,T14,T28	7
					T1,T3,T4,T6,T8,T14,T28	7
19	B3:	iADD	T6,#1	=> T6	T1,T3,T4,T6,T8,T14,T28	7
20		iADD	T28,#8	=> T28	T1,T3,T4,T6,T8,T14,T28	7
21		iCMPGT	T6,T8	=> T24	T1,T3,T4,T6,T8,T14,T28	7
22		iBCOND	T24,B4,B2		T1,T3,T4,T6,T8,T14,T24,T28	8

Figure 2.22 Continued

					T1,T3,T4,T6,T8,T14,T28	8
23	B4:	iSST	(T3),T14		T1,T3,T4,T8	4
24		dSST	(T4),SF1		T1,T3,T4,T8	4
		iSLD	(SP),T5		T1,T3,T4,T8	
25		iADD	T5,#1	=> T5	T1,T3,T4,T5,T8	4
		iSST	(SP),T5		T1,T3,T4,T5,T8	
26		iADD	T3,#4	=> T3	T1,T3,T4,T5,T8	5
27		iADD	T4,#8	=> T4	T1,T3,T4,T5,T8	5
28		S8ADDQ	T8,T1	=> T1	T1,T3,T4,T5,T8	5
29		iCMPGT	T5,T8	=> T9	T1,T3,T4,T5,T8	5
30		iBCOND	T9,B5,B1		T1,T3,T4,T5,T8	5
					T1,T3,T4,T5,T8	5
31	B5:	EPILOG				0

After the LIMIT phase, the compiler knows that the resources are available at each point to perform the operations described in the program flow graph. The remaining phases of the compiler will preserve this invariant whenever they perform a transformation.

2.9 Instruction Scheduling

A modern RISC processor is implemented using what is called a *pipeline architecture*. This means that each operation is divided into multiple stages, with each stage taking one machine cycle to complete. Because each stage takes one cycle, a new instruction may start on each cycle, but it may not complete for some number of cycles after its initiation. Unfortunately, most techniques for code generation attempt to use a value as soon after its calculation is initiated as possible. This was the preferred technique on earlier machines because it limited the number of registers that were needed. However, this order slows down the execution on a RISC processor, since the value is not immediately available. The instruction scheduler reorders the instructions to initiate instructions earlier than their use so that the processor will not be delayed.

Recent RISC processors can start the initiation of several instructions simultaneously. These instructions must be independent and use different function units within the processor. The scheduler must form these groups of instructions, called *packets*. All instructions in a packet can be issued simultaneously.

The original instruction schedulers scheduled instructions within a single block, possibly taking into account the instructions that ended the preceding blocks. They did this by creating a data structure called the *instruction dependence graph,* which contained the operations as nodes and directed edges between two nodes if the first operation must be executed before the second operation. The edges were labeled with the number of machine cycles that must occur between the execution of the two instructions. The scheduler then performed a topological sort of the instruction dependence graph specialized to minimize the total number of cycles that the ordering of instructions required.

Scheduling limited to blocks does not use the multiple instruction-issue character of RISC processors effectively. Blocks are usually small, and each instruction within them depends on some other instructions in the block. Consider the problem of instruction scheduling as filling in a matrix, with the number of columns being the number of instructions that can be issued simultaneously and the number of rows being the number of machine cycles it takes to execute the block. Block scheduling will fill in this matrix sparsely: There will be many empty slots, indicating that the multiple-issue character of the machine is not being used. This is particularly a problem for load, store, multiply, divide, or floating point operations which take many cycles to execute. RISC processors usually implement other integer operations in one cycle. There are several techniques incorporated in the compiler for ameliorating this problem:

- *Unroll:* Earlier phases of the compiler have performed loop unrolling, which increases the size of blocks, giving the block scheduler more chance to schedule the instructions together.

- *Superblock:* When there is a point in a loop where two paths join, it is difficult to move instructions from after the join point to before it. When the succeeding block in the loop is short, the compiler has earlier made a copy of the block so that the joined path is replaced by two blocks, joined only at the head of the loop. This transformation is applied at the same time that loop unrolling is performed.

- *Move:* The normal optimization techniques used for code motion attempt to keep temporaries live for as short a sequence of instructions as is possible. When scheduling, we will schedule each block separately.

For blocks that are executed frequently, we will repeat the code motion algorithm, but allow the motion of instructions from one block to another even when there is no decrease in execution of the instruction.

- *Trace:* Consider the most frequently executed block, *B*, determined either by heuristics or profile information. Find the maximal path including *B* that involves the most frequently executed predecessors and successors of each block on the path. Now consider this path as if it were a block, with some modifications to the dependence graphs to ensure proper actions at condition branches. See if there are any instructions on this path that can be moved to earlier (or later) blocks.

- *Software pipelining:* In the special case of a loop that is a single block, software pipelining can give a good schedule. Software pipelining uses dependence information provided by the dependence graph (not the instruction dependence graph) to overlap the schedules for one iteration of the loop with the following iterations. This does not decrease the length of time that each iteration takes (it may increase it), but allows the iterations to start more quickly, thereby decreasing the execution time of the whole loop. Blocks and loops that can be software pipelined are identified before other scheduling occurs and are handled separately.

During instruction scheduling, some peephole optimization occurs. It can happen during scheduling that instructions that were not adjacent have become adjacent, creating situations such as a store followed by an immediate load from the same location. It is therefore effective to apply some of the peephole optimizations again.

When instruction scheduling is completed, the order of instructions is fixed and cannot be changed without executing the instruction scheduler again. In that case, it may only be necessary to rerun the block scheduler.

We have shrunk the register requirements so the values in registers can fit in the physical registers at each point in the flow graph. Now we will reorder the instructions to satisfy the instruction-scheduling constraints of the target processor. We will assume a processor such as the Alpha 21164, which can issue four instructions on each clock cycle. Many of the integer instructions take one cycle to complete. Most floating point operations take four cycles to complete. In any given cycle one can issue one or two load instructions or a single store instruction. A store instruction cannot be issued in the same cycle as a load instruction. We will assume that the other integer operations can be filled in as necessary. Instructions such as integer multiply or floating point divide take a large number of cycles.

The problem is to group the instructions into one to four instruction packets such that all the instructions in a packet can be issued simultaneously. The compiler also reorders the instructions in an attempt not to use an operand until a number of cycles following the issue of the instruction that computes it to ensure that the value is available.

The load and store operations take a variable amount of time, depending on the load on the memory bus and whether the values are in caches. In the Alpha 21164, there are two caches on the processor chip, and most systems have a further large cache on the processor board. A load instruction takes two cycles for the cache nearest the processor, eight cycles in the next cache, twenty cycles in the board cache, and a long time if data is in memory. Furthermore, the processor contains hardware to optimize the loading of consecutive memory locations. If two load operations are each issued on two consecutive cycles to consecutive memory locations, the processor will optimize the use of the memory bus.

It is important that useless branches are at least not counted when determining scheduling. This is marked with an asterisk (*) in the cycle location.

There are hardware bypasses so that a compare instruction and a branch instruction can be issued in the same cycle. Note that the assignment to SI9 (in B1) can be moved forward eliminating an extra slot. Also note that B12 is only reached from the preceding block, so NOPs do not need to be inserted.

Now note that the inner loop starting with block B2 consists of three blocks. The first block is the conditional test and the third block updates the iterations. All but one of the computations from the third block can be moved to the first block (hoisting), while the remaining instructions can be scheduled more effectively by making a copy of the iteration block (superblock scheduling).

Note that NOPS were inserted in the middle of the code. The machine picks up four instructions at a time, aligned on 16-byte boundaries. It must initiate all instructions in this packet of four instructions before going on to the next packet. To execute the instructions in the smallest amount of time, we must maximize the number of independent instructions in each packet. The resulting scheduled instructions are shown in Figure 2.23.

Figure 2.23 Scheduled Instructions

```
Number      Instruction                         Comment
0     B0:   PROLOG
1           iLDC       1          => T5         /(0) I = 1
2           iSLD       (T2)       => T8         /(0) fetch value of N
3           iBLE       T8,B5                    /(1) no iterations if N <= 0
4           NOP                                 /(1)

5     B1:   iLDC       1          => T14        /(0) LARGE(I) = 1
6           dSLD       (T1)       => SF2        /(0) value A(1,I)
7           CPYS       SF2        => SF1        /(1) DABS(A(1,I))
8           iLDC       2          => T6         /(1)
9           iCMPLT     T8,#2      => T34        /(2) is 2 > N
10          iBCOND     T34,B4                   /(2) yes - no iterations

11    B12:  iADD       T1,#8      => T28        /(0) address(A(2,I)) = address(A(1,I)) + 8
12          NOP                                 /(0) to line up loop entry

13    B2:   dSLD       (T28)      => SF4        /(0) value A(J,I)
14          iADD       T28,#8     => T28        /(0) schedule address update early
15          iCMPLE     T6,T8      => T24        /(1) is J > N
16          iADD       T6,#1      => T6         /(1) J + 1
17          CPYS       SF4        => SF4        /(3) DABS(A(J,I))
18          dCMPGT     SF4,SF1    => SF6        /(7) comparison
19          dBCOND     SF6,B6                   /(11) skip update of variables
20          iBCOND     T24,B2                   /(12)

21    B4:   iSST       (T3),T14                 /(0) store the value into LARGE(I)
22          iADD       T3,#4      => T3         /(0) increment address(LARGE(I))
23          dSST       (T4),SF1                 /(1) store the value into VALUE(I)
24          iADD       T4,#8      => T4         /(1) increment address(VALUE(I))
25          iADD       T5,#1      => T5         /(2) I + 1
26          S8ADDQ     T8,T1      => T1         /(2) increment address(A(1,N))
27          iCMPLE     T5,T8      => T9         /(3) compare fetch(I) ? fetch(N)
28          iBCOND     T9,B1                    /(3) more iterations to perform

29    B5:   EPILOG                              /(0) return from subroutine

30    B6:   d2d        SF4        => SF1        /(0) Infrequently executed code moved
31          iSUB       T6,#1      => T14        /(0) put in register for LARGE(I)
32          iBCOND     T24,B2                   /(1)
33          BR         B4                       /(1)
```

2.10 Register Allocation

The register allocation phase modifies the program flow graph by replacing temporaries with physical registers. There are categories of techniques for performing register allocation on the complete procedure. One is based on graph-coloring algorithms. A graph is formed with each temporary being a node. An undirected edge exists between two nodes if they cannot occupy the same physical register. Register allocation reduces to coloring this graph, where each color represents a different physical register.

The alternative method for register allocation is based on bin packing, where there is a bin for each physical register. Two temporaries can be allocated to the same bin if there is no point in the program where both need to have a value.

Each of these techniques has advantages and disadvantages. The graph-coloring technique is superior when considering conditional branching. Since the bin-packing algorithms typically approximate the set of points where a temporary holds a value by some data structure where it is easy to take intersections of the sets, bin packing does not perform as well as graph coloring with branching.

Bin packing performs better than graph coloring when straight-line code is considered. Since bin packing can traverse the blocks as it performs assignment, it can determine when the same register can be reused immediately. It can also use information about the operations in the program and their order to decide which temporaries to store to memory when too many registers are needed (this can happen even though the LIMIT phase has been executed). Graph coloring has no concept of locality of reference.

This compiler's register allocator combines the two techniques. Because LIMIT has been run, little register spilling will occur. Graph coloring is therefore used to assign registers to temporaries that hold values at the beginning of some block, in other words, in those situations in which graph coloring performs best. A modification of bin packing suggested by Hendron (1993) will be used to schedule temporaries within each block.

Previous attempts at splitting the temporaries that are live at the beginning of blocks (global allocation) from those that are live within a block (local allocation) have encountered difficulties because performing either global or local allocation before the other could affect the quality of register allocation. This problem is resolved by the existence of the LIMIT phase, which has performed spilling of global temporaries before either allocation occurs.

Note that the presence of LIMIT has eliminated most register spilling during register allocation. It does not eliminate all of it. There can be secondary effects of conditional branching that can cause register spilling during either graph coloring or bin packing. This situation is unavoidable, since optimal register allocation is NP-complete. In the situations in which spilling occurs, the register allocator will insert the required store and load operations.

Now we apply register allocation to the example. First the compiler must recompute the points where temporaries are live, because instruction scheduling has changed these points (see Figure 2.24). Note that the scheduler has introduced a redefinition of a local register, so we need to either do superblock scheduling earlier (when we don't know that it will pay off) or redo right number of names, or locally redo right number of names when we create these problems. We only deal with the integer registers here; the floating point registers in this case are simple because they all interfere and so one assigns each to a different register.

After the lifetime information for temporaries has been computed, the compiler uses a graph-coloring algorithm to allocate the registers that are live at the beginning of some block, or registers which are directly assigned to a physical register. The ones assigned to a physical register are preallocated; however, they must be considered here to avoid any accidental assignments. The physical registers will be named using $0, $1, and so on. Note that the temporaries corresponding to formal parameters are assigned to physical registers specified by the calling standard for the target machine. The globally assigned registers are listed in Figure 2.25, together with the kind of register. In this case all of the registers needed are called *scratch registers,* which means that the value in the register need not be saved and restored if the register is used in the procedure.

Figure 2.24 Live Ranges after Scheduling

T1	[1,28],[30,33]	Global
T2	[1,2)	Global
T3	[1,28],[30,33]	Global
T4	[1,28],[30,33]	Global
T5	(1,28],[30,33]	Global
T6	(8,20],[30,33]	Global
T8	(2,28],[30,33]	Global
T9	(27,28)	Local
T14	(5,21),(31,33]	Global
T24	(15,20),[30,32)	Global
T28	(11,20],[30,33]	Global
T34	(9,10)	Local
SF1	(7,23),(30,33]	Global
SF2	(6,7)	Local
SF4	(13,18),[30,30]	Global
SF6	(18,19)	Local

Figure 2.25 Global Register Assignments

```
T1              $16     Parameter
T2              $17     Parameter
T3              $18     Parameter
T4              $19     Parameter
T5              $22     Scratch Register
T6              $23     Scratch Register
T8              $24     Scratch Register
T14             $25     Scratch Register
T24             $20     Scratch Register
T28             $21     Scratch Register
SF1             $f10    Floating Scratch
SF4             $f11    Floating Scratch
Stack Pointer   $30     Stack Pointer
Return Address  $27     Return Address
```

After that the registers that are live at the beginning of any block have been allocated, we can allocate the symbolic registers that are live only within a single block. In this small example there are only a few. In realistic programs, these registers greatly outnumber the globally live registers. These local registers are listed in Figure 2.26. A register is reused if at all possible because the compiler wants to minimize the number of registers used. This avoids the necessity of using a register that is not a scratch register and would thus require that a store operation be inserted at the beginning of the procedure to save its value and a load inserted at the exit to restore the value.

The resulting assembly code is shown in Figure 2.27. The temporaries have all been replaced by registers. There were no spill instructions inserted, so the instruction schedules have not changed.

Figure 2.26 Local Register Assignments

```
T9      $23     Reuse of Register
T34     $21     New Register
SF2     $f10    Reuse of Register
SF6     $f12    New Register
```

Figure 2.27 Code after Register Allocation

```
Number      Instruction                      Comment
0     B0:   PROLOG
1           iLDC     1            => $22    /(0) I = 1
2           iSLD     ($17)        => $17    /(0) fetch value of N
3           iBLE     $17,B5                 /(1) no iterations if N <= 0
4           NOP                             /(1)

5     B1:   iLDC     1            => $24    /(0) LARGE(I) = 1
6           dSLD     ($16)        => $f10   /(0) value A(1,I)
7           CPYS     $f10         => $f10   /(1) DABS(A(1,I))
8           iLDC     2            => $23    /(1)
9           iCMPLT   $17,#2       => $21    /(2) is 2 > N
10          iBCOND   $21,B4                 /(2) yes - no iterations

11    B12:  iADD     $16,#8       => $20    /(0) address(A(2,I)) = address(A(1,I)) + 8
12          NOP                             /(0) to line up loop entry

13    B2:   dSLD     ($20)        => $f11   /(0) value A(J,I)
14          iADD     $20,#8       => $20    /(0) schedule address update early
15          iCMPLE   $23,$17      => $25    /(1) is J > N
16          iADD     $23,#1       => $23    /(1) J + 1
17          CPYS     $f11         => $f11   /(3) DABS(A(J,I))
18          dCMPGT   $f11,$f10    => $f12   /(7) comparison
19          dBCOND   $f12, B6                /(11) skip update of variables
20          iBCOND   $25, B2                /(12)

21    B4:   iSST     ($18),$24              /(0) store the value into LARGE(I)
22          iADD     $18,#4       => $18    /(0) increment address(LARGE(I))
23          dSST     ($19),$f10             /(1) store the value into VALUE(I)
24          iADD     $19,#8       => $19    /(1) increment address(VALUE(I))
25          iADD     $22,#1       => $22    /(2) I + 1
26          S8ADDQ   $17,$16      => $16    /(2) increment address(A(1,N))
27          iCMPLE   $22,$17      => $23    /(3) compare fetch(I) ? fetch(N)
28          iBCOND   $23,B1                 /(3) more iterations to perform

29    B5:   EPILOG                          /(0) return from subroutine

30    B6:   d2d      $f11         => $f10   /(0) Infrequently executed code moved
31          iSUB     $23,#1       => $24    /(0) put in register for LARGE(I)
32          iBCOND   $25,B2                 /(1)
33          BR       B4                     /(1)
```

2.11 Rescheduling

The next phase is a rescheduling phase, which is only executed if the register allocator has changed the set of instructions that are executed. This can happen due to either a peephole optimization or the introduction of spill code. Neither of these occurred in this case, so the rescheduling operation is ignored.

If the register allocator generated any instructions, that is, register spilling occurred, then the instruction scheduler is executed again, but in this case only on blocks where load or store operations have been inserted.

2.12 Forming the Object Module

At last, we near the completion of our task. The instructions have been chosen; the registers have been chosen. All that remains is the clerical task of translating this information and the information about globally allocated data into an object module. This task includes the insertion of debugging information for the debugger. Since our task has been long, I am making light of this last phase. It involves little intricate technology. However, it is complex because the structures of object modules are complex and undocumented. Every document that I have seen describing object module form has serious errors. So this project involves experimental computer science—trying to determine what the linker is expecting. This phase will also generate the assembly language listing for the listing file, if it is requested.

2.13 References

Allen, R., and K. Kennedy. "Advanced compilation for vector and parallel computers." San Mateo, CA: Morgan Kaufmann.

Frazer, C. W., and D. R. Hanson. 1995. *A retargetable C compiler: Design and implementation.* Redwood City, CA: Benjamin/Cummings.

Hendron, L. J., G. R. Gao, E. Altman, and C. Mukerji. 1993. A register allocation framework based on hierarchical cyclic interval graphs. (Technical report.) McGill University.

Hendron, L. J., G. R. Gao, E. Altman, and C. Mukerji. 1993. Register allocation using cyclic interval graphs: A new approach to an old problem. (Technical report.) McGill University.

Morel, E., and C. Renvoise. 1979. Global optimization by suppression of partial redundancies. *Communications of the ACM* 22(2): 96–103.

Wolfe, M. 1996. *High performance compilers for parallel computing.* Reading, MA: Addison-Wesley.

3 GRAPHS

A prime prerequisite for being a compiler writer is being a "data structure junkie." One must live, breathe, and love data structures, so we will not provide the usual complete list of all background mathematics that usually appears in a compiler book. We assume that you have access to any one of a number of data structure or introductory compiler writing books, such as Lorho (1984) or Fischer and LeBlanc (1988). This design assumes that you are familiar with the following topics, which are addressed by each of the data structure books referenced.

- *Equivalence relations and partitions.* The compiler frequently computes equivalence relations or partitions sets. An equivalence relation is frequently represented as a partition: All of the elements that are mutually equivalent are grouped together into a set of elements. Hence the whole set can be represented by a set of disjoint sets of elements. Partitions are frequently implemented as UNION/FIND data structures. This approach was pioneered by Tarjan (1975).

- *Partial ordering relations on sets.* A compiler contains a number of explicit and implicit partial orderings. Operands must be computed before the expression for which they are an operand, for example. The compiler must be able to represent these relations.

The topics that are addressed in this chapter concern graphs. A number of the data structures within a compiler—the flow graph and the call graph, for instance—are represented as directed graphs. Undirected graphs are used to represent the interference relationship for register allocation. Thus these topics are addressed here to the extent that the theory is used in implementing the compiler. The topics addressed are as follows:

Data structures for implementing directed and undirected graphs

Depth-first search and the classification of edges in a directed graph

Dominators, postdominators, and dominance frontiers

Graphs

Computing loops in a graph

Representing sets

3.1 Directed Graphs

A directed graph consists of a set of nodes N and a set of edges E. Each edge has a node that is its tail, and a node that is its head. Some books define an edge to be an ordered pair of nodes—tail and head; however, this makes the description of the compiler more difficult. It is possible to have two edges with the same tail and head. In a flow graph containing a C **switch** statement or a Pascal **case** statement, two different alternatives that have the same statement bodies will create two edges having identical tails and heads.

For a flow graph, there are two distinguished nodes. *Entry* is a node with no predecessors, representing the point where the procedure starts. *Exit* is a node with no successors, where the procedure exits. All execution paths start at *Entry*; all finite paths representing a complete execution end at *Exit*. Note that infinite-length paths are possible, representing infinite loops in the flow graph.

If a procedure has multiple entry points, as is possible in Fortran, then a single *Entry* node is created that contains no instructions, with an edge between *Entry* and each actual entry point. When instructions are emitted, the procedure entry code is inserted at each of the entry points. The existence of the single *Entry* node ensures that the program analysis will be performed correctly. Similarly, if there are multiple nodes with no successors, then a single *Exit* node is created, with an edge between each original exit node and *Exit*.

Each execution of the procedure is represented by a path from *Entry* to *Exit*. Unfortunately, the converse is not true: there are paths from *Entry* to *Exit* that do not represent paths of execution; for example, if there are two conditional branches in the flow graph branching on the same conditional expression. In this case the second conditional branch can only branch in the same direction as the first one. The path that branches the other way is not possible. The compiler cannot identify this situation, so it assumes that all paths are possible. This assumption decreases the amount of optimization.

The graph in Figure 3.1 represents the flow graph for the running example. Node B0 is the *Entry* node. Node B5 is the *Exit* node. Any execution path in the procedure is represented as a path between B0 and B5.

Directed graphs are implemented using two different techniques. Usually the nodes are represented as some data structure and the edges are

66 Building an Optimizing Compiler

Figure 3.1   Flow Graph for MAXCOL

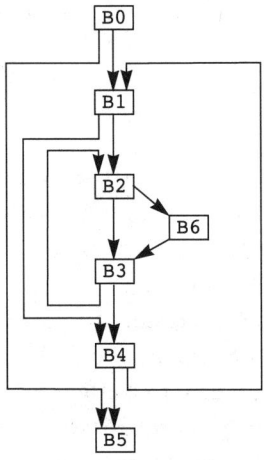

represented by adding two attributes to each node: the set of successors and the set of predecessors of the node. The set of successors of X is the set of nodes Y that are heads of edges, with the tail X. Similarly, the set of predecessors of X is the set of nodes P that are the tails of edges, with head X. Thus in Figure 3.1 the predecessors of B3 are B2 and B6, while the successors of B3 are B2 and B4. Note that any node X satisfies the relation: X is a predecessor of each of its successors, and X is a successor of each of its predecessors. These sets are implemented as linked lists, with the head of the list contained in the data structure representing the node.

An alternative technique is to assign an integer to each node and represent each edge as a bit in a Boolean matrix. If there is an edge between nodes X and Y, then the bit in the position $EDGE[X,Y]$ is set to *true;* otherwise, it is *false*.

The successor/predecessor representation has the advantage that it is efficient to scan through all the edges leaving or entering a node. It is also space efficient if the directed graph is sparse, as is true of most flow graphs. The matrix approach is more efficient in building the directed graph because it is easier to check whether a particular node is already a successor. We will use a derivative of the matrix approach during register allocation; otherwise, the successor/predecessor implementation will be used.

In an undirected graph the edges do not have a sense of direction. One is not traveling from one node to another in a particular direction. Instead, undirected graphs represent the idea of neighbors: two nodes are adjacent or they are not. The techniques for implementing directed graphs are used to implement undirected graphs: for each edge $\{X,Y\}$ in the undirected graph, build two edges (Y,X) and (Y,X) in the implementation. In the matrix form, this means that the matrix is symmetric and only half of the matrix need be stored.

3.2 Depth-First Search

There is no natural order for visiting nodes in a directed (or undirected) graph. Most algorithms in the compiler visit the nodes in the following fashion. The compiler starts by processing some node, usually *Entry* if it is dealing with the flow graph.

Assume the compiler is processing some node X. At some point during the processing of X, the compiler will process the successors of X. Of course, the compiler does not want to process the same node multiple times, so it will not process a successor of X if it has already been processed. Since the algorithm is implemented recursively, when X has undergone processing it will return as a procedure so that the predecessor that started the processing of X can continue processing.

If the directed graph is a tree, the depth-first search corresponds to the walk of a tree. Recall that in walking a tree there are the concepts of a preorder walk, in which a node is processed before its successors are processed; a postorder walk, in which the node's children are processed before the actual work is done on a node; and an in-order walk, in which the work for a node is performed between the processing of the children. A similar idea is available with directed graphs.

During a depth-first search, the algorithm may assign a number to the node in the order in which nodes are visited. This is called the *preorder*. If work is performed on the nodes in this order, it corresponds to the preorder walk of a tree. Similarly, a number is assigned to nodes in the order in which they are completed. This is called the *postorder* and corresponds to a postorder walk in a tree. An important order is the *reverse postorder*, since it corresponds to performing work on a node before processing any of its successors (except possibly for loops).

The depth-first walk algorithm is given in Figure 3.2. This walk classifies the edges into four categories. An edge (n,S) is a tree edge if S has not been processed when n decides to process this successor. In other words, this is the first time that S is being visited. Since each node can have only one predecessor that visits it the first time, the nodes together with the tree edges

Figure 3.2 Basic Depth-First Search Algorithm

```
input:    Program Flow Graph G = (N,E,S)
          Edges are represented by sets of successors
output:   A classification of each edge and ordering of nodes

procedure DFS(n ∈ node)
   n.pre = preorder;
   preorder = preorder + 1;
   for each S ∈ Succ(n) do
      if S.pre = 0 then
         classify (n,S) as "tree edge";
         DFS(S);
      elseif S.rpost = 0 then         /* S is on Stack */
         classify (n,S) as "back edge";
      elseif n.pre < S.pre then
         classify (n,S) as "forward edge";
      else
         classify (n,S) as "cross edge";
      endif;
   endfor;
   n.rpost = rpostorder;
   rpostorder = rpostorder - 1;
end DFS;

preorder = 1;
postorder = |N|;
for each n ∈ N do
   n.pre = 0;
   n.rpost = 0;
endfor;
DFS(S);
```

form a tree or a forest of trees, as shown in Figure 3.3. This tree structure is important because it allows the compiler to use the concepts of tree walks to move around the flow graph.

The second category consists of back edges. These are edges that go from a node to another node that has started processing but has not finished yet. If you look at the algorithm, this means that the edge must go back to a node that is still being processed by a procedure that directly or recursively calls this one: In implementation terms, the head of the edge is a node still on the stack, and that node will be an ancestor of the current node in the depth-first tree. This edge goes from a node to an ancestor in the tree formed of tree edges.

Graphs

Figure 3.3 Depth-First Search Tree for MAXCOL

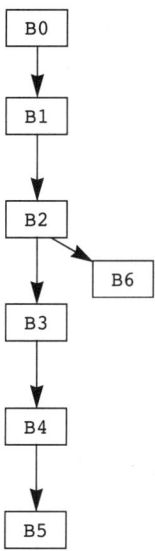

The opposite of backward edges are forward edges. A forward edge from *n* to *S* is an edge that goes from a node to its successor; however, the successor has already been processed. In fact, it was processed as a result of the processing of some other successor of *n*. So this is an edge that goes from an ancestor to a descendent in the depth-first search tree.

No other edge can go up the tree or down the tree, so the fourth category of edges must go from one subtree to another. These are called cross edges. The classification of the edges for Figure 3.3 is given in Table 3.1.

Table 3.1 Classification of Graph Edges

Tree Edges	Forward Edges	Cross Edges	Back Edges
B0 → B1	B0 → B5	B6 → B3	B3 → B2
B1 → B2	B1 → B4		B4 → B1
B2 → B3			
B2 → B6			
B3 → B4			
B4 → B5			

There is a fundamental principle involving depth-first search. Consider a depth-first search that starts at some node n. The set of nodes that will be visited by the depth-first search is exactly the set of nodes that are on some path leaving n. Why? Clearly any node visited by a depth-first search walk is on some path, because the tree edges form a path. Conversely, consider any finite path starting at n. The next node is a successor of n. In a depth-first search, each successor of a node is either visited from that node or has already been visited. Since we are starting at n, this successor is visited from n. The edge from n to that successor can be replaced by a path of tree nodes from n to the successor. Now consider the next node: It is either visited from the second node on the path or has already been visited from the first node. Again a path of tree nodes can be spliced in to create a path from n to the second node. This process can continue until the last node on the path is reached, at which point we have a path of tree edges from n to the end node, indicating that the end node is reached by a depth-first search.

I recommend that you become comfortable with the depth-first search. It is the basis of all other algorithms in the compiler.

3.3 Dominator Relation

Since the program flow graph is used to describe the execution path through the program and optimization is a technique for avoiding repeating work that has already been done, we need some concept of one block always being before another on all execution paths. This concept is called *dominance*.

DEFINITION   **Dominator:** Consider a program flow graph (N, *Entry*, *Exit*), a block $B1$ **dominates** block $B2$ if and only if every path from *Entry* to $B2$ contains $B1$.

Most of the properties of dominators are determined by two kinds of arguments, each based on the definition of dominance. The first form of argument reasons by considering all paths from *Entry* to a block B. Since the dominator is on all such paths, properties of dominators can be determined. The second form of argument reasons by cutting and pasting paths.

Consider a path from *Entry* to B that does not contain a particular block D. This path can be extended to a path to another block by adding an edge at the end; the new path still does not go through D.

LEMMA D1: Each block B dominates itself, since B is on each path from S to B.

LEMMA D2: If B2 dominates B1 and B1 dominates B, then B2 dominates B.

PROOF Consider each path from S to B. By definition of dominance, B1 is on each path. Consider the subpath from S to B1. By definition of dominance, B2 is on this path; hence, B2 is on each path from S to B. That is, B2 dominates B.

LEMMA D3: If B2 dominates B, and B1 dominates B, then either B2 dominates B1 or B1 dominates B2. In other words, the dominators of B form a linearly ordered sequence. The dominator that follows B in this list is called the *immediate dominator* of B and is written *idom(B)*.

PROOF Consider any path from *Entry* to B. If the path is not simple, throw away any loops in the path to make a simple path. Since B2 and B1 both dominate B, they are both on the path. Consider the case where B2 follows B1 on the path (the case where B1 follows B2 is symmetric). We claim that B1 dominates B2. To show a contradiction, assume that B1 does not dominate B2. Then there must be a path from S to B2 that does not contain B1. Replace the first part of the original path from S to B with this new path from S to B2. We now have a path to B that does not contain B1, contradicting the hypothesis that B1 dominates B.

Lemma D3 implies that the dominator relation can be represented as a tree in which the parent of each block is its immediate dominator. We show this tree in Figure 3.4 for the program MAXCOL. Note that the entry node, B0, has no immediate dominator, so it is the root of the tree. Any node that has only one predecessor has the predecessor as its dominator because each path must come through the predecessor. Thus, B2 is the immediate dominator of B6.

The history of computing the dominator relationship is interesting. Early algorithms were slow. One of the first practical algorithms was designed by Purdom (1972). To compute the blocks dominated by B, he pretended that B was not in the graph. He then performed a depth-first search. The blocks that had become unreachable could only be reached by going through B, so B must dominate them. In the program flow graph in Figure 3.1, if we pretend that B2 is not in the flow graph then blocks B2, B3, and B6 are not reachable, so B2 dominates these three nodes. B2 does not dominate B4 since there is an alternate path from B1 to B4 that avoids B2.

Figure 3.4   Dominator Tree for MAXCOL

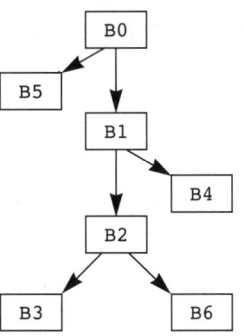

The current algorithm for computing the tree of immediate dominators was developed by Lengauer and Tarjan (1979). This algorithm comes in two forms, with runtime complexity either $O(|N|\ln|N|)$ or $O(|N|\alpha(|N|))$, depending on the complexity of the implementation. I do not state the algorithm here, as it is too complex to describe accurately in the space available. Instead I will give a rationalization for the algorithm and then a simpler algorithm by Purdom that is easy to understand.

Tarjan calculates the dominator using information gathered during a depth-first search of the program flow graph. Note that the dominator of B is an ancestor of B in any depth-first search tree. Frequently it will be the immediate parent in the depth-first search tree. When will it not be so? When there is an edge entering B that is not a tree edge in the depth-first search tree. Such an edge means that there is another way to get to B besides the path in the tree. In that case the closest block that can be a dominator of B is the common ancestor in the tree of B and the tail of the edge. But now things get complex, because that block may not be a dominator because of another edge entering one of the blocks in between.

To resolve these problems and store the information we have been discussing, Tarjan defines a quantity called the *semi-dominator* and computes these values in a bottom-up walk of the depth-first search tree. Having these values, he can easily compute the actual dominators.

The compiler stores the dominator information as a tree. The nodes of the tree are the blocks in the flow graph; however, the tree edges are not necessarily the flow graph edges. The parent of any node in the tree is its

Graphs

immediate dominator. For each block *B*, the compiler keeps two attributes that store the dominator information:

- *idom(B)* is the immediate dominator of *B*.
- *children(B)* is the set of blocks for which *B* is the immediate dominator. Logically this information is a set; however, it is useful to store the information as a linked list, with the successors of *B* that are dominated by *B* coming first in the list. This will make some of the later optimization algorithms work more efficiently.

This tree structure results in the tree in Figure 3.4 for the running example.

The compiler also needs to know the common dominator of a set of blocks. The common dominator is the block that dominates each element of the set of blocks and is dominated by every other block that dominates each of the blocks of the set. This common dominator can be computed as shown in Figure 3.5. The algorithm works by observing that if *Z* does not dominate *B*, and *B* does not dominate *Z*, then one can walk up the dominator tree from one of them to find a block that dominates both.

Although it computes the common dominator of a pair, this algorithm is adequate for any set of blocks because the common dominator can be found by pairwise computing the common dominator of blocks.

Here is a simple algorithm for computing dominators. Recall the basic principle of depth-first searches. A depth-first search that visits a node *n* also visits all nodes reachable from *n*. Now pretend that *n* is not in the graph by pretending that the edges entering *n* do not exist and that *n* does not exist. Perform a depth-first search starting at *Entry* on this mutilated graph. Which nodes are not reachable from *Entry* that were reachable before? A node is not reachable if there is no path to it. If it was reachable

Figure 3.5 Computing the Common Dominator

```
function CommonDominator(Z: block, B: block) returns block;
   if B dominates Z then
      return B;
   endif;
   while Z does not dominate B do
      Z = idom(Z);
   endwhile;
   return Z;
endfunction CommonDominator;
```

before, this means that *n* is on every path to these unreachable nodes. In other words, *n* is a dominator of all of those unreachable nodes. Thus, the algorithm consists of performing a single depth-first search to determine all of the reachable nodes. Discard the unreachable nodes. Now for each node *n* in the flow graph, pretend that *n* is not in the graph and repeat the depth-first search starting at *Entry*. The nodes that are not reachable are the nodes dominated by *n*.

3.4 Postdominators

If the compiler is moving computations to earlier points in the flow graph, then the dominator information gives the safe positions in the flow graph to which to move the computation. The compiler can move the computation to an earlier block that is on each path to the current block. The opposite information is also useful. If the compiler wants to move a computation to a later point, where can it be moved? This question leads to the idea of *postdominance*, which has similar characteristics to dominance with the exception that the path goes from *B* to *Exit* rather than from *Entry* to *B*, and successor blocks are used rather than predecessor blocks.

DEFINITION   **Postdominance:**   A block *X* postdominates a block *B* if and only if each path from *B* to *Exit* contains the block *X*.

The corresponding properties of dominance hold. In fact, postdominance is just the dominance relation on the reverse graph, where successors are replaced by predecessors and vice versa. The same algorithms can be used to compute postdominance by computing dominance on the reversed graph. The information can be stored as a tree, as shown in Figure 3.6. The attributes for postdominance are as follows:

- *pdom(B)* represents the immediate postdominator of *B* and represents the parent of *B* in the postdominator tree.

- *pchildren(B)* represents the set of blocks that are immediately postdominated by *B*. Again this is represented as a set implemented as a linked list with the predecessors of *B* that are also dominated by *B* occurring first in the list.

Figure 3.6 Postdominator Tree for MAXCOL

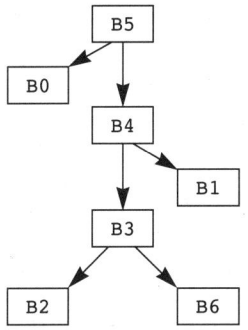

3.5 Dominance Frontier

Consider any path leaving a block *B*. Initially the blocks on the path are dominated by *B*. Eventually a block is reached that is not dominated by *B*. All of the blocks after that are not dominated by *B* unless the path returns to *B*. The first block that is not dominated by *B* is significant because it indicates the range of blocks over which *B* dominates and indicates the limits of optimizations using information about the computations in *B*. Considering all paths, the set of blocks possessing this characteristic is called the dominance frontier of *B*.

Definition **Dominance Frontier:** The dominance frontier *DF(B)* of a block *B* is the set of all blocks *C* such that *B* dominates a predecessor of *C* but either *B* equals *C* or *B* does not dominate *C*.

The definition is a restatement of the preceding motivation. If *C* is a block such that a predecessor is dominated by *B* and *C* is not, then there is a path from *B* to the predecessor. Add the edge from that predecessor to *C* and one has a path matching the motivation. Clearly a path matching the motivation introduces a block into the dominance frontier.

Note that the block *B* is handled specially. A loop starting at *B*, going through blocks dominated by *B* and returning to *B*, introduces *B* into the dominance frontier.

One way of visualizing the dominance frontier is to consider the subtree of the dominator tree rooted at B. A flow graph edge going from one of the blocks in this subtree to a block outside the subtree introduces the block outside the subtree into the dominance frontier. For the sake of this discussion, B is considered to be outside the subtree.

This gives an easy algorithm for computing the dominance frontier. Walk the dominator tree bottom-up, computing the dominance frontier for children before the parent. When considering a block B, there are two cases:

- A flow graph edge leaving B that does not lead to a child of B in the dominator tree must be to a block that is either equal to B or not dominated by B. (If the block were dominated by B, then B must be its immediate dominator, so it would be a child.) Such blocks belong in the dominance frontier of B.

- Consider a block X in the dominance frontier of one of the children C of B, in the dominator tree. If X is not equal to B and is not dominated by B, then it is in the dominance frontier of B. If X is dominated by B, then B must be its immediate dominator, since it is not dominated by C. Since B is not its own immediate dominator, the two conditions can be combined to give the algorithm shown in Figure 3.7.

Figure 3.7   Computing the Dominance Frontier

```
procedure Calculate_Dominance_Frontier(B: Block)
    foreach C ∈ children(B) do
       call Calculate_Dominance_Frontier(C);
    endfor;
    DF(B) = ∅
    foreach X ∈ Succ(B) do
       if idom(X) ≠ B then
          add X to DF(B);
       endif;
    endfor;
    foreach C ∈ Children(B) do
       foreach X ∈ DF(C) do
          if idom(X) ≠ B then
             add X to DF(B);
          endif;
       endfor;
    endfor;
end Calculate_Dominance_Frontier;
```

Table 3.2 Dominance Frontiers

Block	Dominance Frontier
B3	B2 B4
B6	B3
B2	B2 B4
B4	B1 B5
B1	B1 B5
B5	∅
B0	∅

Consider the running example for which the dominator tree is in Figure 3.1. The bottom-up dominator tree walk first visits blocks B3, B6, B2, B4, B1, B5, and then B0. As the walk is performed, the dominance frontier is computed (see Table 3.2). In the calculation of the dominance frontier, B3 finds B2 and B4 in its dominance frontier because they are successors and are not dominated by B3. Similarly, B6 finds B3 in its dominance frontier. During the computation of the dominance frontier of B2, B3 will not be in its dominance frontier because B2 dominates B3. However, B2 is in the dominance frontier of B2.

3.6 Control Dependence

The compiler needs to know the conditions under which the execution of one block leads to the execution of another. The ideas described here are derived from Cytron (1987, 1990 and 1991). Consider two blocks B and X. When does B control the execution of X?

- If B has only one successor block, it does not control the execution of anything. Once B starts executing, it completes executing and goes on to the single next block. Thus B must have multiple successors to be considered a block that controls the execution of X.

- B must have some path leaving it that leads to the *Exit* block and avoids X. If this were not true, then the execution of B would always lead to the execution of X. In other words, B cannot be postdominated by X.

- B must have some path leaving it that leads to X. Again, failure of this condition would violate the idea of control. Thus B can be viewed as a switch: Some way out leads to X, and another way out avoids X.

- *B* should be the latest block that has this characteristic. It's true that an earlier block may similarly control the execution of *X*; however, that block can be viewed as controlling the execution of *B*, which then controls the execution of *X*.

All of these conditions can be summarized in the following definition.

DEFINITION **Control Dependence:** A block *X* is control dependent on a block *B* if and only if

There is a non-empty path from *B* to *X* such that *X* postdominates each block on the path except *B*.

X is either the same as *B*, or *X* does not postdominate *B*.

The first condition summarizes the idea of *B* being the latest block that has a path to *X*. If there were a later block satisfying the other condition, then *X* would not postdominate all blocks on the path. The second condition together with the existence of the path in the first condition gives the switching condition. There is one way through *B* that might avoid *X*, and another way that must lead to *X*.

A more precise definition of control dependence is desired because the compiler needs to know something about the switching mechanism—which edge out of *B* must lead to *X*. This involves an addition to the definition that records the edge involved.

DEFINITION **Control Dependence:** A block *X* is control dependent on an edge (*B,S*) if and only if

There is a non-empty path from *B* to *X* starting with the edge (*B,S*) such that *X* postdominates each block on the path except *B*.

X is either the same as *B*, or *X* does not postdominate *B*.

The definition is unfortunate in that it uses some unknown path. To have an effective way of computing control dependence, the compiler needs a more general condition. Fortunately, the condition is the same as *X* postdominating *S*.

OBSERVATION If *B* and *X* are blocks in a flow graph where there is a path from every block to *Exit*, then *X* postdominates a successor *S* of *B* if and only if there is a non-null path from *B* to *X* through *S* such that *X* postdominates every node after *B* on the path.

PROOF Assume the path exists. Since *S* is on the path, *S* is postdominated by *X*. Conversely, assume that *S* is postdominated by *X*. There is some path from *S* to *Exit*. Since *S* is postdominated by *X*, *X* is on this path. Cut the path short at *X* and add *B* and the edge from *B* to *S* to the beginning of the path. This gives a path from *B* to *X*. Each node except *B* on the path is postdominated by *X*. If it isn't, then there is a path from it to *Exit* and by cutting the original path and pasting in the new path, one can create a path from *S* to *Exit* that avoids *X*, a contradiction. So we have the path.

OBSERVATION If *S* is a successor of *B*, then either *S* is the postdominator of *B* or *pdom(S)* is postdominated by *pdom(B)*.

PROOF Assume *S* is not the postdominator of *B*. Consider any path from *S* to *Exit*. It can be extended to a path from *B* to *Exit*. Thus, *pdom(B)* is on this path. Thus *pdom(B)* is not equal to *S* and is on each path from *S* to *Exit*, so it is a postdominator of *S*. Thus it must postdominate *pdom(S)*.

Now we can give an algorithm for computing the control dependence relation. Look at the definition: the edge (*B*,*S*) is given. What blocks are control dependent on this edge? Any block that postdominates *S* and does not postdominate *B*. These are the nodes in the postdominator tree starting at *S*, *pdom(S)*, *pdom(pdom(S))*, and stopping at but not including *pdom(B)*. The second observation indicates that, traversing the tree upward through the parents (postdominators), the algorithm must reach *pdom(B)* eventually.

The algorithm in Figure 3.8 can be applied to each edge. Actually, it needs to be applied to each edge that leaves a block with multiple successors, since a block with a single successor can have no blocks control dependent on it. For our running example this gives the results in Table 3.3. Sometimes the compiler needs the transpose of this information: for each block, on what blocks it is control dependent. In that case the same algorithm is used; however, the information is stored indexed by the dependent block rather than by the edge leading to the dependence.

Figure 3.8 Calculating Control Dependence

```
function Find_Control_Dependence((B,S): edge)
   depends = ∅;
   X = S;
   while X ≠ (pdom(B) do
      add X to depends;
      X = pdom(X);
   endwhile;
   return depends;
endfunction Find_Control_Dependence;
```

Table 3.3 Control Dependences for the Example Program

Edge (B,S)	Blocks Control Dependent on (B,S)
(B0,B5)	∅
(B0,B1)	B1, B4
(B1,B4)	∅
(B1,B2)	B2, B3
(B2,B3)	∅
(B2,B6)	B6
(B3,B2)	∅
(B3,B4)	∅
(B4,B1)	B1, B4
(B4,B5)	∅

3.7 Loops and the Loop Tree

An optimizing compiler attempts to decrease the number of computations that occur during program execution. Thus the compiler needs to determine those areas of the program that are executed most often and concentrate on improving them. Determining the areas of frequent execution at compile time is not practical or possible. However, parts of the program that execute repeatedly, that is, loops, are the best candidates. So the compiler builds a data structure to represent information about loops.

DEFINITION **Loop:** A loop is a set of blocks, L, such that if $B0, B1 \in L$ then there is a path from $B0$ to $B1$ and a path from $B1$ to $B0$. A block $B \in L$ is an entry block if B has a predecessor that is not in L. A block $B \in L$ is an exit block if B has a successor that is not in L.

In other words, a loop is a region of the program where the path of execution can cycle from one block to another repeatedly. An entry block is a block where execution can enter the loop, and an exit block is a block where execution can leave the loop. Since we assume that there is some path of execution from *Entry* to any block, each loop must have at least one entry block.

The interesting loops are loops with a single entry block, or single-entry loops. For such loops the entry block must dominate all other blocks in the loop. If there is a path that avoids the entry block, then there must be a first block in the loop on the path and this block would be another entry.

The algorithm for computing the blocks in a loop for a single-entry loop is given in Figure 3.9. Consider any block B. The only way that it can be the entry block for a single-entry loop is if there is a back edge in some depth-first search walk of the flow graph. Consider the alternative: An entry block in a loop must be involved in a cyclic path and be the first block in the cycle that is reached in the walk. Thus, all of the blocks in the cycle will be descendents of B in the walk, and the edge leading back to B is a back edge.

The idea behind the algorithm is walking the loop backward. Consider each predecessor of B coming from a back edge. Walk the graph backward from these predecessors. Eventually the walk leads back to B, and all of the blocks in the loop will be visited. The algorithm implements this idea using a work-list algorithm. The set *Queue* contains all blocks that are known to be in the loop but whose predecessors have not been processed yet. Each block is inserted into *Queue* at most once because *Queue* $\subset$ *Loop* and the insertion occurs only when the block is not already in *Loop*.

Later we will generalize this algorithm to handle multiple-entry loops, and use it to compute the nesting structure of loops. The compiler not only

Figure 3.9 Template of Code for Finding a Loop

```
procedure FIND_LOOP(B: block)
      Loop = ∅;
      Queue = ∅;
      foreach P ∈ Pred(B) do
          if (P,B) is a backedge then
              if (P ∉ Loop) ∧ (P ≠ B)then
                  add P to Queue;
                  add P to Loop;
              endif;
          endif
      endfor;
      while Queue ≠ ∅ do
          take X from Queue;
          delete X from Queue;
          foreach P ∈ Pred(X) do
              if (P ≠ B) ∧ (P ∉ Loop)then
                  add P to Queue;
                  add P to Loop;
              endif
          endfor;
      endwhile;
    add B to Loop;
endprocedure FIND_LOOP;
```

needs to know the loops, but needs to know which loops are contained in other loops. Note that the way the compiler computes loops will ensure that the loops identified are either disjoint (no blocks in common) or nested (one loop is a subset of another). The nesting structure is used for three purposes:

1. The compiler uses the loop nest during dependence-based optimization since these phases transform loops to improve program performance.

2. The loop nests are used to perform one kind of strength reduction. Values modified in a regular fashion during each iteration of a loop may be computed in a more effective way; for example, multiplications can be replaced by repeated additions.

3. The loop nests are used during register allocation to find points in the program where values may be stored or loaded from memory.

3.7.1 Infinite Loops

A loop may have no exit blocks, in which case it is an infinite loop. Such loops can occur in real programs. Consider a program that is using the hardware interrupt or signaling mechanism to perform all actions, while the main program remains in a loop. The programmer may write this loop as an infinite loop. These are structural infinite loops. There may be other infinite loops that the compiler cannot determine due to the actual computations that occur during the execution of the program.

Many of the global optimization algorithms can give incorrect results when these structural infinite loops exist. These algorithms are all based on the idea of decreasing the number of computations on paths from *Entry* to *Exit*. If there is a block where there is no such path, the algorithms may perform in unexpected ways.

A simple device eliminates these structural infinite loops: Insert an edge from one of the blocks in the loop to *Exit*. Of course, the edge will never be traversed, because there are no instructions in the blocks that can make the program flow along that edge. However, the optimization algorithms will now perform properly.

How can the compiler identify these infinite loops? A block is in an infinite loop if there is no path from it to *Exit*. So perform a depth-first search on the reverse of the flow graph (consider the predecessors to be the successors and vice versa). The blocks that are not visited are the blocks in infinite loops. After the depth-first search, choose one of the blocks that is

Figure 3.10 Eliminating Infinite Loops

```
procedure FIND_INFINITE_DFS(B: block)
   if B ∉ Visited then
      add B to Visited;
      foreach P ∈ Pred(B) do
         call FIND_INFINITE_DFS(P);
      endfor;
   endif;
endprocedure FIND_INFINITE_DFS;

procedure FIND_INFINITE;
   Visited = ∅;
   call FIND_INFINITE(Exit);
   while Visited ≠ All_Nodes do
      take B from All_Nodes Visited;
      add (B,Exit) as edge in flow graph;
      call FIND_INFINITE_DFS(B);
   endwhile;
end;
```

not visited, create the edge between it and *Exit*, and then attempt to continue the depth-first search using this edge. Figure 3.10 describes this algorithm.

3.7.2 Single- and Multiple-Entry Loops

As noted earlier, loops can be classified by the number of entry blocks. A loop with no entry blocks is unreachable: The instructions cannot be executed, so those loops are already eliminated. Single-entry loops are the most interesting for the optimizer. Multiple-entry loops must be handled because they might occur in programs; however, the optimization techniques will not be as effective. Many of the optimization techniques only work with single-entry loops.[1]

How does the compiler identify multiple-entry loops? A loop is a union of cyclic paths. Consider one of these cyclic paths. During a depth-first

---

1. Single-entry loops are frequently called *reducible loops*. Multiple-entry loops are called *irreducible loops*. This compiler uses techniques that optimize single-entry loops. Multiple-entry loops are identified to ensure that no incorrect translations occur.

search there is a first block *B* on the path that is visited. All other blocks on the cycle are descendants of *B*, and the cyclic edge entering *B* is a back edge. Thus a loop with entry *B* is found as in Figure 3.9 by considering these predecessors and walking the loop backward. The problem with a multiple-entry loop is that this walk can escape from the loop (walking backward through one of the other entries) and eventually lead all the way back to *Entry*. This means that *B* does not dominate these predecessors. Consider the multiple-entry loop {*C,D*} in Figure 3.11. If the depth-first search visits the blocks in order {*A,C,D,E,B*}, then *C* is the first block in the loop that is visited. The edge (*D,C*) is a back edge. When walking backward from *D* one visits {*D,C,B,A*}.

To avoid this problem, the algorithm must be modified to stop the backward walk. But where should the walk stop? The compiler wants a single-entry region, even if it is not a loop. So stop the walk at the block that is closest to the loop and which dominates all of the blocks in the loop. This will be the block that dominates the header *B* and all of *B*'s predecessors that reach *B* by a back edge. Recall that *B* dominates itself. Using this information, the algorithm in Figure 3.9 is modified to the algorithm in Figure 3.12.

The algorithm implements the ideas that we have just discussed. Note that the body of the loop is not computed at this point when a multiple-entry loop is encountered. Instead, the set of blocks that lead to the loop body are recorded in an attribute called *generators*. This set will be initialized to empty before the identification of loops is started. A block that has a non-empty *generators* set is the immediate dominator of a multiple-entry

Figure 3.11 Example Multiple-Entry Loop

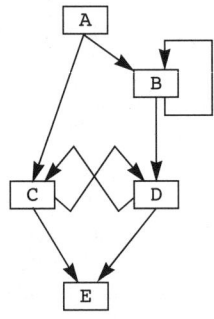

Figure 3.12 Identifying a General Loop

```
function FIND_LOOP(B: block) returns boolean;
   Z = B;                       //Entry block
   Loop = ∅;                    //Blocks in the loop
   Queue = ∅;                   //Unprocessed blocks
   foreach P ∈ Pred(B) do
      if (P,B) is a backedge then
         if (P ∉ Loop) ∧ (P ≠ B) then
            Z = CommonDominator(Z,P);
            add P to Queue;
            add P to Loop;
         endif;
      endif
   endfor;
   if Z ≠ B then
      generators(Z) = generators(Z) ∨ Loop;
      return false;             //False means multiple-entry loop
   endif;
   while Queue ≠ ∅  do
      take X from Queue;
      delete X from Queue;
      foreach P ∈ Pred(X) do
         if P ≠ Z then
            if P ∉ Loop then
               add P to Queue;
               add P to Loop;
            endif
         endif
      endfor;
   endwhile;
   add Z to Loop;
   return true;                 //True means single-entry loop
endprocedure FIND_LOOP;
```

loop. The loop body is not recognized immediately for the following reasons:

- We will see shortly that this whole process is embedded in a depth-first search in which the loop starting at a block is recognized after all blocks later in the walk have been processed. Recording the *generators* set allows this to be true for multiple-entry loops as well.

- More than one multiple-entry loop can have the same immediate dominator. The aggregate will be considered one loop for the process of forming the loop nest.

- We will be able to handle loops contained in this loop more effectively. Consider a multiple-entry loop with entry blocks $B1$ and $B2$ with common denominator C. By delaying the identification of the loop until all successors have been identified, a loop that occurs on the path between C and $B1$ or C and $B2$, will be handled as a nested loop. If this subloop is a single-entry loop, then the full set of optimizations can be applied to it. If the body of the multiple-entry loop were created when either $B1$ or $B2$ was processed, then these subloops would not be considered a separate loop.

We will make a slight modification to *FIND_LOOP* in order to build a tree of tested loops, but this is the basic algorithm. When a single-entry loop is found, the loop body is identified. When a multiple-entry loop is found, the identification of the loop body is delayed until the processing of the block Z. This loop body is identified by the existence of a non-empty *generators*(Z) set.

Later descriptions will divide *FIND_LOOP* into two procedures: The first finds the generators and the second finds the body of the loop. The procedure is split so that finding the body of a multiple-entry loop can use the same code as that for single-entry loops.

3.7.3 Computing the Loop Tree

The compiler needs the complete set of loops and the relationship among the loops. This information is stored as a tree. Loop $L1$ is a child of $L2$ if and only if $L1$ is a subset of $L2$ and is not contained in any other loop contained in $L2$. The algorithm used to compute loops finds the maximum loop with a particular header block. This ensures that two loops are either disjoint or one is contained in the other, a condition allowing the loops to be organized in a tree called the *loop tree*. There are four kinds of nodes in the loop tree:

1. The leaves of the tree are the blocks in the flow graph.

2. Single-entry loops are one form of interior node in the tree.

3. Multiple-entry loops organized as a single-entry region are the other form of interior node. Recall that a multiple-entry loop includes the loop together with all tree nodes back from the loop to the common dominator of all of the blocks in the loop.

4. The root of the tree is a special node representing the whole flow graph. It will not be a loop or block because the flow graph includes two blocks: *Entry* with no predecessors and *Exit* with no successors. These blocks cannot be involved in a loop and are not a single block.

Graphs

To record the tree structure, attributes are added to blocks and the other nodes in the loop tree:

- *LoopParent(X)* is an attribute indicating which node in the tree this node is a child of. It also indicates which loop a loop or block is contained in. *LoopParent(X)* can also be the root, indicating that this block or loop is not contained in another loop. The *LoopParent* of the root is *NIL*.

- *LoopContains(X)* is the set of nodes in the region represented by *X*. For a block, it is *NIL*. For a loop or the root, it is the set of children of *X* in the tree that is the same as the set of loops or blocks directly contained in this region.

- *LoopEntry(X)* is the block that is the entry to this region.

These attributes allow free moment around the loop tree with full knowledge of which blocks and loops are contained in other blocks and loops.

As the loop tree is built, each loop is identified and entered in the tree. Once it has been entered in the tree it is handled as a single entity. Its interior structure is not viewed again during the construction process. The algorithm *FIND_LOOP* is modified to handle tree nodes and augmented to be part of the complete construction process. To form this tree, we need two modifications to the algorithm:

1. Consider the blocks in the graph in postorder. Due to the structure of a depth-first search, a single-entry loop contained in another single-entry loop has an entry block with a smaller postorder number. So by visiting blocks in postorder, the inner loops are identified before the outer loops.

2. Once identified, handle each loop as if it were a single block. This is done by keeping a datum for each block or loop indicating which block or loop it is contained in (if any). When one finds a block, use this datum to scan outward to the outermost identified loop that contains this block.

The compiler now has the complete algorithm. In Figure 3.13 we have the final version of *FIND_LOOP*, which computes the blocks, called the *generators*, that determine all the other blocks in the loop. If it is a single-entry loop, *FIND_LOOP* goes ahead and builds the node in the loop tree using *FIND_BODY*.

FIND_BODY computes the set of nodes in the body of the loop by moving backward from the blocks that generate the loop to the header (see Figure 3.14). All blocks in between are in the loop. It builds the node in the loop

Figure 3.13 Computing Generators of a Loop

```
procedure FIND_LOOP(B: block);
   Z = B;                                  //Entry block
   Loop = ∅;                               //Blocks in the loop
   foreach P ∈ Pred(B) do
      if (P,B) is a backedge then
         Z = CommonDominator(Z,P);         //Find header block
         if (P ∉ Loop) ∧ (P ≠ B) then
            add P to Loop;
         endif;
      endif
   endfor;
   if Z ≠ B then                           //Multiple-entry loop
      generators(Z) = generators(Z) ∨ Loop;
   else                                    //Single-entry loop
      call FIND_BODY(Loop,Z,single_entry_loop);
   endif;
endprocedure FIND_LOOP;
```

tree and fills in all of the attributes. Care must be taken to ensure the distinction between blocks and already computed loops. The loop header and predecessors are always blocks. Before inserting a node into the loop tree, the compiler must find the largest enclosing loop that has already been computed. This is done by *LoopAncestor,* shown in Figure 3.15.

LoopAncestor finds the outermost processed loop that contains the current loop or block by scanning up the *LoopParent* attribute until it finds a node that has a null entry. Since this attribute is updated to a non-null entry by *FIND_BODY* as soon as an enclosing loop has been identified, this algorithm gives the outermost existing loop.

Finally, the main procedure for computing loops can be described (see Figure 3.16). *Calculate_Loop_Tree* first performs a depth-first search to compute the postorder numbers for each node and the back edges. The implementation may perform this depth-first walk at the same time that the rest of the algorithm is being computed—just embed the calculations in a recursive depth-first search procedure after a node is visited.

First *Calculate_Loop_Tree* initializes all of the attributes for blocks. These could be initialized when the blocks were created; however, the step is described here for completeness. Then the procedure visits the blocks in postorder. If the *generators* set is non-empty, then the block is the head of a multiple-entry loop, so that loop is built. Then the procedure checks to see if the block is the head of a single-entry loop. Note that a block may be

Figure 3.14   Computing the Body of a Loop

```
procedure FIND_BODY(Generators: set of block; Head: block, kind: LoopKind)
   Loop = ∅;
   Queue = ∅;
   foreach B ∈ Generators do         //Copy generators to body and Queue
      L = LoopAncestor(B);           //But use outermost containing loop
      if L ∉ Loop then               //Only enter each loop once
         add L to Loop;
         add L to Queue;
      endif
   endfor;
   while Queue ≠ ∅ do                //Work-list algorithm
      take B from Queue;             //Remove arbitrary entry
      delete B from Queue;
      foreach P ∈ Pred(LoopEntry(B)) do
         if P ≠ Head then            //Add in predecessors
            L = LoopAncestor(P);
            if L ∉ Loop then
               add L to Queue;
               add L to Loop;
            endif
         endif
      endfor;
   endwhile;
   add Head to Loop;
   X = new Loop Tree node of type kind;
   LoopContains(X) = Loop;           //Set of attributes of new node
   LoopEntry(X) = Z;
   LoopParent(X) = NIL;
   foreach B ∈ Loop do               //Update parents for components
      LoopParent(B) = X;
   endfor;
endprocedure FIND_LOOP;
```

the head of both a multiple-entry loop and a single-entry loop. In that case, the compiler builds a nest of two loops: the multiple-entry loop is the innermost loop and the single-entry loop is the outer loop. The loop tree for our standing example is given in Figure 3.17.

Figure 3.15   Finding the Outermost Processed Loop

```
function LoopAncestor(B: block) returns LoopNode;
   while LoopParent(B) ≠ NIL do
      B = LoopParent(B);
   endwhile
   return B;
endfunction LoopAncestor;
```

Figure 3.16 Computing the Complete Loop Tree

```
procedure Calculate_Loop_Tree;
   perform a depth first search recording post-order and back edges;
   foreach B ∈ G do                    //Initialize block information
      LoopParent(B) = NIL;
      generators(B) = ∅;
      LoopEntry(B) = B;
      LoopContains(B) = B;
   endfor;
   foreach B ∈ G in post order do
      if generators(B) ≠ ∅ then
         call FIND_BODY(generators(B),B,multiple_entry_loop);
      endif;
      call FIND_LOOP(B);
   endfor;
   call FIND_BODY({Exit},Entry,loop_tree_root);
endprocedure Calculate_Loop_Tree;
```

Figure 3.17 Loop Tree for Example Program

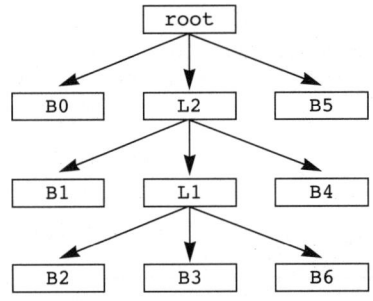

3.8 Implementing Sets of Integers

Throughout the compiler, sets of integers are needed. We have already seen one example: the set of nodes visited during a depth-first search. There are multiple ways to implement these sets, depending on the requirements for computing and using them.

One form of set consists of nodes where the construction algorithm guarantees that we do not attempt to add the same node twice or that the set is small so the search time through the set is small. In this case, sets may be implemented as linked lists. Insertion consists of adding an element to the beginning or end of the list. Deletion consists of removing the element from the linked list, and searching consists of a scan of the list. This form of set is efficient for scanning all of the elements in the set, but is not efficient for insertions or deletions.

Another approach is to use bit vectors to represent sets. Assign a unique integer value to each possible element in the universe of values, starting with 0. Then represent any set as an array of bits whose length is the maximum number assigned plus 1. This technique gives an efficient implementation of insertion (index to find the bit and set it), deletion (index to find the bit and clear it), union, intersection, and search (index to find the bit and check if it is 1). If the sets are not sparse this approach is highly efficient on space. However, it is not efficient for scanning through all the elements in a set. Unfortunately, scanning is a common activity in the compiler.

An alternative technique was developed by Preston Briggs (1993), based on a hint in Aho, Hopcroft, and Ullman (1974). This technique is highly efficient in all of the operations; however, it takes an order of magnitude more space than bit vectors, so one does not want to use it if one needs to have a large number of sets.

Consider our universe of integers, numbered from 0 to *MAX*. Allocate two arrays of *MAX* + 1 elements with initial *INDEX*[0:*MAX*] and *VALUE*[0:*MAX*] and a single integer variable, *NEXTPLACE*.

The idea behind the algorithm (Figure 3.18) is that the elements of the set are stored in *VALUE*, starting at the bottom and piling them up in adjacent slots. As an element *X* is added to *VALUE*, the index in *VALUE* where it is stored is placed in *INDEX(X)*. Otherwise the values of *INDEX* are not initialized. Curiously, the algorithm is dealing with uninitialized data.

How does the algorithm know when a value is in the set? It checks the corresponding *INDEX(X)*. That information may be uninitialized, so first it checks to see if the value is in range. If it is not, then the element is not in the set. If the value is in range it can still be uninitialized, so it checks the corresponding value in the *VALUE* array. If the value matches, then the algorithm knows that the element is in the set.

To remove an element from the set is a bit trickier. The algorithm must run in a constant time so it cannot remove an element and move the others down. Instead it moves the last element in the set down into the position that is being vacated. At the same time it adjusts its *INDEX* value and decreases the counter *NEXTPLACE*.

Figure 3.18 Efficient Set Algorithm

```
procedure MAKE_SET_EMPTY;
   NEXTPLACE = 0;
endprocedure MAKE_SET_EMPTY;

function FIND_ELEMENT(X: int) returns boolean;
   if (INDEX(X)<NEXTPLACE)∧(INDEX(X)≥0) then
      if VALUE(INDEX(X)) = X then return true;
   endif;
   return false;
endfunction FIND_ELEMENT;

procedure INSERT_ELEMENT(X: int);
   if ¬FIND_ELEMENT(X) then
      NEXTPLACE = NEXTPLACE + 1;
      VALUE[NEXTPLACE] = X;
      INDEX[X] = NEXTPLACE;
   endif;
endprocedure INSERT_ELEMENT;

procedure DELETE_ELEMENT(X: int);
   if FIND_ELEMENT(X) then
      VALUE(INDEX(X)) = VALUE(NEXTPLACE);
      INDEX(VALUE(NEXTPLACE)) = INDEX(X);
      NEXTPLACE = NEXTPLACE - 1;
   endif;
endprocedure DELETE_ELEMENT;

Scanning elements in set performed by the macro
   I = 0
   while I < NEXTPLACE do
      X = VALUE(I);
      process X;
   endwhile;
```

The basic operations occur in $O(1)$ time, and scanning the elements in the set is proportional to the actual elements in the set. It does take more space, though. Consider an implementation where the elements are represented by 16-bit numbers. Thus there are 32 bits for each element, indicating that this representation takes 32 times as much space as a bit-vector approach. Thus this representation works well when only a small number of sets (usually one or two) is necessary.

3.9 References

Aho, A. V., J. E. Hopcroft, and J. D. Ullman. 1974. *The design and analysis of computer algorithms.* Reading, MA: Addison-Wesley.

Briggs, P., and L. Torczon. 1993. An efficient representation for sparse sets. *ACM Letters on Programming Languages and Systems* 2(1-4): 59-69.

Cytron, R., and J. Ferrante. 1987. An improved control dependence algorithm. (Technical Report RC 13291.) White Plains, NY: International Business Machines, Thomas J. Watson Research Center.

Cytron, R., J. Ferrante, and V. Sarkar. 1990. Compact representations for control dependence. *Proceedings of the SIGPLAN '90 Symposium on Programming Language Design and Implementation,* White Plains, NY. 241-255. In *SIGPLAN Notices* 25(6).

Cytron, R., J. Ferrante, B. Rosen, M. Wegman, and F. Zadeck. 1991. Efficiently computing static single assignment form and the control dependence graph. *ACM Transactions on Programming Languages and Systems* 13(4): 451-490.

Fischer, C. N., and R. J. LeBlanc, Jr. 1988. *Crafting a compiler.* Redwood City, CA: Benjamin/Cummings.

Lengauer, T., and R. E. Tarjan. 1979. A fast algorithm for finding dominators in a flow graph. *Transactions on Programming Languages and Systems* 1(1): 121-141.

Lorho, B. 1984. *Methods and tools for compiler construction: An advanced course.* Cambridge University Press.

Purdom, P. W., and E. F. Moore. 1972. Immediate predominators in a directed graph. *Communications of the ACM* 8(1): 777-778.

Tarjan, R. E. 1975. Efficiency of a good but not linear set of union algorithm. *Journal of ACM* 22(2): 215-225.

4 FLOW GRAPH

The front end of the compiler has completed its task. It has created an abstract syntax tree and symbol table for each of the procedures being compiled. Now the compiler builds a different representation—one used for improving the procedures (optimization), code generation, instruction scheduling, and register allocation. First, we must make two decisions concerning the structure of the compiler.

4.1 How Are Procedures Stored?

Optimizing compilers use a range of different data structures to represent procedures being compiled. At one extreme the procedure may be represented as a tree; at the other, each procedure may be represented as a sequence of machine instructions for the target machine.

Representing the procedure as a tree makes the original structure of the procedure clear. A procedure consists of declarations, statements, and expressions. Each of these contains components of the same form, so it is natural to represent the procedure as a tree. If a tree structure is used, an abstract syntax tree is the natural choice. The abstract syntax tree is the natural organization for tree-oriented optimization algorithms such as algebraic identities and Sethi-Ullman register numbering.

Representing the procedure as machine instructions makes many optimization algorithms easier. They can each be individually optimized and positioned. The fastest instruction sequence does not naturally match the abstract syntax tree. The individual instructions must be easily manipulated—created, replicated, deleted, or moved—which is more easily done with a sequence of instructions rather than a tree.

Flow Graph

The compiler presented here gains the advantages of both trees and instruction sequences. A procedure is represented as a flow graph of sequences of instructions for an abstract RISC processor. This abstract machine has an inexhaustible supply of registers, called *temporaries*. There is a standard set of instructions for manipulating integers, long integers, floating point numbers, and double-precision numbers.

When tree-oriented algorithms are applicable, the procedure representation is translated into a form called *static single assignment* (SSA) form. When the compiler translates the flow graph into SSA form, the compiler reconstructs the expression trees, which can then be used in the tree-oriented algorithms. The compiler also computes the nested loops of the procedure, providing the tree structure of statements most needed in the compiler.

The assembly language procedure is not represented as text. As noted in chapter 2, it is stored as a directed graph called the *flow graph*. The flow graph is a variant of the idea of flow charts originally used in programming. The flow graph has the following components:

- The *instructions* are much like machine instructions in an abstract RISC processor. Each instruction consists of an operation code (opcode) representing the operation being performed, a set of input operands that are used to perform the operation indicated by the opcode, and a set of output targets that name the values being changed.

- The individual instructions have operands that are constants or *temporaries*. The set of temporaries is an arbitrarily large set of objects, like the physical registers in a real processor. Each temporary holds a value for some portion of the execution of the procedure. Some set of instructions will evaluate an expression and place it in the target temporary. Instructions that use this value as an operand reference the temporary as an operand.

- The instructions form a program in the same manner that assembly code on a real processor forms a program. The execution starts with the first instruction. Instructions are executed in turn until a branching instruction is found. The instructions are broken into sequences called *blocks*. The only instruction that is the destination of a branching instruction is the first instruction in a block. The only branching instructions are the last instructions in the block. At the end of the block there is a branching instruction representing each possible path out of the block.

- The blocks form a *flow graph* having the blocks as nodes in the graph. The edges between the blocks represent the possible execution paths leaving the block. The edge (*B*1,*B*2) indicates that there is some way that the execution of the procedure can travel directly from *B*1 to *B*2. The flow graph will have two distinguished nodes: the start block *Entry* and the exit block *Exit*.

Consider Figure 4.1 as a fragment of a procedure representing the computation of the statement $A = B + C * (B+A)$. The computation is broken into individual computations. Before the value of a variable can be referenced, the address of the variable must be loaded and a load operation for the variable must be executed. All values are loaded into temporaries. For typographical purposes integer temporaries are represented by an integer prefixed with a letter *T*. Note that the addresses of *A* and *B* are used twice and loaded only once. The name *A* indicates the constant address of variable *A*. The value of *B* is used twice and loaded only once. These are examples of redundant expression elimination. The individual operation names (or opcodes) will be described later: iLDC stands for load integer constant, iSLD stands for load integer value from static memory, iADD is integer add, iMUL is integer multiply, and iSST is integer store into static memory. These names are taken from the Massive Scalar Compiler Project at Rice University.

For an example involving loops and branches consider Figure 4.2, which computes an integer power of 2. The argument is the power, and it controls the number of times the loop is executed. The flow graph for this program (Figure 4.3) shows a number of characteristics of flow graphs. Each flow graph starts with a special pseudo-instruction called *prolog* and ends with the instruction *epilog*. These represent whatever computations need

Figure 4.1 Representation of $A = B + C * (B+A)$

```
iLDC    A           => T1    /Get address of A
iLDC    B           => T2    /Get address of B
iLDC    C           => T3    /Get address of C
iSLD    (T2)        => T4    /Get value of B
iSLD    (T3)        => T5    /Get value of C
iSLD    (T1)        => T6    /Get value of A
iADD    T4,T6       => T7    /B+A
iMUL    T5,T7       => T8    /C*(B+A)
iADD    T4,T8       => T9    /B+C*(B+A)
iSST    (T1),T9
```

Flow Graph

Figure 4.2 Sample Program

```
int power2(int i) {
   int p = 1;
   while (i > 0) {
      p = 2 * p;
      i = i - 1;
   }
   return p
}
```

to be performed at the beginning and end of the procedure. Note that prolog takes as an argument the actual parameters of the procedure. In this case the single parameter is *i*, which is stored in temporary T1.

The program flow graph is divided into blocks labeled B0, B1, and B2. They each begin a block in the directed flow graph. The block consists of some number of computational instructions followed by branching instructions that end the block. The conditional branching instructions iBCOND are assumed to be two-way branches, so there is no implied flow of execution from one block to another. The first label is the address to branch to if the condition is true. The second label is branched to if the condition is false.

Figure 4.3 Program Flow Graph for Sample in Figure 4.2

```
B0:   prolog          T1
      iLDC            1             => T3
      i2i             T3            => T2
      iLDC            0             => T4
      iCMPLE          T1,T4         => T5
      iBCOND          T5,B2,B1

B1:   iLDC            2             => T6
      iMUL            T6,T2         => T7
      i2i             T7            => T2
      iSUB            T1,T3         => T8
      i2i             T8            => T1
      iCMPLE          T1,T4         => T5
      iBCOND          T5,B2,B1

B2:   return          T2
      epilog
```

Figure 4.4   Directed Flow Graph for Sample

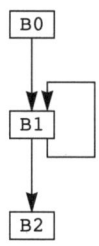

Similarly, branching instructions are included to represent control flow. The intermediate representation is represented as a directed graph, $G = (N,E)$, where each node $B \in N$, called a block, represents a sequence of computational instructions followed by a branching statement (see Figure 4.4). The operands of the branching instructions include the blocks that are possible destinations of the branches. An edge $(P,F) \in E$ occurs when there is a branching statement in P containing a possible destination, F.

4.2 Should the Representation Be Lowered?

Initially the procedure is represented by an abstract syntax tree. It is then translated into the flow graph. As the compiler processes the flow graph, it is gradually modified until the flow graph represents an explicit set of target machine instructions. The gradual modification process is called *lowering*. Thus each phase of the compiler lowers the flow graph, gradually removing source language details and replacing them with target machine instruction details.

Initially the flow graph represents a sequence of computations; however, the level of detail is the same level as the abstract syntax tree. Many computations, such as addition and multiplication, are simple to begin with, so there is no lowering of detail. More complex operations, such as array references and function calls, are represented at an abstract level.

Consider a subscripted array reference, $A[I,J]$, where A is an integer $N \times N$ array with the subscripts running between 1 and N. Such an array is implemented as a block of storage. The individual elements of the array are referenced using the subscript formula (for Fortran),

```
address(A[I,J]) = address(A) + sizeof(int)*(N*(J-1) + (I-1))
```

When the compiler is building the flow graph, it could translate an array reference into a collection of additions and multiplications as given by this formula; however, most information about the actual array reference would be lost. Compiler phases needing information about array references would get imprecise information.

Instead, the compiler creates array load operations and store operations where the array name, subscripts, and bounds are listed as operands. After all uses of array information have occurred, the compiler translates these operations into the simpler arithmetic and memory references implied by the formula. In other words, the level of the flow graph is lowered by replacing higher-level operations by simpler instruction-level operations.

Procedure and function calls are also gradually lowered. There are individual operators for function calls and procedure calls. Initially the arguments of each of these are the name of the subroutine (or an expression evaluating the name of the subroutine) and a list of actual arguments. The details of a procedure call for the target machine are ignored. The level of a function or procedure call is kept at the level of the original program. After interprocedural analysis and in-lining has occurred, the procedure calls are replaced by a set of instructions that compute the effect of calling and returning from the subroutine.

Code generation, or translation into the instructions of the target machine, is a special case of lowering the level. The program flow graph mimics the structure of an assembly language program for an abstract RISC processor. There is a one-to-one correspondence between many of the instructions of the target machine and the operations allowed in the flow graph. If there are operations in the target machine that cannot be represented by a single instruction in the flow graph, then these operations are added to the set of operators. Before the final optimization phases, the flow graph is lowered to only use operators that have a single-instruction representation in the target machine.

Some of the generic operations in the flow graph can be viewed as macros to be expanded. The load and store byte operations on early Alpha processors are an example of this. A multiple-instruction sequence is required to load a byte. If the exact sequence of instructions is generated initially, then some optimizations are lost. Similarly, multiplication by a constant needs to be expanded into a sequence of shifts and adds. Both of these are examples of gradual lowering since each should not be lowered initially, but needs to be done before the final optimization phases so that the individual instructions can be optimized.

Some operations on the target machine may represent several instructions in the flow graph. The easiest example is a load or store operation that takes two arguments, a register and a constant. The address is computed as the sum of the register and constant. This load operation performs two computations: the addition and the fetch. In the initial flow graph, these are represented as two distinct instructions. Before the final optimization phases, these two operations are folded together into a single instruction.

The compiler assumes that all flow of control is explicitly represented in the flow graph. In other words, the flow of control is not gradually lowered. Some flow of control can be hidden within instructions that are not yet lowered, such as maximum and minimum operations. However, each instruction has a set of inputs and outputs, with flow entering the beginning of the instruction and (except for branching instructions) executing the next instruction at the end.

4.3 Building the Flow Graph

This section describes the code in the compiler for translating the abstract syntax tree into the flow graph. First we will consider two situations, an expression and a loop; then we will describe the structure of the code in the compiler.

Consider the statement we discussed earlier: $A = B + C * (B+A)$. The corresponding abstract syntax tree is given in Figure 4.5. The tree is represented

Figure 4.5 Abstract Syntax Tree for $A = B + C * (B+A)$

```
assign
   symbol("A")
   plus
      fetch
         symbol("B")
      multiply
         fetch
            symbol("C")
         parenthesis
            plus
               fetch
                  symbol("B")
               fetch
                  symbol("A")
```

(as before) by the root being the leftmost entry and each child being indented beneath its parent. The tree will be annotated with type information, which is not noted. The transcriptions such as *symbol("A")* are used to indicate a symbol node with a pointer to the symbol table for the variable A.

Recall that the semantics of a language can be divided into two distinct sets of rules: static and dynamic semantics. Static semantics are the set of rules that describe the structural rules of the language (beyond the lexical and parsing structure). For example, a static semantic rule is that a symbol must be declared before it is used. The dynamic semantics are the set of rules that describe the effect of each part of the language. It is part of the dynamic semantics to state that the operands of an addition must be evaluated before the addition is performed (and possibly to specify the order of evaluation of the operands), or that the meaning of an assignment statement is to evaluate the address of the left-hand side, evaluate the value of the right-hand side, and store the value from the right side into the address specified by the left side. These rules are all part of the language standard or language specification.[1]

The language definitions describe the dynamic semantics in terms of the language construct and its operands. To build an assignment statement, the compiler must be able to build the operands. This tree-structured approach is true of each construct. This fact suggests that the flow graph can be built during a bottom-up walk of the abstract syntax tree in which the children are walked in an order described by the dynamic semantics of the language construct. For some tree nodes, such as loops, a bottom-up tree walk is inadequate: Instructions may be generated before, during, and after the generation of the children.

The tree walk is a little more complex than a simple bottom-up tree walk because different operations may be needed depending on the context in which the tree occurs. There are several contexts that occur, but more may be needed depending on the complexity of the language:

Value Context: When the operand is an expression, the compiler will want to walk the expression and create a temporary that contains the

---

1. Many compiler writers, including myself, have made a good living from the fact that many people are not aware of dynamic semantics. Many programmers think that a language is defined if a grammar has been written. The grammar is only a small part of the total effort. The real effort comes in describing the static and dynamic semantics and the interactions between distinct dynamic semantic rules.

corresponding value. As a side effect, it inserts instructions in the flow graph. This walk is implemented by calling the procedure

```
temporary value_walk(ast * node)
```

NoValue Context: When the subtree is a statement or an expression used as a statement, the compiler walks the subtree creating instructions to represent the effect of the subtree, but no temporary is created to hold any final value. There is an opportunity for optimization here—the only instructions that the compiler needs to generate are those representing side effects of the subtree, so some instructions need not be generated. This walk is implemented by calling the procedure

```
void novalue_walk(ast * node)
```

Flow Value Context: If the subtree represents an expression used to determine branching operations, then more efficient instructions can be generated if the compiler walks the subtree generating the testing and branching instructions together. The procedure implementing the flow context walk requires an added two parameters: the blocks to be branched to if the conditional expression is true and if it is false:

```
void flow_walk(ast * node, block * true_block, block
    * false_block)
```

Size Context: If the size of the data represented by the subtree is needed, the subtree must be walked to generate a temporary holding the value of the size of the data. The calling sequence for this procedure is identical to the value context routine. It just computes a different value—the size:

```
temporary size_context(ast * node)
```

Before discussing the structure of each of these tree-walking procedures (they are all similar), we must discuss the structure of the support routines used to build the flow graph. These procedures are structured so that the tree walks will read much like dynamic semantic rules.

4.3.1 Support Procedures for Initially Building the Flow Graph

There are two different sets of support procedures to manipulate the flow graph. The general set of procedures allows the insertion of any instruction in any block, and allows the insertion of one block between two other blocks on edges. Effectively, this is a completely general set of procedures for manipulating the flow graph. These procedures (to be described later) are used to build the following set of procedures for creating the flow graph initially.

The set of procedures for initially building the flow graph work much as an assembly language programmer works. One instruction is added to the flow graph at a time. A block starts after a conditional branch instruction or at an instruction that is branched to. Until a new block, is started all instructions created are added to the end of the current block. When the current block is completed, a new block is started.

The support procedures do differentiate between creating a block and starting a block. A block may be created at any time. When it is created, the block can be involved in conditional branching instructions, that is, it can be branched to. However, the block has yet to have instructions inserted in it. Later the compiler can start the block. This makes the block the current block and all instructions are added to it until the next block is started.

Why this distinction? The compiler must be able to create a conditional branch instruction to a block that is not yet in the flow graph. Consider an **if** statement. When building the conditional branch instruction, neither the **then** part or the **else** part has been processed yet. So the compiler creates the blocks for the start of the **then** part and **else** part before creating the conditional branch instruction. Later it starts putting instructions into the **then** part when that part is processed. This can lead to blocks that remain empty. A separate phase of the compiler will eliminate these empty blocks.

Here are the support procedures for building the initial flow graph:

initialize_graph: This procedure creates an empty data structure for the flow graph and associated tables. It builds two blocks, *Entry* and *Exit,* that are the start and exit blocks for the flow graph. It then makes the *Entry* block the current block so the initial instructions will be in that block.

create_block: This function creates and initializes a new block to be an empty block. It returns the block as the return value.

start_block: This procedure takes a block as argument and makes it the current block. All future instructions will be added to the end of this block.

xxx_instruct: For each class of instructions in the flow graph a separate support procedure is present to create an instruction of that form. The arguments to the instruction are the operation code, the input constants or temporaries, and the output temporaries. For the load and store instructions, further data will be passed indicating what storage locations these instructions might modify.

cond_instruct: The conditional branching instructions have support procedures that terminate the current block and insert edges from the current block to each of the destinations of the conditional branching instruction, thus keeping the edges of the flow graph up-to-date. The arguments for this support procedure are the opcode, the temporary for the value being tested, the destination when the condition is true, and the destination when the condition is false.

uncond_instruct: The unconditional branch instruction has only one argument: the block to be branched to. It terminates the current block and inserts the edge between the current block and the destination of the branch.

new_temporary: This procedure takes an enumeration class as an argument indicating which register class is being referenced. It then initializes the data structures for a temporary and returns it as its value.

There are also support procedures for dealing with temporaries. We assume an infinite supply of temporaries, so we create a new one at any point that a temporary is needed. However, we need some conventions concerning the use of temporaries to ease the work of later optimization phases. Later, during the Limit phase, some of these conventions will be relaxed.

Basic Convention: Each time a formal expression, such as $B + A$ is computed, it is computed in the same temporary. Why? The algorithms for code motion and eliminating redundant expressions need to know where a value is stored. If one instance of $B + A$ is known to be redundant, the compiler wants to delete that computation. To do so, it must search the rest of the flow graph looking for all points where $B + A$ is computed and copying the result into a temporary to be used in place of the redundant expression. Instead, the compiler always computes $B + A$ in the same temporary so that a redundant computation need only be deleted.

The compiler ensures that the convention is met by building a data structure called the *formal temporary table,*[2] consisting of records of the opera-

---

2. This is a simplification of an idea first suggested by Chow (1983) in his thesis and later used by COMPASS in the COMPASS Compiler Engine. The COMPASS approach attempted to use this table for too many purposes.

tion code and inputs for each instruction together with the temporary for the result. There is a unique entry in the formal temporary table even if the instruction occurs multiple times in the flow graph.

Since operands are computed before an expression, temporaries used in expressions are computed before they are used. When an instruction is about to be generated, its operation code and inputs are used as keys in a table lookup on the formal temporary table. If the instruction has already been inserted, the same temporary is used for the target. If this is a new instruction, a new record is inserted in the table together with a new temporary.

4.3.2 Handling Local Variables as Temporaries

Variables with a scope local to a procedure can be handled as temporaries if their addresses are not used. In that case a temporary is used to hold the value of the local variable. The temporary is also used to represent the tree, representing a fetch of the local variable in the abstract syntax tree. If the compiler cannot keep the variable in a register, it will later store it in memory.

This optimization has two advantages. Better code will result if the compiler is optimistic about what it keeps in registers. The elimination of loads and stores is harder than inserting them when they are needed. Secondly, this decreases the size of the flow graph, making all optimizations run faster.

This leads to one of the few situations where the convention is that identical instructions with identical inputs are the only instructions using the same target register. Consider two distinct assignments to i, $i = i + 1$ and $i = i * 3$. Assume that the temporary corresponding to the local variable i is T1. The act of assigning both of these values to i means that there are two distinct register-to-register copy operations that have target T1.

In fact, the temporaries are divided into two distinct classes: the *variable temporaries* and the *expression temporaries*. The expression temporaries satisfy the criteria stated above. All instructions that have one of these as the target register have exactly the same form. The variable temporaries are all others. Different optimizations are used on the two classes of instructions.

4.3.3 Structure of the Tree-Walking Routines

Now we have the infrastructure to describe the tree walks used to implement the flow graph. We will discuss implementing five features: expressions, conditional expressions, branching expressions, structured statements, and **goto** statements.

The structure of the tree-walking procedures can be seen by considering the tree-walking procedure for expressions or nodes that return a value (Figure 4.6). All the other procedures are similar. The structure of the procedure is a **case** statement in which there is one entry for each abstract syntax tree node that can be represented in an expression (for the other tree-walking procedures, different nodes may be present and absent from the alternatives). There is an invariant assertion about each procedure that when a subtree has been walked, all instructions associated with the subtree have been inserted in the flow graph.

Consider the alternative associated with the plus node in the abstract syntax tree. It first walks its children in the order specified by the dynamic

Figure 4.6 Structure of Expression Tree Walk

```
function Value_Walk(n: ast_node) returns temporary;
   case n→operation_code of
      ...
      plus_node:
         begin
            declare
               first: temporary = Value_Walk(n→first);
               second: temporary = Value_Walk(n→second);
               result: temporary;
            enddeclare;
            case n→type of
               integer_type: result = Binary_Instruct(iADD,first,second);
               float_type: result = Binary_Instruct(fADD,first,second);
               double_type: result = Binary_Instruct(dADD,first,second);
            endcase;
            return result;
         end;
      constant_node:
         begin
            declare (result: temporary);
            case n→type of
               integer_type: result = Const_Instruct(iLDC, n→value);
               float_type: result = Const_Instruct(fLDC, n→value);
               double_type: result = Const_Instruct(dLDC, n→value);
            endcase;
            return result;
         end;
      ...
      otherwise:
         call Error("Illegal Abstract Syntax tree");
   endcase;
endfunction Value_Walk;
```

Flow Graph

semantics of the language, in this case left to right. It then adds instructions to the flow graph to perform the appropriate operations to simulate the dynamic semantics. In this case, it checks the type of expression and generates either an integer, floating point, or double-precision addition operation.

The procedure *Binary_Instruct* is called to generate any binary instructions. It takes an instruction operator and two temporaries as operands, generating and returning the temporary of the result. This procedure uses the formal temporary table to ensure that the same temporary is always the result when the operator and operands are the same. It also inserts the instruction as the latest instruction in the current block.

Now consider the entry for constants. Here there is no further tree to walk, so the tree-walking procedure gets the data associated with the node (the constant value in this case) and generates an instruction that has a single constant operand. Again it makes sure that the same temporary is used for all instances of the same constant and that the instruction is inserted at the end of the current block.

If a node of the abstract syntax tree cannot return a value, it has no alternative in the **case** statement. If such a node occurs where an expression is expected, the compiler will give a system error message. This check is valuable because it checks the abstract syntax tree for legal structure at no overhead for correct trees.

Processing Structured Statements

The *NoValue_Walk* procedure is used for statements. For statements like procedure calls, the processing is similar to the processing of expressions. Branching and structured statements are different because they can change the block in which the current instructions are being inserted.

Consider the **case** statement alternative for a **while** loop. Consider the flow graph that the compiler needs to generate (Figure 4.7). This will describe the code in the alternative. The compiler will generate two copies of the loop test. The first copy occurs in the current block to decide if the loop needs to be executed at all. If the loop needs to be executed, then the code for the body of the loop occurs. Another copy of the loop test occurs at the end of the body to decide whether the loop needs to be executed again. This is a more complex representation of the loop than appears in most textbooks. It is chosen to improve the chances for moving code out of the loop.

Thus the compiler is going to start at least two blocks during the processing of a **while** loop. The first block is the block for the body; the second

Figure 4.7 Flow Graph for while Loop

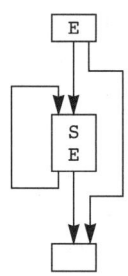

block is the block following the **while** loop. We need the second block because the compiler must be able to branch to the block following the loop.

Recall that a **break** statement can occur inside a **while** statement. To handle such a statement, the translator maintains a stack containing the blocks that follow a looping statement. If a **break** statement occurs, then it is implemented as a branch to the block at the top of this stack. With this information, we can describe the code in *NoValue_Walk* corresponding to a **while** loop and **break** statement (see Figure 4.8).

Conditional Branching Expressions

The short-circuit operators—logical AND, logical OR, and logical NOT—use special processing. A logical AND is false if its first argument is false; otherwise, it has the same value as the second argument. A logical OR is true if its first argument is true; otherwise, it has the same value as its second argument. The *flow_walk* procedure implements these operations, together with conditional branching due to comparisons.

The structure is similar to the other walks, as shown in Figure 4.9. It directly implements the above description of the short-circuit operators. The beauty of this approach is that d'Morgan's laws for logical operations are automatically generated.

The comparison operations call the *Value_Walk* procedure to evaluate the binary operation, called a *comparison*. The result is a Boolean value, which is then tested with the conditional branch instruction.

The opposite situation occurs in *Value_Walk,* which calls *flow_walk* to implement the short-circuit logical AND and logical OR operations. It com-

Figure 4.8 Fragment of Walking Statements

```
procedure NoValue_Walk(n: ast_node);
   case n→operation_code of
      ...
      while_node:
         begin
            declare
               after: block = create_block();
               body: block = create_block();
            enddeclare;
            push after on break_stack;
            call flow_walk(n→conditional,body,after);
            call start_block(body);
            call NoValue_Walk(n→body);
            call flow_walk(n→conditional,body,after);
            call start_block(after);
            pop after from break_stack;
         end;
      break_node:
         begin
            call uncond_instruct(iJMP,top(break_stack));
         end;
      ...
      otherwise:
         call Error("Illegal Abstract Syntax tree");
   endcase;
endprocedure NoValue_Walk;
```

piles them as if they were the conditional expression. In C this would mean that A&&B is compiled as if it were the conditional expression (A&&B?1:0).

Conditional Expressions

Special note is made of conditional expressions because they are one of the few instances where an expression computing a value can have operands or parts of operands in separate blocks. This is one of the reasons that a flow graph approach to the program representation was chosen rather than a tree structure. The concept of a temporary does not depend on being in the same block, so an operand can be computed in one block and used in another.

Consider a conditional expression, (E_0 ? E_t : E_f). The conditional expression E_0 is computed in the current block. There are distinct blocks to compute the other operands. Where is the result value placed? The compiler

Figure 4.9   Structure of *flow_walk*

```
procedure flow_walk(n: ast_node, true_block: block, false_block: block);
   case n→operation_code of
      ...
      and_node:
         begin
            declare (second: block = create_block());
            call flow_walk(n→first, second, false_block);
            call start_block(second);
            call flow_walk(n→second, true_block, false_block);
            call end_block();
         end;
      or_node:
         begin
            declare (second: block = create_block());
            call flow_walk(n→first, true_block, second);
            call start_block(second);
            call flow_walk(n→second, true_block, false_block);
            call end_block();
         end;
      not_node:
         begin
            call flow_walk(n→child, false_block, true_block);
         end;
      less_node:
         begin
            declare (test: temporary = Value_Walk(n));
            call cond_instruct(iBCOND, test, true_branch, false_branch);
            call end_block();
         end;
      ...
      otherwise:
         call Error("Illegal Abstract Syntax tree");
   endcase;
endprocedure flow_walk;
```

needs to generate a temporary to hold that value. That temporary must be handled as a compiler-generated variable temporary. It cannot satisfy the requirement placed on expression temporaries: The instructions for which it is the target register are not all identical.

What about the expression that has a conditional expression as an operand? No problem. The operands may be computed in separate blocks, but that is not a problem for the compiler. The fragment in Figure 4.10, to be added to *Value_Walk,* will handle conditional expressions.

Figure 4.10 Implementing Conditional Expressions

```
conditional_node:
   begin
      declare
         true_block: block = create_block();
         true_register: temporary;
         false_block: block = create_block();
         false_register: temporary;
         result: temporary = new_temporary(n→type);
         after: block = create_block();
      enddeclare;
      call flow_walk(n→conditional, true_block, false_block);
      call start_block(true_block);
      true_register = Value_Walk(n→true_part);
      call CopyRegister(result, true_register);
      call Uncond_Instruct(iJMP,after);
      call start_block(false_block);
      false_register = Value_Walk(n→false_part);
      call CopyRegister(result, false_register);
      call Uncond_Instruct(iJMP,after);
      call start_block(after)
      return result;
   end;
```

goto Statements

goto statements can be a problem with some translation techniques. Here we have developed enough structure that they are quite easy. There are two parts to the processing: the **goto** statement itself and the label position. The following operations need to be performed:

- A label is a symbol in the language. There needs to be a symbol table entry for the label, with a field to hold the block that starts at that label.

- A **goto** statement is translated into an unconditional branch to the block associated with the label. If there is as yet no block associated with the label, use *create_block* to produce one.

- At the point at which the label occurs, insert an unconditional branch to the label in the current block. Effectively end the previous block. Then perform *start_block* on the block associated with the label. If there is no block associated with the label, create one using *create_block*.

This processing translates the **goto** statement into an unconditional branch.

4.4 Structure of Data

Many languages have the ability to initialize data at program initiation. This information is identified by the compiler front end. This section describes how this information is stored so that it can be communicated to the object module.

The compiler must keep a map of data to be included in the object module. This includes COMMON blocks, external variables, and compiler-generated information. The data structure to represent this data is relatively simple—there is only one serious problem.

The compiler adds to the symbol table an extra attribute storing the value to be saved. This data is typically a linked list of values.

The one problem is data that can be repeated a large number of times. This can occur in COMMON blocks or the initialization of arrays in C. A special repeat node must be added to linked lists of data. It has two components: a repeat count and a list of the data to be repeated.

If the data is not constant, then the data is initialized by creating assignment statements in the flow graph.

4.5 Structure of Blocks

Each block is a list of instructions. Since the compiler is frequently inserting and deleting instructions, the lists are implemented as doubly linked lists. The lists represent the order of execution of instructions in the block. Thus a block is the assembly language equivalent of a label followed by a sequence of instructions up to the next branch instruction or label.

In this compiler, a block always starts at a point that is branched to and is completed by a sequence of branching instructions. There are no computational instructions between the instructions at the end of the block. This allows the compiler to reorder and combine blocks.

Later, during instruction scheduling, the blocks will be transformed into a list of small sets of instructions, called *packets*. On multiple-instruction-issue machines, the processor will issue a set of instructions on each cycle. These packets represent the compiler's knowledge of the set of instructions to be issued.

Besides the instructions, each block holds the attributes that describe the edges in the flow graph. Hence each block B holds two attributes: $SUCC(B)$ and $PRED(B)$. $SUCC(B)$ is the set of blocks that can follow B during the execution of the flow graph. $PRED(B)$ is the set of blocks that can precede B during the execution of the program.

4.6 Structure of Instructions

Each instruction, *I*, consists of the following components:

- An operator, represented as an element of an enumeration class, *operation_type*. There is one name for each operation, whether it is a high-level operation that exists initially in the set of instructions or a low-level operation created later during processing.

- A set of temporaries that are queried during the evaluation of the instruction. The values of these temporaries are used to compute a value or effect for this instruction. The pseudo-code will refer to this set of operands as *Operands(I)*.

- A set of temporaries that are certain to be modified by the instruction. Usually there is only one such instruction. However, more registers may be modified by instructions that do not have a simple effect. Thus a procedure or function call may have a larger set of registers that is modified. The pseudo-code will refer to this set of registers as *Target(I)*.

4.7 Structure of Program Flow Graph

Since the graph structure is actually implemented by the successor, *SUCC*, and predecessor, *PRED*, attributes of the blocks, little information is left to be stored in the flow graph. There are the two distinguished blocks: *Entry* and *Exit*. *Entry* is the single block in the flow graph with no predecessors and represents the point where execution starts. *Exit* is the single block with no successors and represents the block where execution ends.

From an implementation point of view, all information about the compilation of this one procedure is grouped together in one data structure as attributes of the flow graph. This is needed for interprocedural analysis. The compiler must be able to store and retrieve all information about a procedure. This eases the problem of compilation during the interprocedural analysis phases.

4.7.1 Critical Edges

Many of the transformations performed by the compiler need to place computations on an edge. Since computations are only in blocks, the compiler must find an equivalent block for the inserted computations. If the tail of the edge has only one successor, the computations can be inserted at the end of the tail since the only way out of the tail is along that edge. If the target block

Figure 4.11 Dividing a Critical Edge

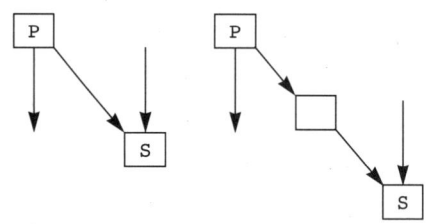

of the edge has only one predecessor the computations can be inserted at the beginning of the target since the only way to the target is along that edge.

The only problems occur when the tail block of the edge has multiple successors and the target block has multiple predecessors, as shown in Figure 4.11. Such an edge is called a *critical edge*. A critical edge can be removed by creating an empty block and replacing the original edge by two edges: one edge with the original source and the new block as target, and another with the new block as source and the original target as target. The two new edges are not critical edges because one of them has a target with only one predecessor and the other one has a source with a single successor.

4.7.2 Classification of Edges in the Flow Graph

The edges in the flow graph can be divided into three categories. Edges that occur because of conditional branches to explicit blocks are called *normal edges*. These are the most frequently occurring edges and the easiest to manipulate. If one needs to change the destination of the branch, it is a straightforward task to modify the instruction and flow graph at the same time. If the compiler can determine that the branch will never be taken or is always taken, then the compiler can change both the set of instructions in the block and the flow graph structure.

For other edges in the program flow graph, the compiler cannot determine the destination of the branch by inspecting the instruction that causes the branch. These edges are called *abnormal edges*. This occurs with the **setjmp/longjmp** operations in C, some implementations of Fortran input/output (I/O), exception handling, subroutine calls with nonlocal branching, and the C **switch** statement in some compilers. In all of these cases a transfer of control may occur and there is no clear way in the set of instructions in the block to determine where the transfer of control leads. The compiler has built a conservative set of successor blocks to ensure that all possible control transfers are accounted for, but the compiler cannot determine exactly where the branch will lead or, in some cases, whether the branch will occur at all.

Abnormal edges are a difficult problem for an optimizing compiler. Most optimizations need to place computations on an edge, which means that critical edges must be removed. This is not possible for abnormal edges because there is no way of modifying the contents of the blocks to reflect the existence of a new block. Furthermore, most abnormal edges are critical edges. The compiler must implement all transformations to avoid problems on abnormal edges.[3]

Another category of edges is *impossible edges*. Many program transformations assume that every block is on some path from the *Entry* to the *Exit* blocks of the procedure being compiled. This will not happen if the block is a member of a loop that has no exits. The compiler must add an edge from some block in such a loop to the *Exit* block. These edges are less of a problem than abnormal edges, because they can never be executed. If a transformation needs to insert a computation on such an edge, simply ignore the insertion because the code will never be executed.

4.8 Classifying Temporaries

Consider an expression $(X+Y) * Z$ consisting of two operands, $(X+Y)$ and Z. The compiler will initially create a sequence of instructions that first evaluates $X + Y$, then Z, and finally $(X+Y) * Z$. When the compiler moves $(X+Y) * Z$ to an earlier point in the flow graph, it must first move $(X+Y)$ and Z. Each of the optimization algorithms uses information about the operands to choose the point to place $(X+Y) * Z$. If the compiler moves the computation of the operands, the information concerning the whole expression is out-of-date. The information must be computed again.

To avoid computing this information again, the compiler enforces a convention on the flow graph that guarantees that the optimization information will still be accurate. Each expression can be viewed as an expression tree. The leaves are the memory loads or uses of temporaries that

---

3. The COMPASS compiler team referred to this problem as the Mangy Dog Problem. It first was observed during the implementation of the register allocator.

represent local variables and special compiler temporaries. The interior nodes are the operators that make up the subexpressions representing the operands. The compiler views the expression as a pure function (without side effects) of the temporaries and memory locations that occur at the leaves of this expression, and not as a function of its immediate operands. Thus, $(X+Y) * Z$ is viewed as a function of X, Y, and Z. It is not viewed as a function of $(X+Y)$. Thus the evaluation of $(X+Y)$ does not inhibit the movement of the complete expression. The compiler depends on two characteristics of the compiler algorithms used here:

1. For any path from *Entry* to the evaluation of an expression and each operand, there is an evaluation of the operand before the evaluation of the expression, and there are no instructions between the two evaluations that might modify the value of the operand. In other words, there is an evaluation of $(X+Y)$ on each path from the entry to the evaluation of $(X+Y) * Z$, and there is no instruction that might modify either X or Y between the two.

2. The compiler establishes a convention that each occurrence of an expression evaluates its value in the same temporary. In our example, suppose X is evaluated in $T1$, Y is evaluated in $T2$, Z is evaluated in $T3$, $(X+Y)$ is evaluated in $T4$, and $(X+Y) * Z$ is evaluated in $T5$. Therefore the instruction representing $(X+Y)$ always represents $T4 = T1 + T2$, and the complete expression is always represented by $T5 = T4 * T3$.

Not all temporaries can be put into this form. A temporary representing a local variable can have different quantities evaluated into it. As we will see shortly, the temporary variables that are the destinations of load operations will also be used as the destination of a copy operation before a store into the same location. For this reason temporaries are divided into two classes: those that satisfy the two above conditions (*expression temporaries*) and those that do not satisfy one or more of the conditions (*variable temporaries*).

To improve optimization, it is helpful to make the set of expression temporaries as large as possible. This may require extra copy operations in the flow graph, which will be removed later during register allocation. Consider the increment operation $I = I + 1$ of a variable temporary I. This can be implemented as a single integer add operation in the flow graph, iADD I,#1=> I. Representing the flow graph in this way violates the second condition on expression temporaries, and the expression $I + 1$ cannot be optimized. Instead, the flow graph represents this computation as two instructions, iADD I,#1=>T1 and i2i T1=>I. With this representation the expression $I + 1$ can be optimized.

For an expression temporary, the only way to change its value is to modify one of the variable temporaries occurring at the leaves of the corresponding expression tree. So optimizers do not consider an evaluation of one of the operands as changing the whole expression. Instead, the optimizer assumes that the modification of one of the leaves modifies all expression temporaries that include that temporary as one of the leaves of its expression tree. Thus the evaluation of a direct operand is not considered an instruction that modifies the whole expression, and the two expressions can be optimized separately.

Independent optimization of expressions and operands assumes that the operands will be moved at least as far back in the flow graph as the whole expression. This is true in the optimization techniques described in this book; however, it is not true of all optimization techniques. Early versions of partial redundancy elimination (Morel and Renvoise 1979) had this problem. It was later solved by (Drechsler and Stodel 1988) and most later authors.

4.9 Local Optimization Information

For efficiency of compilation, the flow graph is divided into blocks such that each block is a sequentially executed sequence of instructions where if the first one is executed, then all of them are executed. For the same efficiency reasons, the optimization computations are divided the same way. The optimization information for blocks is called *local* information, and the optimization for paths through the flow graph is called *global* information.

The difference in information for expression temporaries and variable temporaries concerns the instructions that might modify each temporary. An instruction kills an expression temporary if it assigns a new value to one of the temporaries that occurs at the leaves of the corresponding expression tree. An instruction kills a variable temporary if it modifies the temporary directly. Given the idea of a temporary being killed by an instruction, we can now define the three forms of local optimization information.

DEFINITION **Local Information:** Given a block B and a temporary T then

T is *locally anticipated* in B if there is an instruction in B that evaluates T and there is no instruction preceding that instruction in B that might kill T.

T is *locally available* in B if there is an instruction in B that evaluates T and there is no instruction following that instruction in B that might kill T.

T is *transparent* in B if there is no instruction in B that might kill T. If T is not transparent it is killed in B.

Each definition refers to the concept that one instruction might kill a temporary. For the direct computational instructions, it is easy to determine if one instruction might kill a temporary—that instruction can only modify the output temporaries. Other instructions, such as procedure calls, are more complex. The inner workings of the procedure may not be available and even if available may not indicate which temporaries are modified. In that case the compiler must make a conservative estimate. If the compiler cannot deduce that a temporary is not killed, then it must assume that it is killed.

The language definition may help the compiler make less conservative decisions about the temporaries killed by an instruction. In Fortran, the language standard indicates that a legal program cannot modify the same location using two different names. Thus the compiler can assume that a modification of a formal parameter (dummy argument) does not modify any global variable, local variable, or other formal parameter. In ANSI C, a pointer (when not a pointer to characters) cannot modify a storage location of a different type.

In Figure 4.12 the temporaries I and J are variable temporaries, whereas the temporaries $T1$, $T2$, and $T3$ are expression temporaries. The expression $I * J$, or $T1$, is locally anticipated because it occurs in the block and no preceding instructions can modify I or J. Similarly $I + 1$, or $T2$, is locally anticipated. However, $I * 5$, or $T3$, is not locally anticipated since I is modified before the instruction. Similarly, $T1$ and $T2$ are not locally available, whereas $T3$ is.

Figure 4.12 Sample Block

```
iMUL    I,J     =>    T1
iADD    I,#1    =>    T2
i2i     T1      =>    I
...
iMUL    I,#5    =>    T3
...
```

As shown in Figure 4.13, the compiler computes the local information for each block by simulating the execution of the block. Not knowing the value of temporaries and variables, it only keeps track of the temporaries that are evaluated and killed. A temporary is locally anticipated if the first instruction that evaluates the temporary precedes any instructions that kill the temporary. The compiler maintains a set of all temporaries that have been killed by earlier instructions in the block, making the check for local anticipatability straightforward.

The check for local availability is more difficult because the algorithm does not know which temporaries are killed later in the block while it is simulating the execution. A temporary is locally available if it is evaluated in the block and the temporary is not killed by a later instruction. The

Figure 4.13 Computing Local Information

```
procedure Compute_Local(Block B);
   declare (killed: set of temporary);
   declare (anticipated: set of temporary);
   declare (available: set of temporary);
   killed = ∅;
   anticipated = ∅;
   available = ∅;
   foreach I ∈ B in execution order do
      if |Target(I)| = 1 then        //Normal instruction?
         let T ∈ Target(I);
         if T ∉ killed and T ∉ anticipated then
            add T to anticipated;
            add B to ANTLOC(T);
         endif;
         add T to available;
      endif;
      foreach T ∈ Targets(I) do      //Track temporaries changed
         killed = killed ∪ modifies(T);
         available = available − modifies(T);
      endfor;
   endfor;
for each T ∈ available do
   add B to AVLOC(T);
endfor;
   transp(B) = V − killed;
endprocedure Compute_Local;

foreach B ∈ G do
   call Compute_Local(B);
endfor;
```

algorithm computes this by assuming that a temporary is locally available whenever it is evaluated in the block. When a temporary is killed, it is added to the set of killed variables and is removed from the set of locally available temporaries.

To determine which temporaries might have been modified, the compiler needs a set for each temporary called *modifies*. The set *modifies(T)* contains the set of temporaries and memory locations that are killed by an instruction that has T as a target. For expression temporaries this set is empty. For variable temporaries, it includes the set of all temporaries that have this temporary as a leaf of the corresponding expression tree. The calculation of this set is described in the chapter on alias analysis (Chapter 6).

Apply the algorithm to the block in Figure 4.12 (see Figure 4.13). While simulating the first instruction $T1$ is added to both *available* and *anticipated*. Since $T1$ is an expression temporary, it does not kill any other temporaries. Similarly, the second instruction adds $T2$ to both sets and no temporaries are killed. The copy into I kills $T1$, $T2$, and any other temporaries that use I as an operand. They are both still anticipated; however, they are removed from *available* because a killing instruction follows their evaluation. However, $T3$ is added to *available* and is not later removed. I is both killed in the block and available at the end of the block.

This algorithm may be the most expensive part of the optimizer. The algorithm is simple, but each instruction must be simulated. Other algorithms will consider only the blocks and not the instructions. The data structures need to be tuned for speed and space. Here are the data structure choices that I have found most effective:

- The collection of sets, *modifies(T)*, is large and not dense. For expression temporaries the set is empty. Each of these sets should therefore be stored as a small array of temporaries.

- The sets *available* and *anticipated* occur only once; hence their size is not much of a factor. However, elements are repeatedly being added and union and differences are being taken. The compiler uses the Briggs set implementation technique to store these sets.

- The sets associated with each block, *local_anticipated* and *local_available*, should have an efficient storage. The storage depends on how the global information is computed.

- The set *killed(B)* needs to be efficient. For each of the possible global optimization algorithms, *killed(B)* is best stored as a bit vector.

4.10 Global Anticipated Information

Global information is used to move computations in the flow graph. In reality computations are not moved. Instead, a copy of the computation is inserted at some point in the flow graph. It will then make some other copies of the same computation unnecessary. Insertion and deletion is more effective than moving code because more computations may be able to be deleted than just the copy involved in the move.

To insert a copy of a computation in the flow graph, the compiler must guarantee that every path leaving the point of insertion leads to another point where the computation already occurs. Otherwise, the compiler will be changing the flow graph to execute more instructions, or, much worse, it may introduce an exceptional condition (such as floating overflow) into the flow graph that would not have occurred otherwise. This leads to the definition of anticipation.

DEFINITION **Anticipation:** A temporary T is anticipated at a point p in the flow graph if and only if every path from p to *Exit* contains an instruction that evaluates T and is not preceded on that path by an instruction that might kill T.

The example in Figure 4.14 shows that the temporary T is anticipated at the point p in the flow graph. Each path leaving p goes through an occurrence of the computation computing T before reaching a point where the value of T is killed.

Figure 4.14   Demonstrating Anticipation

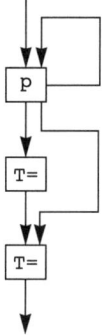

Unfortunately, the definition does not give a direct algorithm for computing anticipation. There are two algorithms in current use. Both will be presented here. The first one is given in most compiler textbooks. The second one is the one recommended for this compiler. However, the time/space trade-offs are such that a switch to the first algorithm may be necessary to improve performance. In other words, the author may be wrong.

To describe anticipation in terms of formulas, consider the Boolean variables $ANTIN(B)$ and $ANTOUT(B)$. $ANTIN(B)$ is true if and only if the temporary T is anticipated at the beginning of block B. Correspondingly, $ANTOUT(B)$ is true if and only if the temporary T is anticipated at the end of block B. What does it mean for $ANTOUT(B)$ to be true? Each path leaving B has a definition of T not preceded by a modification of T. If one looks at the next block on the path, this means that $ANTIN(S)$ is true for each successor of B. Conversely, if $ANTIN(S)$ is true for each successor then consider any path leaving B. The next block in the path is one of the successors, S, and there are no computations between the end of B and S, so each path leaving B has a computation of T before any modification of T.

Now consider a path leaving the beginning of B. This path must travel through B to reach the end of B. Three different events can happen as the path traverses B:

1. There is no instruction in B that either defines T or kills T. In that case nothing happens to T in the block, so the path satisfies the anticipation definition if and only if it satisfies the same definition at the end of the block; in other words, $ANTIN(B) = ANTOUT(B)$.

2. There is an instruction in B that defines T before any instruction that kills T, that is, $T \in local\_anticipation(B)$. Since any path starting at the beginning of the block must go through the block, this means that $ANTIN(B) = $ true.

3. There is an instruction B that kills T before there is any instruction that defines T. (Whether there is an instruction in B that defines T is irrelevant.) Again the block itself is the start of each path, so $ANTIN(B) = $ false.

All of these conditions can be summarized in the set of equations in Figure 4.15. The equations are a direct transcription of the analysis in the form of equations. Unfortunately, there is not a unique solution to the equations.

Consider the flow graph fragment in Figure 4.16. From the definition, one has $ANTOUT(B1) = $ true. But consider the equations. If one inserts the known value for B3 and eliminates the redundant equation, one gets two

Figure 4.15 Anticipatability Equations

$$ANTOUT_B = \begin{cases} \emptyset & \text{if } B \text{ is an exit} \\ \bigcap_{S \in SUCC(B)} ANTIN_S & \text{otherwise} \end{cases}$$

$$ANTIN_B = ANTLOC_B \cup (ANTOUT_B - KILL_B)$$

Figure 4.16 Graph for Multiple Solutions

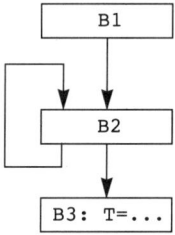

solutions to the equations (see Table 4.1). Which solution represents the collection of points where anticipation is true?

OBSERVATION 1: Given a solution of the anticipation equations. If $ANTIN(B)$ is true then the expression is anticipated at the beginning of B. Similarly, if $ANTOUT(B)$ is true then the expression is anticipated at the end of B.

PROOF We need to verify that the definition is satisfied. Consider any path starting at the start (or end) of B and ending at the exit block. By assumption $ANTIN(B)$ is true. Scan through the blocks in the path, stopping first at the beginning of the block and then the end of the block. If a block is reached when $ANTLOC$ is true, stop,

Table 4.1 Two Different Solutions

Unknown	Solution 1	Solution 2
ANTOUT(B1)	false	true
ANTIN(B2)	false	true
ANTOUT(B2)	false	true
ANTIN(B3)	true	true

because the definition is satisfied. By the equations, if *ANTOUT* of a block is true then so is *ANTIN* of the next block, so the value can only change from true to false as we scan through a block. Stop at the first block *W* where either *Kill(W)* is true or *ANTOUT(W)* is false. Consider the following two cases:

- Consider the case where *Kill(W)* is true. Since *ANTIN(W)* is true, then the expression must be in *ANTLOC(W)* to get the true value for *ANTIN(W)*. Thus an evaluation occurs at the beginning of *W,* verifying the definition.

- Consider the case where *ANTOUT(W)* is false. Since *ANTIN(W)* is true, the expression must be in *ANTLOC(W)* to get the true value for *ANTIN(W)*, again, verifying the definition.

In either case we have a path beginning with a sequence of blocks in which there are no modifications to the operands of the expressions and ending with a block that contains the expression before instructions that modify the operands. The definition is satisfied.

Observation 2: Assume that *ANTIN(B), ANTOUT(B)* is the maximum solution to the anticipation equations. If *ANTIN(B)* is false then *T* is not anticipated at the beginning of *B*.

Proof The proof is given in Appendix A.

4.11 Global Partial Redundancy Information

To compute the anticipated information and to avoid useless optimization computations later, we need another piece of information related to anticipation. *T* is anticipated at *p* if every path leaving *p* leads to an evaluation of *T* before an instruction that kills *T*. What if we are only interested in whether there is at least one path rather than all paths?

Definition **Partial Anticipation:** A temporary *T* is partially anticipated at a point *p* in the flow graph if and only if there is at least one path from *p* to *Exit* that contains an instruction that evaluates *T* which is not preceded by an instruction that might kill *T*.

Partial anticipation means there is some way to get from the point to an evaluation while avoiding instructions that kill *T*. Rather than repeat all of the arguments that gave us the characteristics for anticipation, we will note the differences. As with anticipation, we introduce two Boolean attributes for each block. *PANTIN(B)* being true means that *T* is partially anticipated at the beginning of the block, whereas *PANTOUT(B)* being true means *T* is partially anticipated at the end of the block.

In forming the equations, the information about all paths was used to determine that *ANTOUT* is the intersection of *ANTIN* of the successors. If we are looking for at least one path, then only one of the successors need have the attribute; therefore it is a union rather than an intersection. We thus get the equations in Figure 4.17.

We can make the corresponding observations about partial anticipation as we did about anticipation. Note that the equations do not have a single solution; however, we want the smallest solution rather than the largest. Consider the loop in Figure 4.16 with the evaluation of *T* removed. Nothing is partially anticipated; however, it is possible to get a solution to the equations with *PANTIN(B2)* = *PANTOUT(B2)* = true when the best solution we want has the value false. In anticipation we looked for the largest solution; here we look for the smallest solution.

OBSERVATION 3: Assume *PANTIN(B)* and *PANTOUT(B)* are a set of Boolean values that satisfies the equations in Figure 4.17. If *PANTIN(B)* (correspondingly, *PANTOUT(B)*) is false, then *T* is not partially anticipated at that point.

PROOF Given a solution to the equations, assume *PANTIN(B)* is false. Consider any path from that point to *Exit*. We need to show that we reach a killing instruction or *Exit* before we find an evaluation of *T*. Assume that we reach an evaluation of *T* before a killing instruction. That means we find a block *P* with *ANTLOC(P)* = true. Now walk backward. Since the values are a solution to the equations, *PANTOUT* of the previous block is true also because it is a union operation. By assumption there is no killing instruction in the block, so *PANTIN* is true. Repeat this whole process, walking backward until we reach the original point. We have *PANTIN* being true rather than false. We have a contradiction, the assumption that there is an evaluation of *T* before a killing instruction is false. There is no evaluation, so *T* is not partially anticipated.

Figure 4.17 Partial Anticipation Equations

$$PANTOUT_B = \begin{cases} \emptyset & \text{if } B \text{ is an } Exit \\ \bigcup_{S \in SUCC(B)} PANTIN_S & \text{otherwise} \end{cases}$$

$$PANTIN_B = ANTLOC_B \cup (PANTOUT_B - KILL_B)$$

OBSERVATION 4: Let *PANTIN(B)* (respectively, *PANTOUT(B)*) be true if and only if T is partially anticipated at the beginning (respectively, the end) of B. Then this set of values is a solution to the equation in Figure 4.17.

PROOF We must verify that the values satisfy the equations. Assume they do not. Then there is a block B where the equations are not satisfied. Now look at the possibilities. The equation for *PANTOUT(B)* is satisfied by the nature of the definition. Similarly, the definition implies that the equation for *PANTIN(B)* is also true. Thus a contradiction.

OBSERVATION 5: Let *PANTIN(B)* and *PANTOUT(B)* be the smallest solution to the equation in Figure 4.17, then T is partially anticipated at the beginning of B if and only if *PANTIN(B)* is true.

PROOF This argument mimics the argument for anticipation in the Appendix. The roles of true and false are switched and the smallest solution is used rather than the largest.

4.12 Global Available Temporary Information

The anticipation information describes what happens on paths before evaluations of T in the flow graph. The compiler also needs information about what happens on paths after evaluations of T. This information uses the word "available" rather than "anticipate" and stores information about whether there is an evaluation of T on each path leading to a point. There is also the corresponding partial information.

DEFINITION **Available:** A temporary T is available at a point p in the flow graph if and only if given any path from *Entry* to p there is an evaluation of T on the path that is not followed by any instruction that kills T.

DEFINITION **Partially Available:** A temporary T is partially available at a point p in the flow graph if and only if there is some path from *Entry* to p with an evaluation of T on that path that is not followed by any instruction that kills T.

To illustrate these ideas, consider the flow graph of the running example as shown in Figure 4.18. The temporary T is available at the beginning of block B2 since every path (including the ones that go through B2 and come back again) from B0 to B2 contains an evaluation of T. The temporary S is partially available at the beginning of B2 since the path B0, B1, B2, B3, B2 contains an evaluation of S that is not followed by an instruction that kills it. It is interesting that this evaluation is in B2, and we will later see that this is a potential condition for moving code out of the loop.

Figure 4.18 Flow Graph of Running Example

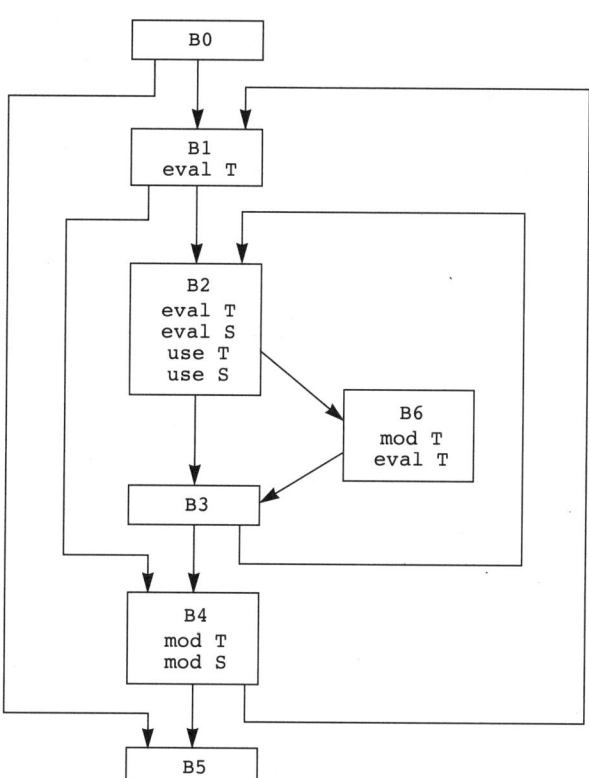

The reasoning that led to the equations for anticipatability can be used to create the equations for availability. The only differences are that predecessors are used rather than successors, and the reasoning involves paths from *Entry* rather than paths to *Exit*. This gives us the equations in Figure 4.19,

Figure 4.19 Equations for Availability

$$AVIN_B = \begin{cases} \emptyset & \text{if } B = Entry \\ \bigcap_{p \in PRED(B)} AVOUT_p & \text{otherwise} \end{cases}$$

$$AVOUT_B = AVLOC_B \cup (AVIN_B - KILL_B)$$

Figure 4.20 Equations for Partial Availability

$$PAVIN_B = \begin{cases} \emptyset & \text{if } B = Entry \\ \bigcup_{P \in PRED(B)} PAVOUT_P & \text{otherwise} \end{cases}$$

$$PAVOUT_B = AVLOC_B \cup (PAVIN_B - KILL_B)$$

whereas before if one has the largest solution, $AVIN(B)$ (respectively, $AVOUT(B)$) is true if and only if T is available at the beginning (respectively, end) of block B.

The equations for partial availability are derived by the same techniques as used for partial anticipatability, giving the equations in Figure 4.20. The smallest solution to the equation in Figure 4.20, $PAVIN(B)$ (respectively, $PAVOUT(B)$) is true if and only if T is partially available at the beginning (respectively, end) of B.

4.12.1 Solving for Partial Anticipatability and Partial Availability

Before computing anticipatability and availability, the compiler performs a preliminary optimization pass that identifies most redundant temporary evaluations: those where one evaluation of T dominates another evaluation of T. Thus, information is needed for a small subset of the total number of temporaries.

Other programmers advocate the use of bit vector techniques to evaluate this information, simultaneously computing the information for all temporaries (Aho 1977). For large flow graphs these bit vectors may be large. On a modern processor, the size of the bit vectors may continuously flush the cache, thus slowing the compiler.

This compiler uses an alternative approach, computing the information for each temporary separately. The information necessary may be sparse, so computing the information separately may save space and avoid flushing the cache during compiler execution. By computing the information on a temporary-by-temporary basis, the compiler can determine early in the algorithm that some optimization will not be effective and avoid computing unneeded information.

So how does the compiler compute partial anticipatability for evaluations of T? Consider the definition. T is partially anticipated at a point if there is a path from that point to an evaluation of T containing no instructions that kill *T*. Looking at this path backward, the compiler can perform a backward graph walk (using predecessors) starting at the evaluations of *T* and stopping when either an instruction that kills *T* occurs, the *Entry* block occurs, or the walk reaches a point that it has already visited. The first two conditions come straight from the definition, and the last one is an optimization: There is no reason to walk a point a second time.

This graph walk can be stated as a work-list algorithm, as given in Figure 4.21. It implements the algorithm described in the previous paragraph. It computes the set *PANTIN* of blocks where *T* is partially anticipated at the beginning of the block. The first loop includes all of the blocks where *T* is locally anticipated. The work list keeps a record of all blocks whose predecessors have not been investigated. The work-list loop takes an arbitrary block *B* and considers each of its predecessors *P*. If *P* is not transparent, then *T* will not be partially anticipated at the beginning of the block unless it is locally anticipated already.

Note that $WORKLIST \subset PANTIN$ because elements are added at the same time and elements are never removed from *PANTIN*. Thus each block can only be added to *WORKLIST* once; hence, the algorithm has time complexity proportional to the number of edges.

For efficient compilation, the structure of each of the sets is important. Consider *WORKLIST* first. The operations performed on *WORKLIST* are insertion, deletion, membership, initialization to the empty set, and testing for the empty set. The maximum number of elements in this set is the

Figure 4.21 Computing Partial Anticipatability

```
WORKLIST = ∅;              //Set of unprocessed blocks
PANTIN = ∅;                //Set of partially anticipated blocks
PANTOUT = ∅;
for each block B ∈ ANTLOC(T) do
    add B to WORKLIST;     //Include all locally anticipated blocks
    add B to PANTIN;
endfor;
while WORKLIST ≠ ∅  do
    take B from WORKLIST;
    for each P ∈ PRED(B) do
        add P to PANTOUT;
        if T ∉ KILL(P) and P ∉ PANTIN then
            add P to PANTIN;   //Include predecessors that are
            add P to WORKLIST;//transparent and not already visited
        endif
    endfor;
endwhile;
```

number of blocks and there is only one instance of the set. Assign distinct integer values to each of the blocks and use the Briggs set algorithm to implement *WORKLIST*.

The operations on *PANTIN* are a subset of the operations on *WORKLIST*. Outside the algorithm the compiler must also scan *PANTIN*, looking at each element in the set. This can be implemented by the Briggs set algorithm also.

KILL is a different matter. This algorithm checks for membership in a collection of sets (indexed by the blocks) of temporaries that may not be sparse. Hence *KILL* should be implemented as an array of bit vectors. The array is indexed by block number, and the bit in the bit vector is indexed by an integer assigned to each temporary T.

The algorithm also computes the blocks *PANTOUT* where T is partially anticipated at the end of the block. This computation is not needed to make the algorithm work, so the two statements involving *PANTOUT* can be eliminated if *PANTOUT* is not needed. *PANTOUT* should also be implemented using the Briggs set algorithm because later use of the data will require a scan of all of the elements.

The computation for partial availability is the same as partial anticipatability except applied to successors rather than predecessors. Note that *PAVOUT* is the quantity computed rather than *PANTIN*, so the algorithm is looking at the ends of blocks rather than the beginning of blocks. All of the same implementations remain for each of the sets. The algorithm is given in Figure 4.22.

Figure 4.22 Computing Partial Availability

```
WORKLIST = ∅;                    //Set of unprocessed blocks
PAVOUT = ∅;                      //Set of partially available blocks
PAVIN = ∅;
for each block B ∈ AVLOC(T) do
    add B to WORKLIST;           //Include all locally available blocks
    add B to PAVOUT;
endfor;
while WORKLIST ≠ ∅  do
   take B from WORKLIST;
   for each S ∈ SUCC(B) do
      add S to PAVIN;
      if T ∉ KILL(S) and S ∉ PAVOUT then
         add S to PAVOUT;        //Include predecessors that are
         add S to WORKLIST;      //transparent and not already visited
      endif
   endfor;
endwhile;
```

Flow Graph

EXAMPLE Consider the temporary S in Figure 4.18. The only instruction that kills S is in B4, so the backward walk implemented by the algorithm indicates that S is partially anticipated at the beginning of blocks B2, B1, B0, B3, and B6. For partial availability one uses a forward walk, so S is partially available at the end of blocks B2, B3, and B6.

4.12.2 Computing Availability and Anticipatability

The partial information can now be used to compute anticipatibility and availability. Just by looking at the definitions, we see that $ANTIN \subset PANTIN$, where $ANTIN$ is the set of blocks in which T is anticipated. Similarly, $AVOUT \subset PAVOUT$.

What is the difference between the blocks that are in $ANTIN$ and the blocks in $PANTIN$? In $PANTIN$ there is a path from the beginning of the block to an evaluation of T, but in $ANTIN$ there must be an evaluation of T on each path from the beginning of the block.

The way to compute $ANTIN$ is thus to start with $PANTIN$ and throw out all blocks that start a path that does not lead to an evaluation of T. In other words, the rejected block leads either to an instruction that kills T or to *Exit*. The algorithm in Figure 4.23 starts with the partially anticipated set and prunes out the blocks that do not satisfy the definition of anticipation. This job requires a work list because the elimination of one block from the set may force multiple other blocks out of the set.

Figure 4.23 Pruning to Correct the Available Set

```
WORKLIST = ∅;
ANTIN = PANTIN;
for each B ∈ ANTIN - ANTLOC do
   if there is S ∈ SUCC(B) such that S ∉ ANTIN then
      remove B from ANTIN;
      add B to WORKLIST;
   endif;
endfor;
while WORKLIST ≠ ∅ do
   take B from WORKLIST;
   for each P ∈ PRED(B) do
      if P ∈ ANTIN - ANTLOC then
         remove P from ANTIN;
         add P to WORKLIST;
      endif;
   endfor;
endwhile;
```

To see that the algorithm is correct, consider the following argument. Consider a block B that is in *PANTIN* but not in *ANTIN*. There is thus some path from the beginning of B to *Exit* that does not contain an evaluation of T before any instructions that kills T. Walk down that path. Since $B \in$ *PANTIN* initially, you come to one of the following situations:

- One arrives at a block that is not in *PANTIN*. The previous block is in *PANTIN*, so the first loop in Figure 4.23 will identify that the preceding block is not in *ANTIN* and remove it from the set, placing it in the work list to remove its predecessors on the path.

- One arrives at a block containing a killing instruction. Since we assumed that this path did not contain a preceding evaluation of T, T is not locally anticipated in the block and therefore the block is not in *PANTIN*, reducing to the previous example.

- One arrives at *Exit*. Since *Exit* $\notin$ *PANTIN*, this also reduces to the first case.

Thus the first loop initializes work by identifying the blocks at the boundaries of paths that violate the definition. Now the work-list algorithm walks backward along the path, successively removing each block until the block B is removed as required by the definition.

EXAMPLE In the example in Figure 4.18, consider the temporary S. We have already computed the points where it is partially anticipated. We must go through that list and throw out any block whose successors are not all in the list. Thus B3 is thrown out because of B4, B6 is thrown out because of B3, B1 is thrown out because of B4, and B0 is thrown out because of B5. Hence S is only anticipated at the beginning of B2.

Now consider the availability of S. It is partially available at the end of blocks B2, B3, and B6. In this case there is nothing to throw out. B2 remains because S is locally available in B2. The only predecessor of B6 is B2. The predecessors of B3 are B2 and B6, where neither of those blocks kills or generates S. Hence the partially available expressions are the available ones in this case.

4.13 Lifetime Analysis

The anticipated and available data are information about the points where a temporary T is evaluated. There is no information about uses. Lifetime information concerns the relation of evaluation points and use points for a temporary T. T is *live* at all points on paths between an evaluation of a temporary and its use.

Flow Graph

> **DEFINITION** **Live:** A temporary T is live at a point p in the flow graph if there is a path from p to a use of T as an operand that does not contain an instruction evaluating T and a path from an evaluation of T to p which does not contain an evaluation of T.

Thus T is live on paths from evaluations of T to uses of T and nowhere else. For an instruction to qualify as an evaluation of T, it must guarantee that a new value for T is computed. If the instruction might modify T then it is not counted as an evaluation of T. This is not a problem for temporaries because temporaries are either modified or not, but we will apply the same ideas to memory references and sometimes the compiler knows one particular memory location that will be referenced and another collection of memory locations that might be referenced.

Computing the points where T is live uses much of the same technology used to compute anticipation and availability. The form of the equations is the same as the form for partial anticipation, except the local information is different.

Given a temporary T, *LiveIn(T)* is the set of blocks B that contain a use of the temporary T that is not preceded by an evaluation of T.

Given a block B, *LiveKill(B)* is the set of temporaries T for which there is an evaluation of T in the block B. Do not count instructions that might change T or change only a part of T.

Global is the set of temporaries that are live at the beginning of a block. This is the same as the union of all of the *LiveIn* sets.

This information can be computed by scanning each block backward. Whenever a use of a temporary is identified, mark the temporary as live. Whenever an evaluation of T is found, add T to the *LiveKill* set and mark the temporary as not live. As the local information is collected, the set *Global* is computed. It consists of all temporaries that are live at the beginning of some block. The local information is summarized in Figure 4.24.

The global information is computed in the same way as partial anticipation. Each temporary is handled separately; however, there is no need to compute anything unless $T \in Global$ because the temporary is only live within a block, not across block boundaries. The algorithm is given in Figure 4.25.

Figure 4.24 Setup to Compute Lifetimes

```
procedure SETUP_LIFETIME;
   declare
      Global: set of Temporary;
      Exposed: set of Temporary;
      LiveIn(Temporary): set of Block;
      LiveKill(Block): set of Temporary;
   enddeclare
   foreach T ∈ Temporaries do
      LiveIn(T) = ∅;
   endfor;
   Global = ∅;
   foreach B ∈ N do
      LiveKill(B) = ∅;
      Exposed = ∅;
      foreach I ∈ B in reverse order do
         LiveKill(B) = LiveKill(B) ∪ ExplicitTargets(I);
         Exposed = (Exposed-ExplicitTargets(I)) ∪ Operands(I);
      endfor;
      Globals = Globals ∪ Exposed;
      foreach T ∈ Exposed do
         add B to LiveIn(T);
      endfor;
   endfor;
endprocedure SETUP_LIFETIME;
```

Figure 4.25 Computing Global Live Information

```
procedure LIVE_WORKLIST(T)
   WORKLIST = ∅;                    //Set of unprocessed blocks
   Live = ∅;                        //Set of blocks where T is live
   for each block B ∈ LiveIn(T) do
      add B to WORKLIST;            //Include B if T locally live
      add B to Live;
   endfor;
   while WORKLIST ≠ ∅ do
      take B from WORKLIST;
      for each P ∈ PRED(B) do
         if T ∉ LiveKill(P) and P ∉ Live then
            add P to Live;          //Include predecessors that are
            add P to WORKLIST;      //transparent and not visited
         endif
      endfor;
   endwhile;
endprocedure LIVE_WORKLIST;
```

To compute the more general definition of lifetime where a temporary is live from an evaluation of T to a use of T, one needs to solve another condition, which is similar to partial anticipatability. One must compute the set of blocks where there is a path to the beginning of the block from an evaluation of T that does not include an instruction that kills T. We will be using this information during register allocation when the compiler is only dealing with single temporaries, so there is no need to consider which instructions kill a temporary. The only thing in that case that kills a temporary is another evaluation of the temporary. The problem thus reduces to a depth-first search starting from the evaluation of a temporary. Any block that is marked live by the work-list algorithm in Figure 4.25 and occurs on the depth-first search walk has the more general property of liveness that we need for register allocation. However, performing the depth-first search has the probability of visiting a large number of blocks. One gets the same result by performing the following processes:

1. Calculate the set of blocks where T is live at the beginning of the block using the work-list algorithm in Figure 4.25.

2. Perform a depth-first search starting at each evaluation of T, but only visit blocks where the work-list algorithm indicated that T might be live.

3. Remove all blocks computed by the work-list algorithm that are not visited during the depth-first search.

4. The result is the set of blocks where T is live at the beginning of the block.

Thus we have the general definition of live easily implemented from the more straightforward definition. Unfortunately, the work list naturally computes the set of blocks where T is live at the beginning of the block. The compiler always needs the set of blocks where T is live at the end of the block, or more correctly, it will need the set of temporaries live at the end of each block. This can be computed from the other information by the algorithm in Figure 4.26.

Note that T is in *LiveOut(B)* if and only if T is live on entry to one of the successors and one can get to B by a depth-first search from some evaluation. The last nested loops in the algorithm compute this fact. *LiveOut* is a sparse set, so it should be implemented as a linked list. The test for membership is easy because all entries for T are made before entries for any other temporary; thus, if T has already been added to *LiveOut* for a block, it is the element at the head of the list. Therefore one need only check the head of the list to see if T has already been added.

Figure 4.26 Total Lifetime Algorithm

```
procedure CALCULATE_LIVE;
   call SETUP_LIVE;
   foreach B ∈ N do
      LiveOut(B) = ∅;
   endfor;
   foreach T ∈ Global do
      call Live_Worklist(T);
      Visit = ∅;
      foreach evaluation of T do
         perform depth first search visiting only nodes in Live: record in Visit;
      endfor;
      Live = Live ∩ Visit;
      foreach B ∈ Live do
         foreach P ∈ Pred(B) do
            if P ∈ Visit then
               add T to LiveOut(P);
            endif;
         endfor;
      endfor;
   endfor;
endprocedure CALCULATE_LIVE;
```

4.14 References

Aho, A. V., and J. D. Ullman. 1977. *Principles of compiler design.* Reading, MA: Addison-Wesley.

Chow, F. 1983. A portable machine independent optimizer—Design and measurements. Ph.D. diss., Stanford University.

Drechsler, K.-H., and M. P. Stadel. 1988. A solution to a problem with Morel's and Renvoise's "Global optimization by suppression of partial redundancies." *ACM Transactions on Programming Languages and Systems* 10(4): 635-640.

Morel, E., and C. Renvoise. 1979. Global optimization by suppression of partial redundancies. *Communications of the ACM* 22(2): 96-103.

5 LOCAL OPTIMIZATION

The most effective transformations in an optimizing compiler are the simplest. Consider the expression $T * 0$. The translation techniques that walk the abstract syntax tree creating the flow graph would naturally compute T, load 0 into a temporary, and perform the multiplication. Algebraic identities can tell the compiler that this expression is 0, so load the constant into a temporary instead.

This chapter discusses these local transformations. The transformations are used in three places in the compiler: during the building of the flow graph, during dominator-based optimization, and later during peephole optimization. The optimizations include the following techniques:

- Apply algebraic transformations to decrease the number of instructions. As an example, the expression $N < 1$ discussed in Figure 5.1 can be replaced by the expression $N \leq 0$, which can be encoded in a single instruction without the need of loading the constant. A large collection of algebraic identities is listed at the end of this chapter.

- The compiler can trace the values stored in temporaries and record the temporaries that have already been evaluated. If the same temporary is evaluated again without an intervening instruction changing the operands, then the instruction may be eliminated. These two operations are combined in a technique called *value numbering*.

- Instructions that are not executed or that generate a temporary that is not used can be eliminated. This is a limited form of dead-code elimination. A more complete form of dead-code elimination occurs later.

These simplifications apply to our running example. Consider the code fragment from the initialization of the outer loop in Figure 2.1 (see Figure 5.2). The left column is the set of instructions generated by translating the

Figure 5.1 Value Numbering and Identities

```
iLDC    1           => T7         iLDC    1           => T7
i2i     T7          => T5         i2i     T7          => T5
iSLD    (T2)        => T8         iSLD    (T2)        => T8
iCMPGT  T5,T8       => T9         iBLE    T8,B5,B1
iBCOND  T9,B5,B1
```

abstract syntax tree into the flow graph; the right column is the resulting set of instructions after local optimization.

The compiler tracks the values in temporaries within the current block and applies algebraic identities. In this case the compiler knows that $T5$ has

Figure 5.2 Value-Numbering Example

```
iLDC    1           => T7         iLDC    1           => T7
iSUB    T5,T7       => T10        iSUB    T5,T7       => T10
iLDC    4           => T11        iLDC    4           => T11
iMUL    T11,T10     => T12        iMUL    T11,T10     => T12
iADD    T3,T12      => T13        iADD    T3,T12      => T13
iLDC    1           => T7
i2i     T7          => T14        i2i     T7          => T14
iSST    (T13),T14                 iSST    (T13),T14
iLDC    1           => T7
iSUB    T5,T7       => T10
iLDC    8           => T15        iLDC    8           => T15
iMUL    T15,T10     => T16        iMUL    T15,T10     => T16
iADD    T4,T16      => T17        iADD    T4,T16      => T17
iLDC    1           => T7
iLDC    1           => T7
iSUB    T7,T7       => T18
iLDC    1           => T7
iSUB    T5,T7       => T10
iSLD    (T2)        => T8         iSLD    (T2)        => T8
iMUL    T8,T10      => T19        iMUL    T8,T10      => T19
iADD    T19,T18     => T20
iLDC    8           => T15
iMUL    T15,T20     => T21        iMUL    T15,T19     => T32
iADD    T1,T21      => T22        iADD    T1,T32      => T33
dSLD    (T22)       => SF2        dSLD    (T33)       => SF2
dABS    SF2         => SF3        dABS    SF2         => SF3
d2d     SF3         => SF1        d2d     SF3         => SF1
dSST    (T17),SF1                 dSST    (T17),SF1
iLDC    2           => T23        iLDC    2           => T23
i2i     T23         => T6         i2i     T23         => T6
iSLD    (T2)        => T8         iSLD    (T2)        => T8
iCMPGT  T6,T8       => T24        iCMPGT  T23,T8      => T34
iBCOND  T24,B4,B2                 iBCOND  T34,B4,B2
```

the value 1. The next computation asks whether $T5 > T8$, which the compiler knows is $1 > T8$. The compiler knows that this is the same as $0 \geq T8$.

After building the program flow graph and performing the initial aliasing analysis, the compiler performs local optimizations and transformations to improve the structure of the program flow graph for the rest of the optimizer and decrease its size so that it takes less time and space. After cleaning up the program flow graph, this phase will perform global constant propagation and folding so that later phases have complete constant information.

Note that most of the algebraic simplifications are applied to integer arithmetic. It must also be applied to floating point arithmetic; however, the compiler must be careful on two points.

The arithmetic must be done at compile time exactly the same way it is done at runtime. Usually this is not a problem. It is a problem if the compiler is not running on the same machine as the machine which executes the program (a cross compiler). It is also a problem if the floating point rounding mode can change. If the rounding mode is not known, constant folding should be avoided.

Precise IEEE floating arithmetic can also be a problem. Full IEEE arithmetic includes the representation of infinities and NaN (Not a Number). The compiler must avoid the evaluation of expressions where one of the operands may be a NaN. It must even avoid replacing $0 * X$ by 0 if X might be a NaN.

5.1 Optimizations while Building the Flow Graph

Building the flow graph can be optimized to eliminate about half of the instructions generated. The idea is that the same computations frequently occur in the same block. This is not true of source code, but it is true of the addressing arithmetic generated by the compiler. These same instructions (and more) could be eliminated later. Eliminating them decreases the storage required for the flow graph and decreases the processing time required in the rest of the compiler. The following instructions can be eliminated from the generated block:

- If a second instance of an instruction is about to be inserted in a block, then it can be eliminated if the arguments of the previous instruction have not been modified.

- If an instruction has constant arguments, then the instruction can be replaced by a load constant instruction. The arithmetic must be done precisely as it would be done on the target machine. If there is any chance that an exception might be raised by the operation, the computation should be left as it is.

- The list of algebraic identities at the end of this chapter should be applied to the instructions as they are generated. The simpler equivalent instruction sequence should be generated when possible.

The effect of these transformations is shown in the code in Figure 5.3 from the running example. The left column is the set of instructions that would be generated by the techniques that have been described in the previous section. The right column contains the instructions that are generated after value numbering and simplification of algebraic identities. Some statistics indicate that these techniques will eliminate about half of the instructions.

Value numbering divides the instructions in a block into equivalence classes: two instructions are equivalent if the compiler can determine that they have the same value. Only one instruction in each equivalence class needs to be generated. The code that generates the flow graph operates as described in Chapter 4, except the procedures that insert instructions into the flow graph maintain data structures to eliminate instructions that are unneeded.

- If the instruction to be inserted is equivalent to an instruction already in the block, then the instruction is skipped and the target register from the equivalent instruction is returned as holding the value needed.
- If the operands of the instruction are constants and the operator has no side effects, then a load constant for the precomputed result is generated instead.

Figure 5.3 Optimizations without Side Effects

```
x = 0        => x           a ∪ true    => true
0 + x        => x           true ∪ a    => true
x - 0        => x           a ∩ false   => false
0 - x        => -x          false ∩ a   => false
x * 1        => x           a ∪ false   => a
1 * x        => x           false ∪ a   => a
x/1          => x           ¬true       => false
x**1         => x           ¬false      => true
a ∩ true     => a           a ∩ a       => a
true ∩ a     => a           a ∪ a       => a
```

Local Optimization

- If the instruction and its operands match a tree corresponding to an algebraic identity, then the simplified form of the tree is generated instead. Changing the instructions may cause some existing instructions to be unused. They will be eliminated later with dead-code elimination.

How does the compiler know when two instructions are equivalent? There are limits to the analysis that the compiler can do. For the purposes of code generation the analysis is simple:

- Two instructions without side effects are equivalent if they involve the same operator and have equivalent inputs.
- Two constants are equivalent if they are identical constants.
- Two load instructions are equivalent if they load equivalent addresses and no store operation has occurred between them that might modify that storage location.
- When in doubt, declare that two instructions are not equivalent. For example, a procedure call may change a number of variables that are visible to it or procedures that it might call. All such variables must be assumed to change at the procedure call.

To implement the value-numbering scheme, the compiler needs to construct tables that will compute this information quickly. The data structures will be described in abstract terms; however, the implementation is simple. The temporaries are represented as small integers, representing indices into tables. Each abstract data structure can thus be represented as an array or a chain-linked hash table. The following data structures are needed:

constant_temporary(temporary) is a data structure that, given a temporary, returns one of the three following classes of values. It returns *top* or $\top$ if the temporary does not contain a value already computed in this block. It can return the value *bottom*, or $\bot$, which indicates that the temporary has been computed in this block but does not have a constant value. Or it can return the constant value that was assigned to the temporary. This is the same information that we will use later when doing global constant propagation. It is used here to combine the answers to these questions: Does the temporary have a constant value? and What is the constant value associated with the temporary? This can be implemented as an array in which each entry is a class or record indicating one of the two alternative values or the value of the constant. The table value is filled in each time a temporary is the target of an instruction.

value_number(temporary) is a data structure that gives the value number associated with the particular temporary. It can be implemented as an array of integers. An entry is filled in each time the temporary is the target of an instruction or an instruction occurs with side effects that invalidate a previous value number.

defining instruction(temporary) is a data structure that returns the instruction that most recently defined the temporary in this block. It is updated as each instruction is generated. If another instruction forces the value number of a temporary to change (due to making the value unknown) or if there is no definition of the temporary in the block, then the entry is *NULL*.

These data structures are used during the generation of the intermediate representation. As an example, consider the generation of a binary operation using the instruction-generation procedure, *binary_instruct*, discussed in Chapter 4. Its implementation will look like the following pseudo-code:

```
temporary binary_struct (opcode, first_operand, second_operand)
    if (constant_temporary(first_operand) is constant)
        ∧(constant_temporary(second_operand) is constant) then
        Get temporary T for loading folded constant from formal
            temporary table;
        Generate iLDC of constant into T
        return T;
    endif;
    Get temporary T for (opcode, first_operand, second_operand) from
            formal temporary table;
    if value_number(T) == NULL then
        Generate the instruction I;
        value_number(T) = new value number V;
        defining_instruction(I) = V;
        return T;
    endif
end procedure;
```

Generating a register copy operation or store operation must destroy the value numbers for any temporaries that use that temporary as an operand. This information is available in the formal temporary table.

5.1.1 List of Local Optimizations

Before all of the other optimizations, some simplifications can be made to the operations in the program flow graph. The compiler front end and the Build phase take a simplistic view of the generation of operations. The program flow graph generated has not taken into account the simplifications that can be made to the program structure. This is as it should be: The simplifications should occur all in one place to avoid repetitive code with compilers for multiple languages. Figure 5.3 is a preliminary list of some of the local optimizations. Others should be added as the quality of the code generated by the compiler is studied and special cases are identified.

Other local optimizations can change the side effects of the program. The language reference manual specifies which side effects must be preserved. For example, in C, integer overflow may be ignored. Thus the compiler may eliminate a computation that has no effect on the values computed by the program even if it eliminates an integer overflow. The set of local optimizations in Figure 5.4 and the similar set for floating point operations in Figure 5.6 can cause side effects, so they must be checked to see that the language description is preserved.

There is also a collection of optimizations based on unary operations (see Figure 5.5). With some of these optimizations the order of use of the operands may change. As long as the actual order of evaluation of the operands in the program flow graph does not change, this is not a problem. This possibility is one of the reasons for choosing the flow graph/operation structure for the internal structure of the program.

The optimization of relational operators in Figures 5.4, 5.5, 5.6 and 5.7 are important in simplifying the flow graph.

Figure 5.4 Optimizations with Side Effects

```
x - x  => 0                         a == a  => true
0 * x  => 0                         a ≤ a   => true
x * 0  => 0                         a ≥ a   => true
0/x    => 0 if x ≠ 0                a ≠ a   => false
x/x    => 1 if x ≠ 0                a < a   => false
x**0   => 1 if x ≠ 0                a > a   => false
1**x   => 1
```

Figure 5.5 Unary Operator Optimizations

```
a + (-a)      => 0              (-a) + b   => b - a
-(-a)         => a              -a < -b    => a > b
(-a) + (-b)   => -(a+b)         -a ≤ -b    => a ≥ b
(-a) - (-b)   => b - a          -a > -b    => a < b
(-a) * (-b)   => a * b          -a ≥ -b    => a ≤ b
(-a)/(-b)     => a/b            -a = -b    => a = b
a + (-b)      => a - b          -a ≠ -b    => a ≠ b
a - (-b)      => a + b          ¬(a=b)     => a ≠ b
(-a) - b      => -(a+b)         ¬(a≠b)     => a = b
(-a) * b      => -(a*b)         ¬(a<b)     => a ≥ b
a * (-b)      => -(a*b)         ¬(a≤b)     => a > b
(-a)/b        => (a/b)          ¬(a>b)     => a ≤ b
a/(-b)        => -(a/b)         ¬(a≥b)     => a < b
a**(-b)       => 1/(a**b)       ¬(¬a)      => a
-(a-b)        => b-a
```

Figure 5.6 Algebraic Identity Optimizations

```
a - a  => 0                 1↑a    => 1
0 * a  => 0                 a = a  => true
a * 0  => 0                 a ≤ a  => true
0/a    => 0 if a ≠ 0        a ≥ a  => true
a/a    => 1 if a ≠ 0        a < a  => false
a↑0    => if a ≠ 0          a > a  => false
```

Figure 5.7 Relational Optimizations (ρ is relational operator)

```
(a-b) ρ 0   => a ρ b              (1/a) ρ (1/b) => b ρ a if b > 0 ∧ a > 0
0 ρ (a-b)   => b ρ a              (a+c) ρ (b+c) => a ρ b
(a/b) ρ 1   => a ρ b if b > 0     (a-c) ρ (b-c) => a ρ c
1 ρ (a/b)   => b ρ a if b > 0     (a*c) ρ (b*c) => a ρ b if c > 0
```

5.2 How to Encode the Pattern Matching

With this number of patterns, how does the compiler writer write the code? There are two ways to do it: use a tree pattern-matching system or write the pattern matches by hand. I am going to take a controversial approach and

Local Optimization

use the handwritten pattern-matching system. Although the set of patterns is large, each of the patterns is simple, involving a small number of operators.

The compiler organizes the code using the operator that is at the root of the tree representing the pattern.

5.3 Why Bother with All of These Identities?

An immediate reaction to this large list of identities is to ask: "Why bother? If the programmer has written an inefficient expression, give him inefficient results." This section attempts to answer this by noting that the compiler is not really concerned with what the programmer wrote. Any improvement in the source code is a fortunate side effect of improving other code. The compiler itself generates expressions, as the following set of instances shows.

- During code lowering, where high-level operations are replaced by lower-level instructions, the compiler will generate expressions. The most common example is the lowering of subscript operations from a subscripted load/store operation to the computation of the address followed by an indirect load/store. The compiler generated the expressions, so the compiler must simplify them: The programmer cannot do it.

- When the compiler in-line expands one subroutine at the point of a subroutine call in another subroutine, the compiler must generate expressions to substitute for the formal parameters at each use. Frequently this is done by creating temporaries at the beginning of the in-line code to hold the values of the parameters and then expanding the body into the flow graph. Many actual parameters are constants or simple expressions; when they are used in the subroutine, many of the simplifications listed here may be applicable.

It can be argued that both of these examples beg the point. If the compiler is generating these expressions, then why not generate the simple expressions rather than the complex ones? The reason is simplicity. If the compiler must include special case code at each point that instructions are generated, the compiler will be large. Furthermore, special cases will be added in one point in the compiler and not at others, so the compiler will be unpredictable. It is better to have a small number of general subroutines that will simplify all generated instructions in the same manner.

5.4 References

Bagwell, J. T. Jr. 1970. *Local Optimization, SIGPLAN Notices,* Association for Computing Machinery 5(7): 52-66.

Frailey, D. J. 1970. *Expression Optimization Using Unary Complement Operators, SIGPLAN Notices,* Association for Computing Machinery 5(7): 67-85.

6 ALIAS ANALYSIS

What does it mean for one instruction to affect another? Remember how the proofs of the theorems about available or anticipated expressions developed. During the proofs a walk is performed backward (or forward) from a point in the flow graph to a point where the desired computation occurs. There must be no instructions on that path that change the computation of the desired expression. In other words, one instruction affects another if interchanging the order of the instructions would change the values in the target temporaries (or memory) after the instruction pair.

This section describes the computation of two attributes for each temporary: *modifies*(T), which is the set of temporaries that are affected by the modification of T, and *store_modifies*(T), which is the set of temporaries whose store operations are affected by a modification of T.

Remember, temporaries are divided into two classes: expression and variable temporaries. Each expression temporary occurs as the target of an instruction that is a pure function of its operands. There may be multiple points where the expression temporary is evaluated. In each case the same instruction occurs, which means the same operator and the same operand temporaries or memory location. Each expression temporary represents an expression tree in which the node representing the temporary is labeled with the operator and the children are the operands. The root and internal nodes of this tree are all expression temporaries. The leaf nodes represent LOAD instructions from memory or variable temporaries. An expression temporary is not considered modified by the reevaluation of one of its operands that is an expression temporary. It is modified if one of the variable temporaries at the leaves of the tree is assigned a new value with a copy operation or if the memory location corresponding to one of the load operations is modified.

Similarly, a store operation can be modified by another store operation. If both store operations may reference the same memory location, then they cannot be reordered.

DEFINITION **Modifies:** A temporary T modifies temporary U if interchanging the order of the instructions that compute the two temporaries will result in different values stored in U.

Consider the fragment of source code in Figure 6.1. Unless there is some unstated relation between A and B, such as the Fortran EQUIVALENCE statement or C language rules for formal parameters, the store into $B(I)$ does not affect the load of $A(I)$ or $A(N)$. Similarly, the store into $A(I)$ does not affect the load of $B(I+1)$. Since the compiler can prove that $B(I)$ and $B(I+1)$ reference different memory locations at each point in the program, the store into $B(I)$ does not modify the value of the load operation $B(I+1)$.

The variable I will be held in a temporary in the flow graph. The increment of I changes the address referenced by each of these STORE and LOAD instructions, so the store into I modifies each of these instructions.

This compiler implements dependence analysis, therefore it can notice that $A(N)$ in Figure 6.1 is not modified by the store into $A(I)$ since the value of I is always less than N in the loop. However, that is not done in this section. Using the techniques in this section, the compiler will be unable to differentiate $A(I)$ from $A(N)$. Compilers without dependence analysis cannot notice this. However, the compiler will identify the following situations:

- When the compiler knows that two addresses are distinct, then no *modifies* relationship will exist between a store and a load. For example, $B(I)$ and $B(I+1)$ are not related by the *modifies* relation. When the compiler

Figure 6.1 Example for Describing Aliasing

```
I = 0;
while I < N do
   B(I) = B(I+1) + 1;
   A(I) = A(I)/A(N);
   I = I + 1;
endwhile;
```

is not sure, it must assume that there is a *modifies* relationship, so $A(I)$ and $A(J)$ must be assumed to be related unless the compiler knows something about the ranges of values that I and J can take.

- The compiler knows that two fields of a nonoverlaid structure cannot be related by the *modifies* relation because they are different offsets from the same address.

- The compiler knows that the *modifies* relation is not transitive. A store into $A(I)$ indicates that the whole array A is modified. The modification of A indicates that $A(I+1)$ is potentially modified. However, the transitive relation "modification of $A(I)$ indicates that $A(I+1)$ is modified" is false.

- Source language restrictions must be taken into account. In C, pointers are typed. Except for pointers to characters (which can point to anything for historical reasons), a storage modification using a pointer can only modify locations of the same type and data structures containing locations of the same type.

The modification information can be expressed as a conjunction (logical AND) of several different factors:

- Consider two different memory references X and Y. If the address of X is never taken in the source procedure and X and Y are not related by some overlaying characteristic of the source language, then a store to X cannot modify the location Y. This is the only modification information used during the creation of the flow graph. It allows the identification of local variables that can be stored in temporaries and allows some efficiency gain by the use of value numbering within a block during the creation of the flow graph.

- There are language-specific rules that also limit the locations that a store to X can affect. In Fortran, the compiler is free to assume that a store to a global variable does not modify a dummy argument (formal parameter). Furthermore, the compiler can assume that a store to a dummy argument does not affect another dummy argument or a global variable. In ANSI C, the compiler can assume that a store through a pointer of one type does not affect a load or store through a pointer of another type unless one of the types is a pointer to a character. The compiler is free to use these rules because the language definition indicates that violation of the rules is a language error, in which case the compiler is free to do whatever it wishes.

- A store to X cannot affect a load or store to Y if X and Y are different offsets from the beginning of the same area of storage. Of course, the difference in offsets must be large enough so that no bit affected by X is in the storage area associated with Y.

These three conditions represent three very different conditions on the store operation. If one of the conditions is not satisfied, then a store to X does not affect the load or store of Y. Thus the modification relation is the conjunction (logical AND or set intersection) of different conditions.

This property can be used to refine the modification information as the program progresses through the compiler. In other words, computing the *modifies* attributes is a process of successive refinement. Early in the compilation process, a less refined version of the modification information is used; in fact, one based on the previous three conditions. Later, more refined information is used that involves analysis of the flow graph. Finally, dependence analysis is used to give the most refined information. This dependence information is used only in some of the phases of the compiler since the more accurate information is not needed in many of the phases.

6.1 Level of Alias Analysis

The rest of this chapter will describe the compiler components that compute this *modifies* relationship. The analysis can be divided into levels. The first and usually only level of analysis is the flow-insensitive analysis. Then some level of flow-sensitive analysis can be included. For this compiler, this step involves dependence analysis. Finally, interprocedural alias information must be taken into account.

Given a STORE instruction I, flow-insensitive alias analysis computes the set of LOAD instructions that might reference the value stored by I and the set of STORE instructions that might replace the value stored by I without considering paths of execution. If I occurs someplace in the procedure, and at another point there is a LOAD instruction referencing the same memory location, then the *modifies* relationship is assumed to hold even though there may be no path from one of the instructions to the other.

Thus flow-insensitive analysis is too conservative. It will deduce that a modification is possible when none is possible. This is the minimal alias analysis. Other algorithms will be used to refine and eliminate parts of the relation determined by the flow-insensitive algorithms.

The second level of alias analysis is dependence analysis. Again there are several levels of dependence. The simplest involves determining whether there is a path from the STORE to the LOADs and STOREs that have a *modifies* relationship with the STORE. The relationship can be ignored if no path exists. For arrays, further analysis can be done to determine the conditions under which the *modifies* relation exists.

Interprocedural analysis, the third level of alias analysis, answers two issues. In the absence of other information, the compiler must assume the most conservative information about formal parameters. This is tempered by the semantics of the source language. For example, Fortran specifies that a variable that is modified within a procedure can only be named in one fashion. This means that the compiler can assume that each store operation involving a formal parameter does not have the *modifies* relationship with any other formal parameter or global variable named in the procedure.

Second, interprocedural analysis records the actions of procedure calls. In the absence of interprocedural analysis, the compiler must assume that every datum addressable by the called procedure has a STORE executed and a LOAD executed. Hence the procedure call is modeled as a collection of simultaneous STORE and LOAD instructions.

With interprocedural analysis, the compiler estimates which data are modified and referenced by each procedure call. With this information, the compiler can model a procedure call by a smaller set of store and load operations. The store operations represent the data that might be modified by the procedure call, and the load operations represent the data that might be referenced by the procedure call.

6.2 Representing the *modifies* Relation

The *modifies* relation is represented in two different ways, depending on whether the flow graph is in normal form or static single assignment form (to be discussed shortly). In either form the compiler must provide enough information so that the algorithms analyzing the flow graph can determine if there is a possibility of a store operation changing a memory location referenced by another load or store operation.

6.2.1 Representing *modifies* in Normal Flow Graph Form

When the flow graph is in normal form, there is a one-to-one correspondence between temporaries and formal expressions. The compiler has built

Figure 6.2 Nodes in Formal Temporary Table

```
formal_node =
   pointer to structure
      op: operator;
      reg: symbolic_register;
      operands: array of formal_node;
   endstructure
```

a data structure, called the *formal temporary table,* to hold this correspondence. This table is represented as a graph in which each node consists of the data structure in Figure 6.2.

The formal temporary table is an acyclic graph, with the load operations being the leaves of the graph and the store or copy operations being the roots. Rather than making additions to the flow graph, the modification information is stored as the *modifies* information that we described earlier. The algorithms operating on the normal form of the flow graph will use this *modifies* information directly to restrict optimizations. This was done earlier when the compiler computed local information for each block in the flow graph.

The *modifies* relation is recorded in terms of the formal temporary table. Each store and copy operation will have an added attribute (called *modifies*) that records the set of load and store operations in the formal computation that have a *modifies* relationship with this operation. The set of instructions that this operation modifies is the set of load operations in its *modifies* set together with all instructions that use the value generated by that load operation either directly or indirectly. Actually the temporary that is the result of the load is used to represent the information. Remember that there is a one-to-one correspondence between the formal load operations and temporaries.

6.2.2 Representing *modifies* in Static Single Assignment Form

Before describing the changes to the flow graph to represent *modifies* information for the static single assignment form of the flow graph, we need to understand something about this form. The basic idea of the static single assignment form of the flow graph is that there is a single instruction that has a particular temporary as its output. The same temporary can be the output of only one single instance of an instruction. This differs from the normal form, where a temporary can be the output of multiple instructions. To compensate for the limitations of static single assignment form, a new operator called the ϕ-node has been added to the instruction set. This operator takes operands from differing predecessors and chooses one of them to be the value copied to the output temporary for the ϕ-node.

With the static single assignment form, all information about changing values is directly encoded in the single evaluation of the temporary and the ϕ-nodes rather than implicitly by using the *modifies* relationship on the side. To do this the compiler introduces the idea of tags.

A *tag* is a memory-based equivalent of the temporaries. Each tag represents an area of memory, and there is a tag for each area of memory that is referenced by instructions in the flow graph. Thus there is a tag for $A(I)$ and another tag for the whole array A. There are tags for each element of each structure referenced and a tag for the whole structure. Furthermore, there is a tag for all the stack-based data and multiple tags for references into the heap.

As you can see, the tags are related. Some tags represent areas of memory contained within other tags. The important thing is that there is a tag for each memory location referenced. There is a tag associated with each load operation. Copy operations do not need tags because the direct relationship between the instruction that evaluates a temporary and the instruction that uses the temporary is recorded in the flow graph when it is in static single assignment form.

Store operations are more complex. There is a primary tag associated with the address that is being modified by the instruction. However, other memory locations (that is, tags) may be modified. To represent the modification of these locations in memory, the STORE instruction must consider each tag that might be modified by the STORE instruction to be a target of the store operation. These indirect targets might be modified, but are not guaranteed to be modified; thus their value must be handled as if they were unknown.

Because of properties of the static single assignment form to be discussed later, the compiler actually handles each of the tags that might be modified as both a target and an operand. Thus each store operation has added a list of pairs of tags. The first element of the pair is the tag considered as an operand; the second element of the pair is the target. When the graph is constructed, both elements of the pair are the same. During static single assignment form construction, the tags are modified so that conditions of a single assignment to the tag are maintained.

6.3 Building the Tag Table

Now that the compiler has the concept of tags, the compiler uses it to compute the *modifies* information in general. The compiler builds a tag for each symbolic memory reference. Hence there is a tag for $A(I)$ and another one for $A(J)$, as well as a tag for the whole array A. These tags will be handled much like registers, except they do not occur as operands of instructions. Instead they occur as attributes of LOAD, STORE, and procedure calling instructions. For the LOAD instruction, the tag indicates the data being loaded. For the STORE and procedure call instructions, it indicates which data may be modified by the instruction.

Each tag structure contains a number of fields representing its relationship to other tag structures:

Temporary: The flow graph always uses the same temporary for loading and storing into the symbolically identical memory location. This temporary is stored in the tag. Although not absolutely necessary, it provides easy access to the temporary and makes table lookup on the tag table easier. At first glance, the reader may consider that there is a one-to-one relationship between tags and temporaries so one or the other of them might be eliminated. However, there are tags that are not related to temporaries: tags for arrays or whole structures. In the case of tags for whole arrays or whole structures the temporary entry is NULL.

Unique: This is a Boolean field indicating that the tag represents a unique area of memory. This attribute is true if the address of the data can be determined at compile or link time or occurs at a fixed offset from the beginning of the stack. It is false for tags representing data in the heap or tags representing array elements whose address is determined at run time.

Kind: The kind of the tag describes the specialized fields that are associated with the tag. The following kinds of tags exist. The list may be expanded if the language being compiled expands.

- Stack: Represents the collection of all data stored in the runtime stack.
- Heap: There is a tag for each type of data stored in the heap. The word "type" refers to the source language type. This allows the compiler to distinguish elements of different types when dealing with pointer dereferencing.
- COMMON block

- Array
- Structure or union
- Atomic: Represents scalars and pointers in memory

Parent: This field is a pointer to the tag representing the parent tag that includes this tag. If there is no parent then the entry is NULL. The following tags have parents:

- An array access has the tag for the whole array as the parent.
- A structure or union access has the tag for the whole structure as a parent.
- An entry in a COMMON block has the tag for the whole COMMON block as the parent.
- Any variable allocated to the runtime stack has the tag for the runtime stack as a parent.
- Any datum residing in the heap (and which is not a component of a larger object) has a parent that indicates a heap object of that type.

Children: This field lists all of the tags that have this tag as their parent. This is the reverse of the parent attribute and is used to scan all of the children whenever necessary.

Offset: If the tag represents memory that is a constant offset within the parent tag, then the offset is placed in this field. Fields of structures or unions are constant offsets from the start of the structure or union. Similarly, references to arrays using constant subscripts give a constant offset from the beginning of the array. If there is no constant offset, then a value $\perp$ is stored in the field to represent the fact that the offset is not known.

Size: The size of the datum represented by the tag is stored in this field. For example, on a 32-bit machine, an integer and float will have a size of 4 bytes, whereas a double-precision number has a size of 8 bytes. Size information is stored for structures and COMMON blocks also. For arrays whose size is not known at compile time, the value $\perp$ is inserted.

6.4 Two Kinds of Modifications: Direct and Indirect

Consider the process of finding all temporaries that are modified by a store operation. Recall that store operations are restricted to using the same temporary to store into a particular symbolic memory location. Thus search the tag table to find the tag that contains that temporary in the temporary attribute. That tag is modified by the store. This is a *direct* modification of a tag.

What other tags are modified by the store operation? Certainly the ancestors on the parent chain are modified. The question is, Are the children of the parents modified? Not necessarily. In fact, modifying all of the children of each parent would generate too many modifications. If one field of a structure is modified, then any field that does not overlap is not modified. These modifications are called *indirect*.

6.4.1 Indirect Modifications in a Structure or Union

The children of a structure or union tag are the tags for the children that have fixed offset attributes. Consider a structure S containing fields a, b, and c. A modification of field $S.a$ indicates that the tag for S is also modified. However, the tags for $S.b$ and $S.c$ are modified if and only if their storage, as indicated by their offset and size attributes, overlaps that of $S.a$.

Thus the algorithm for computing the *modifies* set for a field a of a structure S is as follows. S is the parent tag for $S.a$. Add the temporary for $S.a$ to the *modifies* set and mark S as modified also. If S has a temporary associated with it, then add it to the *modifies* set. At the same time scan the children of S and add each of them to the *modifies* set for $S.a$ if they overlap $S.a$ in memory.

If a structure is contained within another structure, then the same process can be applied at the next level up in the tag table. Recall that only $S.a$ was modified, so we need only look at fields that overlap $S.a$ even though S itself is marked as modified.

This algorithm handles structures, unions (with overlapping fields), and records that have variant fields.

6.4.2 Indirect Modifications in COMMON Blocks

The same algorithm as used for structures can be used for COMMON blocks. Fortran COMMON blocks have the characteristic that they can be viewed with different structures within different procedures. The COMMON block has the same characteristics as a structure, and the same algorithm can be used to determine which variables and arrays within a COMMON block are modified. Each has a fixed size and fixed offset so a scan of the children of the COMMON block tag will find the data that overlap the variable or array that is modified.

6.4.3 Modifications Involving the Fortran EQUIVALENCE Statement

The Fortran EQUIVALENCE statement is handled in COMMON blocks by the same scan for overlapping data. EQUIVALENCE statements indicate that multiple variables overlap (with possibly different types) and indicate the exact offset between each pair of variables. If one of the variables is in a COMMON block, then the other variable is also. It is therefore entered in the list of children with its offset attribute adjusted as indicated by the EQUIVALENCE statement. Now the modification sets will be computed correctly by scanning all of the children to see which overlap.

Assume that *A* and *B* are two variables that occur as a pair in a Fortran EQUIVALENCE statement. If one of them is in a COMMON block, we process them as described in the previous section. Otherwise consider them as two fields of a union, with different offsets within the union as described by the EQUIVALENCE statement. Build a tag for the union and make the paired elements children of the union tag.

If another variable is made equivalent to one of these variables by another EQUIVALENCE statement, add that element to the children of the union with the appropriate offset.

6.5 The Modification Information Used in Building the Flow Graph

The compiler has a chicken-and-egg problem. It cannot compute the *modifies* information precisely before computing the flow graph. While computing the flow graph, the compiler will perform value numbering on the blocks as they are created. This is needed to decrease the size of the flow graph and make it more manageable. To perform value numbering, it must know which memory locations are modified by each store operation so it can invalidate the value numbers for those locations.

The compiler requires the front end of the compiler to compute the set of all variables whose addresses might have been taken.[1] This means computing the variables where the address is copied into a variable for use as a procedure parameter or as the value of a pointer. This is not the same as the

---

1. The compiler cannot always determine all variables whose addresses might have been taken. If there is a procedure call that is separately compiled, then the address might be taken inside the procedure call and stored in a globally available variable. In this case the compiler must assume that all addresses that are visible to the procedure (or any procedure that it calls) might be taken.

situation that occurs during the construction of the flow graph where the address of each variable is loaded whenever it is used. The scalar variables whose addresses are not taken are implemented as temporaries in the flow graph: They can only be modified by explicit reference to them. The other structures and arrays whose addresses are not taken have no hidden side effects, so their information can be traced as the flow graph is constructed.

To handle other cases, the compiler uses a safe approximation to the eventual *modifies* information. As the flow graph is built, the compiler associates a tag with each symbolic memory address encountered. It performs value numbering on single blocks as was described during the construction of the flow graph.

What does it do when it encounters a store operation? If the store operation is to a tag whose address has not been taken, then all explicit tags that overlap this one are assumed to be modified and the value-number information for those tags is invalidated.

If the store operation is to a tag whose address is taken or is a pointer, then the value numbers for all tags that have the same type (assuming the language rules allow it) and involve storage locations whose address might have been taken are considered modified. Any tag representing data that overlap the data for one of the modified tags is also considered modified. That includes any tag containing data structures and fields that overlap a field that is modified.

Since modification information need only be computed for a single block, the compiler need not worry about references in the flow graph that have not been seen yet. The compiler is traversing the block in execution order; it need only invalidate references that have already been seen in this single block. Later references have not been seen so they do not need to be invalidated.

6.6 Tags for Heap Allocation Operations

Getting good modification information for data allocated in the heap is hard. The crudest approach to modification information is to assume that all data on the heap might overlap. In other words, the heap is handled as if it were C-union with each datum allocated on the heap considered a different alternative. This is the typical approach to implementing modification information for heap objects.

If the source language (such as C) has language rules about type compatibility, then the compiler can do better. If the ANSI language rules are in effect and the source language type is not a pointer to a character, then a

Alias Analysis **159**

pointer only points to objects of the same type. Hence only objects of the same type can overlap.

A simple device can sometimes do better. Create a separate tag for each allocation instruction (call on **malloc** in C or the **new** operation in C++). Consider all allocations that occur at that point in the flow graph as potentially overlapping and not overlapping others unless later analysis forces the overlap. Frequently a programmer will use a single allocation statement to allocate all data that match a particular abstract data type. If that is the case, then this device allows the compiler to differentiate this abstract data type from other data types, providing better allocation information.

6.7 More Complete Modification Information

After building the flow graph and before dominator-based optimization, the compiler builds more precise modification information. Before the flow graph was completed, the compiler assumed that all addresses of the same data type (and all structures containing them) overlapped unless the compiler knew the address in terms of constant offset and size from a fixed area of memory. Now the compiler will try to do better by computing the set of tags to which each memory location or temporary can point.

Definition **Points-To Set:** Consider any tag or temporary X. The set of tags to which X can point is the points-to set for X, or $PT(X)$. When X is not used as a pointer, $PT(X)$ is not needed.

$PT(X)$ is flow-insensitive information. There is no indication of the point in the flow graph where this information is being used; it is aggregated over the whole flow graph or the whole program. As we will see shortly, the information will be more precise if it is computed simultaneously over all of the flow graphs for all of the procedures in the program.

The basic algorithm is simple, so I will describe it first. Then I will adjust the algorithm to take care of the problems that we will see in the original description. Initialize all of the sets $PT(X)$ to the empty set, $\emptyset$. Now scan through the flow graph in either normal form or static single assignment form. Scan through the instructions in any order and consider the targets of each instruction.

The instructions can be divided into multiple classes. The largest class of instructions are those that can never be used in an address computation:

They add nothing to the set $PT(X)$ for each X that is a target. The second class includes the instructions that have some unspecified effects such as procedure calls. In this situation the compiler adjusts the $PT(X)$ of each tag or temporary that might be modified in the procedure call. When processing a single flow graph at a time, this means that the set of all memory locations that might be referenced within the procedure call must be added to each $PT(X)$ for each tag or temporary of the same value type. When dealing with all procedures simultaneously, the procedure call can be viewed as a set of copy operations from the actual parameters to the formal parameters. Since the algorithm is flow insensitive, the processing of these copies together with the later processing of the body of the procedure will correctly update all of the $PT(X)$ sets.

The last set of instructions are the instructions that might be involved in an address computation. This includes load and store operations, load constant operations, addition and subtraction of expressions, and the register-to-register copy operations. If the instruction is the load of an address constant, then find the corresponding tag and add it to the $PT(X)$ for each temporary or tag that is an output of the instruction. If it is a register-to-register copy operation, add $PT(Y)$ to $PT(X)$ for the operand of the instruction. If the instruction is a load instruction, add $PT(tag)$ to $PT(X)$, where *tag* is the tag of the memory location and X is the output variable. Addition and subtraction can be considered to not change the point for the purposes of computing $PT(X)$.

As usual, the most difficulty occurs with the store operations. Performing a store adds $PT(Y)$ to $PT(tag)$, where Y is the operand being stored and *tag* is the tag for the primary address in the store operation. There are two cases in considering the other tags associated with the store. If a *tag* represents a memory location that is aligned in the same manner as the primary tag and is the same size, then $PT(Y)$ can be added to *PT(tag)* also.

Where is the problem in this algorithm? What the compiler really wants is to merge the final $PT(Y)$ into $PT(X)$ if Y is an address operand for an instruction computing an address X. What the algorithm above does is merge the current value (at various points in the algorithm) into $PT(X)$. The way to handle this is to build a directed graph, which we will call the *address graph* (the name is not standard). The nodes of the address graph are the tags and temporaries in the set of flow graphs being processed, and there is an edge from Y to X if Y is an address expression (or tag containing a pointer) used to compute X. Instead of scanning the flow graph and updating the $PT(X)$ sets as we go, the compiler scans the instructions, inserting the constants and tags representing memory allocation instructions into the corresponding $PT(X)$ and building this graph as it goes.

Given this graph, the collection of $PT(X)$ sets can be computed in one of two ways (your choice). The first technique is a work-list algorithm. Place all of the nodes that contain non-empty $PT(X)$ sets on the work list. That condition means that the nodes contain constants of memory allocation tags. Then process this work list one node at a time. Assume the compiler is processing the element Y. Then $PT(Y)$ is added to $PT(X)$ for each of the successors X of Y in the address graph. X is added to the work list if $PT(X)$ changes.

Another way of computing the sets is to compute the strongly connected components of the reverse graph of the address graph. Each element X in a strongly connected component has the same value. By processing the nodes in reverse postorder on this (reverse) graph and handling a strongly connected component as a single node, the $PT(X)$ values can be computed in a depth-first search.

6.7.1 An Approximate Algorithm that Takes Less Time and Space

Note that the above algorithm computes $PT(X)$ for each tag and temporary. These sets can overlap; however, if we relax the computation to produce a conservative (larger set) result, then we can store the $PT(X)$ information in linear space. Just expand the sets to be an equivalence class. This means that if $PT(Y)$ is added to $PT(X)$, we simply make X and Y be in the same partition of the equivalence class, and the set $PT(X)$ is all of the address constants and memory allocation tags that are in the same set. This algorithm has been noted by Steensgaard (1996).

The *PT* information can now be implemented using a standard UNION/FIND data structure. When the algorithm would copy $PT(Y)$ into $PT(X)$, simply perform the UNION operation to join these two sets and make them identical (and thus make one of them larger than necessary).

6.8 Including the Effects of Local Expressions

Recall that a tag indicates a memory area and a potential runtime computable offset within the memory area. To correctly compute the *modifies* information, the compiler must take into account these runtime computations. In particular, $A(I)$ must be considered modified if I is modified. In other words, a storage reference is modified if its address changes. The address will change only when the variable temporaries and the temporaries involved in load and store operations within the address expression change. Thus we must compute the *modifies* information for copy operations. The tag representing a memory location is in the *modifies* set of any variable temporary that is a leaf in the expression tree computing the address. How does the compiler compute the *modifies* information for each copy operation? The algorithm here is based on one used in the Rice Massive Scalar Compiler Project.

To compute this information use an auxiliary data structure called *DEPENDS*. There is one *DEPENDS* set for each temporary. Consider two temporaries, T and S. The temporary T is in *DEPENDS(S)* if T is a variable temporary that is used to compute S. These sets can be computed by performing a walk of the flow graph. Recall that all of the operands of any expression temporary must be computed on all paths leading to the occurrence of the instruction computing that temporary. Thus, a depth-first search through the flow graph will visit instructions computing the operands before instructions computing S.

Initialize all of the *DEPENDS* sets to empty. Perform a depth-first search of the flow graph. When processing any instruction computing an expression temporary, make the *DEPENDS* set of the target be the union of the *DEPENDS* sets for the operands. When processing an instruction that computes a variable temporary, make the *DEPENDS* set of the target be the target itself. When the walk is completed all of the *DEPENDS* sets have been computed.

Now scan through the set of all tags, considering the address expression portion of the tag. For the sake of discussion consider a single tag X with an address expression computed into T. X is in the *modifies* set for each temporary in *DEPENDS(T)*.

6.9 Small Amount of Flow-Sensitive Information by Optimization

Later optimization techniques are used to improve the modification information. Consider a particular store operation. What memory locations might be changed by this store operation? Clearly all locations that are in the same points-to set as the address of the store operation and every location that might overlap one of these memory locations.

During the dominator-based optimizations, a degree of flow-sensitive information can be gained by applying the constant propagation algorithm. At that point the flow graph is in static single assignment form, so the set of memory locations that might change is attached to the store operation. A variation on constant propagation can be used to prune this set of memory locations.

Consider a language like C. In C, each pointer must point to a particular data structure. The data structure may be statically allocated, on the heap, or on the stack, but the pointer cannot move from one data structure to another. Here is the idea. Consider an "alternative" value for the address that consists only of the largest data area in which the address points. Thus for an array it is the base of the area. If the address is not knowable, make the value be bottom (see the constant propagation algorithm, described in Chapter 8), which indicates that the compiler has no idea what the value is.

This alternative value has some interesting computational rules. Adding an integer expression to this value does not change it. Hence subscripting does not change it. Similarly, subtracting values does not change it. Thus, constant propagation can be applied and an "alternative value" determined for each store operation. If the alternative value for the address in a STORE is not bottom, then all memory locations that do not overlap this value cannot be changed and can be removed from the list of memory locations that might change.

This algorithm is particularly helpful when arrays are involved or in-line functions have been inserted. It will replace the translation of arrays to pointers and the copying of pointers by array semantics when possible.

6.9.1 Handling the Pointer from a Heap Allocation Operation

Another flow-sensitive refinement of the modification can be performed on the static single assignment form. In this form, each use of a pointer is directly tied to the instruction that computed it. Thus, pointers that have been generated by an allocation instruction, such as **malloc,** can be identified as a walk of the flow graph or the dominator tree is performed. What memory locations can a STORE through this pointer affect?

Initially, the store cannot affect any other memory locations because this is new memory. As the walk continues, a STORE through this pointer can only affect memory locations associated with locations in which this pointer has been stored. This analysis continues until there is a merging of paths in which one value comes from one predecessor and another from an alternate predecessor. Of course, in static single assignment form this means a new temporary name.

Thus a temporary that holds a pointer that is created by a memory allocation operation holds that value for its whole lifetime and can only overlap memory addressed by pointers that are copies of this temporary. This interpretation is safe in this compiler because the compiler never attempts to move instructions when the flow graph is in static single assignment form.

6.10 References

Steensgaard, B. 1996. Points-to analysis by type inference of programs with structures and unions. In *International Conference on Compiler Construction,* number 1060. In *Lecture Notes in Computer Science,* 136–150.

7 STATIC SINGLE ASSIGNMENT

Many optimization algorithms need to know the relationships between uses of temporaries (or variables) and the points where they are evaluated. Each of the algorithms needs to know either the set of points in the flow graph where the value computed by an instruction is used or the set of evaluations whose values might be used at this point in the flow graph. The static single assignment (SSA) form is a compact representation of these facts.[1]

DEFINITION **Static Single Assignment Form:** The flow graph is in static single assignment form if each temporary is the target in a single instruction.

The definition of static single assignment is so restrictive that most programs cannot be translated into SSA form. Consider the left flow graph in Figure 7.1. There are two assignments to the variable X: one outside the loop and one incrementing X inside the loop. There is no way to put X into SSA form without the introduction of a new operator.

To ensure that all program flow graphs can be put in SSA form, another special instruction, called a ϕ-node, is added to the definition of static single assignment form.

DEFINITION **ϕ-node:** Consider a block B in the flow graph with predecessors $\{P_1, P_2, \ldots, P_n\}$, where $n > 1$. A ϕ-node $T_0 = \phi(T_1, T_2, \ldots, T_n)$ in B is an instruction that gives T_0 the value that T_i contains on entrance to B if the execution path leading to B traverses the block P_i as the predecessor of B on the path. The set of ϕ-nodes in B is denoted by $\Phi(B)$.

---

1. An alternative technique called USE-DEF chains can also be used. It frequently requires more space and time to compute and is harder to incrementally update.

Figure 7.1 Graph (left) and SSA Graph Equivalent (right)

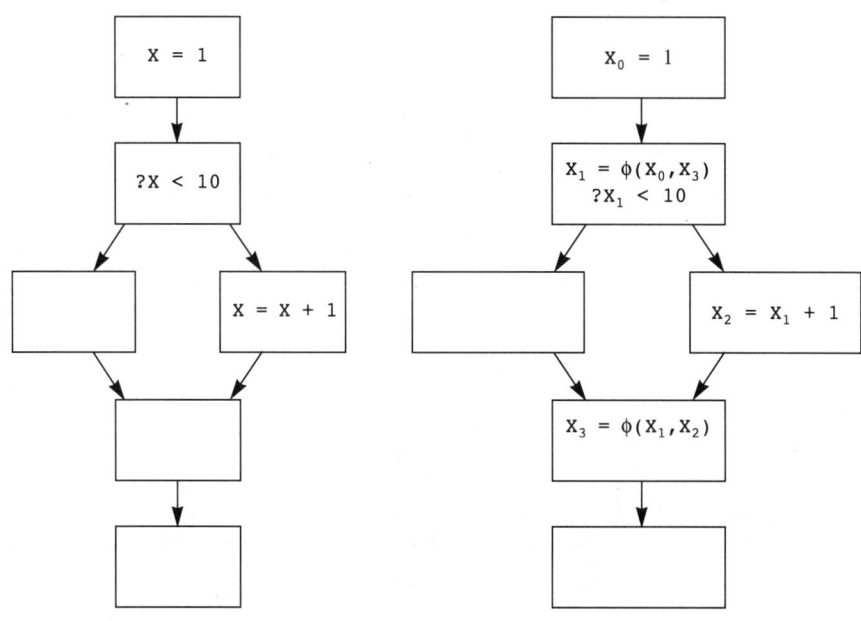

Consider the program flow on the right graph in Figure 7.1. This graph is equivalent to the one on the left (it computes the same values) and is in SSA form. The variable X has been replaced by four variables (X_0, X_1, X_2, X_3) and two ϕ-nodes that indicate the points in the program reached by multiple definitions of X. One of the ϕ-nodes is at the beginning of the loop because there is a modification of X inside the loop and it is initialized outside the loop. The other ϕ-node occurs at the merge of two paths through the loop, where only one path contains a definition of X.

A flow graph in SSA form is interpreted in the same way as a normal program flow graph, with the addition of ϕ-nodes. Consider a path from *Entry* to *Exit*:

- Each normal instruction is evaluated in order, recording the results of each instruction so that these values can be used in the evaluation of later instructions on the path.

- All ϕ-nodes at the beginning of a block are evaluated simultaneously on entrance to the block. The value of target temporary T_0 is T_i if the path came to the ϕ-node through the ith predecessor of the block.

Static Single Assignment

The next two sections describe the fundamental operations of translating a flow graph into and out of static single assignment form. Two areas that are typically overlooked in the literature are emphasized: the simultaneous evaluation of ϕ-nodes at the beginning of a block, and the handling of abnormal edges in the flow graph.

7.1 Creating Static Single Assignment Form

The algorithm for translating the flow graph into static single assignment form treats each temporary independently. In fact, one could partially translate the flow graph leaving some temporaries in normal form and some in SSA form. This compiler does not. The translation takes place in two steps:

1. Determine the points in the program where ϕ-nodes are inserted. In Figure 7.1, there are two points. Insert the ϕ-nodes with the left-hand operand and all right-hand operands being the same value. In Figure 7.1, there would be two insertions of the form $X = \phi(X,X)$.

2. Rename the temporaries so that each instruction and ϕ-node having X as a target is given a new, unique name.

Where are ϕ-nodes needed? Consider a single temporary or variable T and a block B. A ϕ-node is needed at the beginning of B if B has multiple predecessors and different definitions of T occur on distinct paths going through at least two predecessors. This leads to the definition of converging paths.[2]

Definition **Converging Paths:** Two non-null paths, p from B_0 to B_n and q from B'_0 to B'_m, converge at a block Z if and only if

$B_0 \neq B'_0$; in other words, the paths start at different points

$B_n = B'_m = Z$; in other words, both paths end at Z.

If $B_i = B'_j$ then either $i = n$ or $j = m$; in other words, the only point on the paths that is in common is the end point. Note that one of the paths may loop through Z and come back to it.

---

2. Computing these points is not intuitive; thus, we now descend to a theoretical discussion. A more intuitive algorithm was used in an earlier form of static single assignment called p-graphs. P-graphs had all of the characteristics of static single assignment; however, computing the points for the insertion of the birth points was quadratic to the size of the graph, so was not practical in most compilers.

If I_1 and I_2 are assignments to T, then any basic block Z that is the conjunction of two merging paths from I_1 and I_2 will be a point where a φ-node is inserted because two different definitions of T lie on distinct paths reaching that point. But one must go further. Z is now a new definition of T because the φ-node has been inserted, so now it too must be included in the set of definitions of T and the process of computing merge nodes repeated.

Using the notation of Cytron et al. (1991), one obtains the notation and formula shown in Figure 7.2 for the points where φ-nodes need to be inserted for T. The notation is an abstraction of the idea of the previous paragraph. The function J_1 takes a set of blocks as an argument and returns the set of merge points associated with those blocks. However, this process must be repeated with the set of blocks together with the merge point giving J_2. By the definition of merge points, if the argument to J_1 is a larger set, then the result is larger also. In other words, $J_i(S) \subseteq J_{i+1}(S)$. Since there is a finite number of blocks, there must come a point where $J_i(S) = J_{i+1}(S)$. This will be true for all larger values of i, so the formula represented as an infinite union actually represents the value of $J_i(S)$ where the sets stop increasing in size.

It is too difficult to directly compute the merge points; another formulation is needed. An efficient algorithm is based on dominance frontiers. One point before I discuss the algorithm: In forming static single assignment form, each temporary is assumed to have an evaluation at *Entry*. Think of this evaluation as the undefined evaluation. It is the evaluation used when no evaluation has really occurred. If this evaluation is used as an operand, then the operand has an undefined value. This cannot happen with expressions or compiler-generated temporaries. It can happen with user-defined variables stored as temporaries.

Here is the algorithm. Consider two evaluations of T in blocks B and B'. There are three possibilities:

- B dominates B'. Consider a merge point Z for these two blocks. There are disjoint paths from B to Z and from B' to Z. B' cannot dominate Z because then B' would be on the path from B to Z, contradicting disjointness.

Figure 7.2 Join Points for Temporary X

```
S = {B|B contains an assignment to X}
J₁(S) = {Z|∃Z₁,Z₂ ∈ S ∋ Z is merge point for two paths Z₁ →⁺ Z and Z₂ →⁺ Z}
J_{i+1}(S) = J₁(S ∪ J_i(S))
J⁺(S) = ⋃_{i=1}^{∞} J_i(S)
```

Static Single Assignment

- B' dominates B. The same argument as above indicates that B cannot dominate Z.

- Neither B nor B' dominates the other. Then a merge point will not be dominated by either of them because two distinct paths reach it.

Thus the merge points have something to do with the blocks that are not dominated by B. In fact, consider an evaluation of T in B. Follow any path leaving B until you arrive at a block Z that is not dominated by B. By the definition of dominance frontier, $Z \in DF(B)$. Z is also a merge point because there is a path from B to Z and a path from *Entry* to Z. There is an implicit evaluation of T in *Entry*, so $Z \in J(S)$. In other words, we have $DF(S) \in J^+(S)$. We can apply the same repetitive formation method to the dominance frontier, giving the set of equations in Figure 7.3.

The claim is that $DF^+(S) = J^+(S)$ if S contains the entry block. We know that $DF^+(S) \subseteq J^+(S)$ by repetitively applying the inequality $DF(S) \subseteq J^+(S)$. Noticing that the sequence of dominance frontier sets and join sets are each increasing in size, we know that $DF^+(S) \subseteq J^+(S)$, so we need only establish the reverse inclusion. Proving this is a two-step process that is best described in mathematical proofs.

LEMMA Let p: $B \xrightarrow{+} Z$ be a non-null path. Either

B dominates each node on the path p, including Z,

Or there is a block $B' \in DF^+(\{B\})$ on the path p that dominates Z.

PROOF Since we need to establish one or the other of the conditions, we can assume that the first condition is false and establish the second. Assume that there are blocks on the path that are not dominated by B. Consider the first block B_1 on the path that is not dominated by B. Its predecessor is dominated by B, so B_1 is in the dominance frontier of B. Therefore there are blocks in the dominance frontier of B that are on the path. Since $DF(B) \subseteq DF^+(B)$, there are blocks in the iterated dominance frontier of B on the path. Let B' be the last block in $DF^+(B)$ on the path as one walks the path from B to Z. The claim is that B' dominates Z. If B' does not dominate Z, then there is a first block following B' that is not dominated by B'. That block is therefore in the dominance

Figure 7.3 Iterated Dominance Frontier

```
S = {B|B contains an evaluation of T} ∪ {Entry}
DF₁(S) = DF(S)
DF_{i+1}(S) = DF(S ∪ DF_i(S))
DF⁺(S) = ⋃_{i=1}^∞ DF_i(S)
```

frontier of B', so it is in $DF^+(B)$ by the iterative nature of its definition. This is a contradiction since B' was chosen to be the last such block on the path.

A loose interpretation of this proof is as follows: Start at B. Move down the path until one finds a member B_1 of the dominance frontier of B. Now do the same thing starting at B_1. Continue this process until one reaches the end of the path. The last block of this form on the path dominates all the following ones.

LEMMA Let $B \ne C$ be two blocks. If there are two paths p: $B \xrightarrow{+} Z$ and q: $C \xrightarrow{+} Z$ that converge at Z, then $Z \in DF^+(\{B\}) \cup DF^+(\{C\})$.

PROOF Using the previous lemma twice, choose a block $B' \in DF^+(B)$ on p that dominates Z, and a block $C' \in DF^+(C)$ on q that dominates Z. There are three cases:

Suppose B' is on the path q as well as on the path p. By the definition of two paths converging, this means that $B' = Z$, so $Z \in DF^+(\{B\})$.

Suppose C' is on the path p as well as on the path q. Again by the definition of converging paths, this means $Z = C' \in DF^+(\{C\})$.

Suppose that B' is not on path q and C' is not on path p. Now B' dominates Z, which is the last block on the path q. Then B' must dominate the predecessor, Y, of Z on q, because if B' does not dominate Y, a new path between *Entry* and Z can be formed from a path between *Entry* and Y that does not include B' and the edge from $Y \to Z$. Recall that $Y \ne B'$ since B' is not on q. This argument can be repeated for each block on the path q in reverse order so that B' dominates every block on q. Now apply the same argument with C' and p and one finds that C' dominates every block on the path p. So B' dominates and is dominated by C'. The only way that this can happen is that $B' = C'$, which is a contradiction. So this alternative is not possible.

Now recall the definitions of converging paths and the join set $J(S)$. What this lemma shows is that for any set S one has $J(S) \subseteq DF^+(S)$. Now consider the concept of iteration we are using to form DF^+ from DF and similarly J^+ from J. The sequence of sets $DF_1 \subseteq DF_2 \subseteq \ldots \subseteq DF^+$ is a sequence of increasing finite sets with an upper bound being all sets in the graph. Thus there is a point in the sequence where the sets no longer increase; in other words, there is a point where $DF_i = DF_{i+1}$. After this point the sets will always continue to be the same because the inputs on each iteration are the same as the previous iteration. Also note that $DF^+(DF^+(S)) = DF^+(S)$. We have

```
J(S) ⊆ DF⁺(S) for any set S
J₁(S) = J(S ∪ J(S)) ⊆ J(S ∪ DF⁺(S))
      = J(DF⁺(S)) ⊆ DF⁺(DF⁺(S)) = DF⁺(S)
...
J⁺(S) ⊆ DF⁺(S)
```

Static Single Assignment

We can now compute the points at which to insert the ϕ-nodes by computing the points in the iterative dominance frontier.

Computing the iterative dominance frontier can be performed using a work-list algorithm, as shown in Figure 7.4. We have computed the dominance frontier for each block B earlier. The dominance frontier of a set S is just the union of the dominance frontiers of the elements in the set. The iterative dominance frontier means that we must include the dominance frontier of any block that we add into the dominance frontier. This is done by keeping a work list of blocks that have been added to the dominance frontier but which have not been processed to add the elements of their dominance frontiers yet.

Since the algorithm is stated in an abstract fashion, I include a number of implementation hints here:

- The set $DF^+(S)$ is written in the algorithm to indicate that it is dependent on S. The compiler will use it on one set at a time so the algorithm takes a single set as input and computes a single set as output. No indexing is needed.

- The only operation performed on the set S is to scan through the elements to initialize both the *Worklist* and $DF^+(S)$ sets, so it can be implemented using any technique that allows accessing all members in linear time on the size of the set. In this case, the most likely implementation is as a linked list.

Figure 7.4 Iterated Dominance Algorithm

```
Input: A set of blocks S
Output: The set DF⁺(S)
Worklist = ∅;
DF⁺(S) = ∅;
foreach B ∈ S do
   DF⁺(S) = DF⁺(S) ∪ {B};
   Worklist = Worklist ∪ {B};
endfor;
while Worklist ≠ ∅ do
   take B from Worklist;
   foreach C ∈ DF(B) do
      if C ∉ DF⁺(S) then
         DF⁺(S) = DF⁺(S) ∪ {C};
         Worklist = Worklist ∪ {C};
      endif;
   endfor;
endwhile;
```

- The *Worklist* is a set in which the operations are adding an element to the set only when it is known that the element is not in the set, and taking an arbitrary element from the set. Note in the algorithm that an element is added to the *Worklist* at most once because an element can be added to the $DF^+(S)$ at most once because of the conditional test. The most likely implementation of *Worklist* is as an array implementing a stack. The maximum size of the array is the number of blocks in the graph.

- The implementation of $DF^+(S)$ is more subtle. The operations performed on it are initializing to empty, inserting an element, and checking membership. Outside the algorithm, one will need to scan through all the elements in the set. Since it is a subset of the blocks in the graph, its maximum size is known. The most likely implementation for this set uses the set membership algorithm described in Chapter 3. This set algorithm requires that the elements be mapped to a sequence of integers, which can be done using any of the numerical orderings we have computed for the blocks, such as reverse postorder.

Now that we know how to compute $DF^+(S)$, we can piece together the algorithm for computing the places in which to put ϕ-nodes. The basic algorithm, as shown in Figure 7.5, is simple. Handle each temporary or memory location separately. Form the set of all basic blocks that modify the value being considered. Compute the iterated dominators and then insert a ϕ-node at each block that is in the iterated dominance frontier. Initially the node inserted has the same left side and operands. In the renaming phase coming shortly, these names will be changed so that the program satisfies the SSA form conditions.

The algorithm in Figure 7.5 inserts too many ϕ-nodes. It inserts the minimum number of ϕ-nodes to guarantee that each temporary and variable

Figure 7.5 Basic Algorithm for Inserting ϕ-Nodes

```
foreach T ∈ Variables do
    S = {B|B contains definition of T} ∪ {Entry}
    Compute DF⁺(S);
    foreach B ∈ DF⁺(S) do
        n = |pred(B)|;
        Insert an n-operand T = ϕ(T,...,T) in block B;
    endfor;
endfor;
```

Figure 7.6 Inserting Nodes for Global Variables

```
foreach T ∈ Variables do
   if T ∈ Globals then
      S = {B|B contains definition of T} ∪ {Entry};
      Compute DF⁺(S);
      foreach B ∈ DF⁺(S) do
         n = |pred(B)|;
         Insert an n-operand T = φ(T,...,T) in block B;
      endfor;
   endif;
endfor;
```

always has the correct value and the program satisfies the SSA form, but many of these φ-nodes will define temporaries that have no uses, so the φ-nodes can be eliminated. Consider a temporary *T* that is defined and used only in one basic block *B*. The algorithm will still insert φ-nodes at the basic blocks in $DF^+(\{B\})$ even though no uses of *T* occur outside the block. These extra nodes can be eliminated by dead-code elimination; however, they take up space in the compiler and require time to generate, slowing the compiler down. There are two techniques, shown in Figures 7.6 and 7.7, for eliminating some of these nodes.

The first improvement on the basic algorithm is given in Figure 7.6: Do not compute φ-nodes to be inserted for temporaries that do not contain information across a block boundary. If the same temporary is used in multi-

Figure 7.7 Inserting Fewest Nodes

```
foreach T ∈ Variables do
   if T ∈ Globals then
      S = {B|B contains definition of T} ∪ {Entry};
      Compute LiveIn for T;
      Compute DF⁺(S);
      foreach B ∈ DF⁺(S) do
         if B ∈ LiveIn then
            n = |pred(B)|;
            Insert an n-operand T = φ(T,...,T) in B;
         endif;
      endfor;
   endif;
endfor;
```

ple blocks but no information is stored in it at a block boundary, the renaming algorithm will change these into multiple temporaries appropriately.

Recall that *Globals* is the set of temporaries that holds a value at the beginning of some block. This is still too coarse; ϕ-nodes will be inserted at blocks where the value will not be used. In other words, ϕ-nodes need only be inserted where the temporary is live. Figure 7.7 shows the modified algorithm that computes which blocks have T live and only inserts ϕ-nodes in these blocks.

The work-list algorithm for computing *Live* given in Chapter 4 is well suited for this algorithm. The algorithm only processes temporaries in *Global* and the work-list algorithm can then be applied to the small set of temporaries.

7.2 Renaming the Temporaries

At this point we have an algorithm for inserting ϕ-nodes; however, the variables have not been renamed so that there is a single variable name for each definition. We need a consistent renaming of the temporaries in the instructions so that the same name is used when a temporary is evaluated and when it is used. Consider a temporary T in the original program. After the ϕ-nodes are inserted, the uses of T can be divided into two groups:

1. The uses of T that occurred in the original program. All of these uses are dominated by the definition that computes the value used. If this were not true, then there would be another path to the use that avoids the definition, which would mean that there is a point where separate paths from definitions converge between the definition and the use, thus inserting another definition. In other words, each use is dominated by an evaluation of T or a ϕ-node with target T.

2. The uses of T in a ϕ-node. To each such use there is a corresponding predecessor block. This predecessor must be dominated by the definition of T for the same reasons that normal uses of T are dominated.

The renaming algorithm thus reduces to a walk of the dominator tree (see Figure 7.8). Each time one sees a definition of a temporary, a new name is given to the temporary, and that name replaces all of the uses of the temporary that occur in blocks dominated by the definition. After the subtree dominated by the definition has been walked, the previous name is restored so that other subtrees can be walked with the previous name. Uses

Figure 7.8 Basic SSA Renaming Algorithm

```
procedure RENAME(B: Block)
   foreach I := T_0 = φ(T_1,...,T_n) ∈ Φ(B) do
      push NewName() on Top(NameStack(T_0));
      Definition(Top(NameStack(T_0))) = I;
   endfor;
   foreach I ∈ B in execution order do
      foreach T ∈ Operands(I) do
         replace T by Top(NameStack(T));
         add I to Uses(Top(NameStack(T)));
      endfor;
      foreach T ∈ Targets(I) do
         push NewName() on Top(NameStack(T));
         Definition(Top(NameStack(T))) = I;
      endfor;
   endfor;
   foreach S ∈ Succ(B) do
      j = WhichPredecessor(S,B);
      foreach I := T_0 = φ(T_1,...,T_m) ∈ Φ(S) do
         replace T_j by (Top(NameStack(T_j)));
         add I to Uses(NameStack(T_j));
      endfor;
   endfor;
   foreach C ∈ Children(B) do
      call RENAME(C);
   endfor;
   foreach I ∈ B in reverse execution order do
      foreach T ∈ Targets(I) do
         replace T by Pop(NameStack(T));
      endfor;
   endfor;
   foreach T_0 = φ(T_1,...,T_n) ∈ Φ(B) do
      replace T_0 by Pop(NameStack(T_0));
   endfor;
endprocedure RENAME;
foreach T ∈ Variables do
   NameStack(T) = ∅;
endfor;
RENAME(Entry);
```

of a temporary in φ-nodes are handled in the predecessor block. When a block is traversed, all of the φ-nodes in each successor are traversed. Uses of a temporary in the operand position corresponding to this (predecessor) block are renamed in the same way that normal uses are renamed.

The whole point of static single assignment is to provide concise information about the uses and definitions of temporaries, so we need to add attributes to the renaming process that record this information. For each temporary there are two attributes, *Definition(T)* and *Uses(T)*. *Definition(T)* is the single instruction that defines *T*. Recall that there can be more than one temporary defined by each instruction; however, there is only one instruction that defines a particular temporary.

Uses(T) is the set of instructions that uses *T*. This is a set that most likely is implemented as a linked list. Since each instruction is only visited once during the renaming process, the only way that an instruction can be inserted twice into the set is when the same operand is used two or more times in an instruction. I choose to let these multiple insertions occur in the set because later a removal of one operand will only remove one of the uses.

The form of *NameStack* is the implementation issue. *NameStack* is a collection of stacks, one for each temporary. These stacks are implemented as linked lists to avoid excessive storage. The *Push* operation adds an element to the head of the list, and the *Pop* operation removes an element from the head of the list. *Top* looks at the element at the head of the list.

If we are being mathematically pure, we should now prove a lemma that the execution of the static single assignment form computes the same values on each path through the flow graph as are computed with the normal form of the flow graph. The proof is a clerical application of the ideas that we have discussed here, carefully checking that the renaming algorithm is accurate to the execution of the flow graph. If you are not convinced, then we leave the proof to you.

7.3 Translating from SSA to Normal Form

To return the program to normal form involves replacing the ϕ-nodes by equivalent copy operations. The value of a ϕ-node in *B* is the value of its first operand if *B* is entered from the first predecessor, its second operand if *B* is entered from the second operand, and so on. Translation from SSA form to normal form thus consists of replacing the ϕ-nodes by assignments in the predecessor blocks having the same effect, as is shown in Figure 7.9.

Two characteristics of the SSA form make it difficult to translate back to normal form.[3] Consider the flow graph and the corresponding optimized SSA

---

3. These problems were communicated to me by Preston Briggs, now of Tera Computer Company, and elaborated on by L. Taylor Simpson of Rice University. The example is a combination of two examples created by Taylor Simpson.

Static Single Assignment

Figure 7.9 Translation from SSA Form

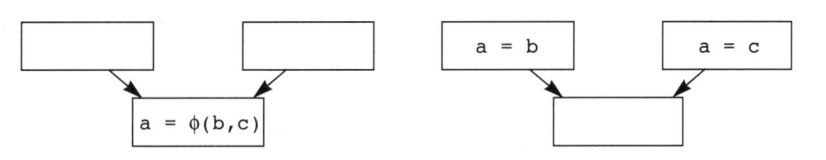

form in Figure 7.10, where only relevant instructions are shown. All ϕ-nodes are evaluated simultaneously at the beginning of a block. In this example, B is also the predecessor and the variables b_1 and a_1 are both used as operands and assigned values in B. The straightforward translation as in the left flow graph of Figure 7.11 destroys b_1 before it is used. The variables a_1 and b_1 are used to define one another. A temporary, t, must be created to hold the value of one while it is receiving a new value.

Also, one of the variables may be modified before it is later used on a different path, as shown in Figure 7.11. In this example u, which is a copy of a_1, is used later in the program. It is eliminated by the optimizer and replaced by a use of a_1. If a_1 is assigned a value at the end of B, then the value of a_1 will be destroyed before its use. But note the following:

- If a B has only one predecessor, then no ϕ-nodes can occur.
- If a predecessor of B only has B as a successor, then there is no possible alternative path out of the block.

Figure 7.10 Normal and Optimized SSA Form

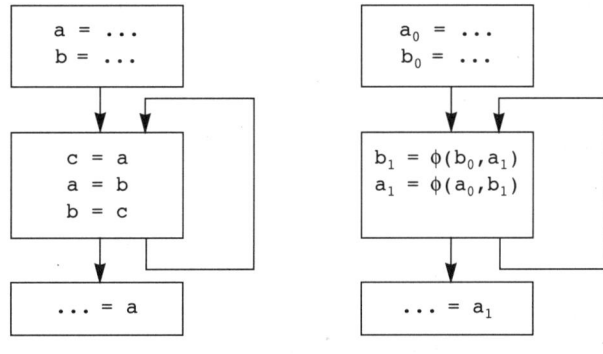

Figure 7.11 Incorrect and Correct Translation

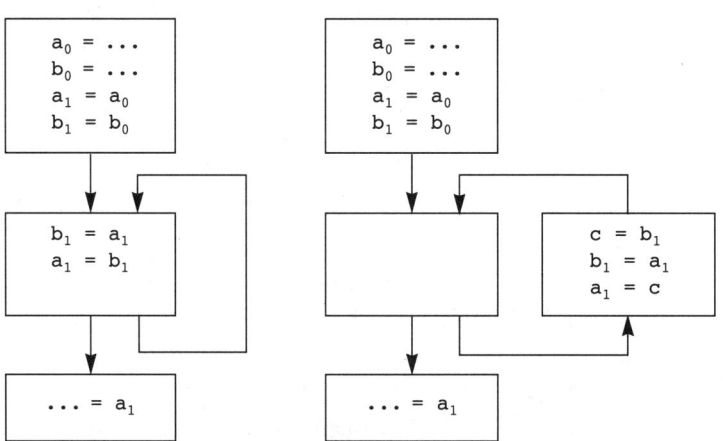

- Thus only critical edges can have this problem, so they must be eliminated before translation by inserting an empty block in the middle of the edge. Since abnormal critical edges cannot be removed, the optimization algorithms using SSA form must ensure that there will be no need to insert a block on an abnormal critical edge.

7.3.1 General Algorithm for Translating from SSA to Normal Form

Given a flow graph $(N, E, Entry, Exit)$ in SSA form and a partition $P = \{P_1, ..., P_r\}$ of the set of all temporaries, rewrite the graph in normal form so that any two temporaries T_1 and T_2 in P_i are given the same temporary name and the ϕ-nodes are replaced by equivalent copy operations. The partition defines an equivalence relation on the temporaries. Equivalent temporaries are renamed to a single temporary in the normal form. The partition must ensure that a valid program will be generated. In particular,

- In each block B, if two equivalent temporaries are targets of ϕ-nodes, then corresponding arguments must be equivalent.
- For each abnormal critical edge (C, B), if $T_0 = \phi(T_1, ..., T_i, ..., T_m)$ is a ϕ-node in B and C is the ith predecessor of B, then T_0 and T_i must be equivalent.

Static Single Assignment

In all of the algorithms in this compiler, the partition of the temporaries will be implemented using the UNION/FIND algorithm of Tarjan (1975) as found in most data structure textbooks (Aho 1983 and Cormen 1990). Initially each temporary is in a partition by itself. Each partition is always represented by a single temporary in the partition. *FIND* takes a temporary as an argument and returns the representative temporary for that partition. *UNION* takes two temporaries, replaces the two partition subsets holding those two temporaries by a single partition subset that is the union of the two, and returns the representative temporary for the union.

Returning to normal form involves two activities: renaming temporaries in ordinary instructions and eliminating φ-nodes (see Figure 7.12). Renaming the temporaries in ordinary instructions is a clerical problem. The compiler scans through all instructions in all blocks and, using the *FIND* function, replaces each temporary by a unique representative from the subset in the partition containing that temporary. The φ-nodes can be eliminated during the same walk of the flow graph in which the temporaries are renamed.

Assume we are considering the edge (C, B) where C is the ith predecessor of B. We insert copy operations into C to simulate the effect of the

Figure 7.12 Renaming to Normal Form

```
procedure NORMAL(N,E,Exit,Entry,P)
   foreach B ∈ N do
      foreach I ∈ B do
         foreach T ∈ Operands(I) do
            replace T by FIND(T);
         endfor;
         foreach T ∈ Targets(I) do
            replace T by FIND(T);
         endfor;
         if I = {U = U} then
            delete I from B;
         endif;
      endfor;
      foreach C ∈ pred(B) do
         call ELIMINATEφ(C,B,WHICHPRED(B,C),FIND);
      endfor;
   endfor;
   foreach B ∈ N do
      remove φ-nodes from B;
   endfor;
endprocedure NORMAL;
```

ϕ-nodes in Φ(B). At the same time we will rename the operands using *FIND*. The compiler must sort the copy operations so that any copy involving a temporary as an operand occurs before the copy involving the same temporary as a destination.

- A temporary (or rather the elements of a partition) can be used multiple times as an operand.
- If equivalent temporaries are targets of ϕ-nodes in B, then corresponding operands are equivalent.
- Some of the copies will be eliminated because the operand and the target are equivalent.

The compiler must sort the copy operations so that uses of a temporary precede their definitions and create temporaries to create copies for mutually dependent temporaries. We describe a graph, $R(B)$, to represent these two relationships.

- The nodes of the graph are the members of the partition P. There is one node of $R(B)$ for each subset in the partition P that contains a temporary occurring in Φ(B). Equivalent temporaries are represented by a single member of the partition.
- There is an edge from $FIND(T_k) \rightarrow FIND(T_l)$ if there are temporaries T_k and T_l such that $T_k = \phi(...) \in \Phi(B)$ with T_l as the ith operand.

How does this graph describe the problem of ordering the copy operations? Each node in the graph corresponds to the representative of a partition element that occurs as the operand or target of some of the ϕ-nodes. Each representative can occur as the target of at most one copy operation. If an ordering is found where uses occur before definitions, then the copy operations can be generated in the same order. This is a topological sort of the reverse graph.

Which nodes generate copy operations? In $R(B)$, there is an edge out of a node if and only if there is a copy operation. So each node in $R(B)$ with a successor generates a copy operation. The other nodes represent temporaries that are used but not defined.

What about the case in which there are mutually dependent temporaries? Then the graph will have a strongly connected region and the topological sort will not succeed. The strongly connected regions must be identified and extra temporaries must be introduced to simulate simultaneous assignment.

Static Single Assignment

The strongly connected regions have a special form because there is at most one edge leaving each node. Look at the definition of an edge; only the ith operand counts, and there can only be one assignment to any temporary in a subset in the partition. If equivalent temporaries are assigned, then the operands must be equivalent. So there can be at most one edge leaving a node in $R(B)$. These two characteristics imply that the strongly connected region has the following characteristics:

- A strongly connected region is a simple cycle. There is a path from any member of the region to any other member. Start at one of the nodes. Since there is only one edge out, there is only one way to leave the node. As you walk from node to node, there are no choices. Eventually you must get to the other node. If you keep walking from node to node, you will eventually get back to the original node. You have a simple cycle.

- The strongly connected region may have multiple predecessors outside the region, but it can have no successors outside the region. The reasoning is the same as before. Since there is only one edge out of each node and the strongly connected region is a cycle, there is no way to get to any successors.

This makes the algorithm simpler. We can use the standard strongly connected region algorithm[4] to identify a reverse postorder for topological sorting and identify the strongly connected regions. Each strongly connected region can be translated as follows:

1. Enumerate the loop in some order where each successive node is a successor of the previous one and the first node is a successor of the last. This can be performed during a depth-first search.

2. Generate one extra temporary, T.

3. Generate an instruction to copy the temporary representing the first node into T.

4. Translate all of the other nodes except the last one as is done for the topologically sorted nodes.

5. Generate an instruction to copy T into the temporary corresponding to the final node.

---

4. Actually there are two related but distinct algorithms. Either one can be used. The one here is in most modern textbooks. The original algorithm is by Tarjan (1972).

Figure 7.13 Mutually Dependent Temporaries

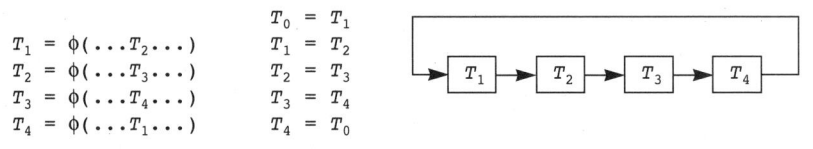

$$T_1 = \phi(\ldots T_2 \ldots)$$
$$T_2 = \phi(\ldots T_3 \ldots)$$
$$T_3 = \phi(\ldots T_4 \ldots)$$
$$T_4 = \phi(\ldots T_1 \ldots)$$

$$T_0 = T_1$$
$$T_1 = T_2$$
$$T_2 = T_3$$
$$T_3 = T_4$$
$$T_4 = T_0$$

Because this algorithm is complex, let's give an example. Consider four temporaries T_1, T_2, T_3, and T_4, which are the nodes in a cycle representing a strongly connected region, as in Figure 7.13. The original ϕ-nodes are shown on the left side, the resulting copy operations occur in the middle column, and the graph representing the copy operations is on the right. An extra temporary T_0 is generated to hold the value of T_1 while all of the nodes are processed. It is the value used to copy into T_4 at the end.

Now that we have all of the principles, it is time to create the algorithm, as shown in Figure 7.14. It involves two parts. The first part creates the directed graph representing the temporaries and is shown in Figure 7.15. Most compiler optimizations attempt to avoid copy operations in the normal form of the flow graph by defining the partition so that both right and left sides of a copy are in the same partition. The algorithm makes special provision to eliminate these extraneous copies.

The graph is represented by a set of nodes called *NodeSet* and two temporary attributes called *ELIM_PREDECESSORS* and *ELIM_SUCCESSORS*, representing the predecessors and successors in the directed graph. *NodeSet* is implemented using Briggs set algorithm because we need to be able to efficiently scan the nodes, check for membership, and insert a node. The predecessors and successors can be implemented using either linked lists or arrays simulating linked lists. I recommend the latter or the use of some collection-based memory allocation method because these data structures are very temporary.

The second part of the algorithm implements the topological sort and identifications of strongly connected regions. These can be done in one algorithm. The topological sort can be performed by pushing each node on a stack after all of its successors have been walked in a depth-first search. The first element in the topological order is on top of the stack, the second element is next on the stack, and so on. Hence the order can be found by listing the elements in the order in which they are removed from this stack.

Figure 7.14 Converting Edge to Normal Form

```
procedure ELIMINATE_ϕ (C: Block, B: Block, i: integer);
   call ELIMINATEBUILD(B,i);
   if NodeSet ≠ ∅ then
      Visited = ∅;                     //Some copy operation required
      Stack = ∅;
      foreach T ∈ NodeSet do           //Build stack from depth first walk
         if T ∉ Visited then
            call ELIM_FORWARD(T);
         endif;
      endfor;

      Visited = ∅;
      while Stack ≠ ∅ do
         pop T from Stack;
         if T ∉ Visited then           //Already processed?
            call ELIM_CREATE(T);       //Create copy operations
         endif;
      endwhile;
   endif;
endprocedure ELIMINATE_ϕ;

procedure ELIM_FORWARD(T: Temporary)
   add T to Visited;
   foreach S ∈ ELIM_SUCCESSORS(T) do
      if S ∉ Visited then
         call ELIM_FORWARD(S);
      endif;
   endfor;
   push T on Stack;
endprocedure ELIMINATE_FORWARD;
```

The strongly connected regions can be identified using the same stack. Before popping an element off the stack, perform a depth-first search using the predecessors rather than the successors of a node. Do not visit any node more than once in this predecessor walk. All of the unvisited nodes reached by this depth-first search of the predecessors are the elements of the strongly connected region containing the predecessor. The algorithm in Figure 7.16 is a transcription of this algorithm (Cormen, Leiserson, and Rivest 1990).

There are three different possibilities when creating the copy to represent a node. If the node has no successor, then there is no copy operation and the node can be ignored. If the node has no unvisited predecessor, then it is a single node that is not in a strongly connected region, so the

Figure 7.15   Building the Auxiliary Graph R(B)

```
procedure ELIMINATEBUILD(B: Block, i: integer)
   NodeSet = ∅;
   foreach T_0 = ϕ(T_1,...,T_m) ∈ Φ(B) do
      if FIND(T_0) ≠ FIND(T_i) then
         call ELIMINATENAME(FIND(T_0));
         call ELIMINATENAME(FIND(T_i));
         add FIND(T_0) to ELIM_PREDECESSORS(FIND(T_i));
         add FIND(T_i) to ELIM_SUCCESSORS(FIND(T_0));
      endif;
   endfor;
endprocedure ELIMINATEBUILD;

procedure ELIMINATENAME(T: Temporary)
   if T ∉ NodeSet then
      add T to NodeSet;
      ELIM_SUCCESSORS(T) = ∅;
      ELIM_PREDECESSORS(T) = ∅;
   endif;
endprocedure ELIMINATENAME;
```

copy operation can be generated where the operand is the successor in the graph and the target is the current node.

The third possibility is a strongly connected region. In that case, perform a depth-first walk using the predecessors until you get back to the current node (see Figure 7.16). Since a strongly connected region is known to be a cycle, this will describe the whole strongly connected region. Before starting the walk create a temporary to hold the value of the first node. Then generate all of the copies except the last after one has completely visited a node (and its predecessors). This will force the copies to be generated in topologically sorted order. The last copy uses the value held in the newly created temporary as its operand. Note that the node at the head of the cycle is not officially visited until the end of the depth-first walk. This forces the copy with the head as target to be generated first.

As you will see in the following example, the additional temporary can be avoided if there is a predecessor to the head. That temporary already holds the value of the target of the first copy instruction and can be used in place of the generated temporary. The algorithm in Figure 7.16 does not include this optimization to make the algorithm clearer; the implementor should include it.

To see how the algorithm works, apply it to the set of ϕ-nodes in Figure 7.17. The ϕ-nodes are in the left column, with the corresponding auxiliary

Figure 7.16 Computing Cycle of Temporaries

```
function ELIM_UNVISITED_PREDECESSOR(T: Temporary): boolean
   foreach P ∈ (ELIM_PREDECESSORS(T) do
      if P ∉ Visited then
         return true;
      endif;
   endfor;
   return false;
endfunction ELIM_UNVISITED_PREDECESSOR;

procedure ELIM_BACKWARD(T: Temporary)
   add T to Visited;
   foreach P ∈ ELIM_PREDECESSORS(T) do
      if P ∉ Visited then
         call ELIM_BACKWARD(P);
         create copy instruction "P := T" at end of C;
      endif;
   endfor;
endprocedure ELIM_BACKWARD;

procedure ELIM_CREATE(T: Temporary)
   if ELIM_UNVISITED_PREDECESSOR(T) then
      create new temporary U;
      create copy instruction "U := T" at end of C;
      foreach P ∈ ELIM_PREDECESSORS(T) do
         if P ∉ Visited then
            call ELIM_BACKWARD(P);
            create copy instruction "P := U" at end of C;
         endif;
      endfor;
   else if ELIM_SUCCESSORS(T) ≠ ∅ then
      add T to Visited;
      take S from ELIM_SUCCESSORS(T);
      create copy instruction "T := S" at end of C;
   endif;
endprocedure ELIM_CREATE
```

graph on the right side. Since there is no order among ϕ-nodes, the order of the nodes has been jumbled. Rather than using names for temporaries involving a subscripted capital *T*, normal letters are used for distinct temporaries to make the graph easier to read.

The results for this example are given in Figure 7.18. The stack generated by the first pass is given in the right column and the generated copies are given in the left. Recall that most edges will not generate any copies at all because the algorithms will eliminate them. This particular example was created to show as much about the algorithm as possible. Note that H is not

Figure 7.17 Example Graph for an Edge

```
F = φ(...B...)
C = φ(...D...)
E = φ(...A...)
G = φ(...H...)
B = φ(...C...)
D = φ(...A...)
A = φ(...B...)
```

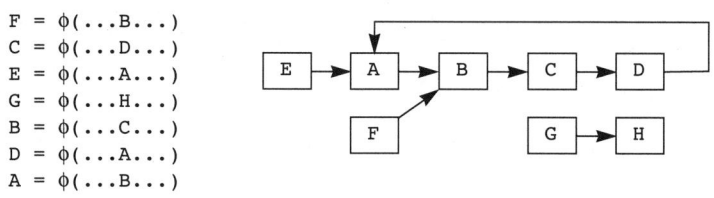

Figure 7.18 Results and Stack for Copy Generation

```
G := H        G
F := B        H
E := A        F
U := A        E
A := B        A
B := C        B
C := D        C
D := U        D
```

the target of a copy since it has no successor. Also note that the new temporary U is not needed since E already holds that value.

7.4 References

Aho, A. V., J. E. Hopcroft, and J. D. Ullman. 1983. *Data structures and algorithms.* Reading, MA: Addison-Wesley.

Cormen, T. H., C. E. Leiserson, and R. L. Rivest. 1990. *Introduction to Algorithms.* New York: McGraw-Hill.

Cytron, R., J. Ferrante, B. Rosen, M. Wegman, and F. Zadeck. 1991. Efficiently computing static single assignment form and the control dependence graph. *ACM Transactions on Programming Languages and Systems* 13(4): 451-490.

Tarjan, R. E. 1972. Depth-first search and linear graph algorithms. *SIAM Journal of Computing* 1(2): 146-160.

Tarjan, R. E. 1975. Efficiency of a good but not linear set of union algorithm. *Journal of ACM* 22(2): 215-225.

8 DOMINATOR-BASED OPTIMIZATION

The compiler now begins global optimization. Global optimization is divided into four components: **VALUE**, **DEPEND**, **RESHAPE**, and **MOTION**, executed in order (Figure 8.1). **VALUE** simulates the execution of the flow graph. If it can determine that the value or structure of an expression can be simplified, it replaces the expression with a simpler form. **DEPEND** performs loop restructuring using dependence-based optimizations. It relies on the simplifications performed by **VALUE** to make dependence analysis more accurate. After loop transformations have been performed, the **RESHAPE** phase is performed. **RESHAPE** includes all of the transformations in **VALUE** together with expression reshaping and strength reduction. **RESHAPE** prepares for the code motion performed in **MOTION. MOTION** performs code motion, including moving loads and stores to complete the global optimization portion of the compiler.

This chapter describes the **VALUE** and **RESHAPE** phases of the optimizer. **VALUE** limits its transformations so that **DEPEND** can operate more effectively. It does not do code motion, because the loop structure may change dramatically in **DEPEND**, and it does not do strength reduction, because **DEPEND** relies on the original form of expressions for analyzing subscripts.

RESHAPE includes all of **VALUE**. It adds strength reduction to modify multiplications in loops to repeated additions. It also applies the distributive and associative laws of arithmetic to integer operations. Several other simplifications are added to improve the flow graph as it is prepared for code motion.

VALUE performs the following transformations. Using the technique of static single assignment (SSA), they are inexpensive and suprisingly effective.

- The compiler can eliminate globally redundant expressions when there is an instance of the expression in a dominator block. This eliminates many of the redundant expressions in the procedure; however, it does

Figure 8.1   Structure of Global Optimizer

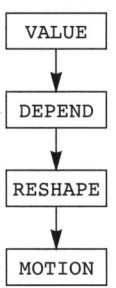

not perform code motion. Later, the compiler uses a technique called *elimination of partial redundancies* to do code motion.

- The compiler performs global constant propagation and constant folding. This is performed in two ways. Initially the compiler performs some constant propagation during the construction of the SSA form at the same time that globally redundant expressions are eliminated. Later a full global constant propagation algorithm is performed. For dependence-based optimizations, it is vital that constants are propagated as thoroughly as possible.

- The compiler can perform transformations that are dependent on the branches previously taken in the procedure. During the construction of the SSA form, the compiler maintains a data structure representing knowledge concerning which branches have been taken. Using this information, the compiler can use the results of relational tests to simplify the program. For example, if a previous computation performed the same comparison and took the TRUE branch then this branch will also take the TRUE branch and thus part of the code may be eliminated.

- Dead code is eliminated. Instructions are dead if their evaluation does not contribute to any value seen outside the procedure being compiled.

After dependence-based transformations have been applied, two further dominator-based transformations are applied to prepare the program for partial redundancy elimination:

- The compiler performs strength reduction. The compiler must identify the variables that are incremented by a fixed amount each time through a loop. This information is then used to simplify expensive computations (such as integer multiply) within a loop by replacing the multiplication with an integer addition and updating the value from a previous time through the loop.

- The compiler reshapes integer expressions using the associative and distributive laws of arithmetic to divide an expression into parts that are unchanging in each of the enclosing loops, allowing the later code motion algorithms to move more expressions out of loops.

8.1 Adding Optimizations to the Renaming Process

During construction of the static single assignment form, the renaming algorithm is easily adapted to include redundant expression elimination, peephole optimization, constant propagation, and expression simplification. Consider two distinct evaluations of $T*R$ in blocks B and B', where B dominates B'. In static single assignment form, the two evaluations will compute the same value if the operands have the same name. So redundant expression elimination reduces to a table lookup problem.

Why can these transformations be performed during the renaming process? If one evaluation of $T*R$ dominates all other evaluations of the same expression with no modifications of either T or R in between, then all of the other evaluations can be eliminated. Conversely, if an occurrence of $T*R$ is redundant, to be eliminated in favor of a single evaluation of $T*R$ this earlier occurrence must dominate the occurrence being eliminated. Otherwise, there would be a path from the start block to the occurrence that avoided the remaining occurrence of the expression.

Redundant expressions can thus be eliminated by performing a walk of the dominator tree looking for multiple occurrences of each expression. When the flow graph is in SSA form, the compiler need only look for identical expressions because the modification of an operand will be recorded by using a completely different temporary. The compiler can maintain a table of the expressions that have occurred on the path through the dominator tree from the start block to the current block. If the next expression is already in that table, then the expression is redundant. When an expression is redundant, do not give the target operand a new name; instead, give it the name of the target of the instruction that is already in the table.

This table has the same characteristics as the available-expression table used during value numbering. Algebraic identities and value numbering can be incorporated in the same way that they were incorporated in the value-numbering algorithm for single blocks. The operations required of this table are as follows:

Initialization: Initialize the available-expression table to have no entries.

Start Block: Begin a basic block. Remember the set of entries currently in the available-expression table so that the entries added during this block can be removed later.

End Block: Restore the available-expression table to the state that it was in when the current block was entered.

Find: Given an instruction I in the flow graph, look up I in the available-expression table using only the operator and operands. Insert I in the table if a matching entry is not already there. Return an indication of whether I was already in the table.

Insert: Insert an expression in the available-expression table even though it is not in the flow graph. This is used to record added information that can be deduced during the dominator tree walk. For example, if a conditional branch tests whether $T = 0$, then the compiler can record that T has the value 0 on one of the alternative branches.

Finalization: Eliminate all storage reserved for the available-expression table.

The available-expression table can be implemented using data structures similar to a scope-based symbol table. It can be viewed as a stack: Elements are pushed onto the stack if they are not already there. The stack is searched from the top of the stack down. Elements are popped off the stack when a block is completed. Of course, the data structure used will be more complex, using a chain-linked hash table to speed up the searches and an auxiliary array to keep track of the elements in each block on the path from the start block to the current block. See the description of symbol tables in McKeeman (1974).

Given the structure of the available-expression table, the full algorithm can be given in Figure 8.2. Each instruction is handled by first renaming its operands. Then any algebraic simplifications are incorporated. Finally, the instruction is entered in the available-expression table and given a new name if it is not in the table already.

If the algebraic simplifications lead to the replacement of conditional branches by unconditional branches, do not update the dominator tree: This would lead to an iterative algorithm. However, the replacement of a

Dominator-Based Optimization

Figure 8.2   Renaming with Optimization

```
procedure OPTRENAME(B: BLOCK)
   foreach T₀ = φ(T₁,...,Tₙ) ∈ Φ(B) do
      push NewName() on NameStack(T₀);
   endfor;
   foreach I ∈ B in execution order do
      StartBlock(B);
      foreach T ∈ Operands(I) do
         replace T by Top(NameStack(T));
      endfor;
      if InAvailableTable(I) then
         T = lhs(I);
         push AvailableTarget(I) on NameStack(T);
         add I to DeadInstructions;
      else
         foreach T ∈ Targets(I) do
            push NewName() on Top(NameStack(T));
         endfor;
      endif;
   endfor;
   foreach S ∈ Succ(B) do
      j = WhichPredeccor(S,B);
      foreach T₀ = φ(T₁,...,Tₘ) ∈ Φ(S) do
         replace Tⱼ by Top(NameStack(Tⱼ));
      endfor;
   endfor;
   foreach C ∈ Children(B) do
      call OPTRENAME(C);
   endfor;
   foreach I ∈ B in reverse execution order do
      if I ∈ DeadInstructions then
         foreach T ∈ Targets(I) do
            Pop(NameStack(T));
         endfor;
         delete I from B;
      else
         foreach T ∈ Targets(I)do
            replace T by Pop(NameStack(T));
         endfor;
      endif;
   endfor;
   foreach T₀ = φ(T₁,...,Tₙ) ∈ Φ(B) do
      replace T₀ by Pop(NameStack(T₀));
   endfor;
   EndBlock(B)
endprocedure;

foreach T ∈ Variables do
   NameStack(T) = ∅;
endfor;
DeadInstructions = ∅;
OPTRENAME(Entry);
```

conditional branch by an unconditional branch may eliminate ϕ-nodes in blocks that have not been processed yet.

8.2 Storing Information as well as Optimizations

The stack nature of the data structures used during SSA creation invite the recording of other information, such as the branches taken in the dominators and why. This information can be used to simplify the program flow graph. Particularly with nested DO loops, the zero-trip test for the outer loop may be the same as in an inner loop.

The algorithm can be modified to store this information also. Consider the point in the renaming algorithm where the children in the dominator tree are visited. Consider a block C with the following characteristics:

B is the direct dominator of C.

B is a direct predecessor of C in the flow graph.

Every other predecessor of C is dominated by C.

In this case the only way into C is through B. Look at the conditional expression controlling the branch from B to C. Perform the following insertions into the available-expression table:

- When the conditional expression has the form $T = constant$, where *constant* is a constant and C is the destination when the condition is true, enter the expression T in the available-expression table with the same name as the constant. The renaming process will now perform constant folding on the blocks dominated by C. Follow the same procedure if the conditional expression has the form $T \ne constant$ and C is the destination when the condition is false.

- If C is the destination when the conditional expression is true, enter the conditional expression in the available-expression table with the same name as the name for the constant *true*.

- If C is the destination when the conditional expression is false, enter the conditional expression in the available-expression table with the same name as the name for the constant *false*.

Now the normal available-expression processing, constant folding, and identities processing will simplify the algorithm. Consider the example

Figure 8.3 Eliminating a Conditional

```
i = 0;                              i = 0;
if (i < n)                          if (0 < n)
   do {                                do {
      j = 0;                              j = 0;
      if (j < n)                          do {
         do {                                a[i,j] = b[i,j];
            a[i,j] = b[i,j];                 j = j + 1;
            j = j + 1;                    } while (j < n);
         } while (j < n);                 i = i + 1;
      i = i + 1;                       } while (i < n);
   } while (i < n);
```

described earlier of two nested loops iterating over a square matrix, as shown in Figure 8.3. The code is written in C, mimicking the code that a front end will generate for a Fortran DO loop or a C **for** loop. The test for zero iterations of the loop is made explicit so that code motion out of loops can be done. The constant propagation modifies the test for the zero-iteration case to test *n* against 0. The occurrence of two tests of *n* against 0 is simplified by eliminating the second one—it is known that the value is true at that point by the information stored in the available-expression table.

The same information can be used to simplify range checks or checks for pointers being null. Although more complex methods can get better results, these tests are a good preamble to the more complex solutions since most cases are eliminated here.

8.3 Constant Propagation

Now that the flow graph is in SSA form, the compiler will perform constant propagation; in other words, it will determine the temporaries that hold a constant value through all possible executions of the flow graph and determine the value of the constant. Some of this has already occurred. The dominator-based value-numbering algorithm performed constant propagation when there was a single load of the constant and all of the uses were dominated by the single load. We must now address the problem of multiple loads of constants (Wegman and Zadeck 1985).

Ideally, the compiler simulates all possible executions of the flow graph and observes the temporaries that are constants. Of course this is impractical, so an approximation to this simulation must be created that can be implemented efficiently. What can the compiler do at compile time?

- If the single definition that defines the temporary is a load constant instruction, the compiler knows that the temporary holds that constant.

- If all of the operands of a ϕ-node are the same constant, the compiler can deduce that the value of the target temporary is the same constant.

- If all of the operands of an instruction are constants or an algebraic identity applies that indicates that a constant value results, then the target temporary is a constant.

- If the compiler can determine that certain paths are not possible because of other constants occurring in branching instructions, the compiler can ignore those paths.

The processing of ϕ-nodes presents the only difficulty. If the compiler has processed all of the predecessor blocks before processing a block that contains a ϕ-node, then the compiler knows whether all of the operands of the node are the same constant so that the target temporary can be described as constant or not. This order is not possible with loops. One of the predecessors cannot be processed before processing other blocks in the loop.

The compiler can make one of two choices when a ϕ-node is found for which all predecessors have not been processed. It can either assume that the node is not a constant (the pessimistic choice) or it can ignore that predecessor and make the determination using the other operands (the optimistic choice) with the understanding that the compiler must come back later and make sure that the additional operand does not violate the optimistic assumption made. During earlier dominator-based value numbering, the compiler made the pessimistic choice. Here the compiler makes the optimistic choice because it will find more opportunities for identifying constants.

8.3.1 Representing Arithmetic

While simulating the execution, the compiler will assign some symbolic value to each temporary. There are only three classes of values that the compiler records: undefined values, known constant values, and nonconstant values. The compiler adds an attribute *value* to each temporary to record the simulated value in this extended set of numbers. The arithmetic system includes the following members:

- A single element called *undefined,* TOP, or $\top$. This value represents the value of a temporary when no value has yet been assigned to it.

- A member for each constant representable in the target machine. We will use this most often for integer constants; however, it can be applied to floating or double-precision constants just as well.

- A single element called *varying*, BOTTOM, or $\bot$. This element represents the value of a temporary that the compiler has determined might not be a constant.

The values for the attribute *value* should be implemented as a variant record, union, or derived class. One field, which we will call *kind*, holds which kind of element this particular value is. The entry for constants will hold an additional field indicating the particular constant.

One important characteristic of this arithmetic system is that the *value* attribute of each temporary can only change twice. All of the temporaries except the formal parameters are initialized to have the value $\top$, indicating that they are undefined. As the algorithm progresses it will either mark a temporary as having a constant value or $\bot$, indicating that it has a varying value. Later the compiler may determine that what it thought was a constant was really varying, so it will change a particular constant value to $\bot$. Once a value becomes $\bot$, it is never changed back to a constant value. Once a value is defined, it can never become undefined. Therefore, the maximum sequence of values that a temporary can take is $\top$, constant, $\bot$.

8.3.2 Simulating the Arithmetic

The compiler needs a function to evaluate the effect of each instruction given the values of the operands in this extended arithmetic system, namely, *CP_EVALUATE,* which takes an instruction as an argument and updates the value of the target temporaries. It returns a Boolean value indicating whether any of the target temporaries has changed value.

CP_EVALUATE has a simple structure: It is one large **switch** or **case** statement with one entry for each opcode. The code for each opcode computes the effect of the instruction on each of the target temporaries and returns the value true if any of them changes value.

What are the arithmetic rules in this extended arithmetic? If you think of $\top$ as undefined and $\bot$ as varying, then the rules are what you would

Figure 8.4 Rules for Addition

Addition	$\top$	c_2: constant	$\bot$
$\top$	$\top$	$\top$	$\top$
c_1: constant	$\top$	$c_1 + c_2$	$\bot$
$\bot$	$\top$	$\bot$	$\bot$

expect. Consider the addition table in Figure 8.4. For two constant values the arithmetic is target-machine arithmetic. If one of the operands is undefined, then the whole value is undefined. If one of the operands has a varying value, then the whole addition has a varying value. The only surprise is that an undefined added to a varying temporary could immediately be declared a varying temporary. This is not done here so that the rules will match the rules for multiplication, where the distinction is important.

For multiplication and the logical operators, algebraic identities can be incorporated. Since $0 * X = 0$, one operand of a multiplication can be a varying temporary and a constant value can result, as long as the other operand is zero. The rules for multiplication (and the logical operators) must be extended to encode this as shown in Figure 8.5.

An undefined value times something else must give an undefined value. If undefined times a varying temporary were encoded as a varying temporary, then when the undefined value was discovered to be 0 and later discovered to be varying, the sequence of values for the target temporary would be $\top, \bot, 0, \bot$. The condition that the values can only change twice would therefore not be satisfied. The restriction does not cause any problems because any temporary that is evaluated in some execution of the flow graph will eventually change the undefined value to one of the other members of the arithmetic system.

Figure 8.5 Rules for Multiplication

Multiplication	$\top$	0	c_2: constant	$\bot$
$\top$	$\top$	$\top$	$\top$	$\top$
0	$\top$	0	0	0
c_1: constant	$\top$	0	$c_1 * c_2$	$\bot$
$\bot$	$\top$	0	$\bot$	$\bot$

Figure 8.6 Rules for Joins

ϕ-node	$\top$	c_2: constant	$\bot$
$\top$	$\top$	c_2	$\bot$
c_1	c_1	$c_1 == c_2\ ?\ c_1 : \bot$	$\bot$
$\bot$	$\bot$	$\bot$	$\bot$

What is the arithmetic of ϕ-nodes? This is where the optimistic view of constant propagation occurs in the algorithm. Any arguments that are undefined or $\top$ are ignored in computing the value of a ϕ-node.

- If any of the remaining arguments has value $\bot$, then the value of the ϕ-node is $\bot$.
- If any two arguments of the ϕ-node are distinct constants, then the value of the ϕ-node is $\bot$.
- If there is at least one constant operand and the previous conditions are met, then the value of the ϕ-node is that constant.
- Otherwise, all arguments of the ϕ-node are undefined, so the value of the ϕ-node is undefined.

For example, consider a block B with two predecessors and a ϕ-node in that block. If all of the operands have the same value, then that is the value of the target temporary. If two of the operands have different defined values (not $\top$), then the target temporary must be a varying temporary, i.e., $\bot$. When one of the operands has value $\top$, we make the most optimistic assumption—that it will later have the same value as one of the other operands. This gives the arithmetic table in Figure 8.6, which uses the C language's condition expression operator to indicate that the value is $\bot$ if the two constants are different.

8.3.3 Simulating Conditional Branches

Many programs are parameterized by constants that are set at compile time or fed as specific constant formal parameters at run time to choose one of several alternative operations within a procedure. This happens particularly when procedures have been inlined and some of the actual parameters were constants. The constant propagation algorithm needs to take advantage of this and eliminate the code that cannot be executed. To this end, we describe a set of rules for conditional branches, and jump-table instructions that will simulate the effect of the destinations of only the branches that the compiler can determine might be executed.

Initially all temporaries are given an undefined value, $\top$. If the argument to a conditional branch is undefined, it indicates that no possible paths out of this instruction are yet known, so the compiler will stop evaluating instructions at this point.

If the temporary involved in a conditional branch is $\bot$, then any possible destination of the branch is assumed to be executable, so both the true and false alternatives are simulated. For jump tables, all of the destinations are simulated.

If the temporary involved in a conditional branch is a constant, then that constant is used to determine which single destination is known to be possible. This destination is included in the simulation.

8.3.4 Simulating the Flow Graph

The compiler uses a simplified technique for simulating the flow graph. Instead of following each possible path through the graph (an impossible task, since some paths are arbitrarily long), the compiler uses the fact that a temporary can only change its value twice. Thus the compiler need only compute the effect of a temporary changing value, and that temporary can only change the effects of the instructions where the target temporaries are used.

These conditions suggest a work-list algorithm. When the compiler knows that an instruction can be executed on some path, it need not keep track of all of the paths. Instead it need only simulate the instruction when one of its operands changes. Since each operand can only change twice, the instruction will be simulated 2^n times, where n is the number of operands.

How does the compiler know when an instruction may be executed? When a block is executed, some of the successor blocks will be executed, depending on the value of the temporary controlling the conditional branch. An unconditional branch with an implicit true for the value of the branching condition will be executed. Since one conditional branch can introduce multiple possible destination blocks, a work-list algorithm is again suggested. So we have two work lists: one for the instructions needing reexecution and another for blocks that have become executable. The algorithm for the two combined work-list algorithms is given later. The algorithm uses the following data structures:

Dominator-Based Optimization

BlockList is a work list of blocks. A block enters the list whenever it is possible that the block might be executed, that is, each time the conditional branch in one of its predecessors indicates that this block has become executable.

Visit is the set of blocks that have been visited. The algorithm initializes this set to empty, inserts blocks, and checks for membership. The Briggs set algorithm is probably the best; however, it is overkill. A bit vector can be used also.

executable is an attribute added to each edge. The attribute has the value true when the edge is known to be executable under some circumstances. It is used to determine the value of φ-nodes, since some instructions in nonexecutable blocks may have been given constant values even though they are not executable.

WorkList contains the set of instructions that need reevaluation. It has the same operations as *BlockList,* so it too should use the Briggs set algorithm.

Before looking at the driver procedure that implements the work-list algorithms, let's first look at the support routines. *CP_Instruction* (Figure 8.7) is called whenever an instruction needs reevaluation. It uses the *CP_Evaluate*

Figure 8.7 Simulating an Instruction

```
procedure CP_Instruction(I: Instruction)
   if I is an arithmetic instruction or φ-node then
      if CP_Evaluate(I) then
         foreach T ∈ Targets(I) do
            foreach J ∈ Uses(T) do
               if J ∉ WorkList then
                  add J to WorkList;
               endif;
            endfor;
         endfor;
      endif;
   else if I is a conditional branching instruction then
      B := block containing I;
      foreach S ∈ Current Possible Destinations for I do
         if ¬ executable(B,S) then
            executable(B,S) := true;
            add (B,S) to BlockList;
         endif;
      endfor;
   endif;
endprocedure CP_Instruction;
```

procedure that we discussed earlier. The instructions that have a value are computed, and if the value has changed, then each of the uses of the resulting temporaries is marked for reevaluation by putting them on the work list.

Conditional branching instructions are checked to see if more destinations can now be reached. The algorithm computes the change using the attribute *executable*. If the attribute is already true, then the block has already been on the work list so it need not be entered again. The attribute is set to true and the destination entered in the work list for all executable blocks that previously had the false attribute.

The current possible destinations for a branching instruction are as follows. If the controlling temporary has value ⊤, there are no destinations. If the controlling temporary is a constant, then it is the corresponding destination for that constant. If the controlling temporary is a varying temporary with value ⊥, then all destinations are possible.

Simulating the execution of the block is shown in Figure 8.8. Each block is simulated again when one of its predecessor edges becomes executable. This changes the values of the ϕ-nodes. In fact, this change of the values of ϕ-nodes is the only reason that the instructions cannot be evaluated just once in an order in which the operands are evaluated before the instruction with the operands (reverse postorder, for instance). When a new edge is present, a new operand becomes relevant in each ϕ-node.

The first time a block is processed, all of the other instructions in the block are evaluated. After that the reprocessing of instructions will be driven by the reprocessing of the instructions to evaluate their operands.

The initialization code is shown in Figure 8.9. All of the sets are initialized to empty, all edges are initialized to not executable, and all temporaries are initialized to have an undefined value. The formal parameters need

Figure 8.8 Simulating a Block

```
procedure CP_Block(B: Block)
   foreach I ∈ Φ(B) do
      CP_Instruction(I);
   endfor;
   if B ∉ Visited then
      add B to Visited;
      foreach I ∈ B do
         CP_Instruction(I);
      endfor;
   endif;
endprocedure CP_Block;
```

Figure 8.9 Initialization of Constant Propagation

```
procedure CP_Initialize;
   foreach temporary T do          //Most temporaries undefined
      value(T) = ⊤;
   endfor;
   foreach formal parameter T do //Adjust formal parameters
      if T is known to be a constant then
         value(T) := that constant;
      else
         value(T) := ⊥;
      endif;
   endfor;
   foreach B ∈ N do
      foreach S ∈ Succ(B) do     //All edges not executable
         executable(B,S) := false;
      endfor;
      foreach I ∈ B do            //Fix unpredictable temporaries
         if I has unpredictable results then
            foreach T ∈ Targets(I) do
               value(T) := ⊥;
            endfor;
         endif;
      endfor;
   endfor;
   Visited = ∅;
   WorkList := ∅;
   BlockList := {Entry};
endprocedure CP_Initialize;
```

to take a different value. If a formal parameter is known to be a constant because interprocedural analysis has indicated that the same value is passed in all procedure calls within this program, then the formal parameter is initialized to have that constant value. Otherwise it is initialized to indicate that it has a defined but unknown value, that is, it is initialized to ⊥.

To start the whole algorithm, the entry block *Entry* is placed on the work list for blocks. There are no ϕ-nodes in *Entry;* however, it will force the evaluation of the instructions in the block and cascade through all of the other blocks as the work-list algorithm progresses.

The algorithms are designed to avoid evaluating instructions until the instruction is known to be executable. This cannot be done because the instructions are put on the instruction work list as soon as an operand changes whether it is in a block that is executable or not. The only place that this can have an effect is in ϕ-nodes. The ϕ-nodes are the collectors of values when there is a merge of control flow.

Figure 8.10 Main Constant Propagation Procedure

```
procedure Constant_Propagation;
   call CP_Initialize;
   while WorkList ≠ ∅ ∨ BlockList ≠ ∅ do
      while WorkList ≠ ∅ do
         take I from WorkList;
         call CP_Instruction(I);
      endwhile;
      while BlockList ≠ ∅ do
         take B from BlockList;
         call CP_Block(B);
      endwhile;
   endwhile;
endprocedure Constant_Propagation;
```

The complete constant propagation algorithm is combined in Figure 8.10. The complexity comes from the existence of two independent work lists. The algorithm completes when both are empty: No more instructions are changing values, and no more blocks are becoming executable. This algorithm is implemented as nested loops, although it could be implemented as one loop with conditional statements. This choice was made because it is expected that many more instructions will be reevaluated than edges made executable.

The constant propagation algorithm does not change the flow graph—it computes information about the flow graph. The compiler now uses this information to improve the graph in the following ways:

- The instructions corresponding to temporaries that evaluate as constants are modified to be load constant instructions.

- An edge that has not become executable is eliminated, and the conditional branching instruction representing that edge is modified to be a simpler instruction. The ϕ-nodes at the head of the edge are modified to have one less operand.

- Blocks that become unreachable are eliminated.

8.3.5 Other Uses of the Constant Propagation Algorithm

The basic constant propagation algorithm can be used in different ways by reinterpreting the ideas of arithmetic. We will see shortly that the algorithm is used to identify induction variables. Here we will describe how to use the algorithm to eliminate redundant checks for null points and to refine the

Dominator-Based Optimization

alias information provided by the static alias analysis component of the compiler.

Eliminating Null Pointer Checks

The compiler may not know the exact address; however, it can sometimes determine when a pointer is null. Consider a temporary that can hold a pointer or a null pointer. Pretend that there are four elements in the arithmetic: $\top$ and $\bot$ as before, and true (when the pointer is not null) and false (when the pointer is null).

- A copy operation gives the target temporary the same value as the source temporary.

- An instruction that checks for a null pointer and traps has as its output the value true. If the operand was a null pointer, the instruction would have aborted the program.

- An instruction that uses this contrived temporary to load a value has as an output the indication that this temporary is not null. This involves the creation of a new temporary and updating the flow graph since the compiler is working in SSA form.

- The flow graph is slightly modified. At a branch that checks for a null pointer, a new instruction with this temporary as target is inserted on the branching, indicating that the temporary is not null. The instruction simply records that the temporary has value "not a null pointer."

- All other temporaries have value $\bot$.

The constant propagation algorithm can now be applied to this contrived arithmetic. At the instructions where this contrived temporary is used, one can check the value to see the character of this temporary as a pointer. If one is executing one of the null-pointer test instructions and the value of the operand is "not a null pointer," then the test can be eliminated.

What we have done is interpreted a different idea as a system of arithmetic and applied the same constant propagation algorithm.

Alias Analysis Information

The alias analysis information can be improved by constant propagation in languages such as C where pointers can be created to any data structure and pointers can be incremented within a data structure.

Associate with each data structure a "tag" naming the data structure. Pretend that each load of an address constant gives a temporary that tag as a value. Normal arithmetic operations such as addition and subtraction take the same tag as one of the operands. Now we can define an arithmetic system containing ⊤, the set of tags, and ⊥.

Constant propagation can now be applied giving each temporary a tag or ⊥. The temporaries that have a tag value represent pointers into the data structure with that tag. A store through that temporary cannot modify the value in memory for any other region.

8.4 Computing Loop-Invariant Temporaries

The compiler is preparing for loop strength reduction: replacing certain multiplication operations by repeated additions.[1] This will involve three different operations. First the compiler must compute the temporaries that do not change in a loop. Second, the compiler will compute the set of induction temporaries: those that vary regularly in a loop. Finally, the compiler will restructure the expressions in the loop to increase the number of expressions that are loop invariant and replace multiplication of induction variables with loop-invariant expressions by a repeated addition.

DEFINITION **Loop Invariant:** A temporary T is a loop invariant in the loop L if it is either not computed in the loop or its operands are loop invariants.[2]

The definition is worded in this fashion to handle the case of loop-invariant temporaries that require multiple instructions to compute. If a temporary T represents the computation $(X + Y) * Z$, then it takes two instructions to compute T. If the definition specified that T is loop invariant if its operands are evaluated outside of L, then this expression would not be loop invariant because $X + Y$ would be evaluated inside the loop. A loop-invariant temporary is one in which the leaves of the corresponding expression tree are not evaluated in the loop.

---

1. There are two different uses of the term *strength reduction* in compiler literature. One use is the replacement of a multiplication by a power of two by a shift or replacing the multiplication by a constant by a collection of shift and add operations. I am using the term to refer to replacing multiplication of a regularly varying temporary by a constant in a loop with an addition.
2. This definition is used by Markstein, Markstein, and Zadeck in the ACM book on optimization that has yet to be published (Wegman et al. forthcoming).

Dominator-Based Optimization

The immediate reaction is to remove loop-invariant instructions from the loop. If they always evaluate to the same value, compute them outside the loop. However, doing so is not safe. A temporary (and its corresponding instruction) is loop invariant irrespective of where it occurs in the loop. It may occur in a conditional statement. Later optimizations will take care of that. The compiler only needs to know what is loop invariant and what is not.

To record the loop-invariant information, we add an attribute to the temporary T called *variant*(T), which contains the innermost loop in the loop tree in which T is not loop invariant. If T is invariant in every loop, then *variant*(T) is the root of the loop tree. If T is not invariant in any loop, then *variant*(T) is null. Recall that this is all being performed on the SSA form of the flow graph, so there is a single definition for each temporary and that definition dominates the uses in instructions.

Before describing the algorithm, let's consider each class of instructions and determine the meaning of loop invariance for each:

- Consider a ϕ-node $T_0 = \phi(T_1, \ldots, T_n)$. To determine that T_0 has the same value each time through a loop, the compiler must know the innermost loop in which each of the operands is invariant and know which block branches to the block containing the ϕ-node. The second condition is impractical to compute, so the compiler will assume that *variant*($T_0 = \phi(T_1, \ldots, T_n)$) is the innermost loop containing it.

- For an instruction that is a pure function, such as addition, multiplication, or disjunction, the instruction varies in the innermost loop in which one of the operands varies.

- A copy operation is a pure function in this situation, so the target is variant in the same containing loop in which the operand is variant.

- A LOAD instruction varies on the innermost loop in which a store operation might modify the same location (that is, the same tag).

The compiler needs an auxiliary function that gives the nearest common ancestor of two nodes of a tree, in this case the loop tree. The algorithm is simple: If either node is an ancestor of the other, then that node is the result. Otherwise choose one of the nodes and start walking toward the root until a node that is an ancestor to (or equal to) the other is found. The algorithm uses the preorder/postorder number test to check if one loop is an ancestor of the other. This check runs in constant time. The algorithm is given in Figure 8.11. The initial test for $L2$ being an ancestor of $L1$ is unnecessary for correct operation of the algorithm, but is included for efficiency.

Figure 8.11 Finding the Nearest Ancestor in a Tree

```
function Loop_Nearest_Ancestor(L1: Loop, L2: Loop) returns Loop;
   if isancestor(L2,L1) then
      return L2;
   endif;
   L := L1;
   while ¬isancestor(L,L2) do
      L := LoopParent(L);
   endwhile;
   return L;
endfunction Loop_Nearest_Ancestor;
```

If it does not improve the performance of the procedure then it should be removed.

For each instruction, the compiler computes the innermost loop in which the computation varies: a direct encoding of the conditions for the varying of any temporary. This algorithm is shown in Figure 8.12. The algorithm processes a block by first processing the ϕ-nodes in the block. The target temporaries are modified in the block and hence are varying in the innermost loop. The other temporaries are processed by looking at each of the operands. Find the innermost common loop for the current block B and the point of definition of the operand. Compare this value with the partially

Figure 8.12 Computing Nested Varying Loop

```
procedure Calculate_Loop_Invariants_block(B: Block);
   foreach T_0 = ϕ(T_1,...,T_n) ∈ Φ(B) do
      variant(T_0) = LoopParent(B);
   endfor;
   foreach I ∈ B in execution order do
      Varying = NULL;
      foreach T ∈ Operands(I) do
         declare (T_varying: Loop = Loop_Nearest_Ancestor(variant(T),B));
         if Loop_Nearest_Ancestor(Varying,T_varying) then
            Varying = T_varying;
         endif;
      endfor;
      foreach T ∈ Target(I) do
         variant(T) = Varying;
      endfor;
   endfor;
endprocedure Calculate_Loop_Invariants;
```

computed innermost varying loop for this instruction, held in *Varying*. If the operand is modified in a more inner loop this becomes the loop in which the instruction varies. After computing the results of all operands, the targets are given this innermost loop on which all of their operands depend.

Recall that static single assignment means that each temporary has a single instruction that evaluates it. It does not mean that each instruction has only one output. In fact, STORE instructions may be viewed as having multiple outputs.

The driving procedure must ensure that *variant* for each temporary is computed before it is used. Since *variant* is computed for each φ-node without using the information for the operands, a dominator tree walk will ensure that all operands have a value for *variant* before the instruction in which the operands are used. Hence the driving procedure uses the algorithm in Figure 8.13.

As with other static single assignment algorithms, this algorithm assumes that all LOAD instructions have another operand, called a *tag*, which is handled like a temporary for the purposes of renaming. Each STORE instruction modifies a particular storage location and a number of tags. There are φ-nodes included for the tags also. The tags are handled just like temporaries for the purposes of SSA computations and are handled like operands in this algorithm for computing invariant temporaries (and tags). Thus a load operation inside a loop will be invariant if the address expression is invariant and the tag is not modified by any store operation in the loop.

As an example, consider the running example and the instruction dSLD (T17) => SF1 in block B2. Consider the flow graph after initial dominator-based optimization has occurred. B2 is a block contained in the loop {B2,B6,B3}, which is contained in the loop {B1,B2,B6,B3,B4}. T17 is assigned a value in block B1, which is in this second loop; hence, *Varying*

Figure 8.13 Driver for Invariant-Code Identification

```
procedure CALCULATE_LOOP_INVARIANTS;
   call CALCULATE_DOMINATOR_TREE;
   call CALCULATE_LOOP_TREE;
   foreach B ∈ N in preorder on dominator tree do
      call Calculate_Loop_Invariants_Block(B);
   endfor;
endprocedure CALCULATE_LOOP_INVARIANTS;
```

starts out pointing at this outer loop. However, the store operation in block B6 also affects the load operation through the tag, so SF1 is marked as varying on the loop {B2,B6,B3}. However, T17 itself is marked as varying on the outer loop.

8.5 Computing Induction Variables

Before the expressions can be restructured to improve loops, the compiler must identify the temporaries that vary in a regular fashion. Now consider a single loop L and a temporary T that varies in L. Temporaries that are incremented by a predictable amount each time through the loop, called *induction temporaries*, are a more tractable form of loop-variant temporary. Operations on these temporaries can frequently be simplified—multiplications replaced by repeated additions, for example.[3] Since the flow graph is in static single assignment form, one cannot talk about incrementing a single temporary. Instead, a set of temporaries defines an induction set.

DEFINITION **Induction Candidates:** Given a loop L, a temporary T is a candidate temporary for L if and only if T is evaluated in L and the evaluation has one of the following forms:

$T = T_i \pm T_j$, where one of the two operands is a candidate temporary and the other operand is loop invariant in L.

$T = T_k$, where T_k is a candidate temporary in L.

$T = \pm T_k$, where T_k is a candidate temporary in L.

$T = T_l$, where T_l is a loop-invariant temporary in L.

$T = \phi(T_1, \ldots, T_m)$, where each of the operands is either a loop-invariant temporary in L or is a candidate temporary in L.

The set of candidate temporaries is computed by looking at the instruction that evaluates each temporary and eliminating those instructions that are not of the correct form. If the instructions are considered in evaluation order, then the compiler knows whether the operands are candidates. As usual, the only problem is that this is not true for ϕ-nodes. Some of the oper-

---

3. The description here is based on a description of strength reduction by Markstein (Wegman et al. forthcoming). That work and this are both based on the original paper by Allen, Cocke, and Kennedy (1981).

Figure 8.14 Finding Candidate Temporaries

```
procedure CALCULATE_CANDIDATES(L: Loop)
   Candidates = ∅;
   WorkList = ∅;
   foreach B ∈ L do                //Initialize sets
      foreach I ∈ Φ(B) ∪ B where I is T = ... do
         if Typeof(T) is integral then
            if T has form T = T_i ± T_j, T = ±T_k, T = T_l, T = φ(...) then
               add T to Candidates;
               add T to WorkList;
            endif;
         endif;
      endfor;
   endfor;
   while WorkList ≠ ∅ do       //Check recursive definition
      take T from WorkList;
      call CANDIDATE_PRUNE(T);
      if T ∉ Candidates then
         foreach I ∈ Uses(T) where I is in L do
            foreach U ∈ Targets(I) do
               if U ∈ Candidates ∧ U ∉ WorkList then
                  add U to WorkList;
               endif;
            endfor;
         endfor;
      endif;
   endwhile;
endprocedure CALCULATE_CANDIDATES;
```

ands of the φ-nodes may not have been processed already, so the compiler reverts to using a work-list algorithm in which all temporaries are first assumed to be candidate temporaries and are eliminated when the assumption is disproved. The algorithm is general; however, we will specifically eliminate nonintegral temporaries (floating-point temporaries in particular) because the compiler will not be applying strength reduction to these types.

A basic work-list algorithm is described in Figures 8.14 and 8.15. The algorithm computes the set of temporaries that are candidates for induction temporaries. It includes each temporary that is computed using the correct form of instruction from the definition and then eliminates temporaries whose evaluating instructions do not have the correct form of operands. When the algorithm stabilizes, the largest set of candidates available has been computed. How does one prove that? Clearly all candidates are in the initial set and only temporaries that would be removed with any set of

Figure 8.15 Pruning to a Valid Set of Temporaries

```
procedure CANDIDATE_PRUNE(T: temporary);
   case on form of I do
      T = ϕ(T_1,...,T_m):
         for i = 1 to m do
            if T_i ∉ Candidates ∧ T_i not loop invariant in L then
               remove T from Candidates;
               return;
            endif;
         endfor;
      T = T_i ± T_j:
         if T_i ∈ Candidates ∧ T_j is loop invariant in L then
            return;
         else if T_j ∈ Candidates ∧ T_i is loop invariant in L then
            return;
         else
            remove T from Candidates;
         endif;
      T = ±T_1 or T = T_1:
         if T_i ∉ Candidates then
            remove T from Candidates;
         endif;
      otherwise:
         system error;
   endcase;
endprocedure CANDIDATE_PRUNE;
```

candidates are removed, so the algorithm computes the maximum set of candidates.

The set of candidates describes the temporaries that are evaluated with the correct instructions in the loop; however, induction temporaries represent temporaries that are incremented in a regular fashion across iterations of the loop, with the value on the next iteration differing by a fixed amount from the values on the previous iterations. There are two possible interpretations of this idea.[4] This compiler uses the following definition.

DEFINITION **Induction Sets and Temporaries:** An induction temporary T in a loop L is a candidate with the following property. Consider the graph with the candidate tempo-

---

4. The other definition of induction variables also requires the induction temporary to change by the same amount each time through the loop following all possible paths through the loop. This is the definition needed for dependence analysis. It is more restrictive than needed for strength reduction.

Dominator-Based Optimization

raries as nodes with an edge between two candidates T and U if T is used to compute the value of U. An induction temporary is a candidate temporary that is a member of a strongly connected region in this graph. The set of temporaries in such a strongly connected region is called an induction set.

In other words, the temporary T is used to compute other temporaries, and those temporaries are used to compute others, until the resulting value is used to compute the value of T on the next iteration. Eventually the value of T is used to compute the value of T. For a single-entry loop, this means that the temporary is involved in a strongly connected region that contains a φ-node at the beginning of the loop.

The algorithm that the compiler used to compute loops cannot be used here. Starting at a φ-node and tracing backward may lead to a number of temporaries that are not in the strongly connected region. Instead, the general algorithm for a strongly connected region must be used. Since the algorithm is applied at several other places in the design, it will not be repeated here. The algorithm is summarized in Figure 8.16.

If the loop is not single entry, we will not bother to apply strength reduction here. A more limited version will be applied later. First calculate the candidate temporaries. Then implicitly create the graph. It does not need to be explicitly created because the form of the instructions evaluating the temporaries in *Candidates* is simple. Perform one of the two standard

Figure 8.16 Pruning Candidates to Induction Sets

```
procedure CALCULATE_INDUCTION(L: Loop)
   if L is of kind single_entry_loop then
      call CALCULATE_CANDIDATES(L);
      Consider graph with nodes being Candidates,
         the roots being the φ-nodes in LoopEntry(L);
         an edge between T and T' if T is used as an
         operand of T'.
      Compute the strongly connected regions of this graph.
      Anchors = {T|T is a target of a φ-node in LoopEntry(L)}
      foreach strongly connected region S do
         if |S| > 1 ∧ Anchors ∩ S ≠ ∅ then
            add S to the collection of induction sets;
         endif;
      endfor;
   endif;
endprocedure CALCULATE_INDUCTION;
```

Figure 8.17 Induction Temporary Example

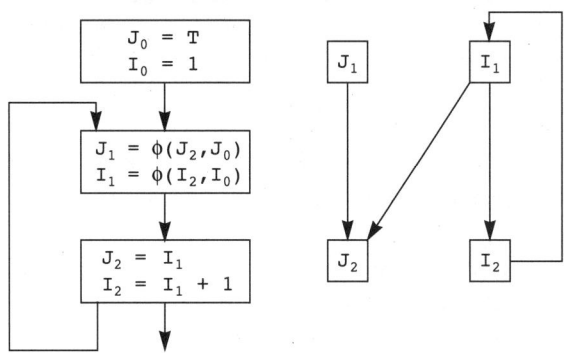

strongly connected region algorithms. Any strongly connected region with at least two members and which includes a temporary that is the target of a ϕ-node at the entry is an induction set.

As an example, consider Figure 8.17. The left column represents the flow graph for the loop, and the right column represents the implicit graph of the candidate temporaries. Note that J_1 and J_2 are not in a strongly connected region and if one had started at J_1 and had traversed the arcs backward one would never return to J_1, unlike the case of computing loops in the flow graph. The set $\{I_1, I_2\}$ represents the induction set in this example.

Consider one induction set $\{T_1, \ldots, T_k\}$. This is a strongly connected region in the graph of *Candidates* temporaries. The only temporaries that can have multiple predecessors in that graph are the ϕ-nodes. So the strongly connected regions have a special form: The normal instructions are divided into subsets that form paths, with the joins and separations occurring at the ϕ-nodes.

Now add one optimization after identifying the induction sets and induction temporaries. Consider three temporaries in an induction set, T_1, T_2, and T_3, where $T_2 = T_1 + RC_1$ and $T_3 = T_2 + RC_2$. Recompute T_3 as $T_3 = T_1 + (RC_1 + RC_2)$.

8.6 Reshaping Expressions

The compiler has now determined most of the expressions that are computed outside a loop, the expressions that are loop invariant in the loop,

Dominator-Based Optimization

and the induction variables within the loop. The compiler can now restructure the expressions to increase the number of expressions moved out of the loop later during partial redundancy elimination. This is done in a phase called **RESHAPE**.

RESHAPE uses the associativity and distributivity rules of integer and logical arithmetic to improve later code motion. Assume that there are n nested loops, L_1 to L_n. The compiler will reorganize each expression E to be of the form

$$E = E' + (LC_1 + (LC_2 + (LC_3 + \ldots + LC_n)))$$

where E' is an expression that is not loop invariant on the innermost loop, LC_1 is loop invariant on the innermost loop, LC_2 is loop invariant on the next-outer loop, and so on, until LC_n is loop invariant on the outermost loop. The same transformation will be made for multiplication and logical operators. This transformation allows the compiler to compute E' in the innermost loop while computing the right-hand operand outside the innermost loop. Similarly, LC_1 can be computed in the next-outer loop while the rest of the expression can be computed outside that loop. This repeats until LC_n can be computed outside the outermost loop.

The expression for E' can be written to expose the induction variables. The most important form of strength reduction involves integer multiplication. If one operand of a multiplication is an induction variable and the other operand does not change in the loop, then the repeated evaluation of the multiplication each time through the loop can be replaced by a repeated addition. To identify these cases, the compiler divides up E' into summands of the form

$$E' = E'' + FD_1 * I_1 + FD_2 * I_2 + \ldots + FD_m * I_m$$

where FD_j is a loop-invariant expression (*FD* is an abbreviation for *first difference*) and I_j is one of the induction variables in the innermost loop. Induction variables for the outer loops are loop constants here, so they are not a part of this expression.

There is danger in this transformation: Wholesale rewriting of expressions may increase the size of the generated code and decrease the execution speed. Most of the time this will not be the case. Consider the running example, in which strength reduction and rewriting the expressions collapses the code remarkably. However, there are cases where this is not true. The compiler attempts to avoid these situations by the following devices.

- It embeds the reassociation in a dominator tree walk used to eliminate redundant expressions. Thus each expression will probably be evaluated once.

- This phase of the compiler does not eliminate the original expressions. Later, after global optimization, dead-code elimination will remove them. Why? One of the problems with reassociation is that it can move expressions into loops. In fact it can move them into conditional expressions within loops. The compiler cannot move them out of these conditional expressions due to safety concerns. So the compiler leaves the original expressions in place, which causes those expressions to be available where the programmer originally placed them. If the compiler has not transformed the expression within the loop, the compiler will find that the moved expression is redundant and eliminate it from the loop.

There are four different categories of operators involved in reassociation. The rest of this discussion will use these names: addition, subtraction, and multiplication. However, there are many other operators that have the same characteristics: logical disjunction, logical conjunction, and logical negation, for instance. The compiler applies the same techniques to all of them. The techniques are not applied to floating-point operations because they are not associative or distributive in the literal sense. When using the term *associative*, the arithmetic must be literally associative, not approximately associative.

Commutative operators such as addition and multiplication have the property that $x + y = y + x$. For these operators, the compiler can reorder the operands in any order desired. In our compiler, the operands are reordered so that the one with the highest reverse-postorder number in the flow graph occurs first. This procedure combined with the *value_table* structure will automatically identify commuted redundant expressions.

Operations such as subtraction that are the combination of a commutative operation (addition) and an inverse operation (negation) are reordered like the corresponding commutative operator; however, an extra flag is maintained, indicating that a negation is also needed. When the instructions are regenerated after processing, the negation flag is used to create a subtraction operation rather than an addition.

Associative operations (such as addition) allow more processing. Assume that an associative operator is the root of an expression tree. Group together all of the operands of the associative operator at the root. In other words, if the compiler has $(x + y) + (w + z)$, handle it as a single operator with a list of operands x, y, w, z. The associative operator can then be rewritten as $(x + (y + (w + z)))$. If the associative operator is also commutative, the operands can be reordered so that the first operand is the one with the highest reverse postorder. This will automatically set up things so that the expressions for the inner loop are computed first, then the operands for the next-outer loop, and so on.[5]

Distributive operations, such as integer multiplication, are the fourth category. The rule $x * (y + z) = x * y + x * z$ can be used to rewrite combinations of addition, subtraction, and multiplication as a sum of products. Each term in the sum of products is the product of a constant (the subtraction contributes a −1 to the constant), induction temporaries, and other temporaries. Now the elements of the products can be ordered using the reverse postorder number as before, and the terms in the sum can be ordered by the maximum reverse postorder number of the components of the product. This gives the expression the form described at the beginning of the section.

Before the dominator walk of the blocks of the loop and at the same time that induction variables are being identified, identify all expressions with the following properties:

- The evaluation of the temporary is implemented with an associative operator. For these purposes, the compiler considers subtraction to be an addition with a negate flag.

- The temporary is used as the operand of an instruction that is not the same associative operator. In other words, the temporary represents the root of an expression tree where the operations near the root are all the same associative operator.

The key insight is that the static single assignment form allows the compiler to view the temporaries in the flow graph as nodes of the original expression trees. Consider two temporaries T_1 and T_2. T_1 can be considered the parent of T_2 in an expression tree if T_1 uses T_2 as an operand. Thus the edge from T_1 to T_2 is given by the *Definition* attribute of the *Operand* set for T_1 to get to the instruction, and the temporary is reached as the *Target* of that instruction.

---

5. This is an observation by Keith Cooper of Rice University.

Given the root of an expression tree, perform a tree walk of that expression tree, analyzing it as a sum of products and combining like terms. This sum of products need not be stored as instructions: It can be stored as a linked list of linked lists in temporary storage. Stop the tree walk when the compiler gets to a constant, LOAD instruction, variable temporary, or induction temporary.

Having recognized the tree, now rewrite it in instructions in the form described above. The only problem is reapplying distributivity. Dividing the expressions into pieces that are invariant in each of the enclosing loops is straightforward: The compiler has already ordered the operands, so the compiler need only divide the sum into the parts invariant in each loop.

For each of these sums, distribution should be applied in reverse. This is a greedy algorithm. Consider a sum and find the component of a term that is an operand of the largest number of terms. Apply distributivity to rewrite those terms as a product of that component with the sum of the other terms involving this component. Keep reapplying distributivity in this greedy fashion until no further rewriting can occur. Each of the products can now be divided into parts that are invariant in each of the enclosing loops by applying the same techniques as were used for addition.

Now we have a reformed expression tree in temporary storage. Rewrite the expressions as instructions in the flow graph. Leave the old expressions there. Use the dominator tree walk to determine if expressions are already available so that they need not be generated again, taking up space and potentially escaping later optimization phases and causing poor runtime performance. At this point go on to the next tree in dominator order.

8.7 Strength Reduction

At this point the hard work for strength reduction has been completed. Consider an incremental expression E having the form

$$E = FD_1 * I_1 + FD_2 * I_2 + FD_j * I_j + FD_m * I_m + (LC_1 + (LC_2 + (LC_3 + \ldots + LC_n)))$$

where I_j are the induction variables and all of the other expressions are loop invariant in the loop L. The idea of strength reduction is to compute this expression before entering the loop and update it each time one of its operands changes. Since the only operands that can change are the induction temporaries, we update E each time one of the induction temporaries changes.[6]

Since the flow graph is in static single assignment form, the compiler cannot update the temporary holding the value for E. Instead, the compiler must generate a collection of temporaries $E_0, \ldots, E_q$: one for each time one of the induction temporaries changes and one for each RC constant involved in a ϕ-node. Assignments to compute the value of each of these temporaries are inserted after the update of each one of the induction temporaries.

Besides generating new temporaries to hold the value of E, the compiler must update uses of the expression E. At each point that E is used, the value is stored in some temporary. The compiler must replace the uses of that temporary with the uses of these new temporaries. This is not difficult: The compiler walks through the loop using the dominator tree and keeps a table of redundant expressions. This information can be inserted in this table as a previous computation of E, which will make the real computation redundant and update the operands.

Where can the induction temporaries change? Let IS_i be the induction set associated with the induction temporary I_i. As noted earlier, the induction set replaces the idea of updating a temporary because the flow graph is in static single assignment form. The expression E changes whenever one of the temporaries in IS_i changes. Consider the cases:

- If T_1 and T_2 are members of IS_i where $T_1 = T_2 \pm RC$, update the value of E by inserting the computation $E_1 = E_2 \pm RC * FD_i$ after the evaluation of T_1. If the table of expressions indicates that $RC * FD_i$ is already available, then the instructions for it need not be inserted at this point in the flow graph; otherwise, insert the multiplication here to be cleaned up by partial redundancy elimination later (one hopes).

- If T_1 and T_2 are members of IS_i where $T_1 = \pm T_2$ (including the case of $T_1 = T_2$), insert a computation $E_1 = \pm E_2$ directly after the assignment to T_1.

---

6. This discussion is glossing over a hard problem. There may be many incremental expressions: Keeping and updating each one ties up most of the registers for the machine. For a few incremental expressions, the discussion given here is best. When there are more incremental expressions, it is probably better to consider the linear function of the induction temporaries as the incremental expression and add in the loop-invariant part separately. The linear function of the induction temporaries is likely to be reused many times in the same loop.

- If T_0 is a temporary in the induction set where $T_0 = \phi(T_1, \ldots, T_m)$, then a ϕ-node for E must be inserted at the head of the same block. Be careful: There may already be another ϕ-node for E in the block that was inserted for another induction set—only insert one ϕ-node for E. Consider each predecessor block in turn:

  - For predecessor block P, if the corresponding temporary T_i is in the induction set for T_0 then the corresponding entry in the new ϕ-node is the temporary holding the value of E at the end of P. Note that P must be in the loop; otherwise, the temporary would not be in the induction set. Also note that the value of E may not be the temporary when T_i was updated since E is updated by each of the induction sets.

  - If T_i is not in the induction set, then insert a computation of E at the end of block P and place the temporary holding that value into the corresponding entry in the ϕ-node. Be careful! There may already be a computation of the same expression available in P, so do not insert it if it is not necessary.

8.8 Reforming the Expressions of the Flow Graph

We have been working on the flow graph in static single assignment form. The compiler must now return the flow graph to normal form. This means that a partition of all the temporaries must be formed to rename them properly. To form this partition, note that no computations have been moved during these optimizations. Some computations have been moved and others reformed. In particular, all load operations are in the same places that they were originally. Some have been eliminated, but none have been moved. This means that the temporaries associated with load operations can all be renamed back to the temporary names that they had originally.

Now consider induction temporaries. Each induction set can be renamed to a single temporary holding the value as it is incremented around the loop. Since no computations have been moved, all of the uses of each of the induction temporaries die with the assignment to the next temporary, so the correctness condition for the partition is satisfied. Inductive expressions that have been reduced by strength reduction are no longer expression temporaries; they become variable temporaries like any other local variable.

All temporaries that are not expression temporaries can be renamed back to the original temporary that created them. Again, no use of the temporary has been moved.

Dominator-Based Optimization **219**

The compiler now has all of the leaves consistently named, so it reconstructs the expression temporary names by using the formal temporary table, as was done during the original building of the flow graph. How is this implemented? When the static single assignment form is created, keep an added attribute that is the original name of the temporary. Also keep a set of temporaries for each induction set.

8.9 Dead-Code Elimination

Two other static single assignment optimizations are described here that are executed later in the compiler. Dead-code elimination and global value numbering occur during the LIMIT phase, where the compiler is reducing the number of physical resources (such as registers and instructions) needed in the program. By describing them here, the reader is still immersed in the SSA formalism.

First consider dead-code elimination. The compiler does not attempt to remove instructions or temporaries as soon as there are no references to them. In fact, there are situations in which the compiler transforms the flow graph so that there are still references to temporaries, but the temporary is not used in computing data that is observable outside the subroutine described by the flow graph. This is particularly true of strength reduction, since all references to the loop index may be removed except the instructions that increment it. So there are still references to the temporary (namely, the instructions that increment it), but no uses of the temporary for computing something worthwhile.[7]

The dead-code elimination algorithm represents a simple idea. First mark the instructions that store into data structures outside the subprogram. These instructions are not dead. Then mark the instructions that compute each of the operands of these instructions. These instructions are not dead. Keep doing this until no more instructions are marked. The unmarked instructions are not used directly or indirectly in producing data that is available outside the subprogram so the instructions can be eliminated.

---

7. One might ask, why not apply dead-code elimination immediately after strength reduction? Because reassociation has occurred earlier. Reassociation has the effect of moving computations into a loop, possibly into a conditional statement within the loop. Partial redundancy will not be able to move the computation back out unless the original occurrence of the expression is still there to make the moved expression redundant.

There are two options for operands of conditional branch statements. The simplest option is to immediately declare that all instructions computing operands of conditional branches are important. The idea is that the path of computation is important.[8] This is a conservative approach, but more instructions can be eliminated by eliminating conditional branches where possible. This can be done with the following steps:

1. Do not initially mark the conditional branching instructions as important.

2. When an instruction in a block B is marked as important, then the appropriate conditional branching instructions that lead to B must be marked as important. Which instructions are these? The definition of control dependence indicates that the conditional instructions are the ones on which the block is control dependent. Therefore mark as important all of the conditional branch instructions for the edge on which the current block is control dependent.

3. After determining the instructions that are not dead, the compiler deals with the conditional instructions that are dead. If a conditional branch is dead, then no block that is control dependent on this edge has any instructions, so generate an unconditional branch to the immediate postdominator of this block.

The algorithm is implemented as a work-list algorithm, as in Figure 8.18. The set *Necessary* is the set of instructions that are needed in the program. Any instruction that is not in *Necessary* is dead and can be eliminated without modifying any data visible outside the subprogram represented by the flow graph. The algorithm initializes *Necessary* and the work list by scanning the flow graph to determine obviously necessary instructions. The obviously necessary instructions include procedure or function calls because they can modify global data, and all input/output (I/O) statements because they change the state of the operating system.

The second component of the algorithm determines all instructions that are necessary by using a work-list algorithm to compute a kind of transitive closure of the uses and *Necessary* relations. When processing an instruc-

---

8. This is what we did in the COMPASS Compiler Engine. The result is that many instructions are eliminated but the framework instructions implementing the flow graph remain, possibly generating loops with no computations within them except the increment of the loop index, or basic blocks with no instructions.

Figure 8.18 Eliminating Dead Code

```
procedure ELIMINATE_DEAD_CODE;
   WorkList = ∅;                  //Find obviously useful instructions
   Necessary = ∅;
   foreach B ∈ N do
      foreach I ∈ B do
         if (I stores into external data) ∨ (I is an I/O instruction) ∨
                (I is a function/procedure call) then
            add I to Necessary;
            add I to WorkList;
         endif;
      endfor;
   endfor;
   while WorkList ≠ ∅ do
      take I from WorkList;
      let B be block containing I;
      foreach edge(C,D) that B is control dependent on do
         foreach J branching statement in C branching to D do
            if J ∉ Necessary then
               add J to Necessary; add J to WorkList;
            endif;
         endfor;
      endfor;
      foreach T ∈ Operands(I) do
         J = Definition(T);
         if J ∉ Necessary then
            add J to Necessary; add J to WorkList;
         endif;
      endfor;
   endwhile;
   foreach B ∈ N do                //Eliminate unnecessary instructions
      foreach I ∈ B do
         if I ∉ Necessary then
            remove I from B;
         endif;
         if I is a branch and I ∉ Necessary then
            change branch to immediate postdominator of block;
         endif;
      endfor;
   endfor;
endprocedure ELIMINATE_DEAD_CODE;
```

tion, the algorithm first makes sure that the branches on which this instruction is control dependent are made necessary. Then it makes sure that all instructions that define the operands are made necessary. Note that this is a standard work-list algorithm: An instruction is only added to the work list the first time that the instruction is inserted into *Necessary*. In fact, the

Figure 8.19 Example of Dead-Code Elimination

```
                    T  = ...
                    I₀ = ...

   = T                          I₁ = φ(I₀, I₂)
                                I₂ = I₁ + 1

                    = T
```

work list is always the subset of instructions in *Necessary* that have not had their operands processed yet.

When the work list becomes empty, all instructions that might affect data outside the subprogram have been processed. All other instructions are eliminated, and branches to blocks that contain no instructions are redirected to the immediate postdominator block. Why the postdominator? If all instructions in the block have also been eliminated, then all branching instructions in the block have also been eliminated, so there are no instructions in blocks that are control dependent on it. But the control flow must branch somewhere. The first available block on any path to *Exit* is the immediate postdominator.

Consider the example in Figure 8.19. It is a simple conditional statement containing a simple loop. Assume that T is used to compute necessary data and the I's are used as a loop index that is no longer needed. That means that the body of the loop is unnecessary. The assignment to I in the initial block can be eliminated. The initial block's branch to the loop is changed into a branch to the join block at the bottom of the example.

8.10 Global Value Numbering

Later the compiler packs multiple temporaries into a single physical register. Two temporaries can be packed into the same physical register only when there is no point in the flow graph where the two temporaries both hold a needed value and the temporaries might contain different values. If they contain the same value, then clearly they can share a register. If the

Dominator-Based Optimization

points where they hold needed values are disjoint, they can also share a register. So the compiler must determine when two distinct temporaries are guaranteed to hold the same value.

Recall our discussion of value numbering for local and global optimization. So far, we have discussed value numbering within a block or between a dominator block and the blocks it dominates. How can the same idea be applied to values that have multiple points of definition? We need to know which temporaries have the same value. In other words, we are forming a partition of temporaries: All temporaries that are known to contain the same value are in the same element of the partition.

Unlike the partitions formed using UNION/FIND algorithms, this algorithm never merges elements of the partition. In fact, one never needs to know all of the elements of a partition. The only useful question is whether two temporaries are in the same partition, that is, whether they are guaranteed to hold the same value. To store this information, the compiler adds an attribute *value_representative* to each temporary. The *value_representative* is a representative member of the partition that is used to name the partition. It is the first temporary that is known to have the common value of all temporaries in this element of the partition. If two temporaries have the same temporary in their *value_representative* fields, they are known to have the same value.

Two temporaries have the same value if they are computed using the same operator and the operands have the same value. If there is ever any doubt, such as a subroutine call instruction or a STORE instruction that may be killing a number of temporaries, then the temporary is assumed to have an unknown value different from any other temporary. In other words, the target temporary is put in a new equivalence class by itself and becomes the representative for all other temporaries added later.

If there are no loops in the flow graph then computing this partition is simple. Visit the blocks in reverse postorder and the instructions within each block in execution order. When there are no loops, this guarantees that the instructions evaluating the operands are processed before the instructions in which they are used.

- Two temporaries that load the same constant are put in the same partition.

- Two temporaries that load a value from memory where the addresses have the same value and the memory locations have the same value are put in the same partition.

- Two instructions that have the same operation code with corresponding operands having the same *value_representative* field will have the same value. That is, the targets of two instructions with operands of the same value and the same operation code will generate the same result.

This bookkeeping can be done in a manner similar to the implementation of value numbering for blocks and dominators. The compiler can build a table called *value_table* that stores each of the instructions indexed by the operation code and the *value_representative* of the operands. A lookup is performed for each instruction as it is processed. If there is already an instruction with the same operation code and equivalent operands in the table, then the target temporary is put in the same partition as the target already in the table.

φ-nodes present two problems. First, these techniques cannot be used to determine if φ-nodes in distinct blocks generate the same result. Implicit in a φ-node is the idea of control flow, so the compiler must include the block as an implicit part of the operation code when dealing with φ-nodes. That is, the *value_table* entry for a φ-node includes the block in which it occurs. Two φ-nodes from the same block may generate the same result.

The second problem is that there is no way to sort the blocks to guarantee that all operands of φ-nodes are processed before the node itself. Consider a loop. There is a φ-node at the beginning of the loop for each temporary (in the normal flow graph) that is modified in the loop. When the compiler attempts to process the instructions in the loop, the tail of the loop has not been processed.

The compiler can handle these problems by iteration over the flow graph. Initially, the compiler makes an assumption about the operands of the φ-nodes and then iterates over the flow graph updating these assumptions. This is inefficient. Instead, the compiler iterates over a data structure called the SSA graph. It is implicit in that the information is already stored; this is just a different way of looking at it.[9]

Consider the set of temporaries to be a directed graph, called the SSA graph, where the nodes are the temporaries and (T_1, T_2) is an edge if T_1 is used as an operand in computing the instruction, with T_2 as a target. Then topologically sorting the SSA graph orders the instructions so that the computations of all operands precede the temporaries they are used to compute. The temporaries that cannot be sorted into such an order are the strongly connected regions of this graph.

---

9. This algorithm is from L. Taylor Simpson's thesis, "Value Redundancy Elimination," at Rice University (1996).

Dominator-Based Optimization

Recall that either standard algorithm for a strongly connected region computes the sets of temporaries that form the strongly connected regions: $C_1, \ldots, C_s$. In the process it also orders these sets of temporaries so that if $T_1 \in C_i$ and $T_2 \in C_j$ where $i < j$, then T_1 precedes T_2 in the reverse postorder of a depth-first search.

What do strongly connected regions look like in this graph? A strongly connected region is either a single instruction or a loop. A single instruction can be processed as discussed above.

All of the instructions in a loop should be processed simultaneously. Of course, this is not possible. The compiler must iterate through the instructions of the loop. The only problem is with the ϕ-nodes. The compiler will make an optimistic assumption about the effects of ϕ-nodes and then iterate through the loop, updating the assumptions until a consistent set of *value_representative* fields is found.

When the strongly connected region contains a cycle, some operands have not been evaluated. These can only occur as operands of ϕ-nodes. First consider what it means to process a ϕ-node. There are three possibilities:

- An entry has already been made in the value table for a ϕ-node in the same block with the corresponding equivalent operands. Thus the *value_representative* field for the target of the current ϕ-node is made the same as that of the ϕ-node in the table.

- If all operands of the ϕ-node are equivalent, then the target is made equivalent to each of the operands and this ϕ-node is entered in the value table.

- If all operands are not equivalent and an equivalent ϕ-node is not already in the value table, then the target of the ϕ-node is placed in a new partition; that is, it is made its own entry in the *value_representative* field and the information is entered in the value table.

Here is where the optimism comes into play. Consider all of the temporaries in a particular strongly connected region in the SSA graph. Order these temporaries in reverse postorder (remember that there is a single instruction with a temporary as the target). Now the instructions evaluating operands will be processed before the uses, except for some ϕ-nodes.

Consider the ϕ-nodes optimistically: If an operand has not been processed yet, assume that it does not affect the result. For each temporary, initially assign it a *value_representative* value of NULL to indicate that the temporary is not processed yet. Then ϕ-nodes are processed by ignoring the operands that have not yet been processed, hoping that they will have the same value as the other operands.

- If a corresponding entry is already available in the value table, then assign the target of this ϕ-node the same *value_representative* value.

- Consider the operands that do not have a *value_representative* attribute of NULL. If at least two of them have different values, then the target of the ϕ-node is placed in a new partition by itself and entered in the table. Since the temporaries are being scanned in reverse postorder, at least one of the operands will have been processed already.

- Consider the operands that do not have a *value_representative* attribute of NULL. If all of them have the same value, then add the target to the same partition (give it the same *value_representative* value) and enter the instruction in the table.

The instructions in the strongly connected region are repeatedly processed until no changes occur, that is, the *value_representative* fields are unchanged during a complete scan of the instructions. This generates two problems: avoiding creation of unnecessary partitions, and the pollution of the value table. During the processing of ϕ-nodes, a new partition is generated for the target if two of the operands differ. The compiler does not need to generate a new partition each time the set of instructions is scanned. Instead, note that if the *value_representative* field for the target of a ϕ-node already has a non-null value different from one of the operands, then it has already been placed in a new partition and so it need not be changed.

Pollution of the value table is good news and bad news. Remember that we are processing the SSA graph. There may be multiple strongly connected regions in this graph for each loop in the flow graph. The false information is good news because it will force potentially equivalent temporaries in another strongly connected region to make the same choices and get the same *value_representative* fields as in the current strongly connected region. It is bad news because false information is stored in the table, which might have adverse consequences later when processing instructions after the current strongly connected region.

The pollution is avoided by creating another table, called *scratch_table*, which has the same structure as *value_table*. During the processing of a strongly connected region, the scratch table is used rather than the value table. After the values have stabilized, the instructions are reprocessed using the value table.

Dominator-Based Optimization

One more point before summarizing the algorithm and giving an example: Algebraic simplification can be combined with this algorithm. Each time the compiler processes instructions, it processes them in execution order. Algebraic simplification and peephole optimizations can be applied during the processing step. In fact, constant folding can be combined with the processing step simultaneously. The description of constant propagation is not included here since constant propagation has already been applied at the point in this compiler where global value numbering is applied.

The algorithm is described in Figure 8.20. Recall that the SSA graph is simply the set of temporaries where (T_1, T_2) is an edge if T_1 is used as an operand of the evaluation of T_2, so the successor relation in this graph is given by the *Uses(T)* attribute and the predecessor in the graph is given by the *Definition(T)* attribute.

The algorithm calls *CALCULATE_GLOBAL_VALUE_SCC* to compute the global value numbers for temporaries in a strongly connected region of the SSA graph. When that calculation is completed, all of the temporaries have the correct *value_representative* field; however, the value table must be updated to reflect the existence of these instructions for future instructions outside the loop.

The description of the algorithm avoids some points that the implementer must face. The semantics of an instruction (such as a copy operation) may indicate that the target operand has the same value as one of the inputs, which the algorithm must reflect. This also occurs with the special processing of ϕ-nodes.

The algorithm in Figure 8.21 describes the processing of instructions in strongly connected regions. The processing is simpler than many algorithms since there are no strongly connected regions within strongly connected regions. The instructions are scanned repeatedly until there are no changes in the *value_representative* attributes. When an instruction is inserted in the tables, the keys for looking up information are the operation code (together with the block if it is a ϕ-node) and the *value_representative* entries for the operands. The value to be retrieved from the table is the *value_representative* value for the target. When an entry is made there are two possibilities: the resulting value is either the same as one of the operands or the resulting temporary is a new entry in a new partition. In the first case, the *value_representative* of the operand is used as the *value_representative* of the target. In the second case, the *value_representative* of the target is made to be itself, indicating a new partition.

Figure 8.20 Main Global Value-Numbering Algorithm

```
procedure CALCULATE_GLOBAL_VALUE;
   Consider the SSA graph SSA: Temporaries is the set of nodes
      and Uses(T) are the successors of T;
   Calculate the strongly connected regions of SSA: C_1,...,C_s
      ordered so that uses out a region precede the region
      and order temporaries in each region in reverse postorder;
   value_table = ∅;
   scratch_table = ∅;
   foreach T ∈ Temporaries do
      value_representative(T) = NULL;
   endfor;
   for i = 1 to s do
      if |C_i| > 1 then              //Strongly connected region
         call CALCULATE_GLOBAL_VALUE_SCC(C_i);
         foreach T ∈ C_i in reverse post-order on Definition(T) do
            I = Definition(T);
            U = value_representative(T);
            apply algebraic simplifications to I;
            if <opcode(I),value_repesentative(Operands(I))>
                     ∉ value_table then
               add <opcode(I),value_repesentative(Operands(I)),U> to
                  value_table;
            endif;
         endfor;
      else if I is a φ-node then
         call CALCULATE_φ_VALUE (I,value_table);
      else                           //Single instruction
         let C_i = {I};
         apply algebraic simplifications to I;
         T = Target(I);
         if <opcode(I),value_repesentative(Operands(I))>
                  ∉ value_table then
            value_representative(T) = T;
            add <opcode(I),value_repesentative(Operands(I)),T> to
               value_table;
         else
            value_representative(T) = value from value_table;
         endif;
      endif;
   endfor;
endprocedure CALCULATE_GLOBAL_VALUE;
```

Consider the fragment of the flow graph in the left column of Figure 8.22. Note that the corresponding *I* and *J* entries always have the same value. The right column represents the SSA graph for the same code. In this example there are four strongly connected regions: $C_1 = \{J_0\}$, $C_2 = \{J_1, J_2\}$, $C_3 = \{I_0\}$, $C_4 = \{I_1, I_2\}$, and $C_5 = \{U\}$. The regions are in the same order in which the

Dominator-Based Optimization

Figure 8.21 Processing Strongly Connected Regions

```
procedure CALCULATE_GLOBAL_VALUE_SCC(C: list of Temporaries);
   change = false;
   repeat
      foreach T ∈ C in reverse postorder do
         I = Definition(T);
         if I is φ-node then
            call Calculate_φ_node_value (I,scratch_table);
         else
            process algebraic simplification but don't change
                  instructions;
            if <opcode(I),value_representative(Operands(I))>
                  ∈ scratch_table then
               let newvalue = value returned by lookup;
            else
               newvalue = temporary representing output value;
               add <opcode(I),value_representative(Operands(I)),T> to
                  scratch_table;
            endif;
         endif;
         if newvalue ≠ value_representative(T) then
            change = true;
            value_representative(T) = newvalue;
         endif;
      endfor;
   until ¬ change;
endprocedure CALCULATE_GLOBAL_VALUE_SCC;
```

algorithm will process them. Note that all operands are evaluated before use when the uses and definitions are in different strongly connected regions and the temporaries are in reverse postorder within a strongly connected region. Now let us walk through the algorithm.

Figure 8.22 Global Value Example

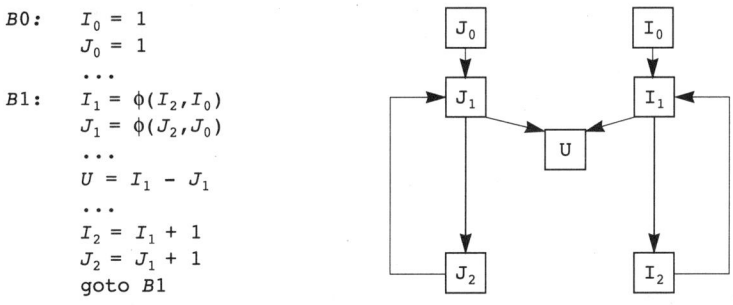

```
B0:    I_0 = 1
       J_0 = 1
       ...
B1:    I_1 = φ(I_2,I_0)
       J_1 = φ(J_2,J_0)
       ...
       U = I_1 - J_1
       ...
       I_2 = I_1 + 1
       J_2 = J_1 + 1
       goto B1
```

Figure 8.23 Entering ϕ-nodes in value_table

```
procedure CALCULATE_ϕ_node(I: Instruction, Tab: table);
   Let I be T_0 = ϕ(T_1, ..., T_n);
   if I ∉ Tab then
      if there is T_i, T_j such that
            value_representative(T_i) ≠ NULL
         ∧  value_representative(T_j) ≠ NULL
         ∧  value_representative(T_i) ≠ value_representative (T_j)
      then
            value_representative (T_0) = T_0
      else
            value_representative (T_0) =
               value_representative(T_i) where
               value_representative(T_i) ≠ NULL
      endif
      Enter I into Tab
   endif
endprocedure CALCULATE_ϕ-node;
```

The temporary J_0 is processed and the corresponding entry is made in the value table, indicating that this temporary has value 1. Now the first real strongly connected region is processed. Initially the algorithm will assume that J_1 is the same as J_0 since the latter is the only processed operand. It will then determine that J_2 must be 2 by algebraic simplification. The algorithm reprocesses J_1 and finds that the two operands of the ϕ-node are different, so J_1 is given itself as a representative of the new partition. Now J_2 does not have any simplification, so J_2 is given itself as a representative of the new partition. There will be no more changes in processing, so all of the real entries are put into the value table. However, the scratch table is left as it is.

The temporary I_0 is processed next. Because the operands of that instruction are the same as J_0, I_0 is given J_0 as its *value_representative* entry. We now come to the strongly connected region $\{I_1, I_2\}$. Initially, I_1 is given the same value as J_0 and I_0 since I_0 is the only processed operand to the ϕ-node. The nodes for this strongly connected region are processed just like the nodes for Js and since the information is in the scratch table, the same representatives are chosen. So, I_1 has the same value as J_1 and I_2 has the same value as J_2.

The compiler can determine that U has value 0 since it is the subtraction of two equal values. This is an example of algebraic simplification. This simplification is limited. If the example was changed so that U was added to I, before I is incremented, the algorithm would be unable to determine that the I and J temporaries were equal.

8.11 References

Allen, F. E., J. Cocke, and K. Kennedy. 1981. Reduction of operator strength. In *Program flow analysis: Theory and application,* edited by S. Muchnick and N. D. Jones. New York: Prentice-Hall.

Markstein, P. Forthcoming. Strength reduction. In unpublished book on optimization, edited by M. N. Wegman et al. Association of Computing Machinery.

Markstein, P., V. Markstein, and F. K. Zadeck. Forthcoming. In unpublished book on optimization, edited by M. N. Wegman et al. Association of Computing Machinery.

McKeeman, W. M. 1974. Symbol table access. In *Compiler construction: An advanced course,* edited by F. L. Bauer et al. Berlin, Germany: Springer-Verlag.

Simpson, L. T. 1996. Value-driven redundancy elimination. Ph.D. thesis, Computer Science Department, Rice University.

Wegman, M. N., and F. K. Zadeck. 1985. Constant propagation with conditional branches. *Conference Proceedings of Principles of Programming Languages XII,* 291–299.

9 ADVANCED TECHNIQUES

Here is the disappointing chapter, which I refer to as the black box chapter. Due to space and time considerations, the book cannot include information on dependence-analysis-based transformations and interprocedural analysis. However, this is the place in the compiler where these techniques are applied. So we will outline the ideas of these phases and refer the reader to the work of Wolfe (1996), Cooper (1988 and 1989), Torczon (1985), Callahan, Cooper, Kennedy, and Torczon (1986), and Hall (1991) for the details.[1]

At this point the flow graph has been simplified by constant folding, elimination of most redundant expressions, and algebraic simplification. The compiler now can do the advanced transformations that are the basis of much recent research. These are the transformations for improving the use of the memory caches and identifying parallel computations.

9.1 Interprocedural Analysis

Initially the compiler compiles each procedure individually, one procedure or flow graph at a time. In fact, the compiler is organized as a production line: Each procedure is translated into a flow graph and fed through the compiler, one at a time, until the results are added to the object file. With this structure, the compiler does not know about the effects of any procedure or function calls. It does not know which variables might be modified by each procedure call, so it must assume the worst.

For interprocedural analysis, this organization must be changed. However the change can be hidden inside the interprocedural analysis phase if

---

1. If a cohesive set of algorithms is not published by one of the researchers, this may be grounds for a second book to complete these ideas. I would rather see a book by one of the researchers that addressed these issues in sufficient detail. But if they do not, then we engineers must publish the work to help ourselves.

Figure 9.1 Schematic of Interprocedural Phase

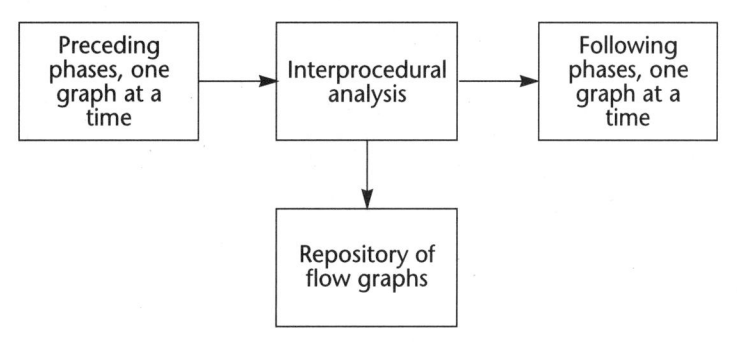

careful data abstractions are maintained. Interprocedural analysis requires information about multiple procedures within the application program, so the compile-one-at-a-time approach must be modified. Instead, the compiler must accumulate the flow graphs (and other data) for each procedure. When all of the flow graphs have been found, the whole program can be analyzed to find the effects of each procedure call more precisely. Then the rest of the compilation can occur, one flow graph at a time (see Figure 9.1).

In other words, the interprocedural analysis phase can be thought of as the stomach of the compiler. It gathers together all of the flow graphs of the application, processes them, and passes each one along to the rest of the compiler to be processed. As each flow graph is passed along, the interprocedural analysis information about its calls and where they are called are available for the optimizers and code generators.

There are many ways in which this repository of information can be stored. One approach is to keep a library of procedures and their flow graphs on the disk as a complex data structure that is updated each time a file in the application is compiled. Another approach is to keep the repository in memory. In our sample case, the whole application will be compiled together. Another alternative is to compile the flow graph into an intermediate form that is kept on the disk in place of the object module. Before linking, the rest of the compilation is completed on this predigested form.

9.1.1 The Call Graph

The important data structure during interprocedural analysis is the *call graph*. This is a directed graph built from the flow graphs of all of the procedures. Each node in the graph is one of the procedures or flow graphs being compiled. There is an arc in the graph between a node N_1 and N_2 if there is a procedure call in N_1 that might call N_2. The edge is annotated with information indicating the binding between formal parameters (dummy arguments) and actual parameters. More properly, this data structure is a multigraph since there may be more than one edge between two nodes.

The definition of the call graph used the word "might" because the compiler cannot always determine which procedure is being called. Each language has a mechanism for dealing with a procedure or function that is not known at compile time. Pascal has procedure/function parameters; C has function variables; Fortran allows the concept of function arguments. In these cases the compiler has more difficulty determining which procedure is being called. When there is a doubt, the compiler must assume that there is a call of each possible procedure.

When there are procedure parameters or variables, the construction of the call graph may be more complex than you might imagine. For normal procedure and function calls, the compiler need only construct an edge from the entry for one procedure to the other. When a procedure variable or parameter is involved, edges might need to be entered each time a new procedure is discovered in the application program. There are two excellent papers on computing the call graph, one by Ryder (1979) and one by Hall and Kennedy (1992).

9.1.2 Simple Interprocedural Analysis Information

Most interprocedural analysis information involves complex properties of the flow graph and usage patterns of variables. However, there is an important collection of simple interprocedural information that are also useful.

Remember our discussion of the three types of edges for a flow graph. To build a safe graph, the compiler is required to create an abnormal edge from blocks containing a procedure call to the *Exit* block. This edge is inserted to model the case in which the procedure call might execute a **longjmp** operation that will cause control flow to exit that procedure and cause the procedure that performed the call to arrive at one of the procedures involved in getting to this point in the application execution. If one knows that there are no **longjmp** or **exit** operations in a procedure or any of the procedures that it calls (a common case), then these edges need not be added.

Advanced Techniques **235**

Often all calls of a procedure will have one of the arguments the same in all calls. Usually, this argument represents some parameter that is always the same in this application, and the user is using some standard library of procedures for some resource. Although we will later allude to techniques to compute when arguments are constants, it is useful to compute the obvious ones initially.

9.1.3 Computing Interprocedural Alias Information

There are four other kinds of information computed during interprocedural analysis:

1. The interprocedural analyzer computes alias information. Consider the point in application execution immediately after a procedure call inside a procedure. Which of its formal parameters (dummy arguments) may reference the same memory location as another variable mentioned in the flow graph? This is only a problem for formal parameters passed by reference so that the actual parameter is a pointer to the data in memory. Interprocedural analysis will compute an estimate of which formal parameters might be sharing the same memory location as other formal parameters or global variables.

2. The interprocedural analyzer computes modification information. The compiler would like to know which variables and memory locations might be modified during a procedure call. This includes both the modification of arguments that are passed by reference and global variables that are modified as side effects. Again, the word "might" is used since it is too difficult to determine whether the data must be modified during a procedure call.

3. The interprocedural analyzer computes the variables that might be used in a procedure. Again, this includes both variables that are modified because they are associated with formal parameters that are passed by reference and global variables. As before, the information is only accurate to "might" rather than "must" standards.

4. The interprocedural analyzer computes the formal parameters that are always bound to a single constant in the application program.

I will not describe the computation of this information here, instead referring you to the papers referenced previously.

9.2 Inlining Procedures

The one part described in this chapter that is needed in any high-performance compiler is procedure inlining. Consider a function such as in Figure 9.2. The cost of calling the function and returning the value is probably more expensive than the actual execution of the function body. These costs can be avoided by substituting the body of the function into the calling procedure rather than inserting a procedure call. During the substitution, the formal parameters must be replaced by the actual parameters in such a fashion that the same computations will be performed after the substitution as would be performed by the function call, and local variables must be renamed so that they do not conflict with the variables in the calling procedure. Of course global variables—variables common between the called function and other functions—must not be renamed.

When should a function be expanded inline? There is no single good answer to that question because of the expansion/contraction problem. The expansion of a function inline within another function initially expands the size of the whole program. On the other hand, this expansion may make possible a number of simplifications that will result in a smaller program. Consider the example of a function that is a large **case** or **switch** statement with each alternative being a single statement. If a function call on that function with a constant actual parameter is replaced by an in-line expansion of the function, the program initially expands in size; however, constant propagation will eliminate all of the code except the corresponding one small alternative, thus making the program smaller and faster. Here is the logic that the compiler should use for deciding whether a function is to be expanded inline:

- If the compiler contains a compile-time command to expand a function inline, then expand it inline. This simply means that the programmer is telling the compiler to do it, so do it. Correspondingly, if a compile-time

Figure 9.2 Example of Function to Inline

```
function maximum(a,b: real) returns real;
   if a <= b then
      return b;
   else
      return a;
   endif;
endfunction maximum;
```

Advanced Techniques

directive indicates not to expand a function inline, then do not do it under any circumstances.

- If there is only one call on a function, then it can be expanded inline. This will decrease the amount of function-call overhead without increasing program size. This situation occurs with programs that are written in a top-down programming style. Such a programming style encourages the writing of functions called only once. If the resulting function is estimated to be larger than some size, such as the size of the fastest cache, then the expansion should not be performed automatically.

- If the compiler estimates that the size of the function body is smaller than the size of the function call, then the function can be expanded inline. The resulting program will be smaller and more efficient.

- If a procedure has one call site that represents a large fraction of all calls of the procedure, then that one call site can be expanded inline, whereas all other calls of the function will be implemented normally. This makes the highly frequent call inlined without inlining all of the calls.

- If the procedure has a flow graph that breaks into many small independent sections of code combined in a branching structure that looks like a **case** or **switch** statement on one of the formal parameters and that formal parameter is always a constant, then expand the procedure inline. In each call, only a small amount of code will remain after dead-code elimination.

- Otherwise, specify a heuristic choice function based on the size of the flow graph being inlined, the number of call sites, and the frequency information for the calls. If the function is small enough, it can always be inlined. If the function is a little bit larger, is frequently called, and has few call sites, then it can still be inlined.

How does the compiler perform in-line expansion? This compiler performs it in the interprocedural analysis phase, so it has all of the flow graphs for the procedures available. These flow graphs have had an initial level of optimization applied to them to clean up the flow graphs. In-line expansion consists of the following steps:

1. Consider the call site where a function is to be inlined. Break the block containing the call site into three parts: the portion before the call, the portion after the call, and the call itself.

2. Replace the block containing the call itself by a copy of the flow graph for the called procedure. In the process, rename the temporary names associated with the flow graph so they are all different from the temporaries that occur in other parts of the larger flow graph. This is a textual renaming problem that can be solved as the copy of the called flow graph is created.

3. In the new block representing the block that is the entry block to the called procedure in the copied flow graph, insert copy operations to copy the actual parameters into the temporaries representing the formal parameters in the called procedure.

For C, this form of in-line expansion is sufficient since all formal parameters are passed by value. For languages with pass-by-reference, a different mechanism should be used. Consider a formal parameter X that is bound to an actual parameter $A(I)$. One could compute the address of $A(I)$ and copy it into a temporary within the inlined called procedure. Each reference to X within the procedure can be replaced by a pointer dereference through the pointer; however, all information about the array A has been lost.

Instead, a more complex mechanism is helpful. Identify all loads and stores of X within the procedure. These are all simple load or store operations. To bind X to $A(I)$, create a new temporary T to hold the value of I and replace each simple load of X by an array load of $A(T)$. Similarly, replace each store of X by an array store of $A(T)$. This matches the semantics of pass-by-reference and keeps all information about A available for use. The temporary for T can be eliminated by optimization.

Before leaving in-line expansion, let's touch on one problem, observed by a number of implementers and studied by Keith Cooper (Cooper, Hall, and Torczon 1992), which involves decreases in performance that may occur with in-line expansion. The problem is exemplified by the procedure *DAXPY* in the *LINPACK* library. This is a simple loop to compute the sum of two vectors, where the second one is multiplied by a constant. If this procedure is expanded inline in *LINPACK*, the program may run slower. Why? This is a Fortran program, so the compiler (using the language rules) can assume that the formal parameters (dummy arguments) do not reference the same memory locations. However, *LINPACK* calls *DAXPY* with two of the arguments referencing the same array. The compiler is in a tough spot: Since the expressions are no longer formal parameters, it cannot assume that they are distinct and will generate slower code to ensure that the program runs properly.

There is no easy solution to this problem. The alias information needs to be expanded to record that within these particular blocks in the flow graph, the compiler may assume that two references to the same array are actually distinct locations. This would require flow-sensitive alias information, which is beyond the scope of this book (or the knowledge of the author).

9.3 Cloning Procedures

Cloning is a generalization of in-line expansion. Consider a procedure P that is called at a number of call sites $C_1, \ldots, C_m$ in the program. Procedure cloning occurs when the compiler notices that the set of call sites can be partitioned into subsets such that different versions of the procedure P can be used. The same version is used at all call sites within the same set in the partition. The different versions will run more quickly than the general procedure in each of the contexts in which the specialized version occurs. This is a research topic. The best discussion available is by Hall (1991).

The partitioning of the call sites involves the identification of some characteristic of the parameters. An easy case is a constant parameter that is used as the stride of a loop. More complex relationships can be identified by determining the dependency information for the flow graph in terms of the formal parameters. When the parameter has certain values, the procedure may be vectorizable, parallelizable, or have a form where the cache usage can be controlled.

There is one case of cloning that should be implemented whether the more advanced technique is implemented or not. Consider a function F that has n different call sites, $S_1, \ldots, S_n$. If there is one call site that is in a frequently executed region of the program and that call site executes a large proportion of all calls on F, then a copy of F should be expanded inline at that site. All other sites should execute a normal call on the original copy of F. The frequency and proportion of the calls is a parameter to be tuned, and the information to make the choice may be gathered by program profiling.

9.4 Simple Procedure-Level Optimization

Whether full interprocedural analysis is performed or cloning is implemented, there are several optimizations that can be made when the body of the calling and called procedures are known at compile time. Consider the two procedures in Figure 9.3. The first column represents the original two procedures. If this section of code is executed frequently, the loop can be

Figure 9.3 Moving a Loop Inside a Procedure

```
procedure CALLER;                          procedure CALLER;
   do I = 1 to n                              call NEWCALLED;
      call CALLED(A(I));                   endprocedure CALLER;
   enddo;
endprocedure CALLER;                       procedure NEWCALLED;
                                              do I = 1 to n
procedure CALLED(X);                             ... X ...
   ... X ...;                                 enddo;
endprocedure CALLED;                       endprocedure NEWCALLED;
```

moved into a new procedure made from a copy of *CALLED* in which the body of the procedure becomes the body of the loop. The parameters for *NEWCALLED* are not listed; however, enough information must be passed to describe the bounds of the loop and the original arguments.

This transformation decreases the amount of procedure overhead. At the same time, it increases the possibilities that the loop can be software pipelined, vectorized, or parallelized.

9.5 Dependence Analysis

Modern reduced instruction set computing (RISC) processors are fast. Most integer instructions take one cycle to execute. Floating-point operations are pipelined so that one or more instructions can be started on each cycle. The major impediment to fast program execution is memory references. The speed of memory is increasing more slowly than the speed of the processors. This chapter discusses the program transformations that can improve the speed of program execution. This discussion is an overview; further details can be found in books by Wolfe (1996) and Kennedy (forthcoming).

To see the kinds of analysis that the compiler must perform, consider the three loops in Figure 9.4. The first loop must be run sequentially. Each iteration of the loop must complete (or nearly complete) before the next itera-

Figure 9.4 Similar Loops, Different Executions

```
DO I = 2,N - 1            DO I = 2, N - 1           DO I = 2, N - 1
   A(I) = A(I-1) + 1.0        A(I) = A(I) + 1.0        A(I) = A(I+1) + 1.0
ENDDO                     ENDDO                     ENDDO
```

tion can begin, since the value $A(I - 1)$ is the value of $A(I)$ computed on the previous iteration of the loop. The iterations of the second loop may be executed in any order because $A(I)$ is not modified or used in any other iteration of the loop. This loop can be optimized for a parallel or vector machine. The third loop can be optimized for a vector machine, since the value of $A(I + 1)$ used is the value that existed before the loop was started. In other words, slight differences in the addresses of the values used in a loop can dramatically change the optimizations that can be applied to a loop.

As you can see, there are several different ways that the stores into $A(I)$ affect and are affected by the load operations from other elements of $A(I)$. The loads and stores involving other arrays do not affect the load or stores into the array A unless the memory for the arrays overlaps.

Definition   **Dependence:** Consider two instructions in the flow graph, I_1 and I_2. The instruction I_2 is dependent on I_1 if and only if there is a path in the flow graph from I_1 to I_2 and the instructions might reference the same memory location. There are several categories of dependence:

- The dependence is a *true dependence* if I_1 is a store operation and I_2 is a load operation. If a true dependence exists, then the compiler must always guarantee that I_1 is executed before I_2 because a value might be stored that is later used in I_2.

- The dependence is an *antidependence* if I_1 is a load operation and I_2 is a store operation. Again the compiler must guarantee that I_1 is executed before I_2; otherwise, I_2 might destroy the value needed by I_1 before it is used.

- The dependence is an *output dependence* if both instructions are store operations. Again the compiler cannot reorder the instructions because the compiler must ensure that the correct value is in memory for later references.

- The dependence is an *input dependence* if both instructions are load instructions. In this case (and in the case of no dependence), the compiler can reorder the instructions because no value can be changed before it is needed.

We have been talking about dependencies on instructions; however, the dependencies are really on the execution instances of the instructions. We summarize the information with respect to individual instructions rather than executions because the compiler will typically not create different instructions for different executions. However, the dependence information is computed with respect to the instances. In the examples above, the first loop has a true dependence, the second loop has no dependences, and the third loop has an antidependence.

Note that although there are paths from each store operation to itself in each of the loops, there are no output dependencies. This is where the different execution instances come into play. The path from the store instruction to itself involves going around the loop, so the store operation is into different memory locations; thus, there is no dependence.

The compiler performs an analysis called *dependence analysis* to determine the character of each of the loops, and records this information in a data structure called the *dependence graph*. The dependence graph contains the set of instructions in the flow graph as nodes. There is an edge between two instructions in the following cases:

- When there is a true, anti-, or output dependence between the instructions. In such cases, one of them must be a store operation and the other either a load or store operation.

- There is a dependence between two instructions I_1 and I_2, and therefore an edge, if I_1 evaluates a value into a temporary T and I_2 uses that temporary.

The compiler builds the dependence graph by considering each pair of memory reference instructions. Consider the first loop in Figure 9.4. There are two memory reference instructions: the store into $A(I)$ and the load from $A(I - 1)$. The compiler must first check to see if there is a path between the two instructions and then check to see if there is any situation where the two references might refer to the same memory location. This need not happen on the same iteration of the loop, so we are looking for two values I and I' such that

$$2 \leq I \leq N - 1$$
$$2 \leq I' \leq N - 1$$
$$I = I' - 1$$

The value of I is the index for the store operation, and I' is the index for the load operation. The first two inequalities indicate that the indices must be within the loop bounds. The equality indicates that the subscripts must be the same to be referencing the same location. Clearly there are values where this set of conditions is satisfied, so there is a dependence. The reference to the memory location by the load occurs on the next iteration after the store.[2]

If the array is multiply subscripted, then there is one equation for each subscript. Assuming that the language standard specifies that array subscripts

---

[2]. The compiler writer wishes to find no dependencies; in other words, one wants no solutions to exist. This will mean that there are no dependencies and the compiler therefore has the maximum flexibility in reordering the instructions.

Advanced Techniques

must be in bounds, the only way that two memory reference instructions can reference the same location is if each of the subscripts has identical value.

If there is more than one enclosing loop, then there would be extra pairs of loop indices: one for each loop, thus generating more inequalities. The problem is to solve both the set of equalities and inequalities simultaneously. There are four distinct techniques for doing this in the literature:

1. Ignore the inequalities and see if there are integer solutions to the equalities. This approach involves the use of Diophantine equation theory from number theory; however, it works well for single subscripts and loops.

2. Ignore the fact that the compiler is looking for integer solutions and consider the problem as a real-valued problem. Consider the inequalities as defining the domain of a real function, and the difference of the left side and right side of the equations as defining a real-valued function. This reduces the problem to determining that there is a zero in the domain. That will be true if the maximum is positive and the minimum is negative. There are clever formulas for estimating the maximum and minimum.

3. A more recent general method called the Omega test (Pugh 1992) will replace these two techniques. It uses a specialized form of integer programming solution that works well with these particular problems. It is much more precise than the previous two techniques.

4. Below you will see a simple test that works the vast majority of the time, leaving the other tests to deal with the difficult problems.

The dependence test given here is sufficient for software pipelining, discussed later. The test is described in terms of a doubly nested loop and a triply subscripted array. Consider the loop in Figure 9.5. It has been made overly complicated to show all of the possibilities. Note that the same loop

Figure 9.5 Simple Dependence Test

```
DO I = 1, N
   DO J = 1, M
      A(c*I+b, d*J+e, f*I+g) = ...
      ... = ... A(c*I+h, d*J+k, f*I+l)
   ENDDO
ENDDO
```

index is used in the corresponding subscript positions in references to A and that at most one loop index is used in any subscript positions. The lowercase letters refer to constants in the program, which are not specified so that a general formula can be obtained. In summary:

- Each subscript has the form *<constant> * <loop index> + <another constant>*

- The same loop index occurs in the same subscript location. This does not mean that the outermost index occurs in the first subscript; it means that if a loop index occurs in one of the positions, then it occurs in the same position in the other array reference.

For this example, one can write down the inequalities and equalities as done earlier. In this case, they will give

$$1 \leq I \leq N$$
$$1 \leq I' \leq N$$
$$1 \leq J \leq M$$
$$1 \leq J' \leq M$$
$$c * I + b = c * I' + h$$
$$d * J + e = d * J' + k$$
$$f * I + g = f * I' + l$$

This seems complex; however, one can directly solve for $I - I'$ and $J - J'$, getting

$$I - I' = (h - b)/c$$
$$J - J' = (k - e)/d$$
$$I - I' = (g - l)/f$$

In this case, there is an integer solution if and only if each denominator divides the numerator evenly and both expressions for $I - I'$ give the same answer. This is adequate to determine most dependencies. Of course the difference must also be less than the upper bound of the loop minus the lower bound so that there are two iterations that provide the difference.

9.6 Dependence-Based Transformations

Although we are not giving the theory for dependence-based transformations, we want to list the important examples that occur. Later we will see the most important one: software pipelining. During the scheduling of loops, the compiler will need to know if it can simultaneously execute parts of different iterations during the same actual loop in the machine. In this way the delays caused by lengthy instruction execution times can be hidden by wrapping the execution of the source loop around a smaller actual machine loop.

For a scalar machine, the actual problem is to avoid load and store operations as much as possible so that the loop is balanced. Consider the number of operations in a loop (usually just the floating-point operations are considered). If most of the time is spent performing the load and store operations, then the loop is memory-bound and the length of time to execute the floating-point operations is unimportant. If most of the time is taken executing floating-point operations, then the memory operations are not important. Unfortunately, loops are usually memory-bound. For a more detailed discussion of these points, see Hall, Kennedy, and McKinley (1991).

One way to decrease load and store operations is to recognize when a value is already in a temporary. We have techniques for doing this within the body of a loop, but dependence information is needed to do this around a loop. In the first loop in Figure 9.4, the value of $A(I - 1)$ loaded on an iteration of the loop is exactly the value of $A(I)$ stored on the previous iteration, so the compiler can remember the value in a temporary and eliminate the load operation, as is shown in Figure 9.6. This is called *scalar replacement*. One load operation was eliminated from the loop, leaving only one store operation.

In Figure 9.4, we saw simple relationships between the subscripts in load and store operations. We must handle more complex situations, as in Figure 9.7, involving multiple nested loops and more complex relationships among the subscripts. Note that in this case the variable I occurs as both the first and second subscripts of some of the memory references. The inner loops are also triangular—the lower bound of the inner loop depends on the loop index of the outer loop.

Figure 9.6 Scalar Replacement

```
IF (3<=N) THEN
   T = A(1)
   DO I = 2, N - 1
      T = T + 1.0
      A(I) = T
   ENDDO
ENDIF
```

Figure 9.7 More Complex Dependence

```
DOUBLE PRECISION A(N,N)
INTEGER I, J, K, N
DO I = 1, N
   A(I,I) = 1.0/A(I,I)
   DO J = I + 1, N
      A(J,I) = A(J,I) * A(I,I)
      DO K = I + 1, N
         A(J,K) = A(J,K) - A(J,I) * A(I,K)
      ENDDO
   ENDDO
ENDDO
```

The laundry list of transformations has already been given in Chapter 2. Instead of repeating the list, we will give the intent of each of the transformations in the following list:

Scalar replacement: As shown above, if the compiler can identify that a value is stored on the previous iteration of the loop, then the loop can be rewritten, eliminating the load and keeping the value in a temporary. This may involve some loop unrolling.

Loop interchange: Besides decreasing the load and store operations, the compiler wants to improve the chances that two references are in the same cache line. Thus the loops may be interchanged so that consecutive values are loaded.

Loop fusion: If there is a sequence of loops, then they may be combined. This will decrease loop overhead. If the loops load the same values it may also remove a number of load operations.

Loop distribution: If a large loop uses too many cache lines, the compiler can divide the loop into multiple loops (under the correct circumstances). This will decrease the cache usage, making it easier to fit the data in the cache.

Unroll and jam: Sometimes two iterations of the outer loop can be merged, decreasing the number of load operations if some load operations are shared between iterations.

9.7 Loop Unrolling

Sometimes the body of the loop is too small to use all of the computational units efficiently. In that case the loop may be unrolled. Consider the loop in the left column of Figure 9.8. It will not be software pipelined on an Alpha because the divide operation is not pipelined. However, the loop can be unrolled to hide as much of the memory latency as possible.

Unrolling the loop is a simple transformation: Make the appropriate number of copies of the loop body and adjust the loop index accordingly. Given the current compiler structure, one need not adjust the loop index, just leave copies of the assignment operation incrementing the index. The loop index will be fixed up by the identification of inductive temporaries and strength reduction during global optimization.

The more difficult issue with loop unrolling is to decide how much to unroll a loop. Some loops, such as those with conditional branching and procedure calls, do not benefit from unrolling. Thus the typical loop to unroll consists of a body that has sequential statements in it without branching. Loops that will be software pipelined should not be unrolled, since they will be unrolled later during the process of software pipelining. Repeating the unrolling will have no benefit and can harm software pipelining. If there are memory references that reference sequential locations in memory, it is probably a good idea to unroll enough to deal with a whole cache line.

There is another form of loop unrolling that applies even when the loop is not a counting loop. This technique has benefits when dealing with WHILE loops in which later instruction scheduling is done globally. Consider the loop in Figure 9.9. The compiler does not know how many times the loop will repeat. It can unroll the loop, leaving the termination conditions in place. In this example it has been turned into a BREAK statement meant to have the same semantics as the **break** statement in C. What is the benefit? Given a smart enough scheduler, the load of *A* can be moved backward to overlap the addition.

Figure 9.8 Loop and Unrolled Loop

```
DO I = 1, N                DO I = 1, N - 3, 4
   A(I) = B(I)/C(I)           A(I) = B(I)/C(I)
ENDDO                         A(I+1) = B(I+1)/C(I+1)
                              A(I+2) = B(I+2)/C(I+2)
                              A(I+3) = B(I+3)/C(I+3)
                           ENDDO
                           DO I = I, N
                              A(I) = B(I)/C(I)
                           ENDDO
```

Figure 9.9 Alternate Form of Unrolling

```
WHILE A(I) > 0 DO                WHILE A(I) > 0 DO
   B(I) = C(I) + A(I)               B(I) = C(I) + A(I)
   I = I + 1                        I = I + 1
ENDWHILE                            IF A(I) <= 0 THEN BREAK;
                                    B(I) = C(I) + A(I)
                                    I = I + 1
                                    IF A(I) <= 0 THEN BREAK
                                    B(I) = C(I) + A(I)
                                    I = I + 1
                                    IF A(I) <= 0 THEN BREAK
                                    B(I) = C(I) + A(I)
                                    I = I + 1
                                 ENDWHILE
```

9.8 References

Callahan, D., K. D. Cooper, K. Kennedy, and L. Torczon. 1986. Interprocedural constant propagation. *Proceedings of the SIGPLAN Symposium on Compiler Construction*, Palo Alto, CA. Published as *SIGPLAN Notices* 21(7): 152-161.

Cooper, K. D., M. W. Hall, and L. Torczon. 1992. Unexpected side effects of inline substitution: A case study. *ACM Letters on Programming Languages and Systems* 1(1): 22-32.

Cooper, K., and K. Kennedy. 1988. Interprocedural side-effect analysis in linear time. *Proceedings of the SIGPLAN 88 Symposium on Programming Language Design and Implementation,* Altanta, GA. Published as *SIGPLAN Notices* 23(7).

Cooper, K., and K. Kennedy. 1989. Fast interprocedural alias analysis. *Conference Record of the Sixteenth Annual Symposium on Principles of Programming Languages,* Austin, TX.

Hall, M. W. 1991. Managing interprocedural optimization. Ph.D. Thesis, Computer Science Department, Rice University.

Hall, M. W., and K. Kennedy. 1992. Efficient call graph analysis. *ACM Letters on Programming Languages and Systems* 1(3): 227-242.

Hall, M. W., K. Kennedy, and K. S. McKinley. 1991. Interprocedural transformations for parallel code generation. *Proceedings of the 1991 Conference on Supercomputing*, 424-434.

Pugh, W. 1992. The omega test: A fast and practical integer programming algorithm for dependence analysis. *Communications of the ACM* 8: 102-114.

Ryder, B. G. 1979. Constructing the call graph of a program. *IEEE Transactions on Software Engineering* SE-5(3).

Torczon, L., 1985. Compilation dependencies in an ambitious optimizing compiler. Ph.D. thesis, Computer Science Department, Rice University, Houston, TX.

Wolfe, M. 1996. *High performance compilers for parallel computing*. Reading, MA: Addison-Wesley.

10 GLOBAL OPTIMIZATION

The compiler next performs a complete optimization phase. Most global optimizations have already been performed. The compiler has performed constant propagation, value propagation, most strength reduction and redundant expression elimination, and has restructured expressions to improve movement of instructions out of loops. All of the optimizations performed so far involved changing the operands used in instructions or the insertion of instructions. No instructions have been moved. Now the compiler will move instructions to less frequent execution points, perform a more complete redundant expression elimination, and perform a different strength-reduction algorithm.

Consider the flow graph in Figure 10.1. The temporary T is evaluated at three points. The modification of T in block B6 means that the previous algorithms will not have eliminated any of the three evaluations. However, the evaluation of T in B2 is redundant due to the other two evaluations of T. Previous redundant expression elimination only identified redundant evaluations when there was a single evaluation in a dominator block. The evaluation of S in block B2 can be moved out of the loop starting at B2 and placed in a new block between B1 and B2.

The algorithm operates on each temporary individually. There are five types of instructions in the flow graph. These instructions can be identified by the operation code for the instruction; however, they also play a role in viewing each expression as an expression tree. At this point the expression tree is implicit, having been translated into individual computations; however, it is useful in understanding the larger structure of this optimizer.

- LOAD instructions are leaves of the expression trees. The LOAD instructions will be moved toward the *Entry* block to a point of less frequent execution. These instructions can be handled much like the normal

Figure 10.1 Opportunities for Global Optimization

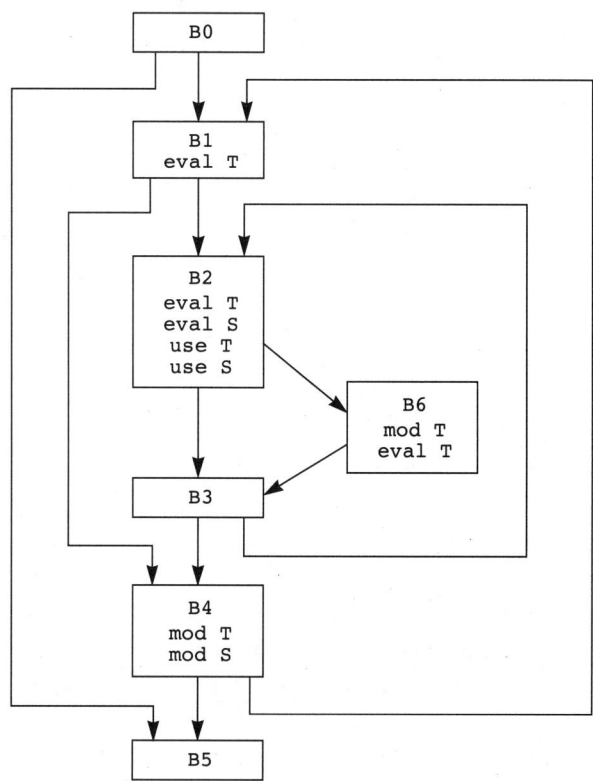

computational instructions, except that LOAD instructions can be killed by STORE instructions and procedure calls. During the transformation, the LOAD instruction is represented by the destination temporary. This is a unique identification by the assumptions we have made about the form of the flow graph.

- COPY instructions play two roles in expression trees. They occur at the roots of the tree, copying the result into the destination temporary or setting up for a STORE instruction. COPY instructions are the most difficult to move in the flow graph because moving the copy operation depends on both the uses and evaluation points of the temporaries involved in the copy. The copy operations will be moved toward the *Entry* block to a point of less frequent execution. This optimization will happen rarely;

Global Optimization

however, it is important when it can happen. During this transformation, the copy operation is represented by a pair: the source temporary and the target temporary. This is a unique representation of the instruction since it completely represents the instruction.

- STORE instructions will be moved either toward *Entry* or toward *Exit*. In effect, they do not occur in the expression trees. Rather, they occur after the copy operation at the root of the tree. During the transformation, the store operation is represented by the temporary being stored. This is a unique representation for all store operations; however, it conflicts with the use of the same temporary for load operations, so separate sets of global and local information are computed for store operations.

- Computational instructions are pure functions that compute a value depending only on their operands. These instructions will be moved toward *Entry* to a point of less frequent execution. We will see that by using this form of partial redundancy elimination these computations can be moved independent of LOAD, STORE, and other computational instructions. During the transformation, the instruction is represented by the destination temporary, which uniquely represents the instruction by the conventions for the flow graph.

- The final class of instructions are those that determine the structure of the flow graph, such as procedure calls and branching instructions. These instructions are left in place by these optimizations and are not moved.

The optimization algorithm computes points in the flow graph where the insertion of evaluations of T will make all present evaluations of T redundant. Then the algorithm eliminates all of the original evaluations. If the algorithm attempts to insert an evaluation into a block that already contains an evaluation, neither the insertion nor the deletion will be performed.

There are three different algorithms depending on the class of instructions to be optimized. The rest of this chapter will describe the algorithms and apply them to the running example.

Partial redundancy elimination (PRE): This transformation includes moving expressions out of loops and eliminating redundant expressions. The compiler determines new positions in the flow graph at which to insert evaluations of temporaries to make all of the original evaluations redundant. The particular form of partial redundancy used here is a derivative of lazy code motion, which ensures that computations are not moved unless there is some path that guarantees a decrease of computations.

Strength reduction (SR): Using a modification of the partial redundancy algorithm, the compiler can further optimize temporaries that are functions of induction temporaries. This handles some of the strength-reduction situations that were not handled earlier in the dominator-based transformation phases.

Load-store motion (LSM): Another generalization of partial redundancy elimination, this technique will move loads of data backward out of loops and move stores forward out of loops in some situations in which the data changes in the loop (that is, the data is not loop invariant).

10.1 Main Structure of the Optimization Phase

The compiler organizes the global optimization phase as a work-list algorithm. The compiler has already identified evaluations of temporaries T that have a single evaluation of T that dominates them and makes them redundant. This category includes most of the redundant evaluations of temporaries. This phase deals with the rarer instances in which evaluations have multiple preceding evaluations that make the current evaluation redundant, and cases in which evaluations are partially redundant.

Since these instances are rarer, the compiler can use a slightly more complex technique for transforming the flow graph that avoids two problems: excessive memory use in the compiler and the necessity of repeated applications of the transformations. Most global optimizing compilers use a set representation to store the information needed for partial redundancy. Some of this information is highly sparse, making the compiler compute a large data structure and then scan it, which is costly in system time and compiler run time. Second, some of these transformations create further opportunities for transformation. The usual solution is to run all or part of the transformation a second or even more times. Again, this is expensive.

The compiler avoids these two problems by treating each temporary individually and using a work-list algorithm to reprocess only those temporaries that might have an opportunity for further improvement. The structure of the phase is given in Figure 10.2. To avoid the problems of intermixing the processing of expressions, copies, and store operations, three different queues are maintained for them. In each pass through the work-list algorithm, the expressions are handled first, then the copies, and finally the store operations. The store and copy operations must update the local information when they move store and copy operations. If the com-

Figure 10.2 Main Global Optimization Procedure

```
procedure GLOBAL_OPTIMIZATION;
    declare
        WorkList: queue of Temporary = Expression and LOAD temporaries;
        STORE_WorkList: queue of Temporary = STORE temporaries;
        Copy_WorkList: queue of Temporary = Copy temporaries;
    enddeclare;
    call COMPUTE_INDUCTION;
    call COMPUTE_LOCAL_INFORMATION;
    while (WorkList ≠ ∅) ∨ (Copy_WorkList ≠ ∅) ∨ (STORE_WorkList ≠ ∅) do
        while WorkList ≠ ∅ do
            take T from WorkList;
            call TRANSFORM_LOAD_AND_EXPRESSION(T);
        endwhile;
        while Copy_WorkList ≠ ∅ do
            take T from Copy_WorkList;
            call TRANSFORM_COPIES(T);
        endwhile;
        while STORE_WorkList ≠ ∅ do
            take T from STORE_WorkList;
            call TRANSFORM_STORES(T);
        endwhile;
    endwhile;
endprocedure GLOBAL_OPTIMIZATION;
```

piler writer finds this process too expensive, the number of iterations of the work-list algorithm can be limited because the flow graph represents a correct program after each transformation.

Each temporary is processed independently. We will show below that there is no interaction between the motion of expression temporaries. For load and copy operations, the interactions are handled by reprocessing. The store operations are reprocessed with the load operations; however, the motion of store operations is less sensitive to the motion of other operations.

10.2 Theory and Algorithms

The execution of the program represented by the flow graph is modeled by a path through the flow graph from *Entry* to *Exit*. When transforming the placement of evaluations of a temporary T, these transformations operate by inserting copies of the evaluation at some points in the flow graph. These insertions make some of the other evaluations of T redundant and thus the latter can be eliminated. There are two limitations on the points at which evaluations of T can be inserted and other copies deleted:

Safety: An evaluation of T can be inserted at a point p only when every path leaving p contains an evaluation of T that is not preceded by an instruction that kills T. Thus an insertion can only occur at points where the temporary is guaranteed to be evaluated later with the same operands. The later evaluation would get the same result with the same side effects, such as division by zero. Recall the definition of anticipation. This condition is identical to saying that T is anticipated at p.

Profitability: Consider any path from *Entry* to *Exit*. The number of evaluations of T on the path after the insertions and deletions must be no larger than the number of evaluations of T on the path before the transformation. The number cannot increase; it is hoped that it will decrease, allowing the program to execute more quickly.

Consider the temporary T in Figure 10.1. The evaluation at the beginning of block B2 is redundant, so it can be eliminated without the insertion of any new copies of the evaluation of T. Any path starting at *Entry* and going to *Exit* will go through either B1 or B6 just before going through B2, so the evaluation will already have occurred.

With the temporary S in Figure 10.1, the transformation will perform an insertion. A new block will be inserted between B1 and B2 containing an evaluation of S. This makes the evaluation of S in B2 redundant. Consider any path going from *Entry* to *Exit*. If the edge between B1 and B2 is traversed, then the loop must be executed at least once, so the new evaluation and the elimination of the old one do not increase the number of evaluations. If the loop is iterated more than once, then there is a decrease in the number of evaluations because the edge from B1 to B2 is outside the loop.

Although we have discussed loops, the algorithms have no knowledge of loops. The loop tree is not needed. Instead the algorithms rely on the concept of paths and the number of occurrences of an evaluation on a path.

10.2.1 Outline of Elimination of Partial Redundancy

Computing the points at which to insert evaluations of T is a two-step process. First the algorithm computes the earliest points in the flow graph (those points nearest *Entry*) where evaluations of T can be inserted without violating safety or profitability. In fact, the algorithm guarantees the minimal number of evaluations of T on all paths. Then the insertion points are pushed later on each path until the last points where the insertions can occur without increasing the number of executed evaluations.

10.2.2 Computing the Earliest Points of Insertion

We will use the lazy code motion[1] variant of partial redundancy elimination.[2] This algorithm determines the earliest points in the program at which evaluations of T can be inserted to make all evaluations of T redundant. These points must satisfy the conditions of safety and profitability.

We will consider the insertion of evaluations of T on the edges of the program flow graph. This means that one needs to evaluate T if one traverses that edge. If the edge has only one predecessor, this is the same as inserting the instruction in the predecessor. If the edge has only one successor, this is the same as inserting the instruction in the successor. If evaluations of T are going to be inserted on each edge into a block, then insert the evaluation in the beginning of the block instead. Otherwise, if the instruction is to be inserted on an edge, create an empty basic block with one successor, the head of the original edge. Make the new block be the successor of the tail. In effect, one has spliced an empty basic block into the middle of the edge.

Now consider an arbitrary edge (P, S). Under what conditions would it be the earliest point at which to insert an evaluation of T?

- First, T must be anticipated at the beginning of S. If it is not, then the insertion is not safe since there is some path to an exit that does not already contain an evaluation of T.

- T should not be available at the end of P. If it is available at the end of P, then there is no point in inserting a new copy, since it would only create two evaluations in succession on some path.

- There must be some reason that the computation cannot be placed earlier. There are only two possibilities: Either T is killed in the preceding block P or T is not anticipated at the end of P. The second condition means there is a path out of P that does not contain an evaluation of T.

---

1. The original algorithm was developed by Knoop, Ruthing, and Steffen (1992). We will use a variant developed by Drechsler and Stadel (1993) because it fits the compiler framework we have developed better.
2. Developed by Etienne Morel (Morel and Renvoise 1979).

Figure 10.3 Earliest Placement Equations

$$EARLIEST_{P,S} = \begin{cases} ANTIN_S \cap \overline{AVOUT_P} & \text{if } P = Entry \\ ANTIN_S \cap \overline{AVOUT_P} \cap (KILL_P \cup \overline{ANTOUT_P}) & \text{otherwise} \end{cases}$$

We can directly translate these conditions into a set of equations, as in Figure 10.3. Unfortunately, the intuition above does not constitute a proof that placing evaluations of T at these points will make all original evaluations redundant or decrease the number of evaluations executed.

LEMMA E1 Consider any path from *Entry* to a block B with $ANTLOC_B$ = true, then either

There is an edge (P,S) with $EARLIEST_{P,S}$ = true and there are no evaluations of T or instructions killing T between the beginning of S and the beginning of B on the path, or

There is some block C on the path that contains an evaluation of T and there are no instructions that kill T on the path between the evaluation in C and the beginning of B.

Informally, this means that on each path through the flow graph each original evaluation of T is either redundant on the path or preceded by an edge where *EARLIEST* is true. So placement of evaluations at each point where *EARLIEST* is true will make all original evaluations redundant.

PROOF Since we have two conditions, we will assume that one is false and prove that the other is true. Assume that walking backward along the path from B one reaches either *Entry* or an instruction killing T before reaching an evaluation of T. In other words, assume that the second condition is false. Consider the subpath consisting of the part of the original path from the killing instruction (or *Entry*) to B.

First note that *AVOUT* is false for each block on this subpath. Remember that *AVOUT* is true only if there is an evaluation on each path leading to the point. The subpath we are considering is one such path that begins either with *Entry* or an instruction that kills T. If *AVOUT* is true, there must be some evaluation of T on the subpath, contradicting the assumption made at the beginning of the proof.

Now consider the two cases:

- Assume that the subpath goes all of the way back to *Entry*. Now start walking backward on the subpath again, starting at B. T is anticipated at B since $ANTLOC_B$ = true and there are no instructions on the subpath that kill T. Walk backward along the path until one comes to a block S where T is anticipated at the beginning of S but not at the end of its predecessor, P. Go back and look at the formulas for *EARLIEST*. They are satisfied for (P, S). If T is anticipated at the beginning of each block, simply make P be *Entry* and S its successor on the path.

- Assume that the subpath starts with a block C that does kill T. Again perform the backward walk starting at B looking for the first block S where T is anticipated in S but not in its predecessor P. Then the formulas for *EARLIEST* are satisfied. If there is no such block, then make P be C and S be the successor of C. Again the formulas are satisfied because the conjunction is satisfied, C killing T.

Before going on we need an auxiliary fact about available temporaries.

LEMMA E2 Assume T is available at the beginning of B. Consider a path from *Entry* to B. Let block C be the last block on the path that contains an evaluation of T. Then $AVOUT_D$ = true for each block from (and including) C up to (but not including) B.

PROOF Since T is available at the beginning of B, each block D (except C) contains no evaluations of T and contains no instructions that kill T. Assume that $AVOUT_D$ = false; then there is a path from *Entry* to D that either does not contain an evaluation of T, or the last evaluation of T is followed by an instruction that kills T. Piece this path together with the original path from D to B. This gives us a path that does not contain an evaluation of T or the last evaluation of T is followed by an instruction that kills T. Thus T is not available at the beginning of B. Thus there is a contradiction.

We now know that insertions at the points where *EARLIEST* is true make the original evaluations redundant. Now we must show that we have not made too many insertions. If an evaluation is redundant, do any insertions occur? No!

LEMMA E3 If T is available at the beginning of block B, then on any path from *Entry* to B there is no edge (P,S) where $EARLIEST_{P,S}$ = true following the last evaluation of T on the path.

PROOF Since T is available at the beginning of T, $AVOUT_C$ = true for each block on the path following the last evaluation of T on the path, by Lemma E2. The equations for *EARLIEST* indicate that none of the edges after that last evaluation can give a result of true.

The more complete question is whether the insertions at these points would be profitable. In other words, is there any path that contains two edges where *EARLIEST* is true that is not separated by an original evaluation?

LEMMA E4 Let (P, S) and (Q, R) be two edges in the flow graph. Assume that there is a path from S to Q that contains no instructions that kill T. If $EARLIEST_{P,S}$ = true and $EARLIEST_{Q,R}$ = true, then there is an evaluation of T on this path.

PROOF Look at the equations for *EARLIEST*. $EARLIEST_{Q,R}$ = true and Q is part of the path, so Q does not kill T. So $ANTOUT_Q$ = false. Assume there is no evaluation of T on the path. Then we have a path from S to Q and extended on that does not contain an evalution of T before an instruction killing T. So $ANTIN_S$ = false by the definition of anticipation. This is a contradiction, since $EARLIEST_{P,S}$ = true requires that $ANTIN_S$ = true.

THEOREM E Consider the program transformation in which evaluations of T are inserted on each edge (P,S) where $EARLIEST_{P,S}$ = true and the initial evaluation of T in each block B where $ANTLOC_B$ = true is deleted. This transformation satisfies the following conditions:

Safety: Every path from a point of insertion to *Exit* arrives at a point of evaluation of T before *Exit* or an instruction that kills T. Thus no new side effects are generated.

Correctness: Each path from *Entry* to a block B where $ANTLOC_B$ = true contains an edge (P,S) where $EARLIEST_{P,S}$ = true. Thus the evaluation of T at the beginning of that block is redundant and can be deleted.

Profitability: The number of evaluations of T on any path from *Entry* to *Exit* after the insertions and deletions is less than or equal to the number of evaluations before the transformation.

PROOF *Safety.* By the definition of *EARLIEST*, T is anticipated at S, so there is an evaluation of T on each path out of S. Hence the transformation is safe.

Correctness. Consider any path from *Entry* to B where $ANTLOC_B$ = true. By Lemma E1, either there is an edge (P,S) where $EARLIEST_{P,S}$ = true not followed by a killing instruction, or an evaluation of T occurs on the path not followed by a killing instruction. In the first case, an evaluation of T is going to be inserted on (P,S) that will satisfy the criteria for availability. If there is an evaluation of T on the path in some block C, then there are two possibilities. If C contains a killing instruction, then that evaluation of T will not be deleted and satisfies the criteria for availability. If C does not contain a killing instruction for T, then $ANTLOC_C$ = true and we can repeat the process on the same path, but only considering the path from *Entry* to C. This process is repeated until a condition for availability is found. The path keeps getting shorter and there are only a finite number of evaluations of T on the path. If one reaches the first evaluation of T on the path without finding the criteria for availability, then Lemma E1 indicates that an earlier edge must have *EARLIEST* being true, so the condition is eventually satisfied.

Profitability. Consider any path from *Entry* to *Exit*. Let $I_1, \ldots, I_m$ be the instructions on the path that are either evaluations of T or instructions that kill T. Let I_0 be a pretend instruction at the beginning of the path that kills T. Now consider each pair of instructions I_k and I_{k+1}.

- If I_{k+1} is an instruction that kills T, then T is not anticipated between the two instructions, so by the equations for *EARLIEST* there is no edge where an evaluation will be inserted.

Global Optimization

- Suppose I_k and I_{k+1} are both evaluations of T. Since we are assuming that local optimization has been performed in a block, we know that I_{k+1} is in a different block than I_k. So I_{k+1} is at the beginning of the block. Thus I_{k+1} will be eliminated by the transformation. Note that only one insertion can occur between the two instructions because of Lemma E4 (there would be no evaluation between the two), so we have one deletion and at most one insertion.

- Suppose I_k is an instruction that kills T and I_{k+1} is an evaluation of T. If they both occur in the same block then there will be no insertions or deletions. Assume they occur in separate blocks; thus again I_{k+1} is at the beginning of a block and will be deleted by the transformation. Again there is at most one insertion and one deletion.

- Following the last evaluation on the path, T is not anticipated, so there are no insertions following the last evaluation.

In summary, the worst case is that there is one deletion for each insertion, that is, profitability is satisfied.

In one sense this transformation is optimal. There is no other set of insertions that is safe, correct and profitable, and that will involve fewer evaluations of T in the transformed flow graph. Later we will see another transformation that is better in a different way.

THEOREM EO Consider another transformation that is safe, correct, and profitable in the sense of Theorem E. The number of evaluations of T on any path from *Entry* to *Exit* after this transformation will be no less than the number of evaluations of T after the *EARLIEST* transformation

PROOF The argument is much like the argument for profitability. Consider a path from *Entry* to *Exit* and list the instructions $I_1, \ldots, I_m$ on the path that are either evaluations of T or instructions that kill T. Pretend that there is an instruction I_0 that kills T at the beginning of the path. Now consider each pair of instructions.

- If I_{k+1} is an instruction that kills T, then T is not anticipated between the two instructions. Since both transformations are safe, neither will insert instructions on any edge between the two instructions.

- Suppose I_k kills T, and I_{k+1} is an evaluation of T. If both are in the same block, then there is no modification of the two instructions and no insertion between them, so assume that they are in different blocks. Thus I_{k+1} is at the beginning of a block and will be deleted, so both transformations must insert an evaluation of T between the two instructions. However, *EARLIEST* will insert only one, by Lemma E4.

- The case where I_k and I_{k+1} are evaluations of T is the difficult case. We are considering one path so we do not know whether T is available or anticipated on the whole path since that involves the flow graph rather than the path: There may be edges entering and leaving the path. Again we are only interested in the case in which the instructions are in separate blocks, since local optimization will remove one of them otherwise. Thus I_{k+1} is locally anticipated in its block. Recall that there are no instructions killing T between these two instructions. Walk backward toward I_k until you find an edge (P, S) where T is anticipated at the beginning of S and not anticipated at the end of P. If no such edge exists, then *EARLIEST* will make no insertions. If the edge does exist, consider two further cases:

- If T is available at the end of P, then there is no insertion for *EARLIEST* by the definining equations.

- Otherwise, T is not available at the end of P, so *EARLIEST* will insert an evaluation on (P, S) and no other insertions between the two instructions, by Lemma E4. We must show that the other transformation must insert a computation between the two instructions also. Since T is not available at the end of P, there is a path from *Entry* to P that contains no evaluation of T after the last instruction killing T. This can be pieced together with the current path between P and I_{k+1}. To satisfy correctness (that is, make T redundant at I_{k+1}), the other transformation must insert a computation on this constructed path after the last killing instruction. This instruction cannot be before P because there is a path out of P to either *Exit* or a killing instruction. That means the inserted evaluation is on the path from I_k to I_{k+1}, proving that at least one insertion happens on this path.

- Consider the portion of the path from I_m to *Exit*. T is not anticipated at any point on this path, so neither transformation will insert an evaluation of T because of safety.

In summary, in each case where *EARLIEST* inserted an evaluation of T, the other transformation was forced to insert an evaluation of T, thus satisfying the theorem.

Investigating the proof of this optimality theorem reveals the reason that this transformation is called *EARLIEST*. It inserts evaluations of T at the earliest possible points that are safe, profitable, correct, and guarantee the fewest number of evaluations.

EXAMPLE In the flow graph of Figure 10.1, the temporary T will not have any insertions and the evaluation in block B2 will be deleted. The temporary S has an insertion on edge (B1, B2) and the evaluation in block B2 is deleted. Now consider a hypothetical evaluation of a constant in block B4 where the constant is not evaluated anywhere else. There are no instructions that kill a constant, so an evaluation will be inserted on the edge (B0,B1) and the evaluation in block B4 will be eliminated. This is the weakness of *EARLIEST*: It can evaluate temporaries long before they are needed.

Global Optimization

The *EARLIEST* transformation has been included here for two reasons. The primary reason is that it is preliminary to the *LATEST* transformation, which we will now describe, and the proof techniques lead one gradually to understand the proof techniques for *LATEST*. Secondarily, the compiler is going to use the *EARLIEST* transformation later during register allocation to move register spilling instructions to earlier points in the flow graph. In that case, moving instructions further will free up more registers and be better.

10.2.3 Computing the Latest Point of Insertion

Inserting evaluations of T on the edges described by *EARLIEST* makes all evaluations of T at the beginning of blocks redundant. In fact, *EARLIEST* gives an optimal solution in terms of number of evaluations performed. However, it is far from optimal when taking into consideration the length of time that values stay in registers.

As an example, consider an instruction that loads a constant into a temporary T. Assume that it is used in the last block of the flow graph, just before *Exit*, in a block that postdominates all other blocks in the flow graph. *EARLIEST* will insert an evaluation of the instruction just after *Entry* although the constant may not be used anywhere else in the flow graph. The word *EARLIEST* means what it says: It places evaluations at the earliest conceivable point in the flow graph. Now we must find a way to delay the evaluations to the latest efficient point.

Form a picture in your mind of the geography of *EARLIEST* insertions and deletions. Consider an original evaluation of T in the graph, and the edges where *EARLIEST* insertions occur. The path from an insertion to an original evaluation may involve branching, joining, and looping; however, Lemma E4 tells us that there are no other edges on that path where *EARLIEST* is true.

Now consider a block B and all paths from *Entry* to B. If each of these paths contains an edge where *EARLIEST* is true and there are no following instructions that evaluate T or kill T, then B is on paths to some evaluations of T. If B does not contain an evaluation of T then the insertions can be delayed until after B. The insertions can occur just before a block that either contains an evaluation of T or has an entering edge coming from an original evaluation of T. In those cases, perform the insertions just before this block. To summarize these ideas we define the equations in Figure 10.4. Unlike *EARLIEST*, these equations need to be solved.

Figure 10.4 Equations for Delaying Insertion

$$LATERIN_B = \begin{cases} \text{false} & \text{if } B = Entry \\ \bigcap_{P \in PRED(B)} LATER_{P,B} & \text{otherwise} \end{cases}$$

$$LATER_{P,B} = (LATERIN_P - ANTLOC_P) \cup EARLIEST_{P,B} \quad \text{if } P \in PRED(B)$$

As with most Boolean equations the compiler encounters, there is not a unique solution to the equations in Figure 10.4. Consider a loop that contains no evaluations of T. As with the equations for anticipatability and availability, one gets different values if one assumes that the values in the loop are true or false. In this case we are trying to push a value back through the loop to before the loop, so we want the maximal solution such that going around a loop does not force the value to false.

10.2.4 Understanding the *LATEST* Equations

Consider a path from *Entry* to *Exit* and a block B where $LATERIN_B$ = true. Walk backward along the path. Since $LATERIN_B$ = true, this means that either $EARLIEST_{P,B}$ = true or $LATERIN_P$ = true and $T \notin ANTLOC_P$, where P is the predecessor of B on the path. If the second case is true, the process can be repeated starting at P rather than B. The result is that any path from *Entry* to B contains an edge (P,S) where $EARLIEST_{P,S}$ = true and no following block up to B contains an evaluation of T before an instruction that might kill T.

Also note that $LATERIN_B$ = true implies that T is anticipated at the start of B. Consider a path leaving B that does not reach an evaluation of T before an instruction that kills T. We can patch together a new path. Start with any path from *Entry* to B and add this path without an evaluation of T. There is an edge where *EARLIEST* is true, so T is anticipated at the head of that edge (look at the formulas). So we have a path from *Entry* to *Exit* that goes through B. T is anticipated at an edge earlier in the path than B and there are no evaluations of T after that edge. So there are no evaluations of T on the path from the head of the edge where *EARLIEST* is true until *Exit*, contradicting the anticipation of T at the head.

10.2.5 Latest Insertions and Deletions

Where does one insert evaluations of T and which evaluations are deleted? As we argued above, we delay the insertion of evaluations to the last possible point. That would be the point where an edge satisfies the conditions for delay but the node at the head of the edge does not because one of the other edges does not have a clear (backward) path to occurrences of *EARLIEST*. The evaluations that are removed are the same as for *EARLIEST*, except in the case in which the *EARLIEST* insertions have been delayed until the block where the evaluation occurs. In that case there is no point in doing the insertions and deletions. This gives the equations in Figure 10.5.

EXAMPLE In Figure 10.1 assume that there is the evaluation of a constant in block B5. *EARLIEST* will insert evaluations of the constant on edges (B0, B5) and (B0, B1). The equations for *LATEST* make it clear that *LATERIN* is true for B5, so no insertion or deletion will occur.

The transformation for *LATER* is less intuitive than the transformation for *EARLIEST*, so it is even more important to prove that the transformation is safe, correct, and profitable. One also needs to prove that it is optimal in two senses: that it has the minimum number of evaluations and the shortest sequence of instructions between the inserted evaluations and the original evaluations.

LEMMA L1 Consider a block B. $LATERIN_B$ = true if and only if each path from *Entry* to B contains an edge (P, S) where $EARLIEST_{P,S}$ = true and there are no evaluations of T or instructions that kill T between the beginning of S and the beginning of B on this path.

PROOF Assume $LATERIN_B$ = true. Consider any path from *Entry* to B. Let B' be the predecessor of B on this path. $LATER_{B',B}$ = true by the equations for *LATER*. This means that either $EARLIEST_{B',B}$ = true, satisfying the condition, or $LATERIN_{B'}$ = true and B' contains no evaluations of T. Walking backward on the path, repeating this argument for each block, one eventually must come to an edge (P, S) where $EARLIEST_{P,S}$ = true

Figure 10.5 Insertion and Deletion Equations

$$INSERT_{P,B} = LATER_{P,B} - LATERIN_B$$

$$DELETE_B = \begin{cases} false & \text{if } P = Entry \\ ANTLOC_B - LATERIN_B & \text{otherwise} \end{cases}$$

and there are no instructions that evaluate T between the start of S and the start of B. Now $EARLIEST_{P,S}$ = true means that T is anticipated at S and there are no instructions between S and B that evaluate T, so T must be anticipated at B and there must be no instructions between S and B that kill T (otherwise it would not be anticipated at S). So the condition is satisfied.

Assume that each path from *Entry* to B contains an edge (P, S) where $EARLIEST_{P,S}$ = true and there are no instructions between the start of S and the start of B that evaluate or kill T. To show that $LATERIN_B$ = true, we assume that $LATERIN_B$ = false and derive a contradiction. Look at the equations.

For $LATERIN_B$ = false there must be a predecessor P_0 such that $LATERIN_{P0}$ = false and $EARLIEST_{P_0,B}$ = false. For the intersection to be false, at least one entry in the intersection must be false. Let P_0 be that predecessor. That means that $EARLIEST_{P_0,B}$ = false, and either $LATERIN_{P0}$ = false or $ANTLOC_{P0}$ = true. However, the assumption is that every path from *Entry* to B contains an edge where $EARLIEST$ is true without any following instructions that evaluate or kill T. So $ANTLOC_{P0}$ cannot be true, because it can be spliced into a path that ends with B.

This whole process can now be repeated with P_0 to get P_1. The process will continue until either one of the predecessors is *Entry* or a loop is formed (remember there is only a finite number of blocks). If *Entry* is reached, then we have constructed a path that does not contain an edge where $EARLIEST$ is true. This is a contradiction.

What if a cycle $P_i, \ldots, P_j$ is formed where $P_i = P_j$ and $i \neq j$? Consider all of the predecessors of all of the blocks in the cycle. Because we are dealing with the maximum solution, $LATERIN$ at any one of the blocks in the cycle is the intersection of the condition $LATER$ from each one of the predecessors for every block in the cycle. This is true because $ANTLOC$ is false for each block in the cycle, so it follows by associativity. For $LATERIN$ for some node to be false, one of the predecessors must have $LATERIN$ false. Add new nodes to the path going from P_j until you get to a node P_k that is a successor of this node. Then add this new node with $LATERIN$ being false into the path. Now continue constructing the path. Each time a cycle is found, the above process can be used to add a new node that is outside the path. Since there are only a finite number of nodes, the process must get to *Entry* and establish the contradiction.

LEMMA L2   Consider a block B and one of its predecessors B'. $LATER_{B',B}$ = true if and only if each path from *Entry* to B' contains an edge (P, S) where $EARLIEST_{P,S}$ = true and there are no evaluations of T or instructions that kill T between the beginning of S and the end of B' on this path.

PROOF   The argument is the same as in Lemma L1. The only addition is that one is dealing with the end of the block B' rather than the beginning of the block B. In this case either $EARLIEST_{B',B}$ is true (in which case the lemma is automatically satisfied) or B' contains no instructions that kill or evaluate T, so the argument for Lemma L1 can be used directly.

We must now repeat the argument for correctness, profitability, and safety that we made for the *EARLIEST* algorithm, but now for the *LATEST* algorithm.

We start with safety. That means that any insertion that is made must lead to an evaluation of T on each path leaving the point of insertion. In other words, we must show that T is anticipated at the head of the edge where an insertion occurs.

LEMMA L3 If $INSERT_{B',B}$ = true, then T is anticipated at the start of B.

PROOF $INSERT_{B',B}$ = true means that $LATER_{B',B}$ = true and $LATERIN_B$ = false (look at the formulas). By Lemma L2, $LATERIN_{B',B}$ = true means that each path from *Entry* to (B', B) contains an edge (P, S) where $EARLIEST_{P,S}$ = true and there are no instructions that evaluate or kill T between the start of S and the end of B'. We proved earlier that $EARLIEST_{P,S}$ = true means that T is anticipated at S. Now there are no evaluations of T between S and the end of B'. Assume T is not anticipated at B. Then there is a path from B to *Exit* that does not contain an evaluation of T before an instruction that kills T. Piece that path together with the path from S to B', and one has a path from S to *Exit* that does not contain an evaluation of T before an instruction that kills T. So T is not anticipated at S. Contradiction.

We next must prove that the insertions are correct. That means that there is an undeleted or inserted evaluation of T on each path from *Entry* to an evaluation that is deleted, so that T is known to be evaluated at the original points of evaluation.

LEMMA L4 Assume that $DELETED_B$ = true. Then after the insertions have occurred, T is available at B.

PROOF $DELETE_B$ = true means that $ANTLOC_B$ = true and $LATERIN_B$ = false. We apply Lemma L1. Consider any path from *Entry* to B. Either there is an edge (P, S) where $EARLIEST_{P,S}$ = true with no instructions between S and B that evaluate or kill T, or there is an evaluation of T on the path not followed by an instruction that kills T. Consider the two cases.

- If there is an evaluation of T on the path, then there are two cases. If that evaluation does not have *DELETE* true, then the condition for availability of this path is satisfied. If the evaluation does have *DELETE* true, then the same argument we are using can be applied to that evaluation. Eventually we will reach either an evaluation with *DELETE* false or the first evaluation on the path, at which point it will be impossible to have a preceding evaluation.

- Suppose $EARLIEST_{P,S}$ = true and there are no instructions between S and B that modify or evaluate T. Then walk down the path from S to B investigating the value of *LATER* and *LATERIN*. Since there are no instructions that evaluate T on the path, and $EARLIEST_{P,S}$ = true, we see by the equations that *LATER* starts out being true and can only become false by *LATERIN* becoming false. So walk the path until we find an edge (P', S') where $LATERIN_{S'}$ = false. We must find such an edge by the time we reach B, since $LATERIN_B$ = false. By the formula for *INSERT*, there is an insertion on this edge. Thus an insertion occurs without following instructions that might kill T.

These two cases together prove that T will become available at B.

We now know correctness and safety. We must prove that the algorithm is profitable. Thus we must show that the number of evaluations of T does not increase on any path from *Entry* to *Exit*. Before the proof, which is similar to the proof for *EARLIEST*, we need to show that there must be an original evaluation of T in the flow graph between any two insertions on a path without instructions that kill T.

LEMMA L5 Consider a path from *Entry* to *Exit*. Let (P, S) and (Q, R) be two edges on the path such that the path from S to Q does not contain instructions that might kill T. If $INSERT_{P,S}$ = true and $INSERT_{Q,R}$ = true, then there is an evaluation of T on the path from S to Q.

PROOF We will use Lemma E4, which is the same lemma about *EARLIEST* rather than *INSERT*. $INSERT_{P,S}$ = true means that $LATER_{P,S}$ = true and $LATERIN_S$ = false. So by Lemma L1 there must be an earlier edge (P', S') on the path such that $EARLIEST_{P',S'}$ = true and there are no instructions between S' and P that evaluate or kill T. Similarly, because $INSERT_{Q,R}$ = true there is an earlier edge (Q', R') where $EARLIEST_{Q',R'}$ = true and there are no instructions between R' and Q that modify or kill T.

Where is the edge (Q',R') in relation to the node S? (Q', R') must be later on the path than S. Assume (Q',R') precedes S on the path. $LATERIN_S$ = false, so Lemma L1 indicates that there is a path from *Entry* to S that does not contain an edge where *EARLIEST* is true without following instructions that evaluate or kill T. Piece this path together with the path from S to Q and we have a path from *Entry* to Q without an edge with *EARLIEST* being true without following instructions that evaluate or kill T. But this contradicts Lemma L1 and the fact that $LATER_{Q,R}$ = true.

Thus we have the edge (P', S') preceding S, which precedes the edge (Q', R'), which precedes Q. *EARLIEST* is true on these two edges and there are no instructions that evaluate T between S' and S or between R' and Q. By Lemma E4, there must be an evaluation of T between the two edges; however, the only place that that evaluation can occur is between S and Q'. Thus we have an evaluation of T between the two edges where *INSERT* is true.

Now we are ready to prove that the transformation is profitable. The proof is an adaptation of the same proof for *EARLIEST*.

LEMMA L6 Consider any path from *Entry* to *Exit*. The number of evaluations of T on the path after the application of *INSERT* and *DELETE* is no greater than the number of evaluations originally on the path.

Global Optimization

Proof Let $I_1, \ldots, I_m$ be the instructions on the path that are either evaluations of T or instructions that kill T. Pretend that there is an initial instruction I_0 at the beginning of the path that kills T. Now consider each pair of instructions I_k and I_{k+1}.

- If I_{k+1} is an instruction that kills T, then T is not anticipated at any block or edge on this piece of the path. Thus there is no edge where *INSERT* is true, so the number of evaluations of T on this piece of the path is the same as the number of evaluations originally.

- Suppose I_k is an instruction that kills T, and I_{k+1} is an evaluation of T. If both instructions occur in the same block, then I_{k+1} is not locally anticipated so there is no insertion or deletion. Consider the case that they are in distinct blocks. Then I_{k+1} is locally anticipated in its block. Thus there is an earlier (P, S) where $EARLIEST_{P,S}$ = true between I_k and I_{k+1}. Thus $LATER_{P,S}$ = true. Now walk down the path from S toward I_{k+1}. Since there are no instructions that can evaluate or kill T, the only way that *LATER* can become false is if *LATERIN* becomes false. There are two cases:

  1. Suppose there is an edge (P', S') between (P, S) and I_{k+1} where $LATERIN_{S'}$ = false. Then $INSERT_{P',S'}$ = true. Since there was only one edge where *EARLIEST* was true, *LATER* and *LATERIN* remain false until we get to the instruction I_{k+1}. In this case, *DELETE* is true for I_{k+1}. We have one insertion and one deletion; thus, there is no net gain in evaluations.

  2. If there is no such edge, we have *LATERIN* being true for the block containing I_{k+1}, so there is no insertion or deletion and no net gain in evaluations.

- Suppose I_k and I_{k+1} are both evaluations of T. Since we are assuming that local optimization has occurred, both evaluations are not in the same block, so I_{k+1} is locally anticipated in its block. There are three cases:

  1. If there is no edge between the two instructions where *EARLIEST* is true, then *LATEST* cannot be true at any edge or block between the two instructions. Thus *LATERIN* is false for I_{k+1}, so I_{k+1} is deleted, thus decreasing the number of evaluations by 1.

  2. If there is an edge where *EARLIEST* is true between the two instructions, and *LATERIN* is true for I_{k+1}, then *LATERIN* and *LATER* are true between that edge and I_{k+1}. If they became false at any point there is no way for them to become true again, since there is only one edge where *EARLIEST* is true. So there is no edge where *INSERT* is true and there is no deletion. Thus there is no change in the number of evaluations.

  3. If there is an edge where *EARLIEST* is true between the two instructions, and *LATERIN* is false, then there is a first block where *LATERIN* is false and the edge preceding it has *INSERT* being true. There can only be one

such edge by Lemma L5. So we have an insertion and a deletion, for no net change in the number of evaluations.

- On the piece of the path after I_m, T is not anticipated, so there can be no insertions.

We have investigated all possible segments, and in each case there was either no increase in the number of evaluations or a decrease in the number of evaluations. Therefore the number of evaluations on the whole path after the transformation is no larger than the number of evaluations originally on the path.

We now know that the transformation is correct, safe, and profitable. Like *EARLIEST*, it is also optimal in that it generates the minimum number of evaluations possible.

THEOREM LO Consider another transformation that is safe, correct, and profitable in the sense of Theorem E. The number of evaluations of T on any path from *Entry* to *Exit* after this transformation will be no less than the number of evaluations of T after the *INSERT/DELETE* transformation.

PROOF We could construct the proof using the same techniques used in Theorem EO; however, a simpler observation makes the job easier. Look at the previous proof of profitability for *INSERT/DELETE*. In the case analysis, whenever an insertion from *EARLIEST* occurred, one of two cases happened with *LATEST*:

- There was an insertion due to *INSERT* being true. In that case, just like the *EARLIEST* case, there was a deletion of the succeeding evaluation of T.

- There was an insertion by *EARLIEST*; however, *LATEST* pushed the insertion all the way down to the next evaluation of T. This happened when *LATERIN* was true for the block containing the next evaluation. In that case there was no insertion or deletion.

In other words, the number of evaluations after *INSERT/DELETE* is exactly the same as the number of evaluations after *EARLIEST*. Since *EARLIEST* is optimal, so is *INSERT/DELETE*.

We now know that *INSERT/DELETE* is as good as the *EARLIEST* transformation. Now we show that it is better by showing that the inserted evaluations are as close to the original evaluations as possible.

THEOREM LC Consider any other algorithm *INSERT'/DELETE'* for insertion and deletion of evaluations of T. Assume that *INSERT'/DELETE'* is safe, correct, profitable, and optimal in the sense that for each path from *Entry* to *Exit* the number of evaluations of T after the transformation is the same as *EARLIEST* or *INSERT/DELETE*. Consider a path from *Entry* to *Exit* with instructions $I_0, I_1, \ldots, I_m, I_{m+1}$, where I_0

is a pretend instruction at *Entry* that kills T, I_{m+1} is a pretend instruction at *Exit* that kills T, and the I_k are all other instructions that either evaluate or kill T. For *INSERT'* and *INSERT*, handle an evaluation of T at the beginning of a block that is not deleted as an insertion on the preceding edge followed by a delete. Consider any pair of instructions, I_k and I_{k+1}, on the path. If any one of the three transformations inserts an evaluation between I_k and I_{k+1}, then all three do, and the insertion for *EARLIEST* occurs before or at the same edge as the insertion for *INSERT*, and the insertion for *INSERT'* occurs before or on the same edge as the insertion for *INSERT*.

This is an involved statement of the fact that *EARLIEST* inserts computations as far away as is possible and *INSERT* inserts evaluations as late as possible to still produce an optimal number of evaluations. Any other optimal transformation must be somewhere in between. A nonoptimal transformation can perform insertions after *INSERT*—just consider the transformation that makes no insertions or deletions. This nonoptimal transformation has its insertion at the last edge.

Proof Go back and look at the proof of Theorem EO. We proved that between any two instructions I_k and I_{k+1}, if *EARLIEST* made an insertion then any other safe, correct, profitable transformation had to make at least one insertion. Thus *INSERT'/DELETE'* must make at least one insertion whenever *EARLIEST* does. It cannot make more than one insertion or make an insertion when *EARLIEST* does not, since then any path including the path from I_k to I_{k+1} would contain more evaluations than for *EARLIEST*. Since *LATEST* makes an insertion whenever *EARLIEST* does, this proves the first part of the theorem.

Consider a pair of instructions I_k and I_{k+1} where all three of the transformations perform an insertion. Since *INSERT'* is safe, the block at the head of the insertion edge must have T anticipated. *EARLIEST* performs an insertion on an edge (P, S) where T is anticipated at S and either T is not anticipated at the exit of P or T is killed in P. So the insertion for *INSERT'* must be either on the same edge as (P,S) or on a later edge, because T is not anticipated at any earlier edge.

Consider the edge (R,Q) where *INSERT* inserts the edge. By the equations, $LATER_{R,Q}$ is true and $LATERIN_Q$ is false. The only way that this could become false is if some other edge had $LATER$ false. By Lemma L1, this means that there is a path from some evaluation of T, call it J, to Q that does not contain any insertion due to *EARLIEST*. Consider a new path from *Entry* to *Exit* that includes the path from J to Q, the path from Q to I_{k+1}, and any path on to *Exit*. If the insertion for *INSERT'* between I_k and I_{k+1} follows Q, then the path from J to I_{k+1} contains an insertion due to *INSERT'* but no insertion due to *EARLIEST* or *INSERT/DELETE*, contradicting the first part of the theorem. Thus the insertion for *INSERT'* must precede the insertion from *INSERT*.

10.3 Relation between an Expression and Its Operands

By handling each temporary independently we have ignored an important implementation detail. The compiler must ensure that temporaries are evaluated before the instructions in which they are used. This is an assumption of the initial flow graph and the definition of expression temporaries. To this end, consider an expression temporary T and one of its operands T'. The following conditions must be true of the original flow graph:

- If T is locally available at the end of a block, then T' must be available at the end of the same block. Since some optimization has occurred earlier, T' might not be locally available; however, it must have been previously computed on all paths. As a formula, $T \in AVLOC(B)$ implies that $T' \in AVOUT(B)$.

- If T is locally anticipated at the beginning of a block, then either T' is locally anticipated or it is already available from previous blocks. As a formula, this means that $T \in ANTLOC(B)$ implies that $T' \in ANTLOC(B) \cup AVIN(B)$.

- If no instruction in B kills T, then no instruction in B kills T'. As a formula, this means that $T \in TRANSP(B)$ means $T' \in TRANSP(B)$.

When the flow chart is initially constructed, the generator guarantees that these conditions are true by ensuring that an evaluation of T' occurs just before the evaluation of T in any block where T is evaluated. Later optimization phases must guarantee that these conditions remain true.

We must ensure that the operands are always evaluated before the instructions in which they are used. Before showing that, we need to know the relationship between the anticipatability of T and of its operand T'.

LEMMA S1 If T is available at the end of block B then T' is available at the end of B. Expanding slightly, T' is available at each point in the flow graph where T is available.

PROOF Consider a point p where T is available, and consider any path from *Entry* to p. Since T is available, there is a point q on the path where an evaluation of T occurs. By the assumptions above, T' is available at q, so there is an earlier point r where an evaluation of T' occurs. There is no instruction between r and q that kills T' and there is no instruction between q and p that kills T. Since an instruction that kills T' kills T, we have no instruction between r and p that kills T'. Since this can be argued for all paths, we have T' available at p.

LEMMA S2 If T is anticipated at p, then either T' is available at p or T' is anticipated at p.

PROOF Since we have two alternatives, we will assume that one is false and show that the other is true. Assume T is anticipated at p and T' is not available at p. That means

Global Optimization

that there is a path from *Entry* to p not containing an evaluation of T', or the last evaluation is followed by an instruction that kills T'. Now consider any path from p to *Exit*. Since T is anticipated at p, there is an evaluation of T at some point q which is not preceded by an instruction that kills T. By the preconditions, there are two possibilities:

- One possibility is that T' is evaluated in the same block as q. The lack of instructions that kill T between p and q means that there are no instructions between p and q that kill T', so there is an evaluation of T' following p on this path with no intervening instructions that kill T'.

- The other possibility is that there is no evaluation of T' in the same block as q. By the preconditions on the flow graph, that means that T' must be available at q. Now we have constructed a path from *Entry* through p to q. This path must contain an evaluation of T' that is not followed by instructions that kill T'. By the construction of the path, this evaluation cannot precede p so it must be between p and q. Lacking instructions between p and q that kill T, and hence T', we have an evaluation of T' with no preceding killing instructions. Thus T' is anticipated at p.

We now have the necessary tools to show that the operands are always evaluated at or before the same point as the instructions of which they are operands.

THEOREM ES Consider a path from *Entry* to *Exit*, T an expression temporary, T' one of its operands, and an edge (P,S) on the path where $T \in EARLIEST_{P,S}$. There are two possibilities:

- There is an evaluation of T' on the path preceding S that is not followed by any instructions that kill T'.

- There is an edge (P', S') on the path preceding S where $T' \in EARLIEST_{P',S'}$ and there are no instructions between the start of S' and the end of P that kill T'.

In other words, in the *EARLIEST* transformation, the operand is either already available or will be inserted on the path before the instruction of which it is an operand.

PROOF $T \in EARLIEST_{P,S}$ means that T is anticipated at the beginning of S and not available at the end of P (look at the formulas). T anticipated at the beginning of S means that T' is either available there or T' is anticipated at the beginning of S. T' available at the beginning of S means that it is available at the end of P.

To show one of two alternatives, we will assume one of them is false and show that the other must be true. Assume that there is no preceding evaluation of T' not followed by instructions that kill T'. Thus T' is not available at the end of P or the beginning of S. Thus T' is anticipated at the beginning of S. March backward along the edge until one of the following conditions occurs (one of them must occur):

- A block P' is reached where T' is not anticipated at the end of P'. Then let S' be the successor on the path, and (P', S') satisfies the condition.

- A block P' is reached where T' is killed by some instruction in P'. Then let S' be the successor on the path, and (P', S') satisfies the condition. Since neither this nor the previous condition has already happened, we know that T' is still anticipated at the beginning of S'.

- *Entry* is reached. Then P' is chosen to be *Entry* and S' is its successor on the path.

There are no other possibilities. While walking backward on the path, one either comes to an instruction that kills T', an instruction that evaluates T', or a point where T' is no longer anticipated. By assumption, the instruction that evaluates T' is not possible. The theorem is therefore proved.

The compiler needs the same result for *INSERT/DELETE*.

THEOREM LS Consider a path from *Entry* to *Exit*, T an expression temporary, T' one of its operands, and an edge (P, S) on the path where $T \in INSERT_{P,S}$. There are two possibilities:

- There is an evaluation of T' on the path preceding S that is not followed by any instructions that kill T'.

- There is an edge (P',S') on the path preceding S where $T' \in INSERT_{P',S'}$ and there are no instructions between the start of S' and the end of P that kill T'.

In other words, in the *INSERT/DELETE* transformation, the operand is either already available or will be inserted on the path before the instruction of which it is an operand.

PROOF Again we assume that the first alternative is not true and show that the second must then be true. Consider the edge (P, S). Assume that there is no preceding evaluation of T' that is not followed by an instruction that kills T'. T is anticipated at the beginning of S, so T' is either available or anticipated at the beginning of S. Since there is no evaluation on this path, T' is not available, so it must be anticipated at the beginning of S.

Since $T \in INSERT_{P,S}$, we know by Lemma L1 that there is an earlier edge (Q, R) with $T \in EARLIEST_{Q,R}$. Now, T is anticipated at all points between the start of R and end of P. Since an instruction that kills T' kills T, and T' is not evaluated on the path, we have T' anticipated between R and the end of P. Walk backward on the path starting at the end of P. As argued in Theorem ES, there is an edge (Q', R') where $T' \in EARLIEST_{Q',R'}$ and this edge must be before (Q, R) since T' is anticipated at each point between R and P. Thus the edge where *EARLIEST* is true for T' precedes the edge where *EARLIEST* is true for T.

Global Optimization

Now we compute *LATEST* for both *T* and *T'*. By Lemma L1, *S* is the first block after *R* on the path with an entering path that contains an evaluation of *T* rather than an edge with *EARLIEST* true. This edge must also contain an evaluation of *T'*; hence during the computation of *LATER* and *LATERIN* for *T'*, one finds that $T \notin LATERIN_S$. So walk in execution order from *R'* toward *S* to find the first block where *LATERIN* is false. The preceding edge has *INSERT* being true. This edge must precede the insertion for *T'* since $T' \notin LATERIN_S$. Thus we have the insertion for the operand preceding the insertion of the instruction in which it is an operand.

10.4 Implementing Lazy Code Motion for Temporaries

Fortunately, the theory we have just described is easily implemented. First order all computations in the program flow graph so that operands occur before the expressions that contain them. We will then optimize each of these computations in order. Consider the evaluation of *T*.

Recall that *EARLIEST* does not require the solution of any equations once availability and anticipatability have been computed, so it can be described by the function in Figure 10.6. The function is being written this way for descriptive purposes; it is probably inefficient in the production version of the compiler since the value of *EARLIEST* will only be asked when the calling procedure knows that *T* is anticipated, thus, we have redundant references to anticipatability. If the compiler used compiling the compiler incorporates in-line expansion of functions, then there should be no inefficiency.

The major computation for *INSERT/DELETE* is the computation of *LATER* and *LATERIN*. We will compute and store the value of *LATERIN* since it is associated with blocks and we will not need to find storage for a value in the data structure representing edges. *LATER* can be computed from *ANTLOC*, *LATERIN*, and *EARLIEST* (Figure 10.7).

The computation of *LATERIN* has much the same form as the computation of availability. It is an intersection of information from all of the predecessors.

Figure 10.6 Pseudo-code for *EARLIEST*

```
function EARLIEST(P: Block, S: Block) returns boolean;
   if (P ∉ AVOUT(T)) ∧ (S ∈ ANTIN(T)) then
      return (P = Entry) ∨ (T ∉ TRANSP(P)) ∨ (P ∉ ANTOUT(T));
   endif;
   return false;
endfunction EARLIEST;
```

Figure 10.7 Computing *LATER* from *LATERIN*

```
function LATER(P,B) return boolean;
   if EARLIEST(P,B) then
      return true;
   endif;
   return (P ∈ LATERIN) ∧ (P ∉ ANTLOC(T));
endfunction ELIMINATE_LATERIN;
```

The major difference is that *ANTLOC* is the information in a block that kills the transmission of *LATER* forward to the next block, and the *EARLIEST* information on an edge is the information that creates the value true rather than the existence of an evaluation at the end of the block.

The compiler uses a work-list algorithm for computing *LATERIN*, much like availability, as is shown in Figure 10.8. The head of each edge that has

Figure 10.8 First Phase of *LATERIN* Computation

```
procedure Calculate_Partial_LATERIN(T: Temporary);
   call Calculate_AVOUT(T);
   call Calculate_ANTIN(T);
   LATERIN = ∅;
   WorkList = ∅;                   //Local data
   foreach B ∈ ANTIN(T) do         //Include heads of EARLIEST edges
      foreach P ∈ PRED(B) do       //Check if predecessor available
         if EARLIEST(P,B) then
            add B to LATERIN;
            add B to WorkList;
            goto B_added;
         endif;
      endfor;
B_added:
   endfor;
   while WorkList ≠ ∅ do            //Compute partially LATERIN
      take B from WorkList;
      if B ∉ ANTLOC(T) then
         foreach S ∈ SUCC(B) do
            if S ∉ LATERIN then
               add S to WorkList;
               add S to LATERIN;
            endif;
         endfor;
      endif;
   endwhile;
endprocedure Calculate_Partial_LATERIN;
```

Global Optimization

EARLIEST true is given the value true for *LATERIN*, then each succeeding block is added if there are no intervening evaluations of *T*. The first phase gives all blocks between an edge where *EARLIEST* is true and the following evaluation of *T* the value of true for *LATERIN*.

The second phase prunes the set of blocks where *LATERIN* is true by eliminating blocks where *LATER* is not true for all predecessors, as shown in Figure 10.9. Initially the algorithm eliminates all blocks that do not have *LATER* true for all incoming edges. At the same time it builds a work list of all blocks that have been eliminated, but whose successors have not yet been processed.

The second part of the work-list algorithm processes each of these eliminated blocks. If the block contains an evaluation of *T* then no further processing is needed since the absence of this block from *LATERIN* cannot affect the presence or absence of its successors. The successors are added to the work list if they are removed from *LATERIN* by the removal of this block. This will happen unless *EARLIEST* is true for the edge between them.

Figure 10.9   Pruning the *LATERIN* Set

```
procedure Calculate_LATERIN(T: Temporary);
   call Calculate_Partial_LATERIN(T)
   WorkList = ∅
   foreach B ∈ LATERIN do              //Start pruning to LATERIN
      foreach P ∈ PRED(B) do
         if ¬LATER(P,B) then
            delete B from LATERIN;
            add B to WorkList;
            goto B_pruned;
         endif;
      endfor;
B_pruned;
   endfor;
   while WorkList ≠ ∅ do
      take B from WorkList;
      if B ∉ ANTLOC(T) then
         for S ∈ SUCC(B) do
            if (S ∈ LATERIN) ∧ ¬EARLIEST(B,S) then
               add S to WorkList;
               delete S from LATERIN;
            endif;
         endfor;
      endif;
   endwhile;
endprocedure Calculate_LATERIN;
```

Figure 10.10 Computing Insertion and Deletion Points

```
procedure LAZY_UPDATE(T: Temporary)
   call Calculate_LATERIN(T);
   foreach B ∈ ANTIN(T) do
      if B ∉ LATERIN then
         foreach P ∈ PRED(B) do
            if LATER(P,B) then
               if |Succ(P)| = 1 then
                  insert evaluation of T at end of P;
               else
                  insert evaluation of T on edge (P,B)
               endif;
            endif;
         endfor;
         if B ∈ ANTLOC(T) then
            delete the evaluation of T from B;
         endif;
      endif
   endfor;
endprocedure LAZY_UPDATE;
```

Now that *LATERIN* has been computed, the compiler must compute the edges on which to perform insertions and the evaluations of T to be deleted. This is done in Figure 10.10. The compiler does not need to look at all blocks to see if they are not in *LATERIN* and the entering edge has the attribute *LATER,* since T is anticipated at a block at the head of an edge where the insertion will occur. Thus we look for blocks in *ANTIN-LATERIN* that have a preceding edge with attribute *LATER*. Insertions occur on these edges. To avoid introducing unneeded blocks, perform a special case check for the situation in which the tail of the edge has only one successor. In that case, insert the evaluation at the end of that block before the unconditional branch.

The algorithm will not attempt to insert an evaluation on an edge where the head of the edge has only one predecessor, since the *LATER* computation will delay the insertion until after the block. If a block has only one predecessor, then $LATER_{P,S} = LATERIN_S$ so it is not possible that $LATER_S$ is false when $LATER_{P,S}$ is true.

10.5 Processing Impossible and Abnormal Edges

The algorithm for placement and deletion of evaluations of T ignores the type of edges that occur in the flow graph. Remember that there are three types of edges. Nearly all of the edges are normal edges, representing branching operations occurring in the blocks. Impossible edges are edges inserted to make the algorithms function properly; they can never be executed in a running program. Finally there are abnormal edges, representing **shortjmp** or **longjmp** forms of instructions or exceptions. Abnormal edges are edges that can be traversed in an executing program; however, there is no mention of the destination block within the tail block for the edge. It is clear how normal edges fit with partial redundancy elimination. How does the compiler deal with the other two kinds of edges?

First consider impossible edges. Note that partial redundancy elimination is one of the algorithms that need the insertion of impossible edges to ensure proper functioning. Recall that each argument about profitability involved a path from *Entry* to *Exit*. Paths that cannot be extended to *Exit* may have more evaluations on them after the transformation than before. The way the compiler solves this problem is to insert an impossible (that is, phony) edge from an infinite loop to *Exit*.

Since an impossible edge cannot be executed, there is no problem with insertions on such an edge. Computations on an impossible edge cannot be executed, so do not insert them. The rest of the algorithm will work properly.

Abnormal edges (P, S) are more difficult because one cannot insert a block in the middle of an edge, since there is no way of modifying P to represent a branch to the constructed block in the middle of the edge. These edges do get executed, so an insertion must occur someplace. There are two techniques that have been used, plus the technique proposed here (making three):

- A pessimistic technique is to pretend that all evaluations are killed at the beginning of S, so $ANTIN_S$ is empty. Thus $EARLIEST_{P,S}$ is false and the $INSERT/DELETE$ computations cannot push the insertion to this edge. This is overkill since it means that there can be no redundant expression elimination in the neighborhood of the edge.

- An alternative approach is to handle the abnormal edge like a normal edge. Hopefully, there will be nothing inserted on the edge. If a computation is inserted on the edge, then insert it into the tail or the head. This is not safe or profitable, but has been done in the Rice Massive Scalar Compiler Project.

This compiler uses a different approach, which counts on the processing of operands before the evaluations that use them. Consider a temporary T.

278 Building an Optimizing Compiler

Apply partial redundancy elimination as described in the previous sections. Usually there will be no insertion on an abnormal edge; in that case, the transformation is complete. The compiler performs more processing if an evaluation is inserted on an abnormal edge.

Consider the set of abnormal edges on which an evaluation of T is inserted. Pretend that T and all temporaries that use T directly or indirectly as operands have another operand. For each abnormal edge (P, S) on which T is inserted, pretend that this added operand is killed at the head of S. This kills all of the instructions dependent on T. Now use partial redundancy to recompute the insertion points. There will now be no insertions of T on the abnormal edges.

Of course, the recomputation may decree that insertions will occur on other abnormal edges that did not have insertions before, so repeat the process until there are no insertions of T on any abnormal edges. This must happen eventually since a safe placement can be determined by killing this phony operand at the head of each abnormal edge in the flow graph, and each iteration will increase the number of abnormal edges that have the phony kill at their head.

10.6 Moving LOAD Instructions

We know how to handle expression temporaries, so now we must address the instructions that occur at the leaves and roots of expression trees. There are two forms of instructions that occur at the leaves: load operations from memory or constants and register-to-register copy operations. At the roots, there are register-to-register copy operations and store operations. The techniques in this phase will move the LOAD, STORE, and computational instructions (Figure 10.11). Copy operations will be addressed in a later section.

The same *INSERT/DELETE* algorithm can be used to move load operations as well. The *modifies* attribute used to compute *TRANSP* already has incorporated all the information needed to limit optimizations when memory changes. If a store operation stores into $A(I)$, then that store operation kills all load operations that load from A.[3] Furthermore, a modification to the value of I kills all references to $A(I)$.

---

3. The compiler may improve on this comment by noticing that the memory locations referenced by $A(I + c)$ are not modified by this store operation, where c is a compile-time constant.

Figure 10.11 Schematic of Code Motion

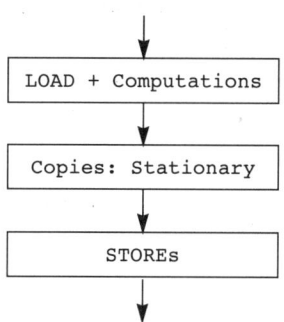

One improvement can be made for load operations. While constructing the flow graph, the compiler always uses the same temporary for the target of a LOAD instruction representing a load from a particular symbolic expression. In other words, all load operations for $A(I)$ use the same target temporary. When the compiler is generating instructions for a store operation, it first copies the value into the same temporary used for a load from the same symbolic expression.

As an example, consider the subscripted reference *VALUE(I)* in the running example with code sequences extracted in Figure 10.12. The address of *VALUE(I)* is always computed into temporary T17. A load operation from *VALUE(I)* always occurs into double-precision temporary SF1. The store operation is implemented as two instructions. First the value to be stored is copied into the temporary representing the fetch of a value, in this case SF1, and then a store operation is inserted from that temporary into memory using the address calculation, in this example, T17.

Although initially inefficient, this code sequence will be improved by later compiler phases. The copy operation will probably be removed by register renaming and register coalescing during the register allocation process.

Figure 10.12 Load and Store Sequences

```
iADD    T4,T16      => T17    /Address(VALUE(I))
dSLD    (T17)       => SF1    /Value of VALUE(I)
...
d2d     SF3         => SF1    /Copy into value of VALUE(I)
dSST    (T17),SF1            /Store it in memory
```

If it is not removed, the store will be moved to a less frequent execution point thus gaining from keeping the value in a register rather than storing it to memory.[4]

The compiler improves the optimization of load operations by observing that a store operation can be viewed as having two actions:

1. First it kills all load operations that load from a memory location that might be modified by this store operation, including the memory referenced by the address specified in the store operation.

2. The store operation can be viewed as implementing an evaluation of the temporary holding the value. In other words, the store can be viewed as a store followed by a load from the same address into the same register.

Note that a store operation can never produce a value in *ANTLOC* for any block, since the memory location is killed before the evaluation. The store operation can contribute to the *AVLOC* information for a block. Since the store operation never contributes to *ANTLOC,* the compiler needs no special checks to avoid deleting a store operation when moving a load. With these comments, the load operation is handled just like expression temporaries.

The temporary T in Figure 10.1 is actually the references to *VALUE(I)*, with the following operations in these blocks:

B1: Initialization of *VALUE(I)*. For complete realism there should have been a modification of T before the evaluation of T in the example, but it would have changed nothing.

B2: The "eval T" is an actual load operation from *VALUE(I)*.

B4: The "mod T" occurs when I is incremented. Changing the address kills the load.

B6: The "mod T" followed by an "eval T" is the store operations updating *VALUE(I)*.

As we see, the store operation contributes to the elimination of the load in block B2.

One further improvement to LOAD optimization is based on the semantics of the source language. Consider an uninitialized variable or data struc-

---

4. The IBM Tobey compiler team (O'Brien, et al. 1985) made the same observation independently.

Global Optimization

ture X that is allocated on the runtime stack. Due to unexecutable paths[5] in the flow graph, the compiler might determine that there are points in the flow graph where the variable is referenced but not initialized. The compiler should pretend that there are load operations for each of the uninitialized elements of the structure at the beginning of the scope. This can be done by adding the load operation to the *AVLOC* information for the block at the beginning of the scope, even though the load is not there. This has the interpretation of an uninitialized value being loaded on all unexecutable paths, making more load operations redundant.

Now that we have the information needed, the same algorithm can be used for load operations as is used for expression temporaries in Figure 10.10.

10.7 Moving STORE Instructions

There are two different ways that store operations can be moved: toward *Entry* and toward *Exit*.[6] Both motions are useful. The store cannot be moved toward *Entry* until the preceding copy operation is moved. The example is a loop such as Figure 10.13. The assignment to T can be moved to before the loop. This is accomplished by first moving the address computation for X, then moving the load of X, then moving the copy operation for X to the temporary for T, and finally moving the store to T.

Figure 10.13 Example of Moving toward *Entry*

```
do I = 1, 10
   A(I) = A(I) + 10
   T = X
enddo
```

---

5. There are paths through many programs that cannot be executed. Consider two IF statements in different parts of the program that use the same conditional expression. It is not feasible for the compiler to determine that both IF statements always branch on the same condition, so the branch on the opposite condition leads to an unexecutable path.
6. Store operations can also be moved toward the *Entry* block. This transformation is less useful than LOAD/STORE motion. The author is not proposing it for the current compiler; however, the technique is discussed at the end of the chapter for reference.

Figure 10.14 Moving the STORE toward *Exit*

```
do I = 1, 10
   A(I) = A(I) + 10
   B(J) = A(I)
enddo
```

Alternatively, the store operation can be moved toward *Exit*. This motion pays off when the address of the store does not change in the loop, but the value being stored does. Consider the loop in Figure 10.14. The value stored in *B(J)* changes with each iteration of the loop; however, the address being stored into does not change, so the store and the copy can be moved to after the loop.

Recall that all store operations have a special form. Each store operation takes two arguments, the address to be stored and the temporary holding the value to be stored. The temporary holding the value is the same as the temporary used to fetch the value with a load operation for the same address. Thus two store operations that store an explicit value into the same address will always use the same temporary to hold the value. Of course there may be other memory locations that might be modified by the store also.

When the compiler moves a store operation toward either *Entry* or *Exit*, it moves the collection of store operations having the same temporary. These are guaranteed to have the same address computation and the same temporary for the address.

10.7.1 Moving the STORE toward *Entry*

The compiler uses the same partial redundancy technology developed for expressions to move the store operation. To do so we must first understand what it means to evaluate a store and to kill a store. The evaluation of a store instruction is an occurrence of the store operation.

What does it mean to kill a store operation? An instruction kills a store (or any other operation for that matter) if the interchange of the execution order of the two instructions might change the values computed by the flow graph. In other words, either the killing instruction does something to the values associated with the store operation (the values in registers or in memory) or the STORE instruction does something to the values used by the killing instruction so that different values either end up in registers or end up in memory. With this understanding, let us identify the instructions that kill the store operation. Consider two instructions, S a STORE instruction and I any other instruction.

- If S kills I then I kills S. To say that S kills I means that I cannot be moved past S. This is the same as I being moved past S. In other words, if S kills any of the operands at the leaves of the expression tree representing I, then we cannot move S past I. This includes other store operations. If I is a store operation, then S can kill I if there is the possibility that they both store values in the same location. Thus the instructions cannot be interchanged.

- If I modifies the temporary holding the value to be stored, then S cannot be moved past I. S cannot be moved past the copy operation that set up the value to be stored.

- If I computes the address expression, then I kills S. The compiler guarantees that no instruction between the computation of the address and the store kills the address computation, so the compiler need only check that it does not attempt to move the store operation past the address computation.

Now that the compiler knows which instructions kill or evaluate the store operation, we can apply partial redundancy to move the store just like any other instruction. The algorithms we have sketched for computing local information for expressions must be expanded to compute the local information for store operations, using the understanding of killing instructions above. Then the lazy code motion equations for moving expressions can be used for moving store operations. Two theoretical problems and one practical problem must be addressed.

The first theoretical problem is, Why should lazy code motion work on store operations? All of the proofs can be repeated, but I prefer another way of looking at the proofs. All of the proofs are based on paths from *Entry* to *Exit* and the possibility of inserting a computation on that path that will compute the same value as was computed later on the path. Rather than viewing the instruction as computing a value, view the instruction as having some effect, where computing a value is one effect. A killing instruction is one that changes the effect. The concept of anticipatability means that it is guaranteed that a later instruction computes the desired effect, whereas the concept of availability means that some earlier instruction has already computed that effect. With these understandings, go back and review the proofs and you will see that the proofs actually show that lazy code motion applies to "effect" rather than "value."

The second theoretical problem is, What about the theorems involving subexpressions? They cannot be viewed as subeffects since there is no such thing. They don't apply, so we make the main procedure apply all transformations for expressions first, then the transformations for copies, and then the transformations for store operations. This also has the advantage that we can avoid trying to move store operations if no copy operations are moved.

The practical problem is as follows. We have used the temporary name to represent the instruction computing it: This does not work for store operations since the temporary is already used to represent load operations. We therefore build a separate set of data structures for store operations. We have *STORE_ANTLOC* rather than *ANTLOC*, *STORE_AVLOC* rather than *AVLOC*, and *STORE_TRANSP* rather than *TRANSP*. Since we compute global information on the fly, the global information is temporary and so it is not a problem.

All of this rationalization now allows the compiler to use the same algorithm for moving store operations toward *Entry* as the compiler uses for expressions and load operations.

10.7.2 Moving the STORE toward *Exit*

This section will discuss moving store operations toward the *Exit* node. This is part of a pair of optimizations called LOAD/STORE motion. We have already implemented the LOAD part, in which the presence of store operations was used to move load operations toward the *Entry* block. By moving the store operations toward the *Exit* block, we will keep the memory value in a temporary as long as it is useful without redundant load and store operations.

The chief advantage of LOAD/STORE motion is in loops. If a datum such as *VALUE(I)* is referenced and changed in a loop, then ordinary code motion cannot move it out of the loop. By performing LOAD/STORE motion, the load can occur before the loop and the store can occur after the loop even though the value is changed in the loop.

The basic idea is to use partial redundancy elimination on the reverse of the flow graph to move store operations toward *Exit*. That means that predecessors are used every place that successors are mentioned in the original theory and vice versa. The ideas of anticipation are turned into a computation like availability, and availability is turned into a computation like anticipation. This duality will be accurate once we specify which instructions can kill and evaluate a store operation.

Global Optimization

What instructions affect the store operation for a temporary T? These instructions must either evaluate or use T, compute the address of the memory location, or be another LOAD or STORE instruction that might reference the same memory location. Let us consider each of the possibilities:

- Instructions that use the value in T do not affect the STORE instruction. Since the value to be stored is always kept in the same temporary as the value loaded using the same address, and since load operations are only moved toward *Entry* and STORE values are moved toward *Exit*, the flow graph guarantees that the correct value is in the temporary at all points where it can be used. The store operation must only guarantee that the value eventually makes it to memory.

- A copy operation into T does not kill the STORE instruction. Moving the store past the copy does change the immediate value that is to be stored in memory; however, there is a store after each copy into T, so interchanging the instructions makes one of the store operations partially redundant.

- Another store operation with the same temporary T has the same temporary for an address so is identical to this store operation. The store operation is the equivalent of the evaluation of T for STOREs (rather than LOADs).

- A load or store involving a different temporary T' that might reference the same memory location kills the STORE instruction. If they might reference the same memory location, then interchanging the order of the instructions might change the value in memory. This is precisely the *modifies* relation for the store operation for T.

- An instruction that kills the address computation for the memory location associated with T also kills the store, since that changes the location in memory being referenced.

- A load involving the temporary T also kills the store. If the store is moved after the load, then the value in memory is not correct and an incorrect value will be loaded. This should be a rare situation since earlier optimization of load operations used the existence of the store operation to make the load redundant. However, some cases involving partial redundancy can still exist.

As with load operations, there is an improvement that can be made for data that is stored on the runtime stack, such as LOCAL variables implementing data structures. Since the data ceases to exist at the end of the execution of the flow graph, the compiler can pretend that there is a store into the memory location in the *Exit* block. This will make some of the other store operations redundant, avoiding those store operations that put data into the memory location that are never loaded again.

We now know the instructions that affect the store operations. Observe that the lazy code motion form of partial redundancy can be recast in terms of the reverse graph. The names that are used are given in Figure 10.15. Rather than using the name *EARLIEST*, the name *FARTHEST* is used to represent the farthest toward *Exit* that the store operation can be moved. Similarly the name *NEARER* is used to represent that the store can be moved nearer to the original position of the store without increasing execution frequency.

The definitions are direct transliterations of the definitions for normal optimization. T being a member of *ST_AVLOC* means that a store of T occurs in the blocks after any instruction that would kill the store. Similarly, $T \in ST\_ANTLOC$ means that a store of T occurs in the block before any instruction which would kill the store. $T \in ST\_TRANSP$ means that no instruction in the block kills a store of T.

From the local information one can compute the global availability and anticipatability information as shown in Figure 10.16. A store is available at a point if each path from the *Entry* to that point contains an instance of the store that is not followed by any instructions that kill T. Similarly, the store is anticipated if every path to *Exit* contains an instance of the store that is not preceded by a killing instruction.

Given this information we can form the analog to *EARLIEST*, which is *FARTHEST*: the edge nearest to *Exit* on which a store can be inserted that will have the same effect as preceding stores. The analog to *LATER* is *NEAR*, which moves the store back toward the original store as far as is pos-

Figure 10.15 Transliteration on Reverse Graph

ANTLOC	⇔	ST_AVLOC
AVLOC	⇔	ST_ANTLOC
AVIN	⇔	ST_ANTOUT
AVOUT	⇔	ST_ANTIN
ANTIN	⇔	ST_AVOUT
ANTOUT	⇔	ST_AVIN
EARLIEST	⇔	FARTHEST
LATER	⇔	NEARER
LATERIN	⇔	NEAREROUT

Global Optimization

Figure 10.16 Global Information for Store

$$ST\_ANTOUT_B = \begin{cases} \emptyset & \text{if } B = Exit \\ \bigcap_{S \in SUCC(B)} ST\_ANTIN_S & \text{otherwise} \end{cases}$$

$$ST\_ANTIN_B = ST\_ANTLOC_B \cup (ST\_ANTOUT_B - ST\_KILL_B)$$

$$ST\_AVIN_B = \begin{cases} \emptyset & \text{if } B = Entry \\ \bigcap_{P \in PRED(B)} ST\_AVOUT_P & \text{otherwise} \end{cases}$$

$$ST\_AVOUT_B = ST\_AVLOC_B \cup (ST\_AVIN_B - ST\_KILL_B)$$

sible without introducing extra store operations on any path. These equations are given in Figure 10.17.

Now that the equations are recorded, each reader should go through the process of convincing himself or herself that the equations do give the correct positions for inserting the store operations nearer to the *Exit* node.

Figure 10.17 INSERT/DELETE Equations for Stores

$$FARTHERST_{P,S} = \begin{cases} ST\_AVOUT_S \cap \overline{ST\_ANTIN_P} & \text{if } P = Exit \\ ST\_AVOUT_S \cap \overline{ST\_ANTIN_P} \cap (ST\_KILL_P \cup \overline{ST\_AVIN_P}) & \text{otherwise} \end{cases}$$

$$NEAREROUT_B = \begin{cases} \text{false} & \text{if } B = Exit \\ \bigcap_{P \in SUCC(B)} NEAR_{P,B} & \text{otherwise} \end{cases}$$

$$NEARER_{P,B} = (NEAREROUT_P - ST\_AVLOC_P) \cup FARTHEST_{P,B} \quad \text{if } P \in SUCC(B)$$

$$ST\_INSERT_{P,B} = NEARER_{P,B} - NEAREROUT_B$$

$$ST\_DELETE_B = \begin{cases} \text{false} & \text{if } B = Exit \\ ST\_AVLOC_B - NEAREROUT_B & \text{otherwise} \end{cases}$$

Convince yourself by going through the proofs, viewing the instructions for their effects rather than the individual value, and see that all of the proofs work on the reverse graph as well as on the original graph.[7]

Now all of the algorithms that we have developed for normal computations can be applied to store operations. When a store operation is moved, there may be more chance for other optimization, so the local information for expressions should be updated and the algorithm rerun for each expression that might be killed by the store. This can be done by adding the expression to the expression work list.

As an example of moving store operations, consider the running example for the book. The store operations into *VALUE(I)* and *LARGE(I)* are moved. The store operations in blocks B1 and B6 are moved into block B3.

10.8 Moving Copy Operations

Moving the copy operations is rarer than moving the load and store operations. Nevertheless, copy operations need to be moved so that whole statements can be moved. The copy operations can be moved either toward *Entry* or toward *Exit*. The same technology can be used to move them as was used to move the load and store operations. We must determine what instructions will kill a copy operation. To make this discussion clearer, consider a copy from a temporary S (source) to a temporary T (target). As with the earlier discussions, an instruction I kills this copy operation if interchanging the two instructions might change the values computed by the flow graph.

- I kills the copy if the copy kills I. This takes care of the case in which the target of the copy is a direct or indirect operand of I.

- I kills the copy if I changes S. Here we have to be more careful, since the theorem about subexpressions does not apply to copies because there are multiple copies with the same target but different sources.

- I kills the copy if I kills S. This is different from the preceding condition, since an instruction that computes S does not necessarily kill S.

---

[7]. The author's first notice of this observation was in a paper by Dhamdhere, Rosen, and Zadeck (1992).

Global Optimization

- *I* kills the copy if *I* is not an identical instruction to the copy and *I* modifies *T*. A different copy can kill this copy also. Interchanging them would change the values computed. However, a copy that has exactly the same form should be viewed as partially redundant, in other words, an evaluation rather than a killing instruction.

Copy operations are different from the expression, load, and store operations we have discussed before in that the copy operation is determined by a pair of temporaries: the source and the target. As noted above, there are multiple copies with the same target and different sources. Rather than optimizing all of the copies together (which cannot be done), each source/target pair is optimized separately. This includes collecting the local information and computing global information on the pair rather than on the single target temporary as in all of the other cases.

With these understandings, the algorithms for moving the copies toward *Entry* can be performed using the same lazy code motion algorithms used for moving all of the other instructions toward *Entry*. While transcribing the algorithms, remember that the compiler is optimizing all of the copies with the same source/target pair at the same time. Remember that *TRANSFORM_COPIES* takes the target temporary as a parameter. This means that there is a loop within *TRANSFORM_COPIES* that loops over all of the possible source temporaries and applies the lazy code motion algorithms to each.

Again, the algorithms for moving store operations toward *Exit* can be applied to copies, with the same understanding that one optimizes a source/target pair rather than a single temporary.

There is no motion of copy operations within the running example. This is not uncommon. The motion of copies will happen more frequently when radical transformations of the loops have been performed by either the dependence analysis phase or a transforming preprocessor. Copies are more likely to be movable when in-line expansion occurs or when the source program was created by an application-dependent preprocessor.[8]

---

8. Compiler writers frequently make the error of thinking the programs are written by programmers. The most troublesome programs are written by other programs. These program generators will generate sequences of statements that no programmer in his right mind would ever consider, for example, 9000 assignment statements in a block.

10.9 Strength Reduction by Partial Redundancy Elimination

While performing lazy code motion, the compiler applies a limited form of strength reduction to handle some situations that are not handled by the loop-oriented strength reduction already performed. This technique is a derivative of the observations made by Joshi and Dhamdhere (1982) and Chow (1983). More recently the idea has been proposed as a derivative of lazy code motion (Knoop, Ruthing, and Steffen 1993).

Why bother, since we have already handled most strength reduction using loop-based methods? In fact, we have handled only the cases where the induction variables are incremented by loop constants rather than constants. The current technique works with increments by constants.

Multiplication by constants is extensive and takes a number of instructions. Usually each instruction is dependent on the previous one, so that during instruction scheduling the multiplication operands become part of the "critical path."[9] Thus every attempt must be made to replace them by less expensive instructions. A common coding idiom is to update an array in a section of code that may involve conditional branching but no loops. Consider the code fragment in Figure 10.18. An array is being built up, with elements being added. Each time an element is added, the index to the loop is incremented. If there were no control flow, all of the increments would have been folded into a single increment earlier in the compiler. That is not

Figure 10.18 Strength Reduction Example

```
A(I) = X
I = I + 1
if Y >= Z then
    A(I) = Y
    I = I + 1
endif
A(I) = Q
I = I + 1
```

- 9. Frequently the argument is made that multiplication and division operations are rare, so they need not be fast. Many times this is true; however, the argument must be refined. Frequency counts should not be used to weight instructions, but rather the total number of cycles that these instructions occupy in computational units in the hardware. Second, it does not matter whether an instruction is rare if the points at which it occurs are in the critical paths of important programs for which the processor was designed. Both of these factors make multiplication and division more important than the usual arguments show.

possible in this case. However, the compiler can maintain a running pointer to $A(I)$ that gets incremented each time that A is incremented. That is what will happen here.

Another case that this technique will handle is when a variable is almost an induction variable. If most modifications of the variable are increments by constants but a few are more complex expressions, then this technique will increment a pointer near the increments by constants and generate a new version of the pointer near the computations that are general assignments.

The technique is based on a simple observation. Consider any computation E of the form $C_0 + I * C_1$ or $I * C_1$, where C, C_0, and C_1 are compile-time constants. When the compiler sees an assignment to a variable of the form $I = I + C$ or $I = I - C$, then pretend that these assignments do not kill computations of the form E. The compiler can pretend not to kill these computations by modifying the gathering of local data *ANTLOC* and *AVLOC*. When the compiler sees an increment or decrement by a constant, the compiler only signals that computations that are not of the form E are killed. Then the compiler performs lazy code motion, which moves the occurrences E using only information about the nonincrement evaluations of I.

After the code motion, the compiler revisits each increment or decrement of I and fixes up the value in the temporary for E so that it has the correct value after the increment. If the assignment to I was an increment, then the temporary is modified by adding $C * C_1$. If the assignment was a decrement, then the value $C * C_1$ is subtracted from the temporary. This need only be done if there is a path from the increment or decrement to a use of E that contains no instruction that evaluates E.

For the example in Figure 10.18 assume that the array A and the values X, Y, and Q are double-precision numbers requiring 8 bytes of storage and that I is not used after the fragment. The result of this strength reduction is then the left column of Figure 10.19. Note that there are two expressions that satisfy the conditions for E: $8 * I$ and *address*$(A) + 8 * I$. Strength reduction is applied to both of them. Note that there is no increment of these two expressions at the end of the code fragment because we are assuming that I is not used later.

Later, dead-code elimination is performed, resulting in the computations in the right column of Figure 10.19. Since I is not used later, the increment to it is removed as well as all references to $I8$ except the first one. The others are not used since the increment of the address expression removes the need for it.

Figure 10.19 Results of Strength Reduction

```
I8 = 8 * I                        I8 = 8 * I
  P = address(A) + I8               P = address(A) + I8
  *P = X                            *P = X
  I = I + 1
  I8 = I8 + 8
  P = P + 8                         P = P+8
  if Y >= Z then                    if Y >= Z then
    *P = Y                            *P = Y
    I = I + 1
    I8 = I8 + 8
    P = P + 8                         P = P + 8
  endif                             endif
  *P = Q                            *P = Q
  I = I + 1
```

There are two shortcomings of this technique. Consider two points in the flow graph, p_1 and p_2, and consider these two possibilities:

- Suppose that p_1 and p_2 are the positions of increment instructions for I with no instructions between them that kill I. If there is no evaluation of E between p_1 and p_2, and there is an evaluation of E after p_2, then the multiplication will be replaced by at least two additions. This is a minor problem since earlier phases of the compiler have eliminated as many repetitive additions as possible. Thus the compiler will ignore this problem.

- If p_1 is the position of the insertion of E or the position of an evaluation of E that is not deleted, and p_2 is the position of an increment of I with evaluation of E between p_1 and p_2, then the strength-reduction transformation would generate a multiplication followed by an addition. On this path there is no point in the first multiplication. The multiplication should be put at p_2 instead, which would change the placement of other multiplications.

The first algorithm needed to implement strength reduction is the computation of the blocks where E must be updated. Start at any block that contains an instance of E that is visible from the beginning of the block ($B \in ANTLOC(E)$). Back up until an edge where an insertion will occur is reached. If the block containing the occurrence of E has *LATERIN* false, then there will be no preceding insertions and the instance of E stays where it is.

Global Optimization

The work-list algorithm is used since earlier algorithms have already removed most multiplications by constants. It is the multiplications by constants that occur outside of loops that are of most importance here. The algorithm is given in Figure 10.20 and is a direct transliteration of the description in the previous paragraph. The result is the set *Update,* which is the set of blocks between an insertion and an evaluation of E that is in the original flow graph. This computation is used with the modified *ANTLOC* that ignores increments and decrements of I.

The second auxiliary algorithm that we need computes the situation in which there is a general assignment to E followed by an increment of I without an evaluation of E in between. The algorithm scans backward starting at each increment. It stops when it comes to an evaluation of E, an instruction that kills I, a point of insertion for E, or a computation of E that is not deleted. It determines that the condition exists if it comes to the evaluation of E or a point of insertion. The algorithm for identifying the unnecessary addition operations is given in Figure 10.21

Now we fit the whole algorithm together (Figure 10.22). It is outlined here in a very high-level pseudo-code. The idea is that lazy code motion is performed under the assumption that all increments of I can be incorporated into the multiplications by additions of constants. Then the increments

Figure 10.20 Blocks in which *E* Is Updated

```
procedure CALCULATE_UPDATE(E);
    WorkList = ∅;
    Update = ∅;
    foreach B ∈ ANTLOC(E) do
        if ¬LATERIN(B) then
            add B to WorkList;
            add B to Update;
        endif;
    endfor;
    while WorkList ≠ ∅ do
        take B from WorkList;
        foreach P ∈ Pred(B) do
            if (¬INSERT(P,B)) ∧ (¬P ∈ Update) then
                add P to WorkList;
                add P to Update;
            endif;
        endfor;
    endwhile;
endprocedure CALCULATE_UPDATE;
```

Figure 10.21 Computing When Extra Additions Will Be Generated

```
function EXTRA_ADDITION(B: Block, E: temporary) returns Boolean;
   WorkList = {B};
   while WorkList ≠ ∅ do
      take from WorkList;
      if C ∈ AVLOC(E) then
         return true;
      endif
      if E ∉ TRANSP(C) then
         return false;
      endif;
      if C ∈ ANTLOC(E) then
         if LATERIN(C) then
            return true
         endif
      endif
   endwhile;
endfunction EXTRA_ADDITION;
```

Figure 10.22 Major Strength-Reduction Algorithm

```
procedure LAZY_STRENGTH_REDUCTION;
   INDUCTION = {Set of increment/decrement STORE operations};
   change = false;
   repeat
      call CALCULATE_LOCAL_IGNORING_INDUCTION;
      call LAZY_CODE_MOTION;
      foreach E of form C₀ + I * C₁ or I*C₁ where I ∈ INDUCTION do
         call CALCULATE_UPDATE(E);
         foreach p ∈ INDUCTION of form I = I + C do
            extra_add = false;
            if p ∈ Update then
               if EXTRA_ADDITION(p,E) then
                  remove p from INDUCTION;
                  extra_add = true;
               endif;
            endif;
         endfor;
         if extra_add then
            change = true;
         else
            foreach p ∈ INDUCTION of form I = I + C do
               insert E = E + C * C₁ after p;
            endfor;
         endif;
      endfor;
   until ¬change;
endprocedure LAZY_STRENGTH_REDUCTION;
```

that cause extra additions are computed. These increments are then handled like normal assignments, and lazy code motion is repeated. If there are no increments that cause extra additions, the algorithm is done. Since this algorithm is used infrequently and the extra additions are infrequent, the repetitions should be few.

10.10 References

Chow, F. 1983. A portable machine independent optimizer—Design and measurements. Ph.D. diss., Stanford University.

Dhamdhere, D. M., B. Rosen, and F. K. Zadeck. 1992. How to analyze large programs efficiently and informatively. *Proceedings of the SIGPLAN '92 Symposium of Programming Language Design and Implementation.* San Fransisco, CA. Published in *SIGPLAN Notices* 27(7): 212-223.

Drechsler, K.-H., and M. P. Stadel. 1993. A variation of Knoop, Ruthing, and Steffen's lazy code motion. *ACM SIGPLAN Notices* 28(5): 29-38.

Joshi, S. M., and D. M. Dhamdhere. 1982. A composite hoisting-strength reduction transformation for global program optimization, parts I and II. *International Journal of Computer Mathematics* 11: 21-41, 111-126.

Knoop, J., O. Ruthing, and B. Steffen. 1992. Lazy code motion. *Proceedings of the ACM SIGPLAN Conference on Programming Language Design and Implementation PLDI92,* 224-234.

Knoop, J., O. Ruthing, and B. Steffen. 1993. Lazy strength reduction. *Journal of Programming Languages* 1(1): 71-91.

Morel, E., and C. Renvoise. 1979. Global optimization by suppression of partial redundancies. *Communications of the ACM* 22(2): 96-103.

O'Brien, et al. 1985. *XIL and YIL: The Intermediate Language of TOBEY, ACM SIGPLAN Workshop on Intermediate Representations,* San Fransisco, CA. Published as *SIGPLAN Notices,* 30(3): 71-82.

11 LIMITING RESOURCES

The compiler is now ready to assign machine resources (registers, condition codes, and so forth) to each computation. There are several available algorithms for resource allocation, each of which performs best on particular classes of programs. Each register allocation algorithm works well when there is an abundance of physical registers available. Each performs badly when the required number of physical registers greatly exceeds the number available.

The algorithm presented here is a wedding of these, attempting to use each type of resource allocation where it works best. The algorithm is structured as a sequence of algorithms that each do a part of the allocation. Previous algorithms organized in this fashion have suffered from the phase-ordering problem: allocating one set of temporary registers has made it more difficult to allocate other sets. The compiler mitigates this problem by performing the LIMIT phase.

The first thing that must be done, therefore, is to reduce the number of required registers. This is done before the register allocation and scheduling phases, allowing each phase to assume that an adequate number of physical registers is available. These functions are performed in the following order, as is shown graphically in Figure 11.1:

1. The LIMIT phase reduces the need for machine resources as much as possible without slowing the execution of the program. It

   - Performs peephole optimization to create the exact sequence of target instructions.
   - Performs register coalescing and register renaming to avoid as many copy operations as possible and replaces each temporary that is used in multiple independent parts of the flow graph by distinct temporaries.

Limiting Resources

Figure 11.1 Back-End Structure

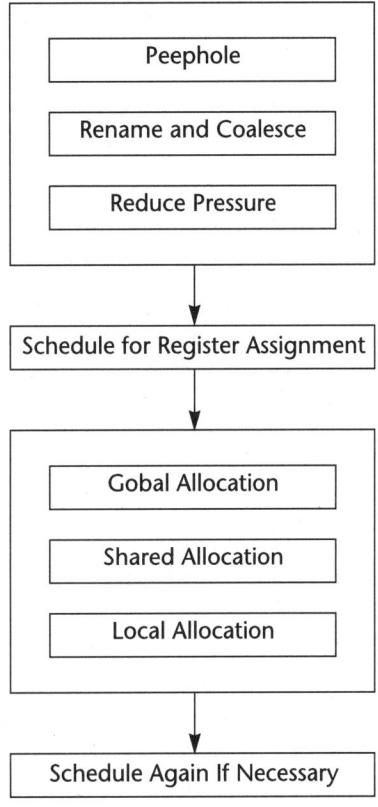

- Reduces the register pressure, limiting the number of registers needed at each program point to fit the physical registers available.

2. The SCHEDULE phase reorganizes the target instructions to reduce the number of machine cycles needed for executing the flow graph. At the same time, it avoids increasing the register pressure beyond the available set of registers.

3. The REGISTER phase assigns the temporaries to physical registers. This is done in three steps.

    - First, temporaries that are live between blocks (global temporaries) are assigned to registers.

- Within a block, temporaries that can share storage with a global temporary are assigned registers.
- Then unassigned temporaries that are live within a block are assigned registers.

4. The RESCHEDULE phase is a reexecution of the SCHEDULE phase. It is only performed if the register allocator has inserted load and store operations.

The register allocation phases must use the target resources effectively. That means using the fewest possible registers. When there are insufficient registers, the register allocator inserts the fewest possible load and store operations. Using the minimum number of registers and inserting the minimum number of load and store operations is unrealistic since the problems are NP-complete. Instead, we use heuristics to do as good a job as possible.

11.1 Design of LIMIT

LIMIT performs four actions to reduce the number of instructions and registers used. These are grouped into two separate subphases. First, LIMIT performs peephole optimization, register renaming, and register coalescing. Then it reduces the number of registers needed (it reduces the register pressure) so that no more registers are needed at any point of the flow graph than exist in the machine.

As noted above, this compiler combines the operations of peephole optimization, register renaming, and register coalescing into a single algorithm. Why? When implemented separately, the algorithms take large amounts of space and time. Consider each of the parts:

- Register renaming involves breaking a single temporary into multiple temporaries if it is used independently in different parts of the flow graph. This involves knowing which evaluations of a temporary may be used at each use. This information can be given by the static single assignment (SSA) form of the graph.

- Register coalescing removes register-to-register copies using a data structure called the conflict graph. The conflict graph can be the largest data structure in the compiler. We observe that much of renaming can occur as renaming on the static single assignment form of the flow graph without the conflict graph. The conflict graph need only be built for a small fraction of the temporary registers, decreasing its size.

Limiting Resources

- Peephole optimization works best when the compiler can inspect the definitions of the operands of each instruction. We have this with the static single assignment form, so peephole optimization can be performed here. It certainly needs to be performed before instruction scheduling.

- As a cleanup phase, dead code must be eliminated. Again this algorithm operates on the static single assignment form of the flow graph.

Since the algorithms all work on the static single assignment form, they can be performed sequentially; however, they can also be combined. Peephole optimization can be performed at the same time that register copies are initially being eliminated for register coalescing. And we will see shortly that register renaming and register coalescing can be combined into one algorithm that computes a partition of the temporaries for reforming the normal flow graph.

After these algorithms based on static single assignment form, the algorithm operates on the normal flow graph and the loop structure to insert load and store operations to reduce the number of registers needed to match the registers available in the target machine. Thus the main procedure for LIMIT has the form shown in Figure 11.2.

The algorithms could be combined further if abnormal edges in the flow graph did not exist.[1] Peephole optimization, local coalescing, and the construction of the static single assignment form could be done simultaneously. Since the compiler must avoid copy operations on abnormal edges, these edges and the corresponding ϕ-nodes must be identified before any coalescing

Figure 11.2 LIMIT Main Procedure

```
procedure LIMIT;
   call CALCULATE_SINGLE_ASSIGNMENT_FORM;
   call LIMIT_PROCESSING_FOR_ABNORMAL_EDGES;
   call PEEPHOLE_AND_LOCAL_COALESCE;
   call RENAME_AND_GLOBAL_COALESCE;
   call DEAD_CODE_ELIMINATION;
   call CALCULATE_NORMAL_FORM;
   call REDUCE_PRESSURE;
endprocedure LIMIT;
```

---

1. By now, you have figured out that abnormal edges are the bane of the compiler writer's existence.

Figure 11.3 Effect of Abnormal Edges

```
procedure LIMIT_PROCESSING_FOR_ABNORMAL_EDGES;
   Occurs_In_Abnormal_ϕ_node = ∅;
   Pairs_In_Abnormal_ϕ_node = ∅;
   foreach B ∈ N do
      if Φ(B) ≠ ∅ then
         for P ∈ PRED(B) do
            if (P,B) is abnormal edge then
               let P be the ith predecessor of B;
               foreach T_0 = ϕ(...,T_i,...) ∈ Φ(B) do
                  add T_0 to Occurs_In_Abnormal_ϕ_node;
                  add T_i to Occurs_In_Abnormal_ϕ_node;
                  add (T_0,T_i) to Pairs_In_Abnormal_ϕ_node;
               endfor;
            endif;
         endfor;
      endif
   endfor;
endprocedure LIMIT_PROCESSING_FOR_ABNORMAL_EDGES;
```

or peephole optimizations are performed. This identification can be done during the construction of the static single assignment form; however, it is described separately for simplicity.

All copies caused by ϕ-nodes on abnormal edges must be eliminated. So nothing can be done to temporaries in these ϕ-nodes that will cause a copy. This is achieved by not changing the points of evaluation or use. Actually, uses can be eliminated but not added. To identify these temporaries, the algorithm in Figure 11.3 is performed, which computes two sets: *Occurs_In_Abnormal_ϕ_node,* which is the set of all temporaries involved in these edges, and *Pairs_In_Abnormal_ϕ_node,* which is the set of pairs that could cause a copy if the compiler is not careful. The algorithm simply looks at all blocks that have any ϕ-nodes and considers each predecessor to see if it is formed with an abnormal edge. If so, each of the ϕ-nodes is scanned and the sets formed.

11.2 Peephole Optimization and Local Coalescing

Peephole optimization is a target-machine-dependent optimization with a machine-independent form (see Figure 11.4). No matter how good an opti-

Figure 11.4 Driver for Peephole Optimization

```
procedure PEEPHOLE_AND_LOCAL_COALESCE;
   change = false;
   initialize information for temporaries to nothing;
   repeat
      Occurs_in_Copy = ∅;
      call PEEPHOLE_BLOCK(Entry);
   until ¬change;
endprocedure PEEPHOLE_AND_LOCAL_COALESCE;
```

mizing compiler is, there are improvements that can be made by performing simple pattern matching on the generated code:

- A load of X may follow a store of X. The compiler has tried to eliminate these; however, phase-ordering problems exist that limit all such attempts.

- A load operation may take an address that is the sum of a temporary and a constant. If the constant is small, the constant can be folded into the offset of the LOAD instruction on the target machine. The same is true of STORE instructions.

- The target machine may have specialized instructions such as the S4ADDQ instruction on the Alpha processor. This instruction multiplies one operand by four and adds the second operand. The instruction is faster than a multiplication since the bits of one operand are directly shifted into the target register.

- The local form of register coalescing—eliminating a copy by using the source operand rather than the target operand in all instructions using the target operand—is a machine-independent form of peephole optimization.

- The compiler can scan through the instructions, symbolically executing them, and remember as much information as possible. A logical AND with a constant generates a result that is 0 in the bits in which the constant is 0. If later instructions attempt to modify or interrogate those bits, then the compiler can change the instruction sequence to generate better code.

Normally, peephole optimization is implemented by scanning through the instructions in each block in execution order. This compiler visits each of the blocks in a dominator walk of the flow graph. This means that each of the operands has been evaluated before the instructions in which they are used. Of course, this is not true for ϕ-nodes. In that case the compiler must make worst-case assumptions: It does not know what is in the temporary. For other temporaries, it records information such as the following:

- If the temporary contains a constant value, record that constant value.
- If the temporary is not a constant value, does the compiler know information about some of the bits? Is the temporary positive? Are certain bits known to be 0 or known to be 1?

The compiler contains a set of procedures for identifying patterns in the instruction stream: There is one procedure for each kind of instruction. That procedure identifies all patterns that end with the particular instruction and performs the transformation required for a better code sequence. It also records the information for each temporary that is the target of that kind of instruction. If the sequence of instructions changes, it restarts the pattern matching with the first instruction in the transformed sequence. Thus multiple patterns may be applied to the same instruction.

Although peephole optimization restarts the scan with the first transformed instruction to allow the identification of multiple patterns, some patterns will still not be identified. The whole peephole optimization phase is repeated until there are no patterns matched. The information gathered from previous iterations is still true for each temporary. This information can be used by ϕ-nodes to get better information on subsequent iterations; however, repetition of the whole peephole optimization phase to gain better information at ϕ-nodes alone should not be performed—there is not enough to be gained by it.

Transformations which involve adding a use of a temporary in *Occurs_In_Abnormal_ϕ_node* or moving the point at which such temporaries are evaluated must be avoided. By doing so, the compiler guarantees that no copies will be introduced later at abnormal edges.

The algorithm in Figure 11.5 describes the processing of a block. The actions in the block are performed in the same order as execution. First the ϕ-nodes are processed. There are only a few transformations that might eliminate ϕ-nodes; however, information can be gained about the value of the result from the information known about the operands.

Figure 11.5 Peephole Optimization of a Block

```
procedure PEEPHOLE_BLOCK(B: Block);
   foreach T_0 = φ(T_1,...,T_m) ∈ Φ(B) do
      call PEEPHOLE_φ_NODE(T_0 = φ(T_1,...,T_m));
   endfor;
   while more instructions I in B do
      applied = false;
      case opcode(I) of
         ...
         iMUL:
            applied = PEEPHOLE_INTEGER_MUL(I);
         i2i:
            applied = PEEPHOLE_INTEGER_COPY(I);
      endcase;
      if applied > 0 then
         change = true;
         repeat processing the last applied instructions in B;
      else
         go on to next instruction in execution order;
      endif;
   endwhile;
   foreach C ∈ Children(B) do
      call PEEPHOLE_BLOCK(C);
   endfor;
endprocedure PEEPHOLE_BLOCK;
```

After φ-nodes are processed, the compiler simulates the execution of the block. This is done by calling the peephole optimization procedure for each instruction in the list. That procedure will perform any transformations. The value true is returned if a transformation is performed. Here is the tricky part of peephole optimization. If no transformations are performed, the compiler wants to go on to the next instruction. If a transformation has been performed, it wants to reprocess the transformed instructions, which may now be a different instruction from the original instruction. Care must be applied to avoid skipping an instruction, attempting to reprocess a deleted instruction, or generally crashing.

After the block has been processed, the walk of the dominator tree is continued by processing the children of the block in the dominator tree.

We will not describe all of the procedures here since their number and patterns depend on the target machine. Instead we will describe the processing of φ-nodes, copy instructions, and integer multiplication. The reader can extrapolate to the structure for all machines.

When creating the procedure for any of the instructions, first consider the transformations that can be applied. With ϕ-nodes, the following transformations are possible when the ϕ-node has the form $T_0 = \phi(T_1, \ldots, T_m)$:

If each of T_1 through T_m are the same temporary, then the ϕ-node can be changed into a single copy operation, $T_0 = T_1$. If neither of these temporaries is involved in an abnormal edge, then the copy can be eliminated.

If all except one of the temporaries T_1 through T_m are the same and that one is the same as T_0, then again the ϕ-node can be turned into a copy operation and potentially eliminated.

Processing a ϕ-node thus consists first of identifying these two possibilities and making the transformation. Afterward, find all the characteristics that are the same between the operands and give the target those characteristics (see Figure 11.6).

As an example of a normal instruction, consider the integer multiplication instruction. What are the peephole optimizations involving it? If it is a multiplication by a constant, it has already been converted to shift and add operations. Just in case some instances slip through or are created after the replacement,[2] the check for some simple cases should be made again. Figure 11.7 gives a fragment of this function. Note that the check for specialized instructions such as the Alpha S4ADDQ is not done here. It is done in the integer add procedure since it is the last operation.

The other instruction to consider here is i2i, which is the integer copy operation in the flow graph. Here there is only one transformation. If the source and target are not involved in abnormal edges, the source can replace all uses of the target, eliminating the target temporary completely. This is illustrated in Figure 11.8. The procedure checks to see if the temporaries involved occur in abnormal edges; if not, all instructions that use the target are modified.

While scanning for peephole optimizations, the compiler precomputes the set of temporaries that occur in either a copy operation or a ϕ-node. Later the conflict graph will be computed for only these temporaries, decreasing the size of the graph and speeding the compiler. The set

---

2. These always seem to happen. The compiler is carefully designed so that all instances of a particular instruction are transformed at a single point in the compiler; however, later transformations might generate the same situation. So if it is not expensive, checks should be made to see that the situation has not already occurred.

Figure 11.6 Peephole Optimizing φ-nodes

```
procedure PEEPHOLE_φ_NODE(T₀ = φ(T₁,...,Tₘ));
   if T₁ through Tₘ are all the same temporary T then
      delete the φ-node;
      insert copy T₀ = T₁ at beginning of block;
      change = true;
   else if T₁ through Tₘ are same temporary T except one T' then
      if T₀ = T' then
         delete the φ-node;
         insert copy T₀ = T at beginning of block;
         change = true;
      endif;
   endif;
   Occurs_in_Copy = Occurs_in_Copy ∪ {T₀,T₁,...,Tₘ};
   find information common to T₁ through Tₘ;
   assign that information to T₀;
endprocedure PEEPHOLE_φ_NODE;
```

Occurs_in_Copy holds the set of temporaries that occur in either a copy or a φ-node. Note that this set is recomputed during each pass through peephole optimization because the processing of copies may change the set of temporaries occurring in copies (Figure 11.8).

Figure 11.7 Peephole Optimization for Integer Multiplication

```
function PEEPHOLE_INTEGER_MUL(I) returns integer;
   let the instruction be T₀ = T₁ * T₂;
   if T₁ and T₂ are both constants then
      calculate value V in the compiler for T₁ * T₂;
      replace instruction by iLDC V => T₀;
      return 1;
   else if T₁ is constant 1 then
      replace instruction by i2i T₂ => T₀
      return 1;
   else if T₂ is constant 1 then
      replace instruction by i2i T₁ = >T₀
      return 1;
   else if T₁ is a power of 2 then
      replace instruction by shift by log(T₁);
      return 1;
   ...
   endif;
endfunction PEEPHOLE_INTEGER_MUL;
```

Figure 11.8 Peephole Optimizing Copy Operations

```
function PEEPHOLE_INTEGER_COPY(I: Instruction) returns boolean;
   let I be the instruction T_0 = T_1;
   if T_0 ∉ Occurs_In_Abnormal_ϕ_node then
      if T_1 ∉ Occurs_In_Abnormal_ϕ_node then
         if T_0 ≠ T_1 then
            foreach J ∈ Uses(T_0) do
               replace uses of T_0 by uses of T_1 in J;
            endfor;
         endif;
         delete instruction I;
         return 1;
      endif;
   endif;
   Occurs_in_Copy = Occurs_in_Copy ∪ {T_0,T_1};
   return ∅;
endfunction PEEPHOLE_INTEGER_COPY;
```

11.3 Computing the Conflict Graph

The algorithm for register renaming and register coalescing needs a data structure called the *conflict graph*.[3] The structure represents the concept that two temporaries contain different values at some common point in the flow graph.

DEFINITION **Conflict Graph:** Given a set of temporaries R, the conflict graph for R is the undirected graph formed from the set of temporaries R as the nodes together with an edge between $T_1, T_2 \in R$ if there is any point p in the flow graph satisfying both of the following conditions:

T_1 and T_2 might contain different values.

T_1 and T_2 are both live at p. This means that there is a path from an evaluation of T_1 to a use of T_1 that includes the point p, and there is a path from an evaluation of T_2 to a use of T_2 that includes the point p. Note that this means that no edge is needed if either temporary is uninitialized.

---

[3] This data structure is normally called the *interference graph*, which reuses the name for the data structure formed during instruction scheduling. Thus I chose to use the name used on the PQCC project at Carnegie Mellon University (Leverett et al. 1979).

How is this data structure represented? The literature describes two representations, which are merged into a single representation in this compiler. Since the temporaries are represented as small integers, the conflict matrix can be represented as a symmetric bit matrix where $C[i,j]$ is true if and only if the temporaries T_i and T_j conflict. This makes the check for a conflict a very fast matrix access; however, determining all of the temporaries that conflict with a particular temporary is slow. Alternatively, the conflict graph can be represented by keeping a list of all conflicting neighboring temporaries for each temporary. This makes the determination of the temporaries that conflict with a temporary easy; however, it makes the determination of the existence of a particular conflict time-consuming.

Unfortunately, the algorithm must perform both checks because checks for existing conflicts are needed during the construction of the graph, whereas later the algorithm needs to know the temporaries that conflict with a particular temporary. Some implementations of the conflict graph first create the bit matrix representation and then translate it into a list of neighbors. This costs significant time to do the conversion. Others keep both data structures simultaneously, using whichever is more efficient for the particular operation. This costs memory in the compiler.

Our compiler optimizes the construction of the conflict graph in two ways. First the conflict graph is only constructed for a subset of the temporaries that are predetermined by the compiler. By keeping the set of temporaries small, time and space are saved. Second, the compiler implements the conflict graph as a combined hash table and the representation of the conflicting neighbors as a list. The data structures are shared between the hash table and graph representation to avoid additional memory consumption.

11.3.1 Representation of the Conflict Matrix

This compiler combines the two representations by using a hash table together with a linked-list representation of an undirected graph. This is done by representing each edge as an entry in a table. This entry is kept on three distinct linked lists:

- The hash table is represented as a chain-linked hash table, so there is one field in the entry called *hashnext* that stores the pointer to the next entry in this chain of the hash table.

- The neighbors of the smaller-number temporary are kept in a list. The field *smallnext* represents the pointer to the next neighbor in the list of conflicting neighbors for the smaller-numbered node.

- Correspondingly, the neighbors of the larger-number temporary are kept in a list, and the field *largenext* represents the pointer to the next neighbor in the list of conflicting neighbors for the larger-numbered node.

For the conflict graph there is no value in representing a temporary that conflicts with itself; thus, an edge is between a strictly smaller-number temporary and a strictly larger-number temporary.

There are two other fields in the entry for the edge:

- The field *smaller* contains the number of the temporary with the smaller value.
- The field *larger* contains the number of the temporary with the larger value.

Note that there is no data stored in the edge. The existence of the edge is the important thing to the algorithms. Thus the data structure for the edge would look something like the description in Figure 11.9.

To check for the existence of a particular conflict, the compiler uses a chain-linked hash table, *ConflictHash*, of some size *HASHSIZE*, which can be a power of two since the hash function is simple. Let T_i be the temporary represented by the integer i and correspondingly let T_j be the temporary represented by the integer j. Since we have no knowledge of the frequencies and interrelationships of the temporary, the hash function consists of linearizing the entries in the corresponding symmetrix bit matrix (which we did not build) and dividing by the size of the table. In other words, the hash function is

```
Conflict(T_i,T_j) = (if i < j then j(j - 1)/2 + i else
                    i(i - 1)/2 + j) mod HASHSIZE
```

Figure 11.9   Structure of a Conflict Entry

```
type ConflictEntry =
        record
            hashnext:      pointer to ConflictEntry;
            smallnext:     pointer to ConflictEntry;
            largenext:     pointer to ConflictEntry;
            smaller:       temporary;
            larger:        temporary;
        endrecord;
```

Figure 11.10 Schema for Referencing Neighbors of T_i

```
p = Neighbors(T_i);
while p ≠ NULL do
    there is conflict between smaller(p) and larger(p);
    if i < larger(p) then
        p = smallnext(p);
    else
        p = largenext(p);
    endif;
endwhile;
```

which generates an index to a chain in the chain table. Of course, *hashnext* is used to scan down the chain until a matching *smaller* and *larger* are found, indicating the presence of the edge.

During insertion, new edges are added at the head of the chain, since locality indicates that once an insertion occurs it is likely that the same insertion will be attempted shortly.

The other operation is finding all of the neighbors of a temporary. Let T_i be the temporary corresponding to the integer i. To scan down the list of temporaries that conflict with T_i, use an algorithm like the one in Figure 11.10.

The compiler will also keep track of the number of a temporary's neighbors. This can be accommodated by adding an attribute to the temporary, called *NumNeighbors*, that is initialized to 0 and incremented each time a conflict is added.

11.3.2 Constructing the Conflict Graph

The definition gives the basic technique for computing the conflict graph. Consider each point in the flow graph. Generate an edge between any two temporaries that are live at that point and are not known to have the same value. This means that the compiler needs to know the set of temporaries live at each point. After live/dead analysis, the compiler only knows the temporaries live at the end of each block. The way to find those live at any point in the block is to scan the block backward, applying the definition of a live temporary to update this set of temporaries, as outlined below:

1. Scanning the instructions backward, first mark as dead any temporary that is the target of the current instruction.

2. Mark as live any uses of temporaries as operands.

3. For each pair (T_1, T_2) live at a particular point, create an edge in the conflict graph between T_1 and T_2.

This approach is inefficient because two temporaries are usually live at a number of points. The algorithm will attempt to insert a conflict at each one of the points. Of course, the compiler will observe that the conflict is already there and not insert it. However, a large amount of time will be consumed attempting these useless insertions. Instead an observation made by Chaitin (1981) is used to decrease the work.

OBSERVATION Consider any path from *Entry* to a point p where T_1 and T_2 are live. One of the following conditions is true:

1. T_1 is live at some instruction on the path that evaluates T_2.
2. T_2 is live at some instruction on the path that evaluates T_1.
3. Either T_1 or T_2 has no evaluations on the path preceding p, so the compiler can ignore the conflict.[4]

PROOF Given a path, start walking backward on the path toward *Entry*. Both T_1 and T_2 are live when you start the walk. Stop at the first instruction where either one of them ceases to be live. Here are the possibilities:

- Neither instruction becomes dead. In that case, there are no instructions that evaluate either of the temporaries on the path before p, so they both contain uninitialized data and the third case occurs.

- One of the temporaries becomes dead because it is the target of an instruction. Since we stopped at the first one that becomes dead, the other one is still live, so we have one of the first two alternatives.

- One of the temporaries becomes dead because there are no preceding evaluations of that temporary on any path starting from *Entry* and reaching the current point in the walk. In that case, there are no evaluations of that temporary on this path, so the third alternative applies.

By the definitions of live and dead, these are the only alternatives, so we have proven the observation.

This observation means that we do not have to create conflicts for each pair of temporaries live at a point. The compiler need only create conflicts between temporaries evaluated at a point and the other temporaries that are live at that point. This gives the algorithm in Figure 11.11. It computes the lifetime information for temporaries that are in *Nodes* in the same way

---

4. A temporary that does not have a value can share a register with any other temporary. Since we do not care what the value is, we can assign it the value in the other temporary.

Figure 11.11 Computing a Partial Conflict Graph

```
procedure CALCULATE_CONFLICT_GRAPH(Nodes: set of temporary);
   ConflictGraph = ∅;
   foreach B ∈ N do
      Live = LiveOut(B) ∩ Nodes;
      foreach I ∈ B in reverse order do
         Live = Live - Explicit(Targets(I));
         foreach T₁ ∈ Explicit(Targets(I)) ∩ Nodes do
            foreach T₂ ∈ Live do
               if Value(T₁) ≠ Value(T₂) then
                  add conflict (T₁,T₂) to ConflictGraph;
               endif;
            endfor;
         endfor;
         Live = Live ∪ (Operands(I) ∩ Nodes);
      endfor;
   endfor;
endprocedure CALCULATE_CONFLICT_GRAPH;
```

that live/dead analysis computes the information and then uses this information and the last observation to add conflicts to the conflict graph.

As an example, consider the straight-line code fragment in Figure 11.12. Assume that T5 is the only register live after the code fragment, and that T0 and T2 are live before the code fragment. Scanning the instructions backward, we get the conflicts listed in the second column, which gives the conflicts created by the instruction.

This algorithm will be used in two places within the compiler. First it is used in the register renaming and register coalescing algorithm. For that purpose it needs a modification described below. Later it is used as stated here for global register allocation.

During register renaming and register coalescing, the compiler computes a partition of the temporaries: Two temporaries in the same partition will be given the same name when the flow graph is translated back into

Figure 11.12 Example Conflict Graph

```
iSLD    0(T0)    => T1     (T0,T1), (T2,T1)
iADD    T1,#1    => T3     (T0,T3), (T1,T3), (T2,T3)
iADD    T2,T1    => T4     (T0,T4)
iADD    T4,T0    => T5
```

normal form. The compiler needs the concept of conflict between two partitions: Two partitions conflict if there is any point at which there is an element of each that is live and not known to contain the same value. In other words, a partition is live at the union of the points where its elements are live. The algorithm for constructing the conflict graph for the partition is the same as for temporaries; however, the edge is constructed between $(FIND(T_1), FIND(T_2))$ rather than between (T_1, T_2), where the partition is represented by use of a UNION/FIND algorithm.

11.4 Combined Register Renaming and Register Coalescing

LIMIT implements a combined algorithm for register renaming, peephole optimization, and partial register coalescing. The combination is based on the observation that both algorithms compute a partition of the temporaries to be used during translation back to normal form. Initially forming the static single assignment form exceeds the requirements of register renaming: It assigns too many new register names and inserts copy operations to copy between them. Register renaming creates the minimum partition that eliminates all of these inserted copies. Rather than eliminating them directly, the elimination of the copies can be combined with the elimination of the copies done in register coalescing.

11.4.1 Register Renaming

Register renaming eliminates the situation in which the same temporary is used in distinct parts of the flow graph to hold different values. Static single assignment form provides a basis for register renaming. Recall that static single assignment form generates a new temporary name for each definition of a value. When translating back into normal form, the names are recombined to eliminate the copy operations implied by the ϕ-nodes. Recall that the translation back to normal form is governed by a relation between temporaries. Two temporaries that are related share the same name in the normal form of the graph.

Register renaming is implemented by constructing the minimal relation that eliminates all copies from ϕ-nodes. This relation is the transitive closure of the condition that two temporaries are related if one is an operand and the other is the target of the same ϕ-node. The relation is implemented using UNION/FIND algorithms to create a partition of all temporaries. Hence the algorithm consists of translating to the minimum SSA form, constructing the partition by declaring that the operands and the target of each ϕ-node are related, and then translating back into normal form.

11.4.2 Register Coalescing

Register coalescing removes as many copy operations as possible. Many of the copy operations have already been eliminated during peephole optimization, which eliminated all copies that were not implied by ϕ-nodes and did not involve temporaries associated with ϕ-nodes at abnormal edges. The largest proportion of the copies are removed in this way. The rest of the copies are eliminated using an observation of Chaitin (1981): If the source and the destination of a copy do not conflict, then the source and destination can be combined into one register. Once the two temporaries have been combined, the algorithm can be applied again to another copy. The observation creates a partition of the temporaries: Two temporaries are in the same partition if they have been combined during register coalescing.

The SSA-form register-renaming algorithm can generate ϕ-nodes associated with abnormal edges in the flow graph. These ϕ-nodes must not generate copy operations when the graph is translated back into normal form. Thus the algorithm must avoid eliminating copies that will cause copies to occur on abnormal edges. As usual, impossible edges are fine since the code on them can never be executed anyway.

The algorithm consists of using the SSA form to eliminate most copies. Initially the temporaries are partitioned so that each temporary is in an element of the partition by itself. Then each ϕ-node and copy instruction is investigated. If an operand and the destination temporaries do not conflict, then both temporaries are put in the same partition. The flow graph is then translated back into normal form.

Note the similarity between register coalescing and register renaming. Both are implemented by creating a partition, and both partitions are created to eliminate the copies at the ϕ-nodes.

11.4.3 Integrating Ideas

Integrating register renaming and register coalescing is straightforward. Each builds a partition of the temporaries for reconstructing the normal form of the flow graph. Build the smallest partition that performs register coalescing, and register renaming will happen for free.

The driver procedure is described in Figure 11.13. The flow graph is already in static single assignment form. First, global value numbering is

Figure 11.13　Coalescing and Renaming

```
procedure RENAME_AND_GLOBAL_COALESCE;
   call CALCULATE_GLOBAL_VALUE;
   foreach T ∈ Temporaries do
      make {T} one partition in equivalence class;
   endfor;
   foreach (T_1,T_2) ∈ Pairs_In_Abnormal_φ_node do
      call UNION(T_1,T_2);
   endfor;
   do
      change := false;
      call CALCULATE_CONFLICT_GRAPH(Occurs_in_Copy);
      call COALESCE_TEMPORARIES;
   while change;
   call Normal_Form;
endprocedure RENAME_AND_GLOBAL_COALESCE;
```

computed so that the compiler knows which temporaries may have the same value: This is used to compute the conflict graph. Initially each temporary is put in a separate element of the partition by itself. Then the pairs of temporaries that occur in copies on the abnormal edges have their partitions merged so that no copies can occur involving them. We have restricted peephole optimization so that this is legal.

Now Chaitin's observation is used to merge partition sets, which is the same as renaming one temporary to be the same as the other. The partition is implemented using a UNION/FIND algorithm with FIND of the elements in the partition being used as the representative temporary. Two temporaries can be combined into one if they do not conflict. At this point the compiler is only interested in combining temporaries that are the source and destination of a copy operation or φ-node. Later during global register allocation, the same observation will be used to allocate registers.

As we will see when we study *COALESCE_TEMPORARIES*, we need to update the conflict graph as we combine two temporaries. However, the update is conservative and not precise, so coalescing is repeated with a recomputed conflict graph until no further copies can be eliminated.

COALESCE_TEMPORARIES in Figure 11.14 performs the walk of the flow graph, checking all copies. As noted above there are two forms of copies: the explicit copies that come from the intermediate representation and the copies implicit in φ-nodes. Since the elimination of some copies may prevent the elimination of others, the flow graph is walked with the most

Figure 11.14 Walking the Graph and Checking Coalescing

```
procedure COALESCE_TEMPORARIES;
   foreach B ∈ N in highest frequency of execution first do
      foreach I ∈ B do
         if I is a copy operation T₀ = T₁ then
            call CHECK_COALESCE(T₀,T₁);
         endif;
      endfor;
      foreach S ∈ SUCC(B) do
         let B be the ith predecessor of S;
         foreach T₀ = φ(T₁,...,Tₘ) ∈ Φ(S) do
            call CHECK_COALESCE(T₀,Tᵢ);
         endfor;
      endfor;
   endfor;
endprocedure COALESCE_TEMPORARIES;
```

frequently executed blocks being processed first. If this information is not available by profiling or static estimates, then walk the innermost blocks of the loops first. Without that information, walk the blocks in any order.

Finally, the real work is done in *CHECK_COALESCE* in Figure 11.15. The conflict information for the partition is stored as the conflict information of the representative temporary, so first find the representative temporaries. If they are the same representative, then the temporaries have already been

Figure 11.15 Coalescing Two Temporaries

```
procedure CHECK_COALESCE(T₀,T₁: Temporaries);
   T₀' = FIND(T₀);
   T₁' = FIND(T₁);
   if T₀' ≠ T₁' ∧ T₀' does not conflict with T₁' then
      call UNION(T₀',T₁');
      T = FIND(T₀')
      foreach S ∈ Conflicts(T₁') do
         add S to Conflicts(T);
      endfor;
      foreach S ∈ Conflicts(T₀') do
         add S to Conflicts(T);
      endfor;
      change = true;
   endif;
endprocedure CHECK_COALESCE;
```

coalesced either directly or indirectly. Second, check to see if they conflict. If they do, then nothing is done; otherwise, the two partitions are merged with a *UNION* operation and the conflict information for the new representative is given the union of the conflict information for the original partitions.

The normal implementation of the UNION/FIND algorithms makes either T_0' or T_1' be the new representative. In that case one of the loops can be eliminated. The elimination of a copy means that *change* is set to true to indicate that some copies were eliminated on this pass. The algorithm can also stop if there are no copy operations left.

What are the advantages of this technique? As noted earlier, local coalescing eliminates most copies without use of the conflict graph. Second, global value numbering allows the elimination of cascading copies without repeated creations of the conflict graph. Third, the algorithm computes the conflict graph only for the temporaries that can be involved in coalescing.

There are some other target architectures that require a form of implied coalescing. If the target machine is not a RISC processor, then it may have instructions in which one of the operands is modified to get the result. With the intermediate representation mimicking a RISC processor, the register allocator wants to make as many of these targets as possible be the same as one of the operands. This is accomplished by substituting two target machine instructions for a RISC instruction: a copy from one operand to the target and the target instruction with the target and the (implied) operand the same. Coalescing is used to eliminate the copy instruction, that is, make the operand and target be the same temporary.

11.5 Computing the Register Pressure

The compiler has reduced the number of temporaries in use as far as possible. Now the compiler needs to determine where in the flow graph each temporary gets assigned to a register. Whenever a temporary is in use, it is in a register; however, it may be spilled to a temporary memory location between uses. We use the register pressure as an approximation to the number of registers that are needed, so the compiler must first compute the register pressure or the number of live temporaries at each point. If there are multiple register sets, such as distinct integer and floating-point registers, then the register pressure is computed separately for each.

Limiting Resources

> **DEFINITION** **Register Pressure:** Given a point p in the flow graph, the register pressure is the number of temporaries that are live at p. If there are separate register sets, the register pressure for each set is computed separately.

The register pressure can be determined by computing the set of temporaries that are live at the end of each block. The size of this set gives the register pressure after the last instruction in the block. Then the compiler walks each block backward, keeping track of which registers are live at each point. The size of the set is the register pressure. At each instruction the compiler will perform the following steps:

1. First, the temporary that holds the value of an instruction is marked dead and removed from the set of live registers. If the temporary was not live before being marked dead, the instruction can be removed.

2. Next, the temporaries that are operands of the instruction are marked live.

3. The register pressure before the instruction is the size of the set of live registers after processing the instruction. Remember, we are processing the instructions in reverse execution order.

Besides knowing the register pressure at each instruction, the algorithm needs to know the maximum register pressure in each block and each loop. For this the compiler uses the loop tree. All of the information about register pressure can be computed in one walk of the loop tree, as described in Figure 11.16.

The register pressure is a synthesized attribute of the loop tree. The register pressure for each node is the maximum of the register pressures for each of the children. So computing the register pressure for a loop is just

Figure 11.16 Finding Register Pressure in Flow Graph

```
procedure CALCULATE_PRESSURE;
   call CALCULATE_LIVE;
   call COMPUTE_LOOP_TREE;
   foreach L ∈ LoopContains(Root_of_Loop_Tree) do
      call CALCULATE_PRESSURE_LOOP(L);
   endfor;
endprocedure CALCULATE_PRESSURE;
```

Figure 11.17 Finding Pressure in a Loop

```
procedure CALCULATE_PRESSURE_LOOP(L: Loop_Node);
   case NodeKind(L) of
   block:
      call CALCULATE_PRESSURE_BLOCK(L);
   single_entry_loop, multi_entry_loop:
      MaxPressure = 0;
      Occur_in_Loop = ∅;
      foreach S ∈ LoopContains(L) do
         call CALCULATE_PRESSURE_LOOP(S);
         MaxPressure = Max(MaxPressure,Pressure(S));
         Occur_in_Loop = Occur_in_Loop ∪ Occurs(S);
      endfor;
      Pressure(L) = MaxPressure;
      Occurs(L) = Occurs_in_Loop;
   endcase;
endprocedure CALCULATE_PRESSURE_LOOP;
```

finding the maximum of the register pressures for the enclosed loops and blocks, as shown in Figure 11.17.

Computing the register pressure in a block is shown in Figure 11.18. The structure mimics the computation of local lifetime information used for live/dead analysis. The block is scanned in reverse execution order and

Figure 11.18 Computing Pressure in a Block

```
procedure CALCULATE_PRESSURE_BLOCK(B: Block);
   Live = LiveOut(B);
   MaxPressure = |Live|;
   Occur = ∅;
   foreach I ∈ B in reverse execution order do
      foreach T ∈ Targets(I) do
         add T to Occur;
         delete T from Live;
      endfor;
      foreach T ∈ Operands(I) do
         add T to Occur;
         add T to Live;
      endfor;
      Pressure(I) = |Live|;
      MaxPressure = Max(MaxPressure,Pressure(I));
   endfor;
   Pressure(B) = MaxPressure;
   Occurs(B) = Occur;
endprocedure CALCULATE_PRESSURE_BLOCK;
```

Limiting Resources **319**

each instruction is executed in backward order. When a definition is found, the temporary becomes dead, and when a use is found, the temporary becomes live if it was not already live. The register pressure is the number of registers that are live between each pair of instructions.

Some processors, such as the INTEL i860, contain instructions that define the target register before the operands are used. In those cases, this code must be changed to reflect the hardware. For those particular instructions, the operands will be referenced first in backward execution order, then the targets will be modified.

11.6 Reducing Register Pressure

The compiler will now simplify the register allocation problem by reducing the register pressure at each point in the flow graph to be no greater than the number of physical registers available. If there are multiple register sets, this is done separately for each set. The compiler identifies points where the register pressure is too large. It stores a temporary in memory before that point and reloads it after the point. The temporary must be in a register at each use of the temporary. The temporary is no longer live between the STORE instruction and LOAD instruction, so the register pressure is decreased.

To summarize this situation, assume that the register pressure is too high at the point p in the flow graph and a temporary T is being spilled to memory. A memory location $MEMORY(T)$ must be assigned to hold the value of T. Then instructions must be added to the program to move T to and from the memory location. If T is live at a point p in the program where the compiler wants to reuse the register holding T, then

> A store operation moving T to $MEMORY(T)$ must be placed on each path between an evaluation of T and p.
>
> A load operation moving $MEMORY(T)$ to T must be placed on each path between p and any instruction that might use T as an operand.

It is not difficult to satisfy these conditions. The compiler could insert a store operation after each instruction that computes a value into T, and a load operation before each instruction that uses the value in T. The problem is that this generates too many memory-reference instructions. On modern processors, memory references are one of the most expensive operations, so the compiler needs to decrease the number of such instructions. These instructions also take up space in the instruction cache, further decreasing performance.

If there is a point in the program where the register pressure exceeds the number of available registers, the compiler will spill a temporary to decrease the register pressure.[5] Since the compiler is trying to decrease the number of load and store operations performed, it will start spilling at the most frequently executed point in the program and attempt to insert the load and store operations at less frequently executed points. To do this it uses a three-step process applied at the point p in the procedure where the register pressure is largest:

1. Find the largest loop (most outward loop) containing p where there is some temporary T that is live throughout the loop and not used within the loop. T is holding a value that is passed through the loop. Insert a single store operation T into $MEMORY(T)$ at the beginning of the loop, and a load operation from $MEMORY(T)$ into T at each loop exit where T is live. Attempt to move the store operations toward the procedure *Entry* as far as is possible without increasing the number of times they are executed. Attempt to move the load operations toward the procedure *Exit* as far as is possible without increasing the number of times they are executed. This may decrease the register pressure at other points.

2. If no loop and temporary T can be found, then apply the same technique to the single block where the register pressure is too high. Find a temporary T that is live throughout the block and not used in the block. Insert the store operation before the block and the load operation after the block if T is live after the block. Again attempt to move the store operation toward the procedure *Entry* block and the load operation toward the *Exit* block.

3. If both previous techniques fail to reduce the register pressure, the load and store operations must occur within the block where the register pressure is too high. Choose a temporary T that is live at p and is not used for the largest number of instructions. Insert a store operation after the definition of T (or at the beginning of the block if there is no definition in the block). Insert a load operation before the next use of T (or at the end of the block if there is not another use in the block). If a load

---

5. There are situations in which the register pressure is not an accurate measure of the number of registers needed. In some situations, more registers are needed due to complex intertwining of register usage patterns. In the presence of uninitialized temporaries and paths through the flow graph that are not executable, fewer registers may be needed. However, the register pressure is typically very close to the number of registers needed.

occurs at the beginning of the block, attempt to move the load as far toward the procedure *Entry* as possible without increasing the frequency of execution. Similarly, move the store operation toward the procedure *Exit* as far as is possible.

Once the compiler has inserted the load and store operations, it uses the techniques of partial redundancy elimination to move the load toward the *Entry* block and the store toward the *Exit* block. The *EARLIEST* algorithm is used so that the operations are moved as far as possible.

Recall that register allocation is an NP-complete problem, so there is no likelihood of finding an algorithm that works well in all cases. This means that the implementer (and the author) must resist too complex allocation mechanisms: Past experience says that they do not pay off.

It is more efficient to compute for each loop the temporaries that are available to spill and then scan from the outermost loop to the innermost, spilling temporaries if the register pressure is too high. An attribute *Through(L)* is computed for the flow graph, each loop, and each block. The algorithm is given in Figures 11.19 and 11.20.

The procedure *COMPUTE_THROUGH* starts the recursive tree walk of the loop tree. Since the attribute is only needed for loops with high register pressure, the attribute is not computed for less complex loops. This will save some time. Note that this is not true of loops contained within other loops. If the outer loop has high register pressure, the register pressure for the inner, less complex loops is still computed. It is too complex to avoid the unneeded computation.

The procedure *COMPUTE_THROUGH_LOOP* handles blocks separately from loops. For a block, a temporary is live throughout the block without references in the block if and only if the temporary is live at the beginning of the block and there are no references. Warning: It is not true that a temporary is

Figure 11.19 Computing Transparent Temporaries

```
procedure COMPUTE_THROUGH;
   call CALCULATE_PRESSURE;
   foreach L ∈ LoopContains(Root_of_Loop_Tree) do
      if Pressure(L) > Max_Physical_Registers then
         call COMPUTE_THROUGH_LOOP(L);
      endif;
   endfor;
endprocedure COMPUTE_THROUGH;
```

Figure 11.20 Main *Through* Calculation

```
procedure COMPUTE_THROUGH_LOOP(L: Loop_Node);
   case NodeKind(L) of
   block:
      Through(L) = LiveIn(L) - Occurs(B);
   single_entry_loop, multi_entry_loop:
      Through(L) = Temporaries;
      foreach S ∈ LoopContains(L) do
         call COMPUTE_THROUGH_LOOP(S);
         Through(L) = Through(L) ∩ Through(S);
      endfor;
      foreach S ∈ LoopContains(L) do
         Through(S) = Through(S) - Through(L);
      endfor;
   endcase;
endprocedure COMPUTE_THROUGH_LOOP;
```

live throughout the block if it is live at the start and end of the block, since it may become dead within the block and then live again. Of course, this cannot happen if there are no references to the temporary in the block.

The set of temporaries that are live everywhere in a loop without references is the intersection of the corresponding set for each component of the loop. The *COMPUTE_THROUGH_LOOP* computes this intersection. The compiler is only interested in the outermost loop in which a temporary is live throughout without references, so after computing the *Through* set for a loop, it removes the references to those temporaries from the inner loops.

For single-entry loops, there is an easier way to compute the *Through* attribute. For a single-entry loop, a temporary is live throughout the loop without references in the loop if and only if it is live at the beginning of the entry block and has no references within the loop. This is true because there is a path from every block to every other block in the loop. This is not true for multiple-entry loops because the compiler has added blocks onto the beginning of the loop to create a single entry region of the flow graph. In these added blocks there is not a path from each block to every other block.

11.7 Computing the Spill Points

The way the algorithm is described, the compiler finds a point where the register pressure is too high and finds a temporary that is just occupying a register throughout a loop and spills it. A simpler implementation occurs by walking down the loop tree. At each loop consider the register pressure. If the pressure is too high, spill a temporary that is live throughout the loop and not referenced in the loop. Keep doing this until the register pressure has been driven down.

This may be inefficient because the algorithm will choose one temporary to spill in one loop and a different one to spill in another; thus, a large number of load and store operations may be inserted between two loops even though a single set of temporaries can be spilled in both loops, avoiding the loads and stores between them. The compiler attempts to avoid this problem by choosing the temporaries to spill based on all of the subloops within a loop. This is only a heuristic because the general problem of choosing which temporaries to spill to get the optimal solution is NP-complete.

The algorithm starts in Figure 11.21 with the driver procedure, which only computes the register pressure and the *Through* sets that contain the temporaries that are live in each loop but not referenced. The procedure then starts the walk of the loop tree. The walk stops when the procedure hits a block or a node that has a pressure lower than the number of registers. Finally it recomputes the pressure for use during instruction scheduling.

There are two fundamental procedures implementing the algorithm: one reduces the pressure in loops (see Figure 11.22), the other uses a different algorithm to reduce the pressure within a block (described later in section 11.7.1). The algorithm we have been discussing reduces pressure in loops. Reducing the pressure within a block is the last resort and is only performed if there are no temporaries that are live throughout the block and unused in it.

Now let's discuss reducing pressure within a loop, as described in Figure 11.22. The algorithm description is more daunting than the actual idea. Compute the set of loops or blocks, *High_Pressure*, which have an internal register pressure that is too high. The compiler needs to spill a temporary that is live in each of these loops if possible. To that end, it computes a priority queue, *Excess_Pressure*, consisting of the loops or blocks contained in

Figure 11.21 Driver for Reducing the Pressure

```
procedure REDUCE_PRESSURE;
   call COMPUTE_THROUGH;
   if Pressure(Root_of_Loop_Tree) > Max_Physical_Registers then
      call REDUCE_PRESSURE_LOOP(Root_of_Loop_Tree);
   endif;
   call CALCULATE_PRESSURE;
endprocedure REDUCE_PRESSURE;
```

Figure 11.22 Spilling Temporaries in a Loop

```
procedure REDUCE_PRESSURE_LOOP(L: Loop_Node);
  case NodeKind(L) of
  block:
    call REDUCE_PRESSURE_BLOCK(L);
  otherwise:
    Exceed_Pressure = ∅;
    High_Pressure
        = {C ∈ LoopContains(L)|Pressure(C) > Max_Physical_Registers};
    foreach C ∈ High_Pressure do
      Excess_Temporaries = Pressure(C) - Max_Physical_Registers;
      if Excess_Temporaries > 0 ∧ Through(C) ≠ ∅ then
          add C to Exceed_Pressure priority Excess_Temporaries;
      endif;
    endfor;
      while Exceed_Pressure ≠ ∅ do
          choose C from Exceed_Pressure with highest priority;
          T = CHOOSE_SPILL;
          call PERFORM_SPILL;
          call OPTIMIZE_SPILL_PLACEMENT(T);
      endwhile;
      foreach C ∈ High_Pressure do
          if Pressure(C) > Max_Physical_Registers then
              call REDUCE_PRESSURE_LOOP(C);
          endif;
      endfor;
  endcase;
  endif;
endprocedure REDUCE_PRESSURE_LOOP;
```

High_Pressure. The priority is given by the excess in register pressure. The algorithm chooses a temporary to spill (described shortly) and then spills it (also described shortly). When as much spilling as is possible has been performed in this loop, spilling is performed in the subloops and blocks if necessary.

How is the temporary to spill chosen? Consider the algorithm in Figure 11.23. The loop (or block) with the most excessive pressure is chosen. Each of the temporaries in *Through* for that loop are candidates for spilling. The one chosen is that which is also a candidate for spilling in the most other loops that need to spill temporaries. This gives the algorithm that optimizes the placement of the load and store operations the biggest chance of avoiding some load and store operations.

The algorithm in Figure 11.24 describes the insertion of the load and store operations. First there must be a memory location to hold the value.

Figure 11.23 Choosing which Loop Temporary to Spill

```
function CHOOSE_SPILL returns Temporary;
   Spill_Candidates = Through(C);    //Possible temporaries to spill
   foreach T ∈ Spill_Candidates do   //Can spill elsewhere?
      Quiet_Regions(T) = {C};
      foreach C' ∈ Exceed_Pressure do
         if T ∈ Through(C') then
            add C' to Quiet_Regions(T);
         endif;
      endfor;
   endfor;
   choose T such that |Quiet_Regions(T)| largest;
   return T;
endfunction CHOOSE_SPILL;
```

Figure 11.24 Inserting Spilled Loads and Stores

```
procedure PERFORM_SPILL(T: Temporary);
   if T does not have associated spill location MEMORY(T) then
      allocate a spill location MEMORY(T) for T
   endif;
   foreach C' ∈ Quiet_Regions(T) do //Spill outside these regions
      add STORE T,MEMORY(T) on entry edge before LoopEntry(C');
      for each block B ∉ C' where B has predecessor P ∈ C' do
         if T is live on entry to B then
            add LOAD MEMORY(T) => T on edge (P,B);
         endif;
      endfor;
      remove T from Through(C');
      if Through(C') = ∅ then
         remove C' from Exceed_Pressure;
      endif;
      call UPDATE_PRESSURE(C');
      Excess_Temporaries = Pressure(C') - Max_Physical_Registers;
      if Excess_Temporaries > 0 then
         change priority of C' to Excess_Temporaries in
               Exceed_Pressure;
      else
         remove C' from Excess_Pressure;
         remove C' from High_Pressure;
      endif;
   endfor;
endprocedure PERFORM_SPILL;
```

Figure 11.25 Updating Pressure

```
procedure UPDATE_PRESSURE(L: LoopNode);
   Pressure(L) = Pressure(L) - 1;
   if Pressure(L) > Max_Physical_Registers then
      foreach C ∈ LoopContains(L) do
         call UPDATE_PRESSURE(C);
      endfor;
   endif;
endprocedure UPDATE_PRESSURE;
```

The same memory location must be used for all references to the same temporary. The store operation is inserted before entry into the loop, and load operations are inserted at the exit points if the temporary is still live there. Since there are no references to the temporary in the loop, this guarantees that the new program has exactly the same computational effect as the original program. Then the data structures are updated. If the loop no longer has excess pressure, then the loop is removed from *Excess_Pressure* and *High_Pressure*. If it still has excessive pressure, the priority is decreased by one.

Updating the register pressure is the most expensive operation, so the compiler uses an approximation that reduces the pressure in the preselected loops and blocks. The optimization of the placement of load and store operations may decrease it in other places. However, the choice to spill the same temporary in as many places as necessary within a loop makes this approximation better. All of the loops or blocks that have high pressure and in which the temporary can be spilled do have the temporary spilled and the pressure adjusted. It is the blocks or loops where the pressure is not too high that fail to have the pressure adjusted. So the algorithm performs a walk of the loop tree, decreasing the recorded pressures by one. It stops when the leaves or a loop with low pressure is reached. The algorithm is described in Figure 11.25 as a simple tree walk down the tree, fixing the values of the attribute *Pressure*.

11.7.1 Reducing the Pressure in a Block

The classic spilling algorithm for one-pass register allocation is used to spill within a block. Scan through the block in execution order. When a point is reached where the register pressure is too high, choose a temporary that is live at that point (so it will reduce the pressure) and whose next use as an operand of an instruction is furthest in the future. Spilling that temporary will maximize the sequence of instructions within the block where the pressure is reduced. For the purposes of choosing this temporary, if there are no further uses of a live temporary in this block, pretend that a dummy use occurs after the end of the block.

The algorithm is implemented in two passes. The first pass scans backward through the block, building a list of the instructions where each temporary occurring in the block is used and computing the register pressure before each instruction (Figure 11.26). It mimics the code that we have used before for computing live/dead information and computing register pressure. Note that register coalescing and register renaming has ensured that there is only one evaluation of a temporary within the block. The list therefore starts at the first point that a temporary becomes live.

The second pass through the block scans forward (Figure 11.27). As it passes each instruction, it removes the instruction from the use lists built in the previous phase so that the lists always hold the uses that remain in the block. As it is scanning forward, it maintains a set of all of the temporaries that are live. When the register pressure exceeds the number of registers, one of the temporaries is stored to memory together with a load operation before the next use. To keep track of the set of temporaries that are live at

Figure 11.26 List of Uses for Reducing Pressure

```
procedure REDUCE_PRESSURE_FIND_USES(B: Block);
   Live = LiveOut(B);
   foreach T ∈ Live do
      create list Reduce_Uses(T) containing end_of_block;
   endfor;
   foreach I ∈ B in reverse execution order do
      foreach T ∈ Targets(I) do
         delete T from Live;
      endfor;
      foreach T ∈ Operands(I) do
         if T ∉ Live then
            create empty list Reduce_Uses(T);
         endif;
         add T to Live;
         add I to head of the list Reduce_Uses(T);
      endfor;
   endfor;
endprocedure REDUCE_PRESSURE_FIND_USES;
```

Figure 11.27 Reducing Pressure in a Block

```
procedure REDUCE_PRESSURE_BLOCK(B: Block);
   call REDUCE_PRESSURE_FIND_USES(B);
   if |Live| ≥ Max_Physical_Registers then
         call REDUCE_SPILL_LOCAL (begin_block)
   endif
   foreach I ∈ B in execution order do
      foreach T ∈ Operands(I) do
         remove I from Reduce_Uses(T);
         if Reduce_Uses(T) = ∅ then
            remove T from Live;
         endif;
      endfor;
      foreach T ∈ Targets(I) do
         while |Live| ≥ Max_Physical_Registers do
            call REDUCE_SPILL_LOCAL(I);
         endwhile;
         add T to Live;
         if Reduce_Uses(T) = ∅ then
            remove T from Live;
         endif;
      endfor;
   endfor;
endprocedure REDUCE_PRESSURE_BLOCK;
```

the beginning of the block, the set *Live* computed in the initial pass is used and the reverse actions are performed on the temporaries as the compiler scans forward through the block.

Which temporary should be stored? The temporary whose next use is furthest in the future. In other words, scan the set of live temporaries and choose the one whose next entry in the use list is latest. This is the classic heuristic used in one-pass register allocators and it makes a register available as long as is possible.

The actual point where the register pressure is too high is within the instruction between the uses of the operands (which might decrease register pressure) and the storing of values in the targets (which increases register pressure). If the pressure is too high, the temporary being spilled is stored before this instruction (the temporary must be one of the operands or another temporary that is live but not used in this instruction). The value must be reloaded before the next use. If there are no more uses in the block but the temporary is live, then the load operations must be placed on each exit edge where the temporary is live and the algorithm to optimize the placement of the spill operations called. Similarly, if the load operation is

Figure 11.28 Inserting a Spill within a Block

```
procedure REDUCE_SPILL_LOCAL(I: Instruction);
   perform_optimization = false;
   Choice = {T ∈ Live| Reduce_Uses(T) most future instruction};
   if MEMORY(Choice) is not allocated then
      allocate memory location for MEMORY(Choice);
   endif;
   insert STORE Choice,MEMORY(Choice) before I;
   remove Choice from Live;
   if I is the first instruction in the block then
      perform_optimization = true;
   Next = Instruction in Reduce_Uses(Choice);
   if Next = end_of_block then
      insert LOAD_MEMORY(Choice) => Choice on exit edges;
      perform_optimization = true;
   else
      insert LOAD_MEMORY(Choice) => Choice before Next;
   endif;
   if perform_optimization then
      call OPTIMIZE_SPILL_PLACEMENT(Choice);
   endif;
endprocedure REDUCE_SPILL_LOCAL;
```

placed at the beginning of the block, then the spill optimizer must be called to improve the placement of the spill (see Figure 11.28).

11.8 Optimizing the Placement of Spill Instructions

Once the initial positions of store and load operations are determined, the compiler optimizes the placement of these STORE and LOAD instructions by moving them to less frequent execution points. The act of moving them decreases the register pressure at the points moved over, making the rest of the pressure-reduction algorithm easier.

To optimize the placement of load and store operations, the compiler keeps the following sets for each spilled temporary. These sets are maintained throughout the spilling process throughout the whole flow graph because spilling a temporary in one region of the flow graph may change the placement of load and store operations in another part of the flow graph.

STORE_IN(T) is the set of blocks in which there is a STORE instruction of *T* into *MEMORY(T)* at the beginning of the block.

STORE_OUT(T) is the set of blocks in which there is a STORE instruction of *T* into *MEMORY(T)* at the end of the block.

LOAD_IN(T) is the set of blocks in which there is a LOAD instruction of *T* from *MEMORY(T)* at the beginning of the block.

LOAD_OUT(T) is the set of blocks in which there is a LOAD instruction of *T* from *MEMORY(T)* at the end of the block.

This section describes an algorithm to improve the placement of these load and store operations. Once the loop-based algorithm has determined the placement of instructions outside of loops, these load and store operations together with the previous load and store operations for the same temporary are used to find better places to put the operations. The algorithm used is the *EARLIEST* algorithm for partial redundancy elimination.

11.8.1 Optimizing the Store Operations

Consider the store operations used to spill *T* to *MEMORY(T)*. These instructions can be viewed as unary operations, depending only on *T*. They can be optimized like any other instruction as soon as we define what it means to evaluate an occurrence of the store and what will kill the store.

What instructions perform an evaluation of the store operation? These are instructions that ensure that the value in memory is the same as the value in *T* after the instruction is executed. Clearly, one of the store operations that the compiler inserts satisfies this condition. However, a load operation from *MEMORY(T)* to *T* also satisfies the condition. Thus, the instructions that evaluate the store operation are both the store and load instructions.

What instructions kill the store operation? These are the instructions that cause the condition that the value in *T* is the same as the value in *MEMORY(T)* to be violated, which will be any instructions that modify *T*. Note that a LOAD instruction first kills *T* and then has the effect of an evaluation of a store operation.

Note that the uses of *T* as an operand do not affect the placement of store operations. The store operations are being moved toward the *Entry* block and never change the value of *T*, so a store can be moved past a use of *T* without affecting any values in registers. This gives us the following definitions for anticipation and availability:

```
STORE_ANTLOC(I) = STORE_IN(T)
STORE_AVLOC(I)  = STORE_OUT(T) ∪ LOAD_OUT(T)
STORE_TRANSP(B) = {T | No instruction in B modifies T}
```

These sets can now be used to compute *STORE_ANTIN*, *STORE_ANTOUT*, *STORE_AVIN*, and *STORE_AVOUT*. Then the formulas for *EARLIEST* can be used to compute *STORE_EARLIEST*. This gives the points at which to insert new STORE instructions and the points at which to delete older instances of STORE instructions.

In contrast to the situation during global optimization of expressions, the STORE instructions should be moved as far as possible. This may decrease the register pressure in other parts of the flow graph and avoid further spills that could not be otherwise identified. Therefore the *EARLIEST* algorithm is used rather than the *LATEST* algorithm.

The computation of *STORE_EARLIEST* uses the formulas for *EARLIEST*, replacing the anticipated and available sets by the corresponding sets described here for stores. The algorithm for inserting and deleting the STORE instructions also uses the formulas describing insertion and deletion for *EARLIEST*.

A further optimization is needed to decrease the number of stores in the flow graph. The *EARLIEST* formulas can describe the insertion of the same computation on all edges leading to a block. In that case, the computation should be inserted at the beginning of the block and not on all of the edges. Also, if the algorithm describes the insertion of a store at the beginning of a block and the deletion of a store at the beginning of the same block, then do not perform either insertion or deletion. This is what happens with *EARLIEST* if a store cannot be moved: The algorithm describes the insertion of a store on each edge leading to the block and the deletion of the store in the block.

The same problem with abnormal edges occurs in this algorithm as with partial redundancy, and the solution is the same. If the algorithm attempts to insert a store on an abnormal edge, the compiler will pretend that there is an instruction that modifies T at the beginning of the head of the edge. Thus T is not anticipated and no insertion will occur on the edge. The algorithm is repeated with this added instruction to determine a new set of points at which to insert the store operations. The complete algorithm is described in Figure 11.29.

11.8.2 Optimizing the Placement of Spilled LOADs

The same techniques can be used to move the load operations, except that the compiler needs to move the load operations toward *Exit*. We apply partial redundancy on the reverse graph, using predecessors everywhere that successors are used in the normal *EARLIEST* algorithm.

To do this, the compiler must know what the evaluation of a LOAD instruction is and what instructions kill a LOAD instruction. An instruction

Figure 11.29 Inserting and Deleting Spilled STOREs

```
procedure MOVE_STORES(T: Temporary);
   call CALCULATE_STORE_LOCAL(T);
   call CALCULATE_STORE_ANTICIPATION(T);
   call CALCULATE_STORE_AVAILABLE(T);
   foreach B ∈ N do
      on_all_edges = ∩ {STORE_EARLIEST_{P,B}| P ∈ Pred(B)};
      if on_all_edges then
         if B ∉ STORE_IN(T) then
            insert STORE T,MEMORY(T) at beginning of B;
            add B to STORE_IN(T);
         endif;
      else
         foreach P ∈ Pred(B) do
            if STORE_EARLIEST_{P,B} then
               if |Succ(P)| = 1 then
                  insert STORE T,MEMORY(T) at end of P;
                  add P to STORE_OUT(T);
               else
                  Recompute placement of STOREs assuming
                   that there is an instruction at beginning of
                   B that kills the STORE T,MEMORY(T).
               endif
            endif;
         endfor;
         if B ∈ STORE_IN(T) then
            delete STORE T,MEMORY(T) at beginning of B;
         endif
      endif;
   endfor;
endprocedure MOVE_STORES;
```

evaluates a LOAD instruction if it guarantees that the value in the temporary is the same as the value in memory. Obviously, a LOAD instruction evaluates a LOAD instruction and so does a STORE instruction.

What instructions kill a LOAD instruction? A use or evaluation of the temporary kills a LOAD instruction. The use kills it because moving the load past the use will destroy the value for the use. An evaluation of the temporary will kill the load since it will generate a value different from the one in memory.

A further optimization can be made by observing that some paths to *Exit* may not contain any further uses of the temporary T. If a LOAD instruction is to be inserted at a point where T is not live, then the insertion can be ignored.

11.9 References

Chaitin, G. J., et al. 1981. Register allocation via coloring. *Computer Languages* 6(1): 47–57.

Leverett, B. W., et al. 1979. An overview of the Production-Quality Compiler-Compiler project. (Technical Report CMU-CS-79-105.) Pittsburgh, PA: Carnegie Mellon University.

12 SCHEDULING AND RESCHEDULING

Reduced instruction set computing (RISC) processors increase execution speed by making the instructions simple (thus keeping the hardware simple) and by a number of other devices for increasing the number of instructions that can be executed in a fixed interval of time.

The processor is *pipelined*. This means that the execution of individual instructions is broken into small tasks that are approximately equal in size. The individual tasks for a single instruction are performed on an assembly line (called a *pipeline*). Pipelining gains the efficiencies of an assembly line. A second instruction can start execution, or be *issued*, when the first instruction is moved from the first stage. One instruction can be issued during each instruction cycle for each pipeline. However, each instruction may not complete its evaluation for one or more cycles after it is issued. If a later instruction attempts to use the value computed in an earlier instruction that has not yet completed all stages of the pipeline, the processor will *stall*, or delay the issuing of the second instruction until the first one has completed. To gain performance, the compiler will reorder the instructions to avoid processor stalls.[1]

The processor will issue multiple instructions at the same time. The processor will load a small set of instructions, called a *packet,* and analyze the relationship between the instructions. If the instructions do not use or change the operands of the other instructions in the set, then the instruc-

---

1. Early RISC processors did not stall when a value was not ready. Instead they executed the instruction using garbage as input. It was the responsibility of the compiler to ensure that such execution did not happen. All recent processors will stall while waiting for operands since the indeterminancy of some instructions, particularly LOAD, multiply, and divide instructions, made scheduling difficult.

tions may be issued at the same time. This gains performance if the processor has more than one computing unit, such as an integer arithmetic unit and floating-point unit.

The processor may have more than one integer unit and more than one floating-point unit. In that case, the packet of instructions that can be fetched is larger and more than one arithmetic instruction may be issued simultaneously. Not all of the arithmetic units may be identical. In that case the compiler will reorder the instructions so that each packet will have instructions that can execute on different arithmetic units.

A processor with these three characteristics is called a *superscalar processor*. Most processors in use today are superscalar. Many of them have an additional characteristic called *out-of-order execution*. Such a processor will operate as described above and will allow later instructions in a packet to execute even when the instructions that precede them are constrained from execution. This later characteristic will not be discussed here since there are few things that the compiler can do to enhance the execution of out-of-order processors that are not important for the normal superscalar processors.

The Digital Alpha 21164 is an example of a superscalar processor. Consider how it matches the criteria above. First, the Alpha is not an out-of-order execution processor. All instructions are executed in order; if the execution of an instruction is delayed, all instructions following it are delayed also.

The Alpha is pipelined. Most instructions for the integer arithmetic units take one cycle; the floating-point instructions take four cycles. Some of the exceptions to these rules are the conditional move, LOAD, multiplication, and floating-division instructions.

The Alpha will attempt to issue four four-byte instructions during each clock cycle. The block of instructions must be aligned on an address that is a multiple of sixteen. If the address is not a multiple of sixteen, then the packet that contains the current instruction is fetched and the initial instructions in the packet are ignored, thus decreasing the number of instruction that can be issued during that clock cycle. If the instructions of a packet contain dependences so that they cannot all be issued, then the initial part of the packet is issued, up to the first instruction that cannot be issued immediately.

The Alpha contains two integer arithmetic units and two floating-point units. Both integer arithmetic units can execute most integer instructions. The exceptions are that shift operations are done on one of the units and branching operations are done on the other. There is a floating-point multiplication unit and a floating-point addition unit. Some instructions are shared between the two units.

Ideally, the Alpha will issue four instructions during a clock cycle. Two of the instructions will be executed by the two integer arithmetic units. One of the other instructions will be an instruction that can be executed by the floating-point multiplication unit, and the final instruction can be executed by the floating-point addition unit. These instructions can occur in any order in the packet of instructions.

There are other characteristics of the Alpha that the scheduler must take into account. Consider load operations. These are performed by the integer arithmetic unit; however, the length of time to fetch data from memory depends on which cache or memory unit currently contains the data.

The Alpha contains three on-chip caches: one for data, one for instructions, and a larger secondary cache. The primary cache contains 8K of data organized as a direct memory-mapped cache with a cache line of 32 bytes. If data is in this cache, a load operation takes two cycles. There is another 8K on-chip cache for instructions; however, it will not be discussed here.

The secondary on-chip cache holds both instructions and data. The cache will hold 96K of information organized as a three-way set-associative cache with each cache line containing 64 bytes of data. A load operation when data is in this cache takes nine cycles, including moving the data into the primary cache.

There is usually a large board-level cache in an Alpha system. This cache contains multiple megabytes of data and is organized as a direct memory-mapped cache with each cache line containing 64 bytes of data. For data in this cache, a load operation takes twenty cycles, including moving the data into the two higher-level caches.

When data is in memory and not in a cache, the load operation takes a long time: somewhere in the range of a hundred cycles, depending on the system involved. This is sufficiently long that there is no point in modeling the exact time in the scheduler. The compiler can handle this in one of two ways. It can optimistically assume that data is in one of the caches and schedule the instructions for that case, or the compiler can be aware that these load operations take a huge amount of time and attempt to move them as early in the schedule as possible.

The effect of pipelining on the execution of a program is that instructions are issued at some point in the program and the result becomes available some number of clock cycles later. Due to hardware optimizations, the number of cycles that the value takes to become available may depend on how it is going to be used, so the delay, or *latency,* is a function of both the instruction computing a value and the instruction that will use the value.

The SCHEDULE phase reorders the instructions in the procedure being compiled to eliminate as many stalls as possible. There are three different types of schedulers, based on the size of the pieces of the procedure that they attempt to reorder:

- *Block schedulers* reorder the instructions within individual blocks. The form of the program flow graph is not changed. The reordering of each block is independent of the reordering of other blocks, with the possible exception of some knowledge about values computed at the end of a block (or used at the beginning of a block).

- *Trace schedulers* reorder the instructions in a simple path of blocks. The paths that are reordered are chosen to be the most frequently executed paths in the program. Instructions may be moved from one block to another. In fact, instructions may be moved to places where the value computed is not guaranteed to be used (speculative execution). By reordering these larger sequences of instructions, more opportunities can be found for eliminating stalls.

- *Software pipeliners* reorder and replicate instructions in loops to eliminate stalls. The result of software pipelining is a new loop in which values are being simultaneously computed for multiple iterations of the original loop.

For a superscalar processor, block scheduling is inadequate. If the machine can issue four instructions on each clock cycle, then a one-cycle delay means that four potential computations are not performed. The compiler must find ways to move computations together so that they can be simultaneously executed. Since most blocks are small, the compiler must combine computations from multiple blocks or multiple iterations of a loop. In other words, the compiler must perform some form of trace scheduling and software pipelining.

Up to this point, we have ignored the amount of time needed to execute instructions and the way that the instructions are issued by the processor. The SCHEDULE phase reorders the instructions to avoid stalls. The Alpha instruction sequence in Figure 12.1 for the statement $A = (B + C) + D * E$ will waste two cycles when the instructions are executed in the order

Figure 12.1 Instructions Before (left) and After (right) Scheduling

0	ldt	f0,B		0	ldt	f0,B
0	ldt	f1,C		0	ldt	f1,C
2	addt	f0,f1,f2		1	ldt	f3,D
2	ldt	f3,D		1	ldt	f4,E
3	ldt	f4,E		2	addt	f0,f1,f2
5	mult	f3,f4,f5		3	mult	f3,f4,f5
9	addt	f2,f5,f6		7	addt	f2,f5,f6
13	stt	f6,A		11	stt	f6,A

described by the source language. The initial load operation takes two cycles to get the data from the data cache. These cycles can be used to execute the later load operations, allowing the loads and the subsequent multiplication and addition to overlap.

Figure 12.1 indirectly shows three other concerns. First, the initial instruction sequence can be executed using only three registers. The reordered sequence requires four registers. Reordering the instructions can increase the number of registers needed, therefore making register allocation harder. There are also cases where instruction scheduling will decrease the number of registers needed; however, these are rare. On the whole, instruction scheduling makes register allocation more difficult.

The second problem is, what happens when register allocation cannot put all temporaries in physical registers? The register allocator will insert store and load operations to move data to and from memory. These instructions destroy the original schedule of instructions, so instruction scheduling may need to be repeated after register allocation. The second time it is called, most temporaries will already have been assigned to physical registers so less movement is possible.

The third problem is implicit in the example shown above. The Alpha processor can issue four instructions at the same time. In this example, there are never more than two instructions available to issue. Many cycles have no instructions to issue, thus many opportunities for starting instructions (cycles) are wasted. How can the compiler reform the program to make more instructions available? We have discussed one method already: loop unrolling. If the code in Figure 12.1 were array references inside a loop, then four iterations of the loop could be executed simultaneously, using many of the wasted cycles.

12.1 Structure of the Instruction-Scheduling Phase

The compiler schedules blocks in groups: Each group is a path within the dominator tree. Note that this is a generalization of an extended block. Since each extended block is a subtree of the dominator tree, a path through an extended block is a path in the dominator tree. One variant of trace scheduling performs scheduling on extended blocks, so this is a generalization of that technique. In scheduling the blocks, the following operations are performed in order:

1. Create the dominator tree. The dominator tree is the basic data structure for global scheduling. The compiler will use it to find paths to schedule together. It will also perform value numbering on the instructions as they are scheduled to eliminate unneeded computations on paths yet to be scheduled.

2. Identify each single-block loop. Perform software pipelining on these loops. This involves the creation of several blocks to hold instructions to start the loop, instructions to end the loop, and an alternative copy of the loop when too few iterations will be performed. These blocks are inserted into the dominator tree, and the initial block is marked as a member of a single-block path that is already scheduled.

3. To perform scheduling the compiler needs to know which temporaries are used or defined between a block and a block it dominates. These are called the *IDEFS* and *IUSE* sets (we will see how to compute them shortly). The compiler computes them before beginning the scheduling.

4. Compute the paths, or *traces,* through the dominator tree to be scheduled together. Two distinct criteria are used for forming the traces. If execution frequency information is available, the most frequently executed path is chosen first, and then the process is repeated on less frequent paths. When two blocks have equal likelihood, the block added to the path is the one more likely to be mergeable with its predecessor or successor.

5. Now perform a depth-first search of the dominator tree. When arriving at a block that starts a trace, schedule that trace. As the compiler walks the tree, it performs value numbering to determine which instructions are available. An available instruction can be eliminated and need not be scheduled. Scheduling consists of two parts: computing the interference graph between instructions and then ordering the instructions to overlap execution as much as possible.

Contrary to other approaches to trace scheduling, this algorithm is applied to the flow graph with temporaries. Registers are assigned later. When the instruction scheduling is applied after register allocation, each trace is made one block long so that instruction scheduling only occurs within a block. In that case only blocks with new instructions inserted need to be rescheduled.

12.2 Phase Order

The scheduler is called twice. It follows the LIMIT phase, so we know that there are enough registers to hold all values needed at each point in the program. It precedes register allocation, so temporaries still exist. It reorders the instructions in the program, leaving a valid representation of the same program. After register allocation the scheduler may be called again if there have been any spill operations inserted into the program. Note that peephole optimization is performed before scheduling. Thus the sequence of phase execution near the scheduler phase is as shown in Figure 12.2.

Since scheduling happens before temporaries are tied to physical registers, there is a larger degree of freedom in moving instructions around. This can increase the number of registers that are live at each point in the program. Thus the scheduler must be constrained to not increase the number of registers needed at each point of the program beyond the number of registers that are available. If this limits the instruction scheduler too much, we

Figure 12.2 Sequence of Phases Involving Scheduling

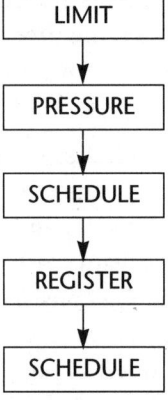

Scheduling and Rescheduling **341**

will change the LIMIT phase to decrease the register pressure further. This can be done experimentally as we test real programs.

Scheduling can create opportunities for peephole optimizations. It can move loads and stores of the same location so that they are adjacent. Hence the scheduler must be prepared to do some limited forms of peephole optimization as it schedules instructions.

After register allocation has been performed, the scheduler can be called again if there are any instructions inserted by the register allocator. If there is no register spilling in the register allocator, then the second execution of the scheduler is unnecessary.

12.3 Example

Two examples are used to illustrate instruction scheduling. First, in Figure 12.3, is the inner loop of the running example. We will schedule the body of the loop, gaining some performance even though the loop has few instructions. This is typical of many loops in real programs.

The corresponding scheduled fragment of the flow graph is given in Figure 12.4. All of the store operations have been removed from the loop and the superblock[2] transformation has replicated the instructions at the end of the loop to improve instruction scheduling.

Figure 12.5 is used as an example for two purposes. The compiler will software pipeline this loop, overlapping the execution of multiple iterations. As well as being used to show software pipelining, we will use this example to illustrate how the compiler would compile a loop that is not software pipelined. Such a loop may be unrolled to gain more instructions for scheduling.

Figure 12.3   Inner Loop of Example

```
DO J = 2, N
   IF (DABS(A(J,I) .GT. VALUE(I))
      VALUE(I) = DABS(A(J,I))
      LARGE(I) = J
   ENDIF
ENDDO
```

---

2. Superblock scheduling is discussed in Appendix B.

Figure 12.4 Instructions in the Inner Loop

```
12 B2:   dSLD      (T28)       => SF4    /value A(J,I)
13       CPYS      SF4         => SF4    /DABS(A(J,I))
14       dCMPLE    SF4,SF1     => SF6    /comparison
15       dBCOND    SF6,B3,B6            /skip update of variables

16 B6:   d2d       SF4         => SF1    /update value of VALUE(I)
17       i2i       T6          => T14    /put in register for LARGE(I)
18       BR        B3

19 B3:   iADD      T6,#1       => T6     /J + 1
20       iADD      T28,#8      => T28    /update value of address(A(J,I))
21       iCMPGT    T6,T8       => T24    /is J > N
22       iBCOND    T24,B4,B2
```

Figure 12.5 Vectorizable Loop

```
DO I = 1,20
   A(I) = B(I) + C(I)
ENDDO
```

Figure 12.6 contains the instructions that are provided after previous compiler phases if the loop will be software pipelined. The body of the loop contains the instructions for one iteration of the loop. Figure 12.7 contains the instructions for the loop that were generated when assuming that the loop would not be software pipelined. The loop has been unrolled four times so that the computations can be overlapped. In this particular case, the compiler might actually unroll the loop more than four times; however, nothing would be gained by depicting more unrolling as an example.

Figure 12.6 Instructions for Vectorizable Loop

```
B2:  dSLD      (T1)        => SF1    /LOAD B(I)
     dSLD      (T2)        => SF2    /LOAD C(I)
     dADD      SF1,SF2     => SF3    /B(I) + C(I)
     dSST      (T3),SF3              /A(I) = B(I) + C(I)
     iADD      T1,+8       => T1     /increment address of B(I)
     iADD      T2,#8       => T2     /increment address of C(I)
     iADD      T3,#8       => T3     /increment address of A(I)
     iADD      T4,#1       => T4     /increment loop count
     iCMPGT    T4,T5       => T6     /check end of loop
     iBCOND    T6,B2,B3
```

Figure 12.7 Unrolled Loop

```
B2:     dSLD    (T1)            => SF1      /LOAD B(I)
        dSLD    (T2)            => SF2      /LOAD C(I)
        dADD    SF1,SF2         => SF3      /B(I) + C(I)
        dSST    (T3), SF3                   /A(I) = B(I) + C(I)
        dSLD    8(T1)           => SF4      /LOAD B(I+1)
        dSLD    8(T2)           => SF5      /LOAD C(I+1)
        dADD    SF4,SF5         => SF6      /B(I+1) + C(I+1)
        dSST    8(T3),SF6                   /A(I+1) = B(I+1) + C(I+1)
        dSLD    16(T1)          => SF7      /LOAD B(I+2)
        dSLD    16(T2)          => SF8      /LOAD C(I+2)
        dADD    SF7,SF8         => SF9      /B(I+2) + C(I+2)
        dSST    16(T3),SF9                  /A(I+2) = B(I+2) + C(I+2)
        dSLD    24(T1)          => SF10     /LOAD B(I+3)
        dSLD    24(T2)          => SF11     /LOAD C(I+3)
        dADD    SF10,SF11       => SF12     /B(I+3) + C(I+3)
        dSST    24(T3),SF12                 /A(I+3) = B(I+3) + C(I+3)
        iADD    T1,#32          => T1       /increment address of B(I)
        iADD    T2,#32          => T2       /increment address of C(I)
        iADD    T3,#32          => T3       /increment address of A(I)
        iADD    T4,#4           => T4       /increment loop count
        iCMPGT  T4,T5           => T6       /check end of loop
        iBCOND  T6,B2,B3
B3:
```

Before describing the scheduling algorithm itself, we will discuss five topics that form the basis for scheduling:

- Rather than scheduling the instructions in a single block, the compiler will schedule instructions in a collection of blocks, called a *trace*. First the compiler must compute the traces. Then it will schedule the instructions in the trace as if they were a single block of instructions.

- As you will see momentarily, the traces are not necessarily sequentially contiguous blocks in the flow graph. When they are not adjacent, the compiler must compute the temporaries that are used or defined between the blocks in the trace.

- When the trace and the interblock information is known, the compiler will compute a data structure called the *interference graph*, which describes which instructions must be evaluated before other instructions and how far in advance these prior instructions must occur.

- Just before the instructions are scheduled, the compiler must compute for each instruction an estimate of how many cycles occur between it and the end of the trace. This is called the *critical path information* and will be used to choose the instructions for scheduling.

- During scheduling the compiler simulates the execution of the instructions and keeps track of which function units within the processor are busy during each execution cycle. This can all be done by maintaining a collection of status information and updating it on each cycle. It is more efficient to precompute all possible states that the function units can be in and represent this as a finite state machine. The update of the state then reduces to a state transition.

We will discuss each of these topics in turn and then give the scheduling algorithm at the end.

12.4 Computing the Trace

The idea of scheduling multiple blocks at a time was made popular with trace scheduling, created by Fisher (1981). He noted that most programs have blocks that are more frequently executed than others. If one chose such a block and extended it by adding blocks that precede and follow it to form a path of blocks, then one could schedule all of the instructions in those blocks together. Of course the compiler had to insert instructions to repair the effects of branches into and out of the path.

Trace scheduling works well, but it has one serious disadvantage. The instructions inserted to fix up the effects of the branches into and out of the trace, called *compensation code,* can be numerous and are not necessarily well scheduled themselves. Thus a flow graph that has a single predominant trace will be scheduled well (most of the time is spent in the single trace). However, flow graphs in which there are multiple important traces or in which it is difficult to find a single predominating trace will perform less well since the compensation code will slow everything down.

Freudenberger, Gross, and Lowney (1994) noticed that the compensation code could be mostly eliminated if the traces were chosen so that there were no branches into a trace from blocks outside the trace and each block in the trace was the successor of only one other block in the trace. This gave nearly as good a performance as the general trace algorithm, with the elimination of most compensation code. These traces are another name for an extended block.

DEFINITION **Extended Block:** An extended block in the flow graph is a set of blocks satisfying the following conditions:

- There is a single block B_0 in the extended block that has no predecessors within the extended block. All of its predecessors occur outside the extended block.
- Every other block $B \neq B_0$ in the extended block has a single predecessor that is a member of the extended block.

In other words, the extended block is a tree of blocks in the flow graph. Lowney proposed that each trace be a path within an extended block.

This scheduler is based on a generalization of this idea by Sweany and Beaty (1992) and later improved by Huber (1995). Sweany chooses traces as paths in the dominator tree. A trace will consist of a sequence of blocks in which each block is the immediate dominator of the next. Then the trace is scheduled as if it were a block of instructions. The instructions are moved around in this trace so that some instructions may be moved to less frequent execution points or moved into slots where their execution time can be hidden.

Sweany's criteria applies to extended blocks. Each block in an extended block is either the entry block or is dominated by its predecessor in the extended block. However, Sweany's trace definition allows other possible traces. Consider a structured **if** statement in a program. If the two alternative branches have nearly equal frequency, it may be better to form a trace consisting of the branching statement at the beginning and the join statement at the end.

How is this movement of instructions different from code motion in the optimizer? The optimizer is limited in how far it can move instructions: It only moves computations to points where they will always be used later, it cannot move a computation to a point where the frequency of execution might increase, and it minimizes the sequence of instructions between computation and use. The instruction scheduler is not so limited. It can move an instruction to a point where its value is not guaranteed to be used, as long as the instruction costs nothing and the register pressure is not exceeded.

DEFINITION **Trace:** A trace is a sequence of blocks $B_1, B_2, \ldots, B_n$ such that for each $1 < i \leq n$ the block B_{i-1} immediately dominates the block B_i. That is, a trace is a path in the dominator tree.

The compiler will divide the flow graph into disjoint traces. The first trace formed should represent the most frequently executed blocks and be expanded in a way to improve the execution of those blocks. The next most important trace is formed from the remaining blocks, and so on. What criteria does the compiler use to choose the blocks in the trace? The following factors have to be considered:

- The trace should include the most frequently executed block B that has yet to be included in a trace. This choice is based on frequency information. This information can be gathered in one of three ways: profiling, static estimation of frequency information as in Ball and Larus (1992), or a rough estimate in which the innermost loop is considered the most frequent and branches are considered equally likely. This block B is called the *anchor* for the trace since the trace is completely determined by the choice of this element. As we will see shortly, the anchor is not the entry point for the trace.

- Consider the successors S of B that have B as their only predecessor and are not included in another trace. Choose the S with the highest frequency of execution. By necessity the frequency of execution will be less than that of B. Include S in the trace and recursively repeat this process for the successors of S. The effect of this process is to include the most frequently executed path through the extended block that starts at B.

- Again consider the immediate dominator D of the anchor B. If it is not already in a trace and is not nested in a loop separate from B, then include D in the trace. Since B has the highest frequency, the frequency of D cannot be higher than B; however, it can be embedded in a loop not containing B. Avoid adding D in that case. Repeat the process for D's immediate dominator, and so on.

- If there are no successors available to extend the trace from B, and a child in the dominator tree is also a postdominator of B and has the same frequency as B, then include this postdominator also.

- If the trace gets longer than a fixed size (determined experimentally), terminate the trace. The size should be measured in terms of instructions. Some of the scheduling algorithms are not linear in the size of the trace, so avoid a trace that is too big. Conversely, if the trace is large then a significant amount of instruction overlapping will already be available, so little incremental advantage can be had by increasing the size of the trace.

Scheduling and Rescheduling

Given these conditions, the algorithm for computing the trace, given in Figure 12.8, is straightforward. Form a priority queue of blocks ordered by execution frequency. Use this queue to find the anchor of a trace and then extend it by the rules mentioned above. Scan backward including the dominators until one must stop the trace. This gives us the entry point. Now

Figure 12.8 Calculating Traces

```
procedure CALCULATE_TRACES;
    Queue = ∅;
    foreach B ∈ N do
        trace(B) = NULL;
        add B to Queue with priority frequency(B);
    endfor;
    while Queue ≠ ∅ do
        take B from Queue;                  //The anchor
        NumberInstructions = |B|;
        C = B;                              //This will become entry
        D = IDOM(C);
        while CAN_ADD_DOMINATOR(D,C) do
            NumberInstructions = NumberInstructions + |D|;
            C = D;
            D = IDOM(C);
        endwhile;
        D = B;                              //Now have entry C
        while D ≠ C do                      //Include blocks in trace
            trace(D) = C;
            remove D from Queue;
            if D = C then break;
            endif;
            D = IDOM(D);
        endwhile;
        D = CAN_ADD_SUCCESSOR(B);
        if D ≠ NULL then
            repeat
                trace(D) = C;
                NumberInstructions = NumberInstructions + |D|;
                D = CAN_ADD_SUCCESSOR(D);
            until D = NULL;
        else if NumberInstructions < MaxInstructions then
            P = PDOM(B);                    //Postdominator
            if P ≠ NULL ∧ (P is child of B) ∧ frequency(B) = frequency(D) then
                trace(P) = C;
                NumberInstructions = NumberInstructions + |P|;
            endif;
        endif;
    endwhile;
endprocedure CALCULATE_TRACES;
```

scan forward from the anchor, including either a path through the extended block or a postdominator. These rules are flexible. The best choices for traces depend on the programming styles of the users and the best programming styles in the source language, so be prepared to modify this code to meet these needs.

The compiler needs to have a means to name a trace. The name the compiler uses is the block that is the entry to the trace. Each block has an attribute *trace(B)*, which is either NULL because the block has yet to be inserted in a trace or is the block that is the entry to the trace. Given this attribute, it is easy to find all of the blocks in the trace. The trace consists of a set of blocks forming a path in the dominator tree starting at the entry block to the trace. Simply scan down the tree looking at each child. If there is a child with the same value for *trace*, then the trace includes that child. If no child has the same value of *trace* as its parent, then the trace ends.

Note that we use the vertical lines, $|B|$, to represent the number of instructions in B. This is a reasonable notation since the vertical lines are used in mathematics to represent cardinality.

The decision process for adding the dominators of the anchor to the trace is given in Figure 12.9. The dominators are added if there are any (the compiler must stop at the root) and they are not already in a trace. If the trace has gotten too long, stop the trace. The compiler must also check whether the dominator is in a loop that does not include the anchor directly or indirectly. It is appropriate for the dominator to be in an outer loop, but not a loop in which the anchor is not directly or indirectly included.

Figure 12.9 Determining Whether Dominators Can Be Added to a Trace

```
function CAN_ADD_DOMINATOR(D: Block, B: Block) returns boolean;
   if D = NULL then
      return false;
   endif;
   if trace(D) ≠ NULL ∨ NumberInstructions ≥ MaxInstructions then
      return false;
   endif;
   L = LoopParent(D);   //Uses loop tree
   if L is ancestor of B in loop tree then
      return true;
   else
      return false;
   endif;
endfunction CAN_ADD_DOMINATOR;
```

Scheduling and Rescheduling

Figure 12.10 Determining Whether a Successor Can Be Added to a Trace

```
function CAN_ADD_SUCCESSOR(B: Block) returns Block;
   BestS = NULL;
   foreach S ∈ SUCC(B) do
      if trace(S) = NULL ∧ |PRED(S)| = 1 then
         if frequency(S) > frequency(BestS) then
            BestS = S;
         endif;
      endif;
   endfor;
   return BestS;
endfunction CAN_ADD_SUCCESSOR;
```

For extending the trace from the anchor into an extended block, the algorithm in Figure 12.10 is used. Find a successor that has only one predecessor. Choose the successor with the highest frequency and that is the next block to add to the trace.

Now consider the running example we have been using throughout the book. We will use the flow graph without superblock formation occurring. Forming superblocks will make for a better trace, but that is for later discussion. Assume that each loop is executed one hundred times, so the inner loop is actually executed nearly ten thousand times. We assume that the maximum value is changed about ten times each loop, so that the number of executions of block $B6$ will be one thousand (see Table 12.1).

The compiler forms the priority queue of blocks and chooses one of the most frequently executed. There is not a unique choice here. One possibil-

Table 12.1 Hypothetical Frequencies

Block	Number of Executions
B0	1
B1	100
B2	9900
B3	9900
B4	100
B5	1
B6	1000

ity is that block B3 will be chosen first. Then the immediate dominators of that block will be scanned, giving a first trace of {B0, B1, B2, B3}. The next trace would be the single block {B6}. Then block {B4} forms a trace, with the final trace being {B5}.

Another possibility is that the block B2 is chosen to form the anchor of the first trace. The dominators will be added and the successor in the extended block B6 can be added. This gives the first trace as {B0, B1, B2, B6}. Then {B3} will form a trace by itself, as will {B4} and {B5}.

12.5 Precomputing the Resource Information

This scheduler deals with traces that are paths through the dominator tree. There may be multiple blocks between a block and its dominator. The compiler must know what temporaries and memory are used and modified in these blocks.

12.5.1 Definition and Use Information

The scheduler chooses a sequence of blocks $B_1, B_2, \ldots, B_n$ such that each block is the immediate dominator of its successor. It then schedules these blocks together, potentially moving computations from one block to a previous or later one. To do this, the compiler must know which temporaries are modified or used between the two blocks. The algorithm here is based on an algorithm of Reif and Lewis (1978), which was specialized by Sweany and Beaty (1992) for instruction scheduling.

DEFINITION **OUT:** For each block B, $OUT(B)$ is the set of temporaries that are modified by the execution of B.

DEFINITION **IDEFS:** For each block B, $IDEFS(B)$ is the set of temporaries that are defined on some path from $IDOM(B)$ to B. This does not include definitions that occur in B or in $IDOM(B)$.

In Figure 12.11, $IDEFS(B4)$ includes T2 and T3 but does not include T1 or T4. T2 and T3 are included because each is defined on a path from B1 to B4 where B1 is the immediate dominator of B4.

Scheduling and Rescheduling

Figure 12.11 Flow Graph for *IDEFS* Compuation

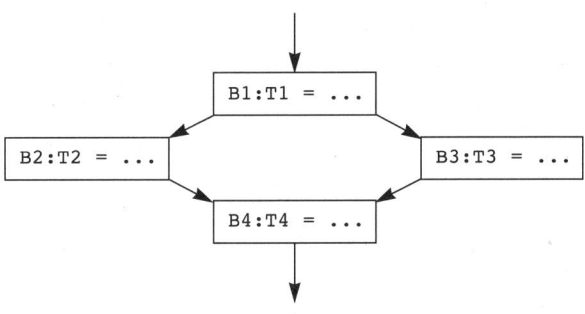

A similar set of information exists for uses rather than definitions. The idea is identical and the computations that we see below are identical. The only difference is that the occurrences of uses of temporaries and variables as operands are measured rather than the targets of instructions.

DEFINITION **IUSE:** For each block B, $IUSE(B)$ is the set of temporaries that are used as operands on some path from $IDOM(B)$ to B. This does not include uses that occur in B or in $IDOM(B)$.

12.5.2 Computing the Instruction Interference Information

Two observations and a data structure description will describe the technique for computing the *IDEFS* and *IUSE* sets. Consider any path $IDOM(B) = B_0, \ldots, B_n = B$ from B's dominator to B. Note that each B_i is dominated by $IDOM(B)$.

Begin walking the path starting at $IDOM(B)$. B_1 must be a successor of $IDOM(B)$ in the flow graph. This means that $IDOM(B)$ is the immediate dominator of B_1. Label B_1 as the block Z_1. Continue walking the path. Initially the blocks (possibly an empty set) are dominated by Z_1, but eventually one either comes to the end of the path or finds a block that is not dominated by Z_1. Call this block Z_2. The claim is that $IDOM(B)$ is also the immediate dominator of Z_2. Well, it is dominated by $IDOM(B)$ and is not dominated by any other block after $IDOM(B)$ on the path, so its immediate dominator must be $IDOM(B)$. Continue this walk until one finds a block not dominated by Z_2, call it Z_3. Continuing the whole process, a sequence of blocks $Z_1, \ldots, Z_m$ is found on the path, where each of these blocks is a child of *IDOM(B)* in the dominator tree. What we need to do is find the temporaries modified on each of the segments between Z_i and Z_{i+1}. From this information we can compute the *IDEFS(Z_i)* sets, as we will see shortly.

The other observation tells us how to compute the temporaries modified between Z_i and Z_{i+1}. Look at Z_{i+1}. In the flow graph we know each of its predecessors. One of these predecessors is the block on the path before Z_{i+1}. That predecessor is dominated by Z_i. If the compiler knows the *IDEFS* information for all of the blocks dominated by Z_i, then it can compute the set of temporaries modified on any path from Z_i to this predecessor (and then combine this with OUT for the predecessor to get the information from Z_i to Z_{i+1}).

Before describing this computation, the compiler needs the formula for relating *IDEFS* to the set of temporaries potentially modified between two blocks P_0 and P_r, where P_0 dominates P_r. Consider the sequence of blocks $P_0, \ldots, P_r$, where P_{i-1} is the immediate dominator of P_i. Any path between P_0 and P_r contains all of these blocks, and the definition of *IDEFS* indicates that the set of temporaries that might be modified on any path between the two, *DEFS*, must satisfy the following equation:

$$DEFS(P_0, P_r) = IDEFS(P_r) \cup \bigcup_{i=1}^{r-1} IDEFS(P_i) \cup OUT(P_i)$$

We have the basic information. How does the compiler piece this together into an algorithm? First the compiler must compute this information bottom-up in the dominator tree: It needs the information for dominated blocks to compute the information for dominator blocks. Because of the way *IDEFS* is defined, and the previous observation that the information for one child in the dominator tree can affect the information for the other children of a block, the information for all children of a node are computed simultaneously.

The compiler needs to know *DEFS(Z_i,P)* where P is a predecessor of Z_{i+1}. This is the difficult information to store efficiently. The storage uses a UNION/FIND algorithm. Consider a block B_0 that is the current block being processed. Let Z_1 through Z_n be the children of B_0 in the dominator tree. Thus each block dominated by B_0 is a member of one of the subtrees rooted at one of the Z_i. If one has a block P that is a predecessor of Z_{i+1} on the same path, then one can walk up the dominator tree from P to the corresponding child of B_0 that is the root of the tree. As one performs this walk, one can compute *DEFS(Z_i,P)* using the formula above. By adding in

$OUT(P)$ one computes the temporaries potentially modified between Z_i and Z_{i+1}. This is the information we need.

However, this tree walking is inefficient. A shadow data structure is therefore created that contains the same information as walking the tree. The data structure is collapsed as the walk progresses. This data structure is based on a UNION/FIND tree with the addition of EVAL operations to compute the sets. Here is how it is structured. When a block is processed, it is added into a UNION/FIND structure in which the representative of the partition is the block at the root of the subtree that has been processed and all blocks in the subtree are dominated by the representative. Of course the standard UNION/FIND collapsing occurs to make this tree much shallower than the actual dominator tree. Associated with each edge in this UNION/FIND structure is the *DEFS* set between the parent in the structure and the child. When collapsing occurs, the *DEFS* set is updated to represent the new parent and the child. When EVAL is called, collapsing occurs and the resulting *DEFS* set is returned as the value.

We now have everything for the algorithm except the mutual computation of the *IDEFS* sets for the children of a particular node. What does the previous discussion tell us? We can view the children of B_0 as a new graph where there is an edge between the two children if there is a path from one to the other that does not go through the parent. Given this new graph, the set of temporaries in *IDEFS* becomes the set of temporaries modified on any path from the roots of the graph (they are the children that are direct successors of the parent) to the nodes. This can all be done by topologically sorting the children. Of course there can be strongly connected regions. Their effect is that arbitrary paths through the strongly connected regions can occur, so the union of all temporaries modified in a strongly connected region must be computed.

Figure 12.12 shows the algorithm for performing this computation. The children, the *Z*s, are formed into a graph by looking at each child's predecessors and finding the alternate child that dominates that predecessor. This gives the edge between two of the children. As noted earlier, this could have been done by walking up the dominator tree. Instead it is done with a UNION/FIND algorithm so that paths may be collapsed. Then the strongly connected components are computed and ordered in reverse postorder. Now we have the effect of a topological sort. Predecessors occur before successors except for strongly connected regions.

Since a path can go around a strongly connected region any number of times, the effect of a strongly connected region is the union of the effects of the blocks within it. For a single block, there is no effect between the

Figure 12.12 Algorithm for *IDEFS*

```
procedure CALCULATE_IDEFS;
  call IDEFS_INITIALIZE;
  foreach B ∈ N in postorder on the dominator tree do
    let Z_1,...,Z_n be the children of B in the dominator tree;
    Edges = ∅;
    foreach Z_i do      //Form Graph of the Zs
      foreach P ∈ Pred(Z_i) do
        add (IDEFS_FIND(P),Z_i) to Edges;
      endfor;
    endfor;
    Now consider the Zs with edges Edges as directed graph W;
    compute strongly connected regions S of W;
    foreach S in reverse postorder do
      CurrentDEFS = ∅;
      if S is strongly connected then
        foreach C ∈ S do
          CurrentDEFS = CurrentDEFS ∪ OUT(C);
        endfor;
      endif;
      foreach C ∈ S do
        foreach P ∈ Pred(C) do
          CurrentDEFS = CurrentDEFS ∪ IDEFS_EVAL(C) ∪
                        OUT(C)
        endfor;
      endfor;
      foreach C ∈ S do
        call IDEFS_UNION(B,C,CurrentDEFS);
      endfor;
    endfor;
  endfor;
endprocedure CALCULATE_IDEFS;
```

predecessor and the current block. Having computed the summary effect, that information is added to the information already computed for the predecessors to give the information about what can be computed on a path from the direct dominator through one of its successors that is also a child (and root) to the current node. This information is then added to the dominator tree to store the result.

Figure 12.13 gives the support procedures for implementing the UNION/FIND and EVAL. They are included because the EVAL operation is rarely used in the literature. There are two attributes implementing these operations. *DEFS* indicates the set of temporaries that are changed between the parent and the child; the information is stored with the child. *FindParent* indicates the parent of a block. If it is null then this is the root of the current tree.

Scheduling and Rescheduling

Figure 12.13 Algorithms for UNION/FIND/EVAL

```
procedure IDEFS_INITIALIZE;
   foreach B ∈ N do
      FindParent(B) = NULL;
   endfor;
endprocedure IDEFS_INITIALIZE;

function IDEFS_FIND(B: Block) returns Block;
   Parent = B;
   while FindParent(Parent) ≠ NULL do
      Parent = FindParent(Parent);
   endwhile;
   call IDEFS_COLLAPSE(Parent,B);
   return Parent;
endfunction IDEFS_FIND;

procedure IDEFS_UNION(Parent, Child: Block, Info: Set of Temporary);
   FindParent(Child) = Parent;
   DEFS(Child) = Info;
endprocedure IDEFS_UNION;

function IDEFS_EVAL(B: Block) return set of Temporary;
   Parent = IDEFS_FIND(B);
   return DEFS(B);
endfunction IDEFS_EVAL;

procedure IDEFS_COLLAPSE(Root, Child: Block);
   Parent = FindParent(Child);
   if Parent ≠ Root then
      call IDEFS_COLLAPSE(Root,Parent);
      DEFS(Child) = DEFS(Parent) ∪ OUT(Parent) ∪ DEFS(Child);
      FindParent(Child) = Root;
   endif;
endprocedure IDEFS_COLLAPSE
```

The initialization consists of simply setting all *FindParent* attributes to null. The *DEFS* attribute need not be initialized since it will only be used after being set. The FIND operation consists of walking up the tree to find the root. Once that has occurred, the tree is collapsed using the collapsing procedure to shorten any future walks.

The UNION operation has a fixed block that is made the parent. It is guaranteed to be fed two blocks with *FindParent* being null, so no collapsing will occur. The other attribute is the set of blocks modified between the parent and the child, which is simply stored in the data structure.

The EVAL operation uses FIND to find the root. At the same time a collapse occurs (within the FIND). Hence the EVAL consists of simply returning the stored data that has now been updated to be between the root (now the parent) and the current block.

The real work occurs in the *COLLAPSE* procedure. If the parent is not the root, collapse the parent first. Now there are two hops to the root. Collapse it to one hop by using the definition of *DEFS* to compute the temporaries modified between the root and the current block.

This is sufficiently complex that an example is necessary. Consider the normal flow graph for the running example (refer back to Figure 2.1, p. 13). We will deal with a single temporary. In that case we can refer to Boolean values rather than sets: The value true occurs if the temporary is in the set. Note that block $B1$ dominates block $B2$ and block $B4$. Assume that a temporary T is modified in block $B6$. What is $IDEFS(B4)$?

Before processing block $B1$ (which computes the value of $IDEFS(B4)$), the algorithm most process $B2$ (which computes the values of $IDEFS(B3)$ and $IDEFS(B6)$). The blocks $B3$ and $B6$ form a graph, with $B6$ preceding $B3$. When the algorithm is applied, one gets the value of $OUT(B6)$ added into $IDEFS(B3)$ so that $IDEFS(B3)$ is true.

Now apply the algorithm to $B1$, computing the values of $IDEFS(B4)$ and $IDEFS(B2)$. One of the predecessors of $B4$ is $B3$, which is dominated by $B2$, so the graph of children is formed with $B2$ preceding $B4$. When computing the *IDEFS* set for $B4$, its predecessor $B3$ is interrogated and we find that $IDEFS(B3)$ is true so $IDEFS(B4)$ is true.

The same algorithm can be applied to compute the *IUSE* sets using the *IN* set of temporaries that are used as operands instead of the *OUT* set of temporaries modified.

12.6 Instruction Interference Graph

Now that the compiler has determined the set of instructions to schedule, it builds the data structures used for scheduling.[3] The instruction interference graph records the limitations on the ordering of instructions. It is built for each trace and records which instructions must occur before others and how many cycles before so that the values will be available when used in the later instruction (see Figure 12.14).

---

3. Note that I said *used* rather than *needed*. It is possible to perform scheduling without building the interference graph. Instead, the graph can be implicitly built by keeping track of the instructions computing the operands and their placement. It is easier and more effective to build the interference graph, although this takes time and space.

Figure 12.14 Computing the Interference Graph

```
IDG = ∅;
for R ∈ Resources do
    LastWrite(R) = ∅;
    LastRead(R) = ∅;
endfor;
foreach B ∈ Trace in dominator order do
    foreach I ∈ B in execution order do
        add I to IDG;
        foreach T ∈ Operands(T) do
            if LastWrite(R) ≠ ∅ then
                choose J from LastWrite(R);
                if I ∉ Succ(J) then
                    add I to Succ(J);
                    add J to Pred(I);
                    delay(J,I) = MachineDelay(J,I);
                endif;
            endif;
            add I to LastRead(R);
        endfor;
        foreach T ∈ Targets(I) do
            for J ∈ LastRead(R) do
                if I ∉ Succ(J) then
                    add I to Succ(J);
                    add J to Pred(I);
                    delay(J,I) = AntiDependenceDelay(J,I);
                endif;
            endfor;
            if LastWrite(R) ≠ ∅ then
                choose J from LastWrite(R);
                if I ∉ Succ(J) then
                    add I to Succ(J);
                    add J to Pred(I);
                    delay(J,I) = 1;
                endif;
            endif;
            LastWrite(R) = {I};
            LastRead(R) = ∅;
        endfor;
    endfor;
endfor;
```

Definition **Interference Graph:** Given a trace of blocks $\{B_0, \ldots, B_n\}$ the instruction interference graph is an acyclic directed graph. There are three different kinds of nodes in the graph:

- Each instruction in the trace is a node in the graph. These are the essential elements of the graph.

- For each block *B* in the trace, there is a *Block_Start* node that will be referred to as *Block_Start(B)*. This node is present to determine where each block starts. It will also carry dependence information necessary to inhibit reordering of instructions that might destroy data needed later.

- For each block *B* in the trace, there is a *Block_End* node referred to as *Block_End(B)*. As with the *Block_Start* nodes, it is present to determine which instructions are in each block and to carry dependence information necessary to inhibit invalid reordering of instructions.

An edge (*Tail, Head*) between two nodes indicates that *Tail* must precede *Head* in the final order of instructions. The absence of an edge between two nodes means that they can be arranged in any order. Each edge is labeled with an integer *delay*((*Tail, Head*)) indicating the number of cycles after *Tail* issues that *Head* may issue. If the *delay* is 1 then *Head* may issue on the cycle following *Tail*. It is possible for the delay to be 0. This usually means that there is specialized hardware present to make the value of one instruction available to another faster than the normal pipeline timing.

When is there an edge between two nodes? Two conditions are necessary. *Tail* must precede *Head* in the initial instruction order; that is, *Tail* is executed before *Head*. Second, both instructions must either use or define the same resource. There are four cases:

True dependence: If *Tail* modifies some resource that is later used by *Head*, then there is a true dependence. An edge exists between the two nodes, with a delay indicating the length of time needed for *Tail* to complete the modification of the resource. The length of the delay depends on both *Tail* and *Head* since the time for the resource to be available is different for different instructions pairs.

Antidependence: If *Tail* uses a resource that is later modified by *Head*, there is antidependence. Reordering the instructions cannot be allowed: If *Head* occurred before *Tail* then *Head* would destroy the value needed by *Tail*. Normally the delay is 1, indicating that only the order of the store and load is important; however, the architecture may indicate a different delay. On the Alpha 21164 the delay is 3 for an antidependence edge between a STORE and a LOAD instruction since it is more difficult to access data that has just been stored.

Output dependence: If *Tail* and *Head* both modify the same resource, then the initial order must be preserved so that later nodes will get the value of the resource modified by *Head*. Normally the delay is 1, indicating that only the order counts.

Input dependence: There is no restriction on order if both *Tail* and *Head* use a resource without modifying it. No ordering of the instructions is required, so no edge is created.

A *resource* is any quantity that indicates a change of execution state of the program. Hence each temporary is a resource. Thus, there is an edge from an instruction that evaluates a temporary to each instruction that uses the temporary. There is an edge from an instruction that evaluates a temporary to the next instruction that evaluates the same temporary. And there is an edge from each instruction that uses a temporary to the next instruction that evaluates it.

If the target machine has condition codes, they are a resource. They are handled like temporaries. If the set of instructions that set condition codes is pervasive, as in some complex instruction set computing (CISC) architectures, then the condition codes should be handled specially since the size of the interference graph will be huge. In most RISC architectures only a few instructions set condition codes (if they exist) and a few read them. In that case the condition codes are handled as implicit operands or targets of the instructions, just as the temporaries are handled as actual arguments.

Interferences for LOAD and STORE instructions are computed using the region of memory that each can reference. Each region of memory that the compiler can identify is a resource; hence the tags previously used for alias analysis indicate separate resources. The edges for the load and store operations match the kinds of dependencies that occur:

- There is an edge between each store operation and each succeeding load operation from the same area of memory. If the compiler can determine that the memory regions do not overlap, then no edge is necessary. The compiler can determine this if the areas of memory are different, if the addresses are known to be different (for example, if the addresses differ by a constant), or if the dependence analyzer leaves information indicating that the store and load do not reference the same location in memory.

- There is an edge between each store operation and each succeeding store operation. The same considerations as with load operations apply.

- There is an edge from each load operation to the next store operation into the same region of memory. Of course if the addresses are known to be different, the edge is not inserted.

Not all edges need be inserted in the graph. Assume the compiler is building an edge (*Tail, Head*) and there are already two edges (*Tail, Middle*) and (*Middle, Head*) in the graph with

```
delay((Tail, Head)) ≤ delay((Tail, Middle)) + delay((Middle, Head)),
```

then the new edge is unnecessary. The edges already in the graph place stronger restrictions on instruction order than the new edge. Three occurrences of this are easy to identify:

- Consider a node *Head* that uses a resource *R*. By the definition, there must be an edge from every preceding node modifying *R* to *Head*. The compiler need only record the edge from the last preceding node that modifies *R* to *Head*. The set of nodes that modify *R* form a list of edges in the graph since there is an output dependence from each such node to the next one.
- There is a similar situation with output dependences. If *Head* modifies resource *R*, then there need only be one output dependence edge from the preceding node that modifies *R* to *Head*.
- Consider a node *Tail* that uses a resource *R*. There is an edge from *Tail* to the next node that modifies *R*, recording an antidependence; however, there is no need to record the antidependences with later nodes that modify *R* since that antidependence is subsumed by the initial antidependence and the sequence of output dependences between nodes that modify *R*.

What are the conditions for interferences with *BlockStart(B)* and *BlockEnd(B)*? These nodes represent the boundaries of each block, so the compiler must ensure that the *BlockStart* node occurs before the *BlockEnd* node and that the *BlockEnd* node for the dominator occurs before the *BlockStart* node of the dominated block. The other way to view the *BlockStart* node is that it represents all instructions that occur before the block and after the dominator. These ideas give us the conditions for interferences with *BlockStart* and *BlockEnd*:

- There is an interference edge between *BlockStart(B)* and *BlockEnd(B)* and an interference edge between *BlockEnd(IDOM(B))* and *BlockStart(B)*. Thus, the *BlockStart* and *BlockEnd* nodes form a linked list in the graph. This can be implemented by either forcing these edges to exist or by introducing an artificial resource that is written by each *BlockStart* node and read by each *BlockEnd* node. This creates the same edges as noted above.

- Pretend that *BlockStart(B)* reads every resource that is read by an instruction between B and *IDOM(B)* and writes each resource that is defined between B and *IDOM(B)*. In other words, make the set of resources used by *BlockStart(B)* be *IUSE(B)*, and the set of resources defined by *BlockStart(B)* be *IDEFS(B)*.

12.7 Computing the Priority of Instructions

The compiler next computes the priority of each instruction, in other words, how important an instruction is to the overall schedule for instructions in the trace. If the compiler delays the scheduling of some instructions, the so-called critical instructions, it will make the execution time for the whole trace longer. Other instructions have more latitude in their scheduling.

The priority of an instruction is the minimum time from the place where the instruction is scheduled to the end of the execution of the trace. Consider the unscheduled instruction with the longest time interval from the point where it will be scheduled until the end of the trace. If we delay the scheduling of this instruction by one cycle, we extend the execution length of the whole trace by one cycle. Thus the most important instruction to schedule is the one with the longest time interval from its execution to the end of the trace. The compiler approximates the time interval from the issue of an instruction until the end of the trace by computing the longest path in the interference graph from the instruction to the leaves of the interference graph.

Why is this an approximation? There are two major reasons why this number might not be exact. Using the solution to the longest path problem as the length of time assumes that there are sufficient function units so that each instruction can be scheduled on any cycle. It also assumes that each function unit is available on each cycle. If sufficient function units are not available, then some instructions must be delayed for a cycle. On some of the Alpha processors, the multiply instruction can only be issued every four cycles.

Since the interference graph is acyclic, the longest path can be computed efficiently and at the same time the approximation can be improved to partially compensate for these two conditions. The compiler must compute an attribute *priority(I)* for each instruction *I*. This can be done by performing a depth-first walk through the interference graph, computing the priority of successors in this graph before computing the priority of a node:

```
priority(J) = max{delay(J, I) + priority(I)|I ∈ Succ(J)}
```

Since not all instructions are implemented in a simple pipelined fashion, the formula must be made more complex. Consider the following two cases in the Alpha 21164 as representative cases:

- Integer multiply instructions cannot be issued more frequently than every four to twelve cycles, depending on the instructions and sources of the operands. The latency of each multiply instruction is eight to sixteen cycles, so the multiply instructions are partially pipelined.

- A floating divide instruction cannot be issued until results of the previous divide instruction are available.

To compute a more accurate value for *priority,* the compiler must compute the total latency caused by instructions in each of these classes. The *priority* cannot be less than each of these values.

The compiler computes these total values by keeping temporary attributes, *multiply_latency* and *divide_latency*, for each node in the instruction dependence graph. These attributes are only needed to compute *priority* and can be discarded after its computation.

The algorithm is described in Figure 12.15. It is a direct implementation of the previous discussion. The form of the algorithm is a depth-first search where successors are processed before the current node. The maximum length of time to the end of the block is computed using the measures we have discussed. If there is other information that should be included, it too can be added to the algorithm.

Figure 12.15 Computing Instruction Priority

```
procedure COMPUTE_PRIORITY(instruction J)
   add J to Visited;
   multiply_latency(J) = Time_for_Multiply(J);
   divide_latency(J) = Time_for_Divide(J);
   priority(J) = 0;
   for I ∈ Succ(J) do
      if I ∉ Visited then
         call COMPUTE_PRIORITY(I);
      endif;
      multiply_latency(J) = multiply_latency(J) + multiply_latency(I);
      divide_latency(J) = divide_latency(J) + divide_latency(I);
      priority(J) = max(priority(J), priority(I) + delay(J,I));
   endfor;
   priority(J) =
            max(priority(J),multiply_latency(J),divide_latency(J));
endprocedure COMPUTE_PRIORITY;

Visited = ∅;
create priority;
create multiply_latency;
create divide_latency;
for J ∈ IDG do
   if J ∉ Visited then
      call COMPUTE_PRIORITY(J);
   endif;
endfor;
destroy multiply_latency;
destroy divide_latency;
```

12.8 Simulating the Hardware

One view of instruction scheduling is that the compiler simulates the hardware keeping track of which functional units are in use on each clock cycle. It then chooses the instruction to issue based on which functional units are not currently in use and will not be in use at each cycle that the instruction to be issued needs them.

To perform this simulation, the compiler must have a mechanism for tracking the function units currently in use. The compiler needs this to be an efficient mechanism, preferably taking a single load instruction to determine the current state of all of the function units.

Historically, the state of the function units has been modeled by a Boolean matrix. Each clock cycle is represented by a column, where the first

Table 12.2 Hypothetical Machine State

	Cycle 0	Cycle 1	Cycle 2	Cycle 3
Integer	true	false	false	false
Floating Add	false	false	false	false
Floating Multiply	false	false	false	false

column is the current clock cycle. Each function unit represents a row with the value true in any column (that is, clock cycle) where the function unit has already been reserved for use. Similarly, each instruction is modeled by a matrix of the same form (clock cycles representing columns, function units representing rows). The instruction can be scheduled if it does not use any function units during any of the subsequent cycles that are already reserved, in other words, if the element-by-element AND of the two matrices results in a zero matrix. If the instruction can be scheduled, then the state can be updated by replacing the state by the OR of the previous state and the instruction being scheduled.

Eventually, no instructions will be able to be scheduled either because the function units are busy or there are dependencies on previous instructions that are still executing. In that case the compiler advances to scheduling the next machine cycle. This consists of shifting the state matrix so that the second column becomes the first column, the third column becomes the second, and so on.

To illustrate this idea, consider a hypothetical machine with an integer functional unit, a floating-point addition unit, and a floating-point multiplication unit. Assume that we are in the middle of scheduling a machine cycle, as shown by the machine state in Table 12.2. This state indicates that we have already scheduled something that is using the integer unit.

Tables 12.3–12.5 represent the resource matrices for individual instruction classes. More than one instruction may share the same pattern of func-

Table 12.3 Resource Matrix for Integer Operations

	Cycle 0	Cycle 1	Cycle 2	Cycle 3
Integer	true	false	false	false
Floating Add	false	false	false	false
Floating Multiply	false	false	false	false

Table 12.4 Resource Matrix for Floating Add

	Cycle 0	Cycle 1	Cycle 2	Cycle 3
Integer	false	false	false	false
Floating Add	true	true	false	false
Floating Multiply	false	false	false	false

Table 12.5 Resource Matrix for Floating Multiply

	Cycle 0	Cycle 1	Cycle 2	Cycle 3
Integer	false	false	false	false
Floating Add	false	false	false	false
Floating Multiply	true	false	false	false

tion usage, so these may be combined together in a class to make smaller data structures.

The integer class does everything in one cycle, so it ties up the function unit for a cycle and is completed. The floating-point add instruction uses the floating-point unit for two cycles, so it is not fully pipelined. It can only start a floating-point instruction every other cycle. The floating-point multiply instruction is fully pipelined. Actually, it should be represented as multiple function units with one stage for each cycle; however, these function units are only used by the floating-point multiplier and are completely determined by the first stage in the pipe, so the machine model can be simplified to show only the first stage.

If the scheduler schedules first a floating-point add instruction and then a floating-point multiply instruction in the same cycle, then the machine state looks like Table 12.6. There are no more instructions that can be scheduled in this cycle.

Table 12.6 End of One Cycle

	Cycle 0	Cycle 1	Cycle 2	Cycle 3
Integer	true	false	false	false
Floating Add	true	true	false	false
Floating Multiply	true	false	false	false

Table 12.7 Machine State at Start of Next Cycle

	Cycle 0	Cycle 1	Cycle 2	Cycle 3
Integer	false	false	false	false
Floating Add	true	false	false	false
Floating Multiply	false	false	false	false

To start the next cycle, the machine shifts all of the columns left by one to indicate that the current cycle is completed and the next clock cycle has become the current clock cycle. This gives us the state in Table 12.7. Note that the machine can issue an integer instruction or a floating point multiply. However, the floating add instructions cannot be issued since the function unit is still busy. Recall that the floating add unit used the same resource twice.

This description has been a simplified one. There are many more function units and they are not all directly connected to the instruction class. For example, there may be an integer register write function unit that writes the resulting data into the register file. Also some instructions will use multiple major function units: A copy integer to floating register instruction will involve some of the integer function units and some of the floating function units.

The problem is that computing the machine state in this fashion is time consuming and requires specialized code in the scheduler. This compiler uses a technique described by Bala and Rubin (1996) for simplifying and speeding the processing of state.

12.8.1 Precomputing the Machine State Machine

The idea is simple. Represent the machine state as a finite state machine. Look at the description given above. View each machine state matrix as a state in a finite state machine. Look at each instruction class as an element of the vocabulary in which the transition from one state to the next is represented by ORing the matrices together as noted above. This gives a nondeterministic finite state machine. Form the deterministic finite state machine associated with the nondeterministic one, and one can use this machine rather than the matrices. Thus all state transitions are reduced to a lookup in a matrix.

There is one problem with this dream. The number of states may be large: in the tens of thousands. This makes the storage for the finite state machine excessive. However, Bala and Rubin note that processors have a very regular structure. The integer unit has very little to do with the individual floating-point units. It is time to review the cross-production of finite state machines. Consider two finite state machines with states S_1 and S_2, then one can form the cross-product finite state machine (S_1, S_2) consisting of ordered pairs of states from S_1 and S_2. The transition from one state to the other is performed by doing the transition for each element of the ordered pair and taking the ordered pair of the results: that is, $\tau(s_1, s_2) = (\tau(s_1), \tau(s_2))$.

Here is the plan. Divide the processor up into major functional elements. Form the machine for each part. Note that all instructions are part of the vocabulary for each machine; it is just that the integer instructions will rarely change the state of the floating-point machine and vice versa. Store both machines and perform the lookup using two matrices. The machines for each major functional part are in the hundreds of states and you are storing two of them. Thus the state can be expressed as a pair of 16-bit numbers.

Note that the finite state machine may be nondeterministic. Why? Isn't the construction we have just described deterministic? If there are single function units for each function, then yes. If there are multiple units for the same operation (multiple integer function units, for example), then there will be multiple transitions under the same instruction class to distinct states.

What are the start states for this machine? Clearly the state representing the matrix of all false values is a start state; however, there are two other classes of start states:

- When one machine cycle is completed, the state of the machine must be initialized for the next cycle. This involves shifting the matrix left one. So we need a function *STATE_SHIFT(S)* that takes a state S and gives the state that represents the matrix with all values shifted left one column. The range of this function must be considered a start state for the scheduling of the next cycle. This function is represented internally as a vector indexed by S and giving the state number for the state at the beginning of the next cycle. To decrease the number of start states, we require the scheduler to issue NOP instructions for all function units if it has no other instructions to schedule in a given cycle. This means that all the initial function units will be occupied in a state that ends a cycle and we do not have to perform the shift for intermediate states.

- At the beginning of a block, the compiler needs to make an estimate for the state of the machine after executing one of the preceding blocks. This does not need to be exact: The more accurate a computation, the fewer stalls that will occur. Since the compiler does not know which block is actually the predecessor, it forms a state from the state at the end of each of the predecessor blocks by ORing the state matrices together. Actually we need only consider two predecessors because more can be handled by applying the process successively to the rest of the predecessors in pairs. So we must form the OR of any two states that end a block and introduce those as new start states. We need a function $COMBINE\_PRED(s_1, s_2)$ that takes the OR of the two matrices and returns the shifted result as the start state for the first instruction in the block.

We have outlined the procedure. All of this computation is done during the compiler construction so that the code in the machine consists of matrices representing the transition functions and the *COMBINE_PRED* function and a vector representing the *STATE_SHIFT* machine. This is very much like the tables required in the use of LEX or YACC.

The algorithm is outlined in Figure 12.16. Initially the machine starts with a single state, which is the state with nothing busy. The algorithm is written in terms of matrices; however, each matrix for a state is stored once and a unique integer to represent the state is used to represent the matrix in all tables that are generated for use in the compiler.

There is a waiting list called *StateQueue* that holds each state after it is created. Each state only enters that queue once because it is entered into the *StateTable* and the *StateQueue* at the same time and nothing is ever removed from the *StateTable*. When a state is processed, the generator attempts to create a transition under every possible instruction class.

If there are no transitions generated, then the machine is full for the current clock cycle and the compiler must generate a transition to a new start state for the next cycle. This is done by performing that manipulation on the matrix for the state and then seeing if a corresponding state already exists. If not, add it to the set of states also.

The whole process is continued until all states have been processed so that all transitions are known. After the algorithm is performed, the equivalent deterministic finite state machine must be found.

12.8.2 Looking at the Instruction Schedule Backward

For some optimizations of the schedule and for software pipelining, the compiler sometimes wants to scan backward through the instructions to insert an instruction into an already scheduled list. The state of the machine as recorded in the resource matrices and states that we have just computed tells us whether an empty slot exists where an instruction can be inserted. It does not tell us whether inserting an instruction there will interfere with

Scheduling and Rescheduling

Figure 12.16 Generating State Machine

```
procedure BUILD_SCHEDULE_FSM;
   TransitionTable = ∅;
   StateTable = ∅;
   StateQueue = ∅;
   let FM be matrix with all false;    //Enter start state
   add FM to StateTable;
   add FM to StateQueue;
   while StateQueue ≠ ∅ do
      take F from StateQueue;
      get matrix FM for F;
      foreach instruction class I do
         get matrix IM for I;
         if FM ∩ IM = ∅ then
            D = FM ∪ IM;
            if D ∉ StateTable then
               add D to StateTable;
               add D to StateQueue;
            endif;
            add transition from F to D under I to TransitionTable;
         endif;
      endfor;
      if no transitions out of F then
         let D be FM shifted left by one column;
         if D ∉ StateTable then
            add D to StateTable;
            add D to StateQueue;
         endif;
         record STATE_SHIFT(FM) = D;
      endif;
   endwhile;
endprocedure BUILD_SCHEDULE_FSM
```

a later instruction that has already been scheduled. For this we need the reverse finite state machine.

Consider the same set of states, but build the transitions in the reverse direction. This gives us a very nondeterministic finite state machine from which we can build a deterministic finite state machine. After we have scheduled a block, we run the reverse state machine on the block to give a pair of state numbers for each instruction. The forward state numbers indicate what legal instructions can occur in the future, and the backward state numbers indicate what legal instructions can occur in the past.

We now have a representation of the state of the machine before an instruction is executed and a representation of the machine following the instruction that is executed. We store this information with each instruction. Give each instruction two temporary attributes that exist during instruction scheduling and register allocation. *ForwardState(I)* is the state of the machine before the execution of instruction *I*. *BackwardState(I)* is the state of the rest of the instructions after *I*.

12.8.3 Replacing One Instruction by Another in a Schedule

Normal instruction scheduling only needs *ForwardState(I)* to perform list scheduling. In fact it need not be stored as an attribute since the compiler only needs the current state, which can be stored as a global variable. There are three instances when instructions are scheduled in a nonsequential order:

- During normal scheduling one must ensure that a critical instruction is scheduled in the cycle that ensures the minimum length of the block. Having done that, there are less critical instructions that can be scheduled before it, as long as they do not delay the scheduling of this critical instruction. The scheduling can be done by scheduling the next critical instruction and then inserting the other instructions before it.

- During software pipelining, the compiler will pretend that the scheduling of one instruction will actually schedule shadow versions of the same instruction in regularly spaced later cycles. The compiler must record the fact that shadow instructions will occur at fixed points later in the schedule. Thus, some later instructions must be scheduled before the next current instruction.

- Rarely during register allocation, instructions will be spilled into memory. This requires the insertion of load and store operations into the schedule. The best way to do this is to find an empty slot in the schedule that can be replaced by the LOAD or STORE instruction and directly place the instruction in the proper place in the schedule.

We therefore need to know the conditions under which one instruction can be replaced by another. This includes the possibility of inserting an instruction into an empty slot in the schedule.

Assume that we have the states *ForwardState(I)* and *BackwardState(I)* for each slot in the schedule, whether there is an instruction there or not. Thus we can implement the schedule as a sufficiently large array in which each instruction will occupy a slot. At the beginning we initialize the *ForwardState* and *BackwardState* attributes to the start state for each of the machines, indicating that all of the resource matrices are empty.

Now consider the conditions under which an instruction *I* can be inserted in slot *IS*. To be able to be inserted in that position means that the instruction cannot conflict with any instructions that have been scheduled in the past. This is the same as having a transition out of *ForwardState(IS)* because we only created transitions when there was no conflict. The *BackwardState(IS)* attribute indicates whether there is a future instruction already scheduled that will conflict with *I*. If no future instruction conflicts with *I*, then there is a valid transition out of *BackwardState(IS)* under *I*.

If the instruction *I* can be placed in slot *IS*, then the *ForwardState* and *BackwardState* attributes of the slots must be updated. This involves recomputing the *ForwardState* attribute forward from the slot *IS* and recomputing the *BackwardState* backward from *IS*. This is less expensive than it seems. Since we are dealing with finite state machines, we need only scan forward (or backward) as long as the newly computed state differs from the previously stored state.

The recomputation of states will only differ for a few slots. Why? Remember the construction of the finite state machine, which involved resource matrices and the shifting of columns. As soon as all columns involving the current instruction have been shifted to the left, the current instruction will not be visible in the state of the machine. In other words, only a few shifts (the maximum number of columns in a matrix) can occur. Practically, only a few iterations are required.

The pseudo-code summarizing the insertion is given in Figure 12.17. It elaborates the discussion above. The value false is returned if the instruction

Figure 12.17 Inserting Instructions in Slots

```
function INSERT_INSTRUCTION(I:Instruction, IS:slot) returns boolean;
   if τ(ForwardState(IS),I) ≠ Error ∧ τ(BackwardState(IS),I) ≠ Error then
      place I in slot IS;
      J = IS;
      State = ForwardState(IS);
      repeat                   //Fix up forward direction
         State = τ(State,Instruction_in_slot(J));
         J = J + 1;
      until State = ForwardState(J);
      J = IS
      Bstate = BackwardState(IS);
      repeat                   //Fix up backward direction
         BState = τ(BState,Instruction_in_slot(J));
         J = J - 1;
      until Bstate = BackwardState(J);
      return true;
   else
      return false;
   endif;
endfunction INSERT_INSTRUCTION;
```

cannot be inserted. Otherwise, the insertion occurs and the states are updated.

12.9 The Scheduling Algorithm

The scheduler forms the instructions in the trace into packets. The set of instructions in each packet can be issued in the same clock cycle. The instructions in the next packet can be issued in the next clock cycle, and so on. For the Digital Alpha 21164, the scheduler will attempt to issue four instructions: two integer operations, a floating add, and a floating multiply. If there are no more instructions to issue for a particular clock cycle, the scheduler will issue NOP operations for each of the unused function units. Thus each packet is always full; however, it may contain NOP instructions. Later the compiler will combine packets to eliminate NOP operations. This will not speed the execution of the processor directly; however, it will decrease the number of instructions and thus use the instruction cache more effectively.

Thus the SCHEDULE phase attempts to divide the instructions into packets that can be issued simultaneously. To do this, it must group the instructions into packets in such a fashion that the instructions in a packet do not conflict with one another.

As noted earlier, this scheduler uses a concept of trace based on the dominator tree. The first thing that is done is to compute the auxiliary information: the traces, *IDEFS,* and *IUSE* sets. Then a walk of the dominator tree is started, as noted in Figure 12.18. The basic structure is to choose a trace, schedule it, and then walk down the blocks in the trace performing a trace on the other children not in the trace. As we do this, we keep track of the instructions that have already been scheduled using value numbering on the dominator tree. The value table is indexed by opcode and the value

Figure 12.18 Driver for the Scheduler

```
procedure Schedule;
   call Calculate_Traces;
   call Calculate_IDEFS;
   call Calculate_IUSE;
   Initialize value numbering tables to empty;
   call ScheduleTrace(Root);
endprocedure Schedule;
```

Figure 12.19 Example of Hoistable Instruction

```
if X <= 0 then
   G = A * B + 1;
else
   G = A * B + 2;
endif;
```

number of the operands. When a temporary is modified, it is either reentered in the table with the new operator and operands or is entered with no known instruction but a new value number (as with *IDEFS* computations).

Why the use of value numbering here? Are not all redundant expressions eliminated? No! Instruction scheduling can introduce redundant expressions. Consider the source statement in Figure 12.19. If one of the branches is included in a trace with the conditional expression at the beginning, then it is quite likely that $A * B$ will be scheduled before the conditional branch. It is therefore available before the beginning of the other trace.

Figure 12.20 gives the actual algorithm for walking the dominator tree. First the trace is determined as described earlier. It is headed by a block with $Trace(B) = B$. At most one child in the dominator tree has the same value of trace, and so on down the tree until no child has the value of B for the *Trace*. Then that trace is scheduled by a call to *SchedulePackets*. After

Figure 12.20 Determining the Trace and Walking It

```
procedure ScheduleTrace(B: Block);
   let Trace = {B_0,...,B_t} be the trace rooted at B;
   call SchedulePackets(Trace);
   foreach C ∈ Trace in dominator order do
      foreach I ∈ C after scheduling do
         enter I in value number table keyed by operands, operator
         if unknown modification occurs, give new value number
      endfor;
      foreach D ∈ Children(C) do
         if Trace(D) = D then
            call ScheduleTrace(D);
         endif;
      endfor;
      remove value number table information for C;
   endfor;
endprocedure ScheduleTrace;
```

the trace is scheduled, then trace an instruction at a time, entering the instructions into the value table. When a block boundary is reached, the walk continues at the child in the trace; however, the instructions for each of the other children are scheduled before that since such blocks must be the beginning of a trace.

The real work starts in Figure 12.21. *SchedulePackets* (notice the plural) first computes the interference graph. From this it initializes the attributes *Ready(I)*, which is the first clock cycle where the instruction can be scheduled without instruction stalls, and *PredLeft(I)*, which is the number of predecessors that have not yet been scheduled. *PredLeft(I)* is the same attribute used in many topological sorting algorithms to control a topological sort. After all, an instruction schedule is a topological sort of the interference graph. *Ready(I)* is the maximum of the times where the operands are available. The operand is available after its instruction is scheduled and the delay associated with the pair of instructions has occurred. Since it is a maximum, we initialize *Ready(I)* to 0 and increase it whenever we find an operand that gives a larger value.

Before scheduling the instructions, the procedure checks to see if the instructions at the root of the conflict graph are available outside the trace. If they are, the instruction is replaced by a COPY instruction. We would

Figure 12.21   Starting Trace and Scheduling Packets

```
procedure SchedulePackets(Trace);
   call Calculate_Interference_Graph(Trace);
   foreach I ∈ Trace do
      Ready(I) = 0;
      PredLeft(I) = |Interfere_Pred(I)|;
   endfor;
   let Available = {I|PredLeft(I) = ∅};
   foreach I ∈ Available do
      if I matches entry J in value table then
         replace I by copy from destination of J to
            destination of I;
      endif;
   endfor;
   IS = 0;
   State = Initial_State
   while Available ≠ ∅ do
      call SchedulePacket;
      IS = IS + 1;
   endwhile;
endprocedure SchedulePackets;
```

like to do better, but we have a phase-ordering problem here. Register coalescing has already occurred. We will attempt to make the register allocator allocate the registers to the same register; however, this cannot be guaranteed, so the copy must be made, which inhibits other optimizations.

The set *Ready* contains all of the instructions that can be scheduled on this cycle without delay. The set *Available* is the set of instructions that are available to schedule during this or a future cycle. In other words, all of the instructions that a member of that set interferes with have been scheduled. To compute this set we keep an attribute for each instruction called *PredLeft(I)*, which is the number of predecessors in the conflict graph that have not been scheduled. When this attribute reaches 0, the instruction is added to the *Available* set.

With all of this machinery, the procedure *Schedule_Packet* in Figure 12.22 chooses the instructions from *Ready* that can be scheduled. It chooses the most important instructions first and only instructions that do not conflict with instructions that are already scheduled. After all of the instructions have been scheduled, the *Available* set is updated. The

Figure 12.22 Scheduling a Packet

```
procedure SchedulePacket;
   Packet = ∅;
   Ready = {I ∈ Available |IS ≥ Ready(I)};
   foreach I ∈ Ready in decrease value of Schedule_Importance(I) do
      if τ(State,I) ≠ Error then
         remove I from Available;
         add I to Packet;
         State = τ(State,I);
      endif;
   endfor;
   add function unit NOP operations until full packet;
   place Packet in slot IS in schedule;
   foreach I ∈ Packet do
      foreach J ∈ Interfere_Succ(I) do
         if IS + delay(I,J) ≥ Ready(J) then
            Ready(J) = IS + delay(I,J);
         endif;
         PredLeft(J) = PredLeft(J) - 1;
         if PredLeft(J) = 0 then
            add J to Available;
         endfor;
      endfor;
   endfor;
endprocedure SchedulePacket;
```

PredLeft attribute of each successor of an instruction in the packet is decremented. When it reaches 0 its instruction is added to the *Available* set.

What is *Schedule_Importance*? This determines the instructions in the *Ready* set that are scheduled first. It is a lexographic sort on the instructions in the *Ready* set and is based on the ideas of the RS6000 instruction scheduler described in Warren (1990). For each major function unit the instructions are sorted separately, in the following order.

- Consider the subset of instructions with the maximum value of *Priority*(*I*). These instructions are more important than the others, hence they are scheduled first. *Ready* has already been chosen to include the instructions whose operands are now in registers. Compute first the instructions that determine the length of the execution sequence.

- Of this smaller set of instructions, the instructions that decrease register pressure are more important than the instructions that increase register pressure. Increasing the register pressure is one of the dangers of instruction scheduling. In fact, if you track the register pressure, avoid increasing it past the number of registers available.

- Of this smaller set of instructions, the instructions that have more successors are more important than the instructions with fewer successors in the interference graph. Scheduling instructions with more successors increases the size of the *Available* set more quickly, so there is likely to be more instruction that can be scheduled in the near future.

- If there is still not a single best choice, choose the instruction that is earliest in the original trace.

Of course this is a heuristic ordering. Scheduling is an NP-complete problem in general. Other criteria can be added for particular processors. For example, on the newer Alpha processors there is an advantage to having multiple stores to sequential locations in memory be adjacent. This can be added as a criterion. If the previous cycle contained a store to a location that precedes the store location for an instruction in the *Ready* set, then give this instruction priority.

12.9.1 Refinements

There are two refinements to this scheduling algorithm that may improve it. It will depend on the processor and the set of programs typically scheduled. The first refinement involves looking at *Schedule_Importance*. If there is a critical instruction to schedule, we schedule it; however, an earlier instruction that was not critical and was scheduled in an earlier slot may prevent the scheduling of the critical instruction. How can the scheduler be modified to (sometimes—remember this is all NP-complete) prevent this?

Consider the set *Available,* which contains all of the instructions whose operands have begun being evaluated. Choose the instruction in this set with the largest *Priority*. Compute the instruction slot where that instruction will have its operands available. Then before executing the normal scheduling process, schedule this critical instruction in this slot.

This is a major modification to the scheduling algorithm; however, it may be useful on some processors. This algorithm no longer schedules the instructions in order so that we need only keep track of the *ForwardState*. Now the instruction schedule is considered to be a large array of instructions, initially empty, with the *ForwardState* and *BackwardState* for each empty instruction slot being the initial state. The insertion of an instruction in the schedule must then use the replacement algorithm rather than simple insertion. For processors with complex processor architectures, this modification is worthwhile.

The other modification to the scheduling algorithm is to schedule the instructions backward. In other words, schedule the last packet first, then the preceding packet, and so on back to the initial packet. To do this the compiler must build the reverse of the interference graph and compute the number of cycles from an instruction to the beginning of the block rather than to the end of the block. Otherwise the algorithm is identical.

There are two advantages to scheduling the trace backward. First, the scheduler can track exact register pressure. As we have seen before, tracing through a sequence of instructions backward allows the compiler to see which instruction is the last use, so the compiler knows when a temporary is live or dead.

The other advantage to scheduling backward is more subtle. When scheduling instructions forward, there are points at which there are no important instructions to schedule; however, there may be other instructions that could be scheduled later but will be scheduled early because there is nothing else to do. This needlessly increases the register pressure. By scheduling instructions in reverse order, the compiler will schedule an instruction at nearly the latest time possible for the value to be available when needed.

The disadvantage of backward trace scheduling is more of an unknown. Trace scheduling has typically scheduled instructions in a forward order. How scheduling backward fits with instruction scheduling needs some experimentation. What one would like is to schedule instructions away from the most frequently executed blocks in a trace. How does one do this?

A final refinement to the scheduling algorithm can be made. If some of the predecessors of the head of the trace have been scheduled already, then the beginning state is not the initial start state of the finite state machine. Instead some of the function units may already be busy. In building the finite state machine we computed the *Join* of two states. This can be used on the predecessors to compute the initial state. If a predecessor has not been processed, then ignore that predecessor in forming the *Join*.

12.9.2 *Block_Start* and *Block_End*

During the discussion of scheduling, we have not discussed the *Block_Start* and *Block_End* nodes in the interference graph, which were inserted to mark the boundaries of blocks and to make sure that legal schedules were maintained. How do they fit into the whole scheduling process?

Block_Start and *Block_End* are treated just like instructions. These are the only instructions that reference a fictitious function unit. There is also a fictitious slot in each packet that can hold one of these pseudo-instructions. Now perform the scheduling just as the algorithm specifies. The packets that contain a *Block_Start* pseudo-instruction represent the start of that block, and the packets that contain a *Block_End* pseudo-instruction represent the end of the block. Thus the schedule can be parsed back into the original blocks.

12.10 Software Pipelining

There is a specialized form of scheduling for simple loops. If the body of the loop is scheduled as described above, then there is nothing going on at the beginning of the loop. During the loop, the function units become active, and at the end of the loop body, the function units are again unused. This is an inefficient use of the function units.

There are two ways to mitigate this problem. First the compiler can unroll the loop some number of times and then schedule the unrolled loop body. This decreases the problem since between copies of the loop body in the unrolled loop the function units may be kept busy; however, the problem still occurs at the front and back of the unrolled loop. Furthermore, the body of the loop may become large and cause problems with the instruction cache.

Scheduling and Rescheduling

An alternative way to schedule the loop is software pipelining. Consider some loop L where the compiler knows the number of iterations to be executed before the loop begins. If the compiler can arrange that the first iteration begins execution shortly before the second iteration, and so on, then the compiler will keep the function units busy at the end of each iteration.

Of course, this is not possible as it is stated. There is only one instruction stream. But the compiler can generate separate instruction streams for the first iteration, and the second, and so forth, and then attempt to interweave the instruction streams into one instruction stream. Actually what the compiler does is more properly modeled by the right-hand column of Figure 12.23. The compiler determines a number referred to as II, or the initiation interval. It starts the first loop II cycles before the second loop, which is started II cycles before the third loop, and so on. The resulting code consists of three sections. The prologue is the code to get the execution of the loop going. It consists of the instructions for most of the first iteration of the loop, somewhat less code for the second iteration of the loop, and so on. The purpose is to begin the computations continued cyclically in the software-pipelined loop.

The software-pipelined loop is the important concept. Multiple iterations of the loop are folded upon one another. The first time through the software-pipelined loop, the compiler completes the last instructions for the first iteration of the loop, earlier instructions for the second iteration of the loop, and so on. During the next iteration, the first iteration is already

Figure 12.23 Schematic of Pipelined Loop

Iteration 1					Prologue
	Iteration 2				Software-Pipelined Loop
		Iteration 3			
			Iteration 4		Epilogue

completed. The instructions executed for the second iteration are the same as those for the first iteration during the previous loop body execution, except they are for the following iteration.

The software-pipelined loop contains instructions for multiple iterations of the loop. We will see how to compute the number of iterations shortly. It is also unrolled to some extent to allow renaming of the temporaries to allow valid use of the physical registers. An important point is that each instruction in the original loop occurs once in the software-pipelined loop (if the loop is unrolled, it occurs the number of times the loop is unrolled).

What is the benefit? Software pipelining works well when the separate iterations of the loop reference independent data. In that case, the computations in one iteration have nothing to do with computations in another iteration, so the execution of multiple iterations allows a tighter scheduling of instructions (usually much tighter).

The software-pipelined loop executes until almost all iterations of the loop are completed. It then exits into the epilogue code, which completes the final iterations of the loop.

If the number of iterations of the original loop are small enough, there is no advantage to software pipelining. In fact it makes the implementation of the software-pipelined loop more difficult. Also it will be simpler to implement software pipelining if the number of iterations of the loop are a multiple of some number (to be determined later). These two ideas can be combined by generating two copies of the loop: one is the sequential copy and the other is the software-pipelined copy. The compiler compiles the code as in Figure 12.24. The constant D, which is the number of iterations

Figure 12.24 Combining Unrolling and Start

```
DO I = L,H                I = L
   Body                   IF (H >= L + D) THEN
ENDDO                         WHILE I <= H - S DO
                                  Body 1
                                  Body 2
                                  ...
                                  Body S
                                  I = I + S
                              ENDWHILE
                          ENDIF
                          WHILE I <= H DO
                              Body
                              I = I + 1
                          ENDWHILE
```

before software pipelining is useful, and the constant *S*, representing the number of iterations of the loop, are determined during the construction of the software-pipelined loop.

The compiler must generate the prologue, epilogue, and the software-pipelined loop. Actually, it will generate the software-pipelined loop first, and all of the other computations are determined by the loop. The agenda is as follows:

1. Determine one schedule of a single iteration of the loop constrained so that it can be folded on itself. Think of rolling up a piece of transparent paper with marks on it so that no two marks overlap and the marks are evenly spaced when rolled up.

2. In this schedule for a single iteration, determine the maximum number of cycles that a temporary assigned in the loop is live. This will determine *S* and together with the schedule determine *II* and the software-pipelined loop.

3. Then build the prologue by overlaying multiple executions of the first few iterations of the loop as sequential (rather than looping) code.

4. Build the epilogue in the same way. Overlay the final executions of the loop as sequential code.

To begin the process we need an estimate for the initiation interval. That is the length of the software-pipelined loop. This is an initial estimate that will change for several reasons while we determine the loop.

12.10.1 Estimating Initiation Interval and Limiting Conditions

There are conditions that must be met for software pipelining to apply. We will work with the simplified assumption that each iteration of the loop is independent of the others. This condition can be checked using differing methods:

- If the compiler contains a data dependence analyzer for loop transformation, then this can also be used to check if a loop has no loop-carried dependences.[4] This is the best technique for testing and will find more loops for software pipelining.

---

4. A loop-carried dependence occurs when a store on one iteration of a loop stores a value that might be loaded on a separate iteration of the loop, or a load occurs on one iteration of a loop where a store may occur into the same location on another iteration of the loop. Similarly for a store and a store.

- The iterations are independent if the array that is stored into on all of the left-hand sides of the assignment statements in the loop is not the same as the arrays on the right-hand side. The one exception is that a load from the same location that is stored into can occur on the right-hand side. This is the minimal condition. It will find a number of the loops for software pipelining but will not find many that occur in linear algebra codes.

- Loops can be software pipelined if all load and store operations are referenced through temporaries that change by the same amount through each loop and they can be seen to reference different areas of memory. Suprisingly this is a special purpose and a general technique. It is specialized because it can only see a few of the cases. However, if it is used to generate two copies of the loop, one for sequential execution and one for pipelined execution, the choice between loops can be made at the beginning of the loop by comparing pointers.

This book is performing a limited form of software pipelining. It is possible to software-pipeline when there are loop-carried dependences. The same techniques as we will discuss here apply, with added dependences in the interference graph. The number of situations in which this gives an advantage over simple unrolling is limited.

Having said all of this, what is the initial estimate for the initiation interval *II*? Consider the loop *L*. It is composed of a number of instructions. Each instruction must be executed in the software-pipelined loop. Sort the instructions into buckets, one bucket for each class of function unit: various floating-point units, integer units, and load/store units. Divide the number of elements in each bucket by the number of units of that type. In the Alpha there are two integer units, so divide the number of integer instructions by two.[5] The maximum of these ratios is the estimate for the initiation interval *II*.

This estimate simply means that we must have enough slots in the packets to put all of the instructions. So make *II* be the smallest value at which there are enough slots in the packets.

12.10.2 Forming the Schedule for a Single Iteration

To form the software-pipelined loop we first determine the schedule for a single iteration of the loop that will be rolled back on itself to make the

---

[5]. Yes, I know they are not identical units. This process is to get an approximation. If it does not work, it will be increased later.

software-pipelined loop. The same techniques for scheduling are used that we discussed with traces. However, there are two major differences: First, we are dealing with a single block that forms a loop; and second, we are not going to schedule instructions in order.

This means that we will use the algorithm for replacing instructions in slots that we discussed in the section on state machines. Lay out the schedule initially as a large array of packets with each slot empty. Initialize the *ForwardState* and *BackwardState* attributes to indicate that no function units are busy. Now compute the conflict graph just as we did for traces. There is no need is include *Block_End* or *Block_Start* pseudo-instructions.

Now perform the scheduling in the way described for traces, with one modification. When an instruction is placed into a slot in a packet, insert a copy of the instruction in the same slot in the packet II cycles later, $2 * II$ cycles later, . . ., II cycles earlier, $2 * II$ cycles earlier, and so on. In other words, there will be a copy of that instruction in the same slot in the packets that differ in clock cycle by a multiple of II.

Since we are simultaneously placing copies of the same instruction in the slots, the compiler does not have to check each of the slots to see if the insertion can occur. Each slot has the same *ForwardState* and *BackwardState* as its copies. If they do not, then the initiation interval is too small, so restart the process with a bigger initiation interval.

It is possible that no schedule can be found. An instruction will need to be inserted, but there is no place to put it. In that case, stop, increase the initiation interval, and try again.

We repeat this process until we get a schedule with copies of the same instruction a distance of II cycles apart. Note that this process must terminate. If the initiation interval II gets to be the same as the length of a single schedule for a block, then one will get the same schedule without conflict. However, the performance of software pipelining is proportional to the ratio of the original length of a schedule divided by II, so when II gets close to the length of the longest path through the interference graph, then the whole process should be stopped and loop unrolling used instead.

The idea is to roll this schedule up into a loop that is II packets long. This does not quite work because of temporary names and physical registers. If we rolled the loop up completely, each temporary would be clobbered each time through the loop, although the time delay between the point of evaluation and the point of use in the sequential execution of instructions may be much longer. The initiation interval could be two cycles while the time between evaluation and use is four cycles, for instance. So we must first unroll this loop the minimum amount needed to avoid this problem.

12.10.3 Unrolling Loops and Renaming Temporaries

For the moment, ignore the copies of instructions in the schedule. Consider only the instructions inserted for one iteration. Compute the maximum number of cycles TL that a temporary is live. This is done in the usual way that we have used throughout the compiler. Scan the schedule backward, recording when a temporary becomes live and when it becomes dead. The maximum length is the maximum lifetime.

Now form the kernel version of the software-pipelined loop by forming a schedule II long using the last II packets of the schedule determined above (now including the copy operations). Unroll this loop $S = \lceil TL/II \rceil$ times to ensure that enough distance occurs between definitions and uses.

We must next rename the temporaries to ensure that the patterns of uses and definitions match the original schedule (before all the copies and unrolling). To do this, consider all of the temporaries that are evaluated inside the loop: $\{T_1, \ldots, T_k\}$. Generate S different copies of these registers: one for each iteration of the loop in the unrolled loop. The original set can be used as one of the sets if you like.

Now simultaneously go through the original schedule and unrolled schedule, modifying the temporaries in the formed loop so that all temporaries that apply to one iteration of the original loop use the same set of temporaries. This can be done by looking at each instruction in the rolled schedule. Look at the same instruction in the original schedule. For the temporaries that instruction defines, consider all of the uses. The instructions in the unrolled loop need to use the same temporary. The instructions can be found in the unrolled loop because they are the same distance from the original instruction there as they were in the original schedule (taking the wrap around at the end of the loop into account).

We now have the software-pipelined loop. It consists of S copies of the kernel loop with renaming to ensure value use/definition relationships. But we are not done. The register pressure should now be computed. If the register pressure is too high so that register spilling will occur, then the initiation interval needs to be increased and the whole process repeated until the pressure is brought down. Register spilling will circumvent all advantages of software pipelining.

12.10.4 Forming the Prologue

To form the prologue, consider the software-pipelined loop. Assume that the prologue had been created. The loop itself represents S iterations of the real loop and has length $II * S$. When the program has executed the first II cycles of the kernel loop, we have completed the first iteration of the original loop. Since that kernel copy consists of the last II instructions of the original schedule, the prologue can be initialized to all but the last II instructions of the original schedule together with the temporaries renamed to match the temporaries for the first iteration.

When the compiler has finished the second II cycles, we have completed the second iteration of the original loop. The last II packets of that schedule performed in this kernel, and the previous II packets were performed in the previous kernel. So the prologue can have all but the last II packets of an iteration added to it, shifted late by II packets, and renamed to use the temporaries from the second iteration. This continues until there are no more instructions to be added.

Although these instructions in the prologue form a valid schedule, the schedule should be combined with other surrounding code and can be scheduled better. Thus the prologue should be scheduled as part of a trace containing the head of the loop.

Note that at the end of the unrolled loop, we have executed S iterations of the original loop. The complete execution of the unrolled loop will therefore represent some multiple of S iterations of the original loop.

12.10.5 Forming the Epilogue

The epilogue is computed in the same manner as the prologue. When the unrolled loop has been executed, an iteration (which is a multiple of S) has been completed. There are $\lceil \textit{(length of schedule)}/II \rceil$ iterations still in execution. The epilogue can be formed by initializing it to the last II of the original schedule, with the temporaries renamed to match the next to the last loop body in the unrolled loop. Then add on the last $2 * II$ packets in the original schedule, renaming to match the previous copy of the kernel in the unrolled loop, and so on.

Note that this number of iterations can be bigger than S, so the process may cycle back to the last kernel loop in the unrolled loop. If all instructions in the loop take a single cycle, then there is no advantage to software pipelining at all. The loops that profit are loops that have floating-point computations or load operations. On the Alpha, a floating-point operation takes four cycles. This latency is hidden during software pipelining, so a possible speedup of a factor of four is possible. Of course this much improvement may not occur if there are already some computations that can be executed in parallel. Load operations can give a better payoff. Loads from the S-Cache on the Alpha are eight or nine cycles. Software pipelining can hide much of this latency; however, the more latency means the more registers, which will limit software pipelining.

We now have the whole loop, prologue, pipelined loop, and epilogue. What is the maximum payoff that can be achieved by software pipelining? Ideally, each function unit executes an instruction each cycle. In the worst case, each function unit is executing at most one instruction at a time, so the best possible speedup is the length of the pipeline. The target payoff is for load operations, which may take a large number of cycles.

12.11 Out-of-Order Execution

Recent RISC processors have included out-of-order execution. This means that the processor keeps a buffer of instructions that are prepared to be issued. The processor fetches instructions into this buffer and then issues an instruction when its operands are available. If a particular instruction's operands are not available then it waits. It is possible that a later instruction will have its operands available and execute before an earlier instruction, thus the name.

How does the compiler simulate out-of-order execution? This has not been settled in the literature. Here are my views on scheduling for out-of-order execution.

Pretend that the compiler is able to do perfect scheduling so that each instruction is prepared for execution at exactly the time that the operands become available. Then there are no delays or stalls and the processor will run at full speed. It does not matter what size the instruction buffer is. The instructions are available to be executed at exactly the point they are needed. Effectively the buffer is an infinite size: It will never overflow with instructions to be executed.

Perfect scheduling is not possible for two reasons. Some instructions, such as LOAD instructions, execute for a period of cycles that is impossible to compute. The compiler can only make guesses at the timing of these instructions. Second, the processor makes guesses about which path will be executed out of a conditional branch. If the guess is incorrect, the processor must back up and reexecute instructions.

I view out-of-order execution as handling these uncomputable events: loads and branch prediction. The compiler should schedule the instructions as if the processor were not an out-of-order execution processor. The more effective this schedule is, the larger the size of the effective instruction buffer. The role of the out-of-order component is to handle the unpredictable events. In other words, the compiler uses the instruction buffer to hold instructions that are limited by these unpredictable events and buffer against the time losses caused by them.

Schedule as if it were an in-order execution processor and allow the hardware to take care of events that are not predictable. This is a reasonable initial guess at scheduling for such processors. It remains to be seen if better scheduling can be done in the future.

12.12 References

Bala, V., and N. Rubin. 1996. Efficient instruction scheduling using finite state automata. Unpublished memo, available from authors. (Rubin is with Digital Equipment Corp.)

Ball, T., and J. R. Larus. 1992. Optimally profiling and tracing programs. *Proceedings of the Nineteenth Annual ACM SIGPLAN-SIGACT Symposium on Principles of Programming Languages, POPL92,* Albuquerque, NM. 59–70.

Fisher, J. A. 1981. Trace scheduling: A technique for global microcode compaction. *IEEE Transactions on Computers* C-30(7): 478–490.

Freudenberger, S. M., T. R. Gross, and P. G. Lowney. 1994. Avoidance and suppression of compensation code in a trace scheduling compiler. *ACM Transactions on Programming Languages and Systems* 16(4): 1156–1214.

Huber, B. L. 1995. Path-selection heuristics for dominator-path scheduling. Master of Science thesis, Michigan Technical University.

Reif, J. H., and H. R. Lewis. 1978. Symbolic program analysis in almost linear time. *Conference Proceedings of Principles of Programming Languages V, Association of Computing Machinery.*

Sweany, P. H., and S. Beaty. 1992. Dominator-path scheduling: A global scheduling method. *Proceedings of the 25th International Symposium on Microarchitecture (MICRO-25),* 260–263.

Warren, H. S. 1990. Instruction scheduling for the IBM RISC System/6000 processor. *IBM Journal of Research and Development* 34(1).

13 REGISTER ALLOCATION

The compiler has already performed register renaming and register coalescing, reduced the register pressure, and scheduled the instructions. It is time to assign registers to each temporary. The register allocator must satisfy the following constraints in order of importance:

Correctness: The compiler must assign distinct temporaries to distinct registers if there is a point in the flow graph where both temporaries might contain distinct values and both are used later. If either of the temporaries is uninitialized at that point, then the compiler is free to assume that the two temporaries have the same value.

Avoid spilling: The compiler should assign temporaries to registers so that the number of LOAD and STORE instructions inserted by the register allocator are as small as possible during the execution of the program.

Use few registers: The compiler should use as few registers in the register set as possible. Registers that are saved by the calling procedure should be used before registers saved by the called procedure.

Many compilers take a simplistic view of register allocation. They describe register allocation in terms of some algorithmic problem—such as graph coloring or bin packing—and then use some heuristic solution for that particular formulation. Such register allocators perform well on problems needing few registers; however, if the number of registers needed is significantly greater than the number of registers available, each of these register allocation methods generates a large number of spill instructions, namely, the loads and stores to memory generated by the register allocator.

The problem is that each of these allocation techniques uses one of the two types of information available. The graph-coloring allocators use the con-

Register Allocation

cept of interference or conflict graphs. The conflict graph has no concept of which instructions are near each other, so it performs poorly on blocks. The bin-packing register allocators perform well on blocks, but have to use an approximation to handle control flow. It is possible to create situations where one algorithm will work better than another. This approach to register allocation was chosen to expose the best attributes of each of the algorithms.

This compiler combines the two. Recall that the compiler has already inserted spilling instructions to reduce the register pressure to less than or equal to the number of registers available. The compiler will now use three distinct allocation algorithms to allocate registers:

- The compiler uses a derivative of graph-coloring register allocation introduced by Preston Briggs (1992) to perform allocation of temporaries that are live across block boundaries.

- The compiler uses a derivative of the FAT algorithm introduced by Laurie Hendron (1993) to perform allocation of the local temporaries that can be allocated to the same registers as global temporaries.

- The compiler uses the standard single-pass register allocation algorithm to allocate registers to temporaries that are live only within a single block. This is a bin-packing algorithm that allocates the local temporaries one at a time as the block is walked in reverse execution order.

By separating the assignment of local and global temporaries, the compiler introduces the possibility of a phase-ordering problem: The assignment of global temporaries may inhibit the assignment of local temporaries. This is unavoidable since the optimal allocation of registers is an NP-complete problem. The design is such that the particular choice of algorithms to use will avoid as much of the problem as is possible.

To illustrate the interplay between global and local register allocation, consider the pictorial representation of a block in Figure 13.1 The set of instructions

Figure 13.1 Pictorial Representation of Block

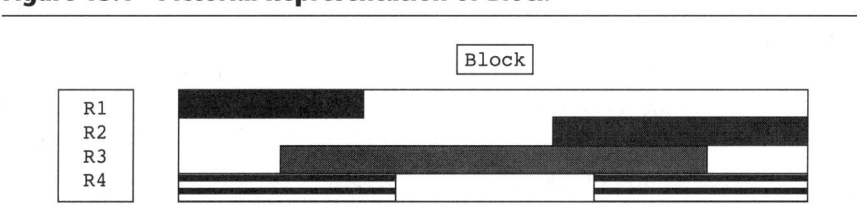

Figure 13.2 Driver for Register Allocation

```
procedure REGISTER_ALLOCATION;
   call GlobalAllocate;
   foreach B ∈ N from innermost loop outward do
      call LocalAllocate(B);
   endfor;
endprocedure REGISTER_ALLOCATION;
```

where a temporary is live is represented by a horizontal distance. Each temporary is represented by a distinct row. The global register allocator will create situations such as R1, R2, and R4. R1 contains a value assigned in another block and used for the last time in this block. R2 is assigned a value in this block and used in another block. R4 combines the two: R4 is assigned a value in this block, control flow leaves the block, and returns to the block using the value earlier in the block. R3 is a typical local temporary. It is assigned a value in the block and used for the last time later in the block. In large procedures, this is most of the temporaries. R1, R2, and R4 are allocated by the global allocator. R2 and R4 are combined with other local temporaries by the FAT algorithm. R3 is allocated using the local allocator.

Recall that all of these algorithms are approximations to an optimal allocation. An optimal allocation can be discovered by solving an integer programming problem; however, this technique is too expensive for a production compiler.

The main algorithm for register allocation is to perform each form of allocation in turn. The FAT algorithm and the local register allocator work together by the FAT algorithm creating data structures that are used by the local register allocator. The calling structure is shown in Figure 13.2. First, perform global register allocation and then apply the FAT algorithm and local register allocation algorithms on each block.

13.1 Global Register Allocation

First, the compiler allocates registers to temporaries that hold a needed value at the boundary of blocks. Usually this means the temporary is evaluated in one block and used in another; however, it is possible that the temporary is evaluated in this block and control flow leaves the block, returning later, and the value is used earlier in the same block.

Register Allocation

The global allocator is based on the Preston Briggs (Briggs, Cooper, and Torczon 1994) modification of the Chaitin (1981) graph-coloring register algorithm. It uses the conflict graph and the concept of interference or conflict that was introduced earlier during the LIMIT phase. Two temporaries can be assigned to the same physical register if there is no point in the flow graph where they both hold potentially different values that will be used later, that is, they do not conflict.

So the allocation problem is to assign a register to each node (temporary) so that two nodes that are connected by an edge are not assigned the same register. This is the graph-coloring problem, where the set of registers is the set of colors. Unfortunately, graph coloring is an NP-complete problem, so there are no known good algorithms for solving it.

Chaitin resurrected a heuristic for graph coloring that works effectively for complex control flow.[1] A node in the conflict graph having fewer neighbors than the number of colors (physical registers) can always be colored, since it can be assigned any of the colors different from the colors of its neighbors. In that case the node can be removed from the graph to be colored later, after all of its neighbors have been colored. This process is repeated until all of the nodes have been removed from the graph (if possible). Then the process is reversed. Each node is added back into the graph and given a color different from each of its neighbors currently in the graph.

Frequently, all nodes can be removed from the graph using this heuristic. In that case the observation above gives a complete algorithm for coloring the graph. Chaitin originally proposed an algorithm that stopped when there were no nodes with fewer neighbors than colors. The algorithm then chose a node to spill to memory.

The heuristic and a more recent improvement are illustrated by the conflict graph in Figure 13.3. There are four temporaries with the edges representing the conflicts. S3 has one neighbor, so it can be removed from the graph, leaving S0, S1, and S2. After removing S3, each of them has two neighbors, so any one of them can be removed from the graph next, say S0, and then S1, followed by S2. In the end we have a sequence of temporaries (S2, S1, S0, S3) that need to be assigned registers. S2 is first. Put it back into the graph and assign it to any register, say R0. S1 is next: Put it back into the

---

1. As Chaitin also noted, one can construct a program to have any undirected graph as its conflict graph, so very general graphs can occur. However, most graphs are simpler. For example, most temporaries have only one point of definition, and programs are mostly structured so the interactions between temporaries are much more limited.

Figure 13.3 Example Conflict Graph

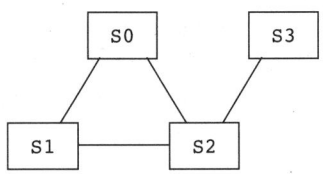

graph and assign it any register except the one assigned to S2, say R1. Similarly for S0, assigning it R2. Finally, S3 needs to be assigned a register. It conflicts only with S2 (which is assigned R0), so it can be assigned to either R1 or R2. Thus the algorithm can assign registers even though S2 has three neighbors.

Although the algorithm has been described in terms of sequences, one sees that the nodes are removed from the stack in the opposite order to the order of assigning registers. Thus the nodes are pushed on a stack as they are removed and popped off the stack as they are reinserted in the conflict graph.

Of course, the nodes themselves are not removed from the conflict graph. All that the algorithm uses as the nodes are removed is the number of neighbors in the conflict graph. Thus the algorithm must keep a count of the number of neighbors still in the graph and update it as nodes are removed.

13.1.1 When the Heuristic Does Not Work

The description of the heuristic is not a complete algorithm. It is possible that no node in the conflict graph will have fewer neighbors than the number of colors. This will occur more rarely in the current compiler since the early reduction in the register pressure makes fewer temporaries live at each point, so there are fewer conflicts. However, it is possible.

Chaitin originally suggested that a temporary that is least important and has the most neighbors should be chosen and spilled. Insert store operations into a memory location after each definition of the temporary, and insert load operations into the temporary before each use. This will remove all edges to the node from the conflict graph and the algorithm can continue removing edges from the graph, hopefully removing more nodes from the conflict graph. When the nodes are being removed from the stack and being assigned a color, there is always a color available.

Preston Briggs has suggested a modification of Chaitin's original algorithm that gives better results. The problem with Chaitin's suggestion is that the coloring heuristic is too coarse. It assumes that each neighbor of a temporary will be assigned a different register, so the number of registers needed for other temporaries is the number of neighbors. Actually, several neighbors may be given the same color. If that is the case, Chaitin's suggestion would have inserted unneeded store and load operations.

Briggs, copying Chaitin, suggested that the least important temporary be chosen; however, instead of inserting the load and store operations immediately, simply push the temporary on the stack that is being formed. Now when nodes are being removed from the stack and being assigned a color, there will be situations in which no colors are available. In that case, spill that temporary as was done in Chaitin's algorithm.

Both Briggs and Chaitin repeat the register allocation in a loop until all temporaries have been assigned registers. When register spilling occurs, a pass through the register allocator can complete without assigning physical registers to all temporaries. The registers for holding spilled values just before they are used and just before they are stored need to be assigned. Since these registers do not exist until the middle of a register allocation pass, the most effective way to deal with them is to repeat the coloring algorithm using the complete set of registers.

The proposed register allocator does not need to repeat the graph-coloring algorithm. The new temporaries introduced by spilling are loaded and stored within single blocks, so they can be handled later by the local scheduler. This implies that the register pressure may exceed the number of physical registers during local register allocation.

To summarize, the registers that cannot be colored are assigned spill locations in memory exactly as the earlier LIMIT phase assigned spill locations. The determination of the load and store locations together with the assignment of registers for these temporaries occurs later, during local register allocation. To do this the global allocator performs the following transformations when the temporary T is to be spilled:

- It allocates a memory location for the spilled temporary, *MEMORY(T)*, if it is not already allocated.

- It adds the temporary to the set *SpillRegisters,* which indicates to the local register allocator that a LOAD instruction should be inserted before the first use (if not preceded by a definition) and a store operation should occur after the last definition (unless the temporary is no longer live).

Note that this is the reverse of the role that spilling played in LIMIT. In LIMIT the compiler assumed that temporaries are in registers and only moved the temporary to memory when absolutely necessary. Here the temporary is assumed to be in memory and is moved to a register when needed. So the load operations happen before the block and store operations occur after the block. The load operation cannot be moved backward, nor can the store operation be moved forward without affecting other already allocated temporaries. The placement of these operations thus cannot be improved without moving the operations into the block.

13.1.2 Overall Algorithm

This compiler combines these ideas into an algorithm (see Figure 13.4). First the compiler recomputes the conflict matrix for the temporaries that are live at the beginning of any block. A counter *NeighborsLeft* is associated with each node (that is, temporary) of the conflict graph. It is initialized to be equal to the number of neighbors this node has. At the same time that *NeighborsLeft* is initialized, the nodes are bucket-sorted into buckets. All nodes in the same bucket have the same number of neighbors.

13.1.3 Building the Stack of Temporaries to Color

The heuristic is then used to remove nodes from the conflict graph and push them on the register stack *Stack*. Since the nodes are bucket-sorted, the compiler need only look at one of the buckets.

Figure 13.4 Driver Procedure for Global Allocation

```
procedure GLOBAL_ALLOCATION;
   call Compute_Conflict_Graph(GlobalVars);
   MaxNeighbors = MAX{|Conflict(T)| where T ∈ GlobalVars};
   for i = 0 to MaxNeighbors do         //Initialize buckets
      Bucket(i) = ∅;
   endfor;
   foreach T ∈ GlobalVars do            //Bucket sort temporaries
      add T to Bucket(|Conflict(T)|);
      NeighborsLeft(T) = |Conflict(T)|; //Initialize for stacking
      InGraph(T) = true;                //Initialize for coloring
   endfor;
   call BUILD_ALLOCATION_STACK;
   call ASSIGN_GLOBAL_REGISTERS;
endprocedure GLOBAL_ALLOCATION;
```

Register Allocation

Which buckets should be inspected first, the ones containing nodes with the most edges or the ones with nodes containing the fewest edges? This is not clear to the author. If one looks at nodes with the most edges first, then the total number of edges being removed with each node is greater and it is likely that more nodes will have fewer edges than the number of registers. If one looks at nodes with fewer neighbors first, then the nodes with fewer neighbors will be the last nodes to be colored where there is less latitude. The nodes with more neighbors will be colored first, when there are more registers available. There is no clear answer. This design pushes the nodes with fewer edges first because it makes the pseudo-code simpler. The only change to experiment with different orders is in the loop that references the buckets.[2]

The stacking algorithm, as described in Figure 13.5, has been stated without some of the optimizations and data structure choices that can be made. Here are some notes.

- *Stack* can be implemented as an array that is preallocated. Its size cannot be any larger than the number of global temporaries.

- The compiler must be able to delete arbitrary nodes from buckets. The buckets can be implemented as doubly linked lists. Insertions into buckets can always occur at the beginning of the list.

- The algorithm has written the manipulation of i as simply as possible. One can experiment with the order in which nodes are chosen. One can also decrease the number of increments. Consider the algorithm as stated. If the current node is in *Bucket(i)*, then the next node by necessity will be in *Bucket(j)*, where $j >= i - 1$ so the loop can restart at that point rather than 0.

13.1.4 Assigning Registers to Temporaries on the Stack

After the temporaries have been formed in a stack in which simpler-to-allocate temporaries are at the bottom of the stack and hard-to-allocate temporaries are at the top of the stack, the algorithm in Figure 13.6 goes

---

2. Keith Cooper of Rice University has commented that any plausible improvement to a register allocation algorithm can only be validated by experimentation. From my own experience, many changes to algorithms that should theoretically only improve the performance of the allocator have decreased the performance. This is the nature of NP-complete problems.

Figure 13.5 Building Stack of Temporaries to Allocate

```
procedure BUILD_ALLOCATION_STACK;
   ComputedPriority = false;              //No spill information yet
   Nodes = GlobalVars;                    //Nodes yet to pushed
   Stack = ∅;                             //Stack for coloring
   while Nodes ≠ ∅  do
      i = 0;                              //Find non-empty bucket
      while Bucket(i) = ∅ do
         i = i + 1;
      endwhile;
      if i > MaxPhysicalRegisters then    //Satisfy heuristic?
         if ¬ComputedPriority then        //Have we computed spill info?
            ComputedPriority = true;
            call ComputePriority;
         endif;
         choose T from {U|Priority(T)/NeighborsLeft(T) is minimum};
         delete T from Bucket(NeighborsLeft(T));
      else
         choose T from Bucket(i);
         delete T from Bucket(i);
      endif;
      delete T from Nodes;
      push T on Stack;
      InGraph(T) = false;
      foreach U ∈ Conflict(T) do          //Update neighbors
         if InGraph(U) then
            delete U from Bucket(NeighborsLeft(U));
            NeigborsLeft(U) = NeighborsLeft(U) - 1;
            add U to Bucket(NeighborsLeft(U));
         endif
      endfor;
   endwhile;
endprocedure BUILD_ALLOCATION_STACK;
```

through the stack assigning colors to the temporaries. Each temporary must be assigned a color different from the neighbors.

Note that the algorithm does not attempt to keep the number of neighbors that have been returned to the graph up-to-date. It does keep the attribute *InGraph* up-to-date because it is used to signal that a temporary has been colored.

If there are no registers left after looking at all of the neighbors, the temporary is spilled. This consists of leaving the *InGraph* attribute false to indicate that it has no associated physical register and adding the temporary to *SpillRegisters*. The local register allocator will take care of inserting load and store operations to effect the spilling.

Figure 13.6 Register Coloring Algorithm

```
procedure ASSIGN_GLOBAL_REGISTERS;
   AlreadyAssigned = ∅;         //Assigned physical registers
   SpillRegisters = ∅;          //Registers to spill
   while Stack ≠ ∅ do
      pop T from Stack;
      UnavailableRegisters = ∅;
      foreach U ∈ Conflict(T) do
         if InGraph(U) then
            add Color(U) to UnavailableRegisters;
         endif;
      endfor;
      if |UnavailableRegisters| = MaxPhysicalRegisters then
         if MEMORY(T) is not allocated then
            allocate location for MEMORY(T);
         endif;
         add T to SpillRegisters;
      else
         Color(T) = ChooseRegister(T);
         add Color(T) to AlreadyAssigned;
         InGraph(T) = true;
      endif;
   endwhile;
endprocedure ASSIGN_GLOBAL_REGISTERS;
```

13.1.5 Choosing the Actual Physical Register

Any physical register that is not already assigned to a neighboring temporary is an appropriate choice for the register to assign; however, there are certain choices that may improve the final result. If there is a physical register that has already been used somewhere else in the procedure, then it is preferable to reuse that register. If only unused registers are available, then the compiler must take into account the calling standard of the processor. Certain registers are saved and restored by the calling procedure. These registers are temporary registers that can be used by the current procedure without added cost. Other registers must be saved and restored by the called procedure. The first time that these are used within a procedure, code must be inserted in the procedure prologue and epilogue to save and restore these registers.

The algorithm in Figure 13.7 implements these ideas with one addition. Consider the temporary T that is being allocated a register. Some of its neighbors (those with *InGraph* false), call one of them U for the moment, have not yet been allocated a register. If T can be allocated to the same register as

Figure 13.7 Choosing the Register

```
function ChooseRegister(T: Temporary) return PhysicalRegister;
   foreach U ∈ Conflict(T) do
      if ¬ InGraph(U) then
         foreach Z ∈ Conflict(U) do
            if InGraph(Z) ∧ T ∉ Conflict(Z) then
               return Color(Z);
            endif;
         endfor;
      endif;
   endfor;
   foreach U ∈ AlreadyAssigned do
      if U ∉ UnavailableRegisters then
         return Color(U);
      endif;
   endfor;
   foreach U ∈ CallerSave do
      if U ∉ UnavailableRegisters then
         return Color(U);
      endif;
   endfor;
   foreach U ∈ CalleeSave do
      if U ∉ UnavailableRegisters then
         if MEMORY(U) not allocated then
            allocate memory for MEMORY(U);
         endif;
         insert STORE U,MEMORY(U) in prologue;
         insert LOAD MEMORY(U) => U in epilogue;
      endif;
   endfor;
endfunction ChooseRegister;
```

one of the other temporaries that conflict with U, then it might be easier to allocate U when the time comes.

If this heuristic does not work, then attempt to assign T to a physical register that has already been used. This will keep the number of registers used down. Remember that scheduling has already occurred, so the compiler has already reordered instructions and nothing will be gained by using more registers.

If no register is available that has already been used, then use one of the *CallerSave* registers because there is no cost for saving and restoring them. Failing that, use a *CalleeSave* register; however, code must be inserted in the prologue and epilogue of the flow graph to save and restore the physical register.

13.1.6 Implementing Spilling

Although described in the pseudo-code, we have not discussed the choice of temporary to push on the stack when no temporary satisfies the heuristic. We have discussed what to do when there is no register available during the assignment of registers. In that case the temporary is placed in a set *SpillRegisters* and the spilling process is delayed until local register allocation.

This compiler uses Chaitin's method for choosing a temporary to push on the stack (Chaitin 1982). More complex techniques have been proposed more recently; however, their value in the current design is undetermined. The more complex techniques seem to work better with straight-line code or situations with large register pressure; however, we are dealing with these situations differently.

There are two factors in choosing a temporary to push on the stack. Since registers are colored in reverse order to the order in which they are placed on the stack, the compiler should push the least important temporary on the stack. Second, the compiler should push a temporary that conflicts with a large number of temporaries that are not yet on the stack. This will decrease the number of edges in the conflict graph and make it more likely that more nodes will satisfy the coloring heuristic. The compiler must piece these two criteria together into a single algorithm or formula to describe the priority of a node. Many formulas would do; we use Chaitin's, which chooses the temporary with the smallest value:

$$\frac{\Sigma\{\texttt{frequency(p)} | \texttt{p is a point where } T \texttt{ is used or defined}\}}{\texttt{NumberLeft}(T)}$$

Unfortunately, the compiler cannot precompute this information and save it for all cases where spilling might occur, since the attribute *NumberLeft(T)* keeps changing during the process of pushing temporaries on the stack. Instead, the compiler precomputes the following formula and then performs the division when spilling is necessary:

$$\texttt{Priority}(T) = \Sigma\{\texttt{frequency(p)} | \texttt{p is a point where } T \texttt{ is used or defined}\}$$

As far as the code is concerned, the subroutine *Compute Priority*[3] does a walk over the flow graph identifying all load and store operations involving

---

3. The code for *Compute Priority* is not included as pseudo-code. It is a clerical walk of the flow graph using the frequency information stored with the block and the occurrences of load and store operations to accumulate the information.

temporaries and computing the numerator of this expression. It stores it in the attribute *Priority(T)*. Later, when a temporary must be chosen to push on the stack, the division by the denominator is performed and the smallest value resulting is chosen.

13.2 Local Register Allocation

Global register allocation is completed. Now we must allocate registers that are live in blocks. This allocator has a different structure because the regions of the procedure where each temporary is live are more regular. The instructions of a block can be enumerated in the order that they are executed. If there were no global temporaries already assigned, there are simple algorithms for doing good local allocation in straight-line code. This compiler does use these ideas eventually, but first it must deal with the global temporaries that have already been assigned registers, so that they do not foul up the simple straight-line algorithm (Figure 13.8).

Before local register allocation, the compiler must fix up the global temporaries that were not allocated by the global register allocator. These are the temporaries in the set *SpillRegisters*. The compiler must go through the

Figure 13.8 Main Local Allocation Procedure

```
procedure LOCAL_ALLOCATE(B: Block);
   if SpillRegisters ≠ ∅ then call INSERT_GLOBAL_SPILL(B);
   call endif;
   call LOCAL_CLASSIFY(B);
   call BUILD_LOCAL_CONFLICT(B);
   call BUILD_LOCAL_BUCKETS;
   Stack = ∅;
   NumRegisters = MaxPressure;
   i = 0;
   while LiveStart ≠ ∅ do
      call ADD_TO_LOCAL_STACK;
      take T from LiveStart;
      delete T from LiveStart;
      call ALLOCATE_WITH_GLOBAL(T);
   endwhile;
   call ADD_TO_LOCAL_STACK;
   if any unstacked temporaries then call ONE_PASS_ALLOCATE(B);
   call endif;
   call GIVE_STACKED_TEMPORARIES_COLOR;
endprocedure LOCAL_ALLOCATE;
```

block and perform three functions. First it must insert a STORE instruction into memory after the last assignment of a value to one of these temporaries. Second, it must put a load operation before the first use of one of these temporaries if that use is not preceded by an assignment to the temporary. Finally, a new name must be given to the temporary within this block. Since a single name is associated with each temporary, the compiler must create a new name whenever it splits the references to a temporary into separately allocated portions. By giving it a new name the temporary can be allocated to different registers in different blocks.

The algorithm in Figure 13.9 performs these three tasks in a two-step process. A backward pass is performed that determines the last instruction that places a value in one of these temporaries. A store operation is inserted after those instructions. At the same time, it determines which temporaries need a load operation inserted before them. The algorithm does this by assuming that the load is needed and deleting the assumption if an earlier assignment to the temporary is found.

The second pass is a forward pass, using the attribute *NewName* to hold the local name for the spilled temporary and inserting the load operation before the first use of the temporary name.

After the spilling of global temporaries, the local register allocator classifies the types of temporaries that occur in the block. Before this is described, the reader should be made aware that all of the walks in the register allocator mimic the computation of live information. In fact, most compute live information. They all perform a reverse-execution walk of the flow graph, either implicitly or explicitly computing live information and performing whatever processing takes place at the same time. In the case of classifying the temporaries, the information collected is a set of sets of temporaries and the maximum register pressure, that is, the maximum number of temporaries live at any given time. These sets are listed below:

LiveThrough: The temporaries that are live at each point in the block. They may be referenced in the block and possibly modified; however, there is no point between instructions where these temporaries are not live. Thus each one of them occupies a physical register for the complete block, effectively removing that physical register from any consideration for local allocation.

LiveStart: The temporaries that are live at the beginning of the block and become dead after some instruction in the block. These are the global temporaries that will cause the local register allocator problems. This

Figure 13.9 Spilling and Classifying Temporaries

```
procedure INSERT_GLOBAL_SPILL(B: Block);
   InsertSTORE = SpillRegisters; InsertLOAD = ∅;
   foreach I ∈ B in reverse execution order do
      foreach T ∈ Targets(I) do
         if T ∈ SpillRegisters then
            if T ∈ InsertSTORE then
               delete T from InsertSTORE;
               insert STORE T,MEMORY(T) after I;
            endif;
            delete T from InsertLOAD;
         endif;
      endfor;
      foreach T ∈ Operands(I) do
         if T ∈ SpillRegisters then add T to InsertLOAD; endif;
      endfor;
   endfor;
   NewName = ∅;
   foreach I ∈ B in execution order do
      foreach T ∈ Operands(I) do
         if T ∈ SpillRegisters then
            if NewName(T) = NULL then
               NewName(T) = new temporary name;
            endif;
            if T ∈ InsertLOAD then
               delete T from InsertLOAD;
               add LOAD MEMORY(T) => NewName(T) before I;
            endif;
            replace T by NewName(T) in I;
         endif;
      endfor;
      foreach T ∈ Targets(I) do
         if T ∈ SpillRegisters then
            if NewName(T) = NULL then
               NewName(T) = new temporary name;
            endif;
            replace T by NewName(T) in I;
         endif;
      endfor;
   endfor;
endprocedure INSERT_GLOBAL_SPILL;
```

local register allocator walks the block backward (remember the simulation of live computation) to allocate temporaries, and it must take great care not to overlap the use of a temporary that it allocates with a physical register allocated to a temporary in *LiveStart*. The allocator uses the FAT heuristic for doing that.

LiveEnd: The temporaries that are live at the end of the block and became live at some instruction in the block. These will cause the compiler no problems with local register allocation. In effect, they are preallocated local temporaries for the purposes of allocation within this block.

LiveTransparent: The temporaries that are live throughout the block and not referenced in the block. As with *LiveThrough*, these temporaries occupy a physical register throughout the block. However, they are useful when the register pressure is too high because they can be spilled before and after the block, as was done in the LIMIT phase.

LocalRegisters: Local temporaries that become live within the block and later become dead within the block. In computationally intensive programs this is the largest class of temporaries. Allocating physical registers to these temporaries is the whole point of this section. Note that the newly created temporaries associated with spilled temporaries are in this class.

The algorithm in Figure 13.10 is precisely a recomputation of live information within the block and uses this live information to classify all of the temporaries using the definitions above. For example, a temporary in *LiveTransparent* is live on exit from the block and has no references to it. Thus *LiveTransparent* is initialized to be the set of temporaries live on exit and then a temporary that is referenced is removed. The others are handled similarly.

Having classified the temporaries, it is now time to prepare for register allocation. Suprisingly, the compiler computes the conflict graph for the block. Although graph coloring is not the basis for this allocator, the graph-coloring heuristic can be viewed in the following useful way: A temporary that has fewer neighbors than available colors is always easy to color, thus it can be put aside. By repeating this process, the easy temporaries are all put aside, leaving only the temporaries that are difficult to color to be dealt with in a specialized way. In fact, the removal of these easy registers removes the clutter, making the hard decisions apply only to the hard temporaries.

The compiler computes two data structures for the local register allocator (see Figure 13.11). The first is the local conflict graph, in which the only temporaries that occur in the graph are the temporaries that occur in this block. This makes for a small graph, one hopes. There are cases where one

Figure 13.10 Classifying Temporaries in a Block

```
procedure LOCAL_CLASSIFY(B: Block);
   LiveTransparent = LiveOut(B);
   LiveThrough = LiveOut(B);
   LiveStart = ∅;
   LocalRegisters = ∅;
   Live = LiveOut(B);
   MaxPressure = |Live|;
   foreach I ∈ B in reverse execution order do
      foreach T ∈ Targets(I) do
         delete T from Live;
         delete T from LiveTransparent;
         delete T from LiveStart;
         if T ∉ Operands(I) then
             delete T from LiveThrough;
         endif;
         if Color(T) = NULL then
             add T to LocalRegisters;
         endif;
      endfor;
      foreach T ∈ Operands(I) do
         add T to Live;
         delete T from LiveTransparent;
         add T to LiveStart;
         if Color(T) = NULL then
             add T to LocalRegisters;
         endif;
      endfor;
      Pressure(I) = |Live|;
      MaxPressure = max(MaxPressure,Pressure(I));
   endfor;
   LiveEnd = LiveOut(B) - LiveThrough;
endprocedure LOCAL_CLASSIFY;
```

procedure is a large (think thousands of lines of code) block. In that case, the global conflict graph is small and this one is big.[4]

The algorithm also computes the range in which the temporary is live. This information is needed by the FAT algorithm. The information is recorded by assigning two numbers to each instruction. The end of the block is numbered 0, and the numbers increase toward the beginning of

---

[4]. Compiler writers frequently forget that there are two categories of program writers. Human program writers are more easily dealt with. The compiler can estimate the patterns of usage. Programs that write programs are much more difficult, creating programs with horrid structure.

Register Allocation

Figure 13.11 Building Lifetimes and Local Conflict Graph

```
procedure BUILD_LOCAL_CONFLICT(B: Block);
   LocalConflict = ∅;
   Live = LiveOut(B) - SpillRegisters;
   TimeCount = 0;
   foreach T ∈ Live do
      EndTime(I) = TimeCount;
   endfor;
   foreach I ∈ B in reverse execution order do
      TimeCount = TimeCount + 1;
      EndTime(I) = TimeCount;
      foreach T ∈ Targets(I) do
         StartTime(T) = TimeCount;
         delete T from Live;
         foreach U ∈ Live do
            create entry (T,U) in LocalConflict;
         endfor;
      endfor;
      TimeCount = TimeCount + 1;
      StartTime(I) = TimeCount;
      foreach T ∈ Operands(T) do
         EndTime(T) = TimeCount;
         add T to Live;
      endfor;
   endfor;
   TimeCount = TimeCount + 1;
   foreach T ∈ Live do
      StartTime(T) = TimeCount;
      foreach U ∈ Live - {T} do
         create entry (T,U) in LocalConflict;
      endfor;
   endfor;
endprocedure BUILD_LOCAL_CONFLICT;
```

the block. The smaller number of the pair represents the portion of the instruction that performs modifications of registers. The larger number represents the portion of the instruction that fetches the operands.

There are two attributes associated with each temporary. *StartTime(T)* is the counter associated with the instruction that writes the temporary. If the temporary is live at the beginning of the block, then it references a value preceding the block. *EndTime(T)* references the operand section of the last instruction to reference the temporary. If the temporary is live at the end of the block, then the attribute references off the end of the block. These attributes are computed in a single walk through the block that simulates the live computation and assigns *EndTime* the first time the temporary becomes live and assigns *StartTime* when the temporary becomes dead.

After the register allocator has computed the conflict and lifetime information, it prepares to do the standard graph-coloring heuristic to remove easy temporaries. Just as with the global allocator, the temporaries are bucket-sorted (see Figure 13.12). The same attributes are set up in the same way as in the global register allocator.

Now we will describe the algorithm out of order for ease of understanding. What we want to do is go through the block assigning physical registers to temporaries as we go. This algorithm is described later in Figure 13.15. Before allocation begins, all of the physical registers are placed in a set called *FreeRegisters,* indicating that they are available for use. As we scan through the block (again in reverse order, simulating live computation), we assign one of the *FreeRegisters* to a temporary the first time that we see it become live; that is, we find the last use of the temporary. We return the physical register allocated to a temporary to *FreeRegister* at the point where it is defined (if the temporary is not also used as an operand).

The problem is that this does not work if there are global temporaries already allocated physical registers at the other end of the block. We may pull a physical register out of *FreeRegister* and assign it to a temporary whose lifetime overlaps a global temporary that is already using that register.

The solution is to preprocess the global temporaries that are live at the other end of the block (in this case, the start of the block since we are going through the block backward). This is the FAT heuristic. Take one of

Figure 13.12 Build Buckets for Local Coloring

```
procedure BUILD_LOCAL_BUCKETS;
   MaxNeighbors = MAX{|Conflict(T)| where T ∈ LocalRegisters};
   for i = 0 to MaxNeighbors do
     Bucket(i) = ∅;
   endfor;
   foreach T ∈ LocalRegisters do
     add T to Bucket(|Conflict(T)|);
     NeighborsLeft(T) = |Conflict(T)|;
     InGraph(T) = true;              //Initialize for coloring
   endfor;
endprocedure BUILD_LOCAL_BUCKETS;
```

these temporaries, call it T. The FAT heuristic does the following operations:

1. It scans through the block finding all of the points where the register pressure is maximum. These are called the FAT points.

2. For each of these FAT points, it chooses a local temporary that is live at that FAT point. We say that the temporary covers that FAT point. The temporaries are chosen so that each FAT point is covered and no two temporaries chosen have overlapping lifetimes or lifetimes that overlap with T. This may not be possible; in that case, there will be further spilling. After all, this is a heuristic, not an algorithm.

3. Each one of these temporaries covering the FAT points are assigned the same physical register as the T.

4. The physical register associated with T and the temporaries that cover the FAT points is taken out of consideration for further allocation. The register pressure is reduced by 1 at each of the instructions where one of the covering temporaries is live. In other words, we ignore the physical register, T, and the temporaries that cover the FAT points.

5. We now repeat this process with the other global temporaries live at the beginning of the block until we have processed them all.

6. At this point there are no temporaries live at the beginning of the block that we care about so we can apply the one-pass local register allocator as described above.

This is the algorithm we use. The only modification is that between the processing of each of these temporaries the compiler applies the coloring heuristic to remove easy registers. This is the algorithm that we describe in Figure 13.8. We now describe the support procedures.

The graph-coloring heuristic is implemented by two procedures, *ADD_TO_LOCAL_STACK* (Figure 13.13) and *GIVE_STACKED_TEMPORARIES_COLOR* (Figure 13.14). The algorithms are copies of the algorithms used during global allocation and will not be described further. Note that the variable *NumberRegisters* starts out being the same as the constant *MaxPhysicalRegisters* and keeps decreasing each time the FAT algorithm is applied.

Note that there should be no spilling involved with the coloring heuristic. Temporaries are pushed on the stack when they have fewer neighbors than colors. Nothing is pushed on the stack that violates that condition. When the FAT heuristic is applied, one physical register is taken out of participation, so

Figure 13.13 Building Local Graph-Coloring Stack

```
procedure ADD_TO_LOCAL_STACK;
    i = ∅;
    while i < NumberRegisters do
        if bucket(i) ≠ ∅ then
            take T from bucket(i);
            push T on Stack;
            foreach U ∈ Conflict(T) do
                if InGraph(U) then
                    InGraph(U) = false;
                    delete U from bucket(NeighborsLeft(U));
                    NeighborsLeft(U) = NeighborsLeft(U) - 1;
                    add U to bucket(NeighborsLeft(U));
                    if i > NeighborsLeft(U) then i = NeighborsLeft(U);
                    endif;
                endif;
            endfor;
        else
            i = i + 1;
        endif;
    endwhile;
endprocedure ADD_TO_LOCAL_STACK;
```

the number of neighbors allowed is decreased by one. This does not affect any earlier temporaries pushed on the stack.

The one-pass register allocator is described in Figure 13.15. It is a single pass, simulating live computation (so it can know when a temporary

Figure 13.14 Coloring the Easy Local Temporaries

```
procedure GIVE_STACKED_TEMPORARIES_COLOR;
    while Stack ≠ ∅ do              //No spilling possible
        pop T from Stack;
        UnavailableRegisters = ∅;
        foreach U ∈ Conflict(T) do
            if InGraph(U) then
                add Color(U) to UnavailableRegisters;
            endif;
        endfor;
        Color(T) = ChooseRegister(T);
        add Color(T) to AlreadyAssigned;
        InGraph(T) = true;
    endwhile;
endprocedure GIVE_STACKED_TEMPORARIES_COLOR;
```

Figure 13.15 One-Pass Register Allocation

```
procedure ONE_PASS_ALLOCATE(B: Block);
   GlobalRegisters = {Color(T)|T ∈ LiveStart}
   FreeRegisters = All physical registers;
   for T ∈ LiveEnd do
      delete Color(T) from FreeRegisters;
      InGraph(T) = true;
   endfor;
   FreeRegisters = FreeRegisters - GlobalRegisters;
   Live = LiveEnd;
   for I ∈ B in reverse execution order do
      foreach T ∈ Targets(I) do
         delete T from Live;
         if (T ∉ Operands(I)) ∧ (Color(T) ∉ GlobalRegisters) then
            add Color(T) to FreeRegisters;
         endif;
      endfor;
      foreach T ∈ Operands(I) do
         if T ∉ Live then
            add T to Live;
            if Color(T) = NULL then
               if FreeRegisters = ∅ then
                  call LOCAL_SPILL_REGISTER(I,B);
               endif;
               choose S from FreeRegisters;
               delete S from FreeRegisters;
               Color(T) = S;
               InGraph(T) = true;
            endif;
         endif
      endfor;
   endfor;
endprocedure ONE_PASS_ALLOCATE;
```

becomes live) and parceling out free physical registers when a temporary becomes live. If a temporary already has a color, then it need not be assigned one. Due to failures of the FAT heuristic, it is possible that spilling will be required within the block.

The FAT heuristic in Figure 13.16 is a direct implementation of the original description. The nonoverlapping lifetimes are chosen by use of the *FinishTime* local variable. This variable indicates that point at which the most recent addition to the covering set becomes dead again in the reverse-execution walk. The attribute *BeginTime* indicates the point where the global temporary that is going to be sharing a physical register with all of these

Figure 13.16 FAT Heuristic

```
procedure ALLOCATE_WITH_GLOBAL(B: Block, G: Temporary);
   BeginTime = EndTime(G);
   FinishTime = 0;                   //The end of the block
   foreach T ∈ LiveEnd do
      if Color(T) = Color(G) then
         FinishTime = StartTime(U);
         break;
      endif;
   endfor;
   Live = LiveOut(B);
   foreach I ∈ B in reverse execution order do
      foreach T ∈ Targets(I) do
         delete T from Live;
      endfor;
      foreach T ∉ Operands(I) do
         add T to Live;
      endfor;
      if I precedes FinishTime then
         if |Live| ≥ NumberRegisters + |LiveThrough| then
            while T ∈ Live do
               if EndTime(T) is later than FinishTime then
                  next iteration of loop;
               endif;
               if StartTime(T) precedes BeginTime then
                  next iteration of loop;
               endif;
               Color(T) = Color(G);
               FinishTime = StartTime(T);
               break;
            endwhile;
         endif;
      endif;
   endfor;
   NumberRegisters = NumberRegisters - 1;
endprocedure ALLOCATE_WITH_GLOBAL;
```

temporaries becomes dead. So the next temporary to be chosen has to be live at a point of maximum pressure and not have a lifetime that overlaps the global at the beginning or the previous temporary in the covering set.

When spilling is needed, the classic spilling heuristic is used (Figure 13.17). Consider the register allocation process at an instruction I where there is an operand that needs a temporary assigned to a physical register. There are not enough physical registers, so choose the temporary whose previous use is the furthest away. By inserting a load operation after I and a store operation after the last definition of the temporary, a register is freed up for use for the largest possible period of time in the block.

Figure 13.17 Spilling within the Block

```
procedure LOCAL_SPILL_REGISTER(I: Instruction, B: Block);
   Scan the block in execution order finding the T ∈ Live with
      earliest previous use or definition;
   if MEMORY(T) is not allocated then
      allocate MEMORY(T);
   endif;
   insert LOAD MEMORY(T) => T after I;
   Insert a STORE T,MEMORY(T) after the previous use;
   Get a new temporary name;
   Scan from the previous use back to the beginning of the
      block renaming all references to T with this new name;
   delete Color(T) from FreeRegisters;
endprocedure LOCAL_SPILL_REGISTER;
```

13.3 References

Briggs, P., K. D. Cooper, and L. Torczon. 1992. Coloring register pairs. *ACM Letters on Programming Languages and Systems* 1(1): 3-13.

Briggs, P., K. D. Cooper, and L. Torczon. 1994. Improvements to graph coloring register allocation. *ACM Transactions on Programming Languages and Systems* 16(3): 428-455.

Chaitin, G. J. 1982. Register allocation and spilling via graph coloring. *Proceedings of the SIGPLAN '82 Symposium on Compiler Construction,* Boston, MA. Published as *SIGPLAN Notices* 17(6): 98-105.

Chaitin, G. J., et al. 1981. Register allocation via coloring. *Computer Languages* 6(1): 47-57.

Hendron, L. J., G. R. Gao, E. Altman, and C. Mukerji. 1993. Register allocation using cyclic interval graphs: A new approach to an old problem. (Technical report.) McGill University.

14 THE OBJECT MODULE

The compiler has now determined the exact instructions, the order of the instructions, and the layout of data. The only four jobs left to do are generate the object, assembly, error, and listing files. These are clerical jobs. This does not minimize their difficulty or importance. There is little theory applicable to these tasks.

To understand the generation of object files, remember the four different concepts of time that the compiler must understand. Events that happen during *compile time* are events that happen within the compiler—analyzing the program and generating output that will be used to create the program. Events that happen at *link time* are operations that happen while the linker is running. This includes the layout of the executable program and the modification of some addresses to represent the actual locations in memory rather than the relative addresses specified by the compiler. There is a tight correlation between some link-time operations and compile-time operations. The compiler must create a collection of commands to specify the operations that the linker must perform to create the image. The creation of the commands is a compile-time operation; the execution of the commands is a link-time operation.

For completeness, there are two more time intervals: *load time* and *run time*. Operations that happen at load time include further relocation of relative addresses and setting the addresses of shared libraries. Load-time operations are the execution of commands that are left in the executable image created by the linker. Thus load-time operations are execution of commands created at link time, which further are the effects of commands created at compile time. Finally, runtime operations are the processes that occur during the execution of the program. Although all instructions are

The Object Module **413**

executed at run time, the term usually refers to the creation of data structures, such as the static nesting stack, that are maintained at run time.

As you can see, all of these processes are controlled by commands created by the compiler at compile time and inserted into an output file called the *object file* or *object module*.

14.1 What Is the Object Module?

The object module is a collection of commands to the linker describing how data must be stored in memory and how that data must be modified when the data is placed in one position rather than another. Consider a particular procedure such as the running example we have used throughout the book, *MAXCOL*. This procedure consists of a contiguous sequence of numbers representing the instructions in the procedure, a set of data representing the storage locations for data in the procedure, and a set of storage locations holding the constants that require more storage than the immediate field of the instructions.

The compiler knows the relative locations of the instructions in the procedure; however, it does not know the absolute locations since it has no knowledge of the other procedures and data that will be loaded with this one. Hence the compiler cannot determine the absolute locations for instructions or data; it can only determine the relative locations with respect to the other instructions and data in the procedure. If required to do so, the linker must adjust the addresses created by the compiler to be absolute addresses rather than the relative addresses created by the compiler.[1] This process is called *relocation*.

To represent contiguous sequences of numbers, either instructions or data, the object module has the concept of a *section* of data. A section of data consists of the following parts.

- Each section has a unique name. Two sections that have the same name are either concatenated together or overlaid by the linker. Thus multiple object modules can contribute to the same section by using the same name. Similarly, separate parts of the same object module can contribute to the same section.

---

1. Some instructions represent addresses as offsets from the current program counter. In this case the linker does not need to adjust the addresses. Many processors have a set of relative branches together with the absolute jump instruction.

- Each section has a set of attributes. The most important attribute is whether this section involves concatenation of data from separate section commands or overlaying of data from separate section commands. Other attributes include the read and write attributes of the section. The object module can specify that a particular section can be read-only or read-write. This information can be used by the operating system to invoke page protection when possible.

- Each segment has an alignment. Since some data must begin at an address that is a multiple of some specified power of two, the segment command must allow the compiler to describe the multiple of two on which this portion of the segment must begin. This allows the compiler to allocate packets of instructions for multiple issue or data that must be aligned at specified addresses.

- Each section command indicates a size. This is the number of bytes of memory (or whatever memory units are used) to be allocated by this section command.

- The section may have data stored in the storage represented by this section command. Frequently this data will be instructions; however, it can be data or constants.

- Each section contains a collection of other commands, which will be specified below, for performing relocation on the data in the section and storing information about important locations in the section.

The compiler represents absolute addresses as a section name together with an offset within the section. The linker will replace this pair by the absolute address. When the compiler is storing an absolute address in an instruction or data, it will actually store the offset and create a command to indicate to the linker that the address of this part of the section must be added in also. There is a subtle point here: The linker keeps track of which section command is associated with each component of the section and will add in the relative offset of the beginning of the data for that section command.

The object module contains the following commands besides the segment commands above.

- A *definition command* defines a symbol. It contains two parts: the name of the symbol being defined and an expression representing the symbol. For our purposes that expression need only be a segment name and an offset. Thus the name *MAXCOL* in our running example must be made known to other procedures so it can be called. The entry point is described by a definition command, which represents the offset within the segment representing the instructions where the entry point occurs.

- A *use command* indicates that a symbol described by a definition command is to be used. It has three parts: the name of the symbol, the location in the section where the symbol is to be used, and an indication of whether the symbol is to be added or subtracted. When the symbol used is a section name, the value added is the beginning address of the piece of the segment created by this current section statement. Hence relocation can occur by this command.

These two commands are used by the compiler to instruct the linker on where to adjust data and where to place addresses. More complex commands may be available in the object module; however, these are what are needed for basic compilation. Another commonly available command is one to expand the current section by a fixed amount of initialized data. This will decrease the size of the object modules considerably.

There are other parts of the object module for debugging. These are less standardized and can vary from language compiler to language compiler on the same machine. The basic form of this data is tables of information. There must be a table that describes the address of each variable in the program indexed by the location where the program has stopped. The data may be in memory, on the stack, or in registers, and the debugging symbol table must store this information. Furthermore, a table of line numbers or program statements must be included, indexed by the program counter where the program has stopped.

Originally, each machine had a distinct object module format. This is still true, although many of the object module formats are based on COFF or ELF, which are formats that have developed within the UNIX community. However, each manufacturer has developed additions or slightly different implementations so that even these are not standard. This is particularly true in the area of the debugging tables.

The major problem with object modules, in my experience, is that all descriptions of object modules are inaccurate. The only real definition of an object module is what the linker accepts. The only way to find this out is by experimentation. Implementing the object module generator once the object module format is known is easy. Finding out what the object module format actually *is* (not what it is described to be) is difficult.

14.2 What Segments Are Created by the Compiler?

The compiler will generate several object module segments to represent the compiled procedure. Typically each of these segments will have a name that is a function of the procedure name, for example, the procedure name together with a character that is impossible in a procedure name followed by some unique set of characters.

One of the segments will hold all of the instructions. There are usually other segments, although they can be combined together:

- A segment to hold all local initialized static data. The name of this is frequently a function of the procedure name; however, the data could be placed in one large segment with all other static data.

- A segment to hold all local uninitialized static data. Again the name can either be a function of the procedure name or one large segment for all uninitialized data.

- Similarly, segments for initialized and uninitialized external data. This is data that can be referenced by other procedures. It could be combined with the local data if desired. Actually, each external variable may be placed in a segment by itself. This can be useful in languages where the originator of the data is not known (such as C or common blocks in Fortran). In that case each procedure can create the segment for the data and mark it as an overlay segment. Then only one area of storage will be allocated.

- A segment may be created to hold all constants referenced in a procedure. Again this segment can be combined with others in a number of fashions.

14.3 Generating the Object File

How does the compiler generate this collection of object module commands? At this point of the compilation, the compiler has a direct representation of each instruction and the order of instructions. It knows the exact size of each datum and the initialization of each datum. In other words, the compiler has a little bit more knowledge than the input to an assembler. It knows more information since the instructions have already been scheduled and peephole-optimized, taking advantage of any special characteristics of the instructions.

Thus the compiler need only simulate a two-pass assembler to generate the object module. What does a two-pass assembler do? It scans through the instructions pretending to generate the object module. Instead of generating the object module, it keeps track of each address that is associated with the beginning of a block in the flow graph. Since each instruction has a fixed size, this can be done in one pass. At the same time each set of variables is scanned and the relative address within the segment is determined, just as described in introductory compiler textbooks describing the layout of data.

During the second pass, the compiler does generate the object module. It now knows all addresses relative to their corresponding segments, so it can lay out the segments. As it creates the segments it keeps a table of definition and use commands to describe the operations that must be performed to update each datum or instruction. Thus an instruction that includes an absolute address is represented as a fixed number in the segment together with a command describing the use of the segment name to be added into the number to represent the full address.[2]

After all of the segments for data have been generated, the segments for the debugging tables must be generated. They are usually handled like any other data (although they may not be loaded in the executable by the linker). Thus the debugging symbol table will have a collection of absolute data, such as the names of the symbols. However, references to memory locations in the program will be represented by the use of a defined symbol or by a segment name plus offset.

14.4 The Complication: Short versus Long Branches

We have not described one problem with the formation of the object module: the generation of short or long branches. Most RISC processors contain a set of relative branches, which can branch at an offset from the program counter. This usually includes the conditional branch instructions. If the distance that is being branched is short, then this is very efficient. Unconditional longer branches are implemented by loading the address of the instruction to be branched to and performing the unconditional jump instruction. Long conditional jump operations are implemented by using a short conditional branch instruction on the negation of the condition to

---

2. With RISC architectures, the addresses are rarely included in the instruction. Instead the addresses are included in the constants, which are loaded into registers to perform an absolute branch. This simply replaces the updating of instructions by the updating of constants for relocation.

branch around a long unconditional branch instruction. Thus there are three different sizes for branch instructions:

- A short conditional or unconditional branch instruction. This will typically be one instruction, thus 4 bytes on most RISC processors.

- A long unconditional jump instruction. This will require two instructions, one to load the address constant and one to perform the jump operation. Thus this instruction sequence requires 8 bytes on most RISC processors.

- A long conditional jump instruction will require three instructions: A short conditional branching instruction, the loading of an address constant, and the performance of an unconditional jump instruction. This requires 12 bytes on most RISC processors.

There is a phase-ordering problem with the translation of branching instructions into short instructions or long instructions. Short instructions do not require extra registers; however, long instructions require a register. Thus the compiler wants to translate the branches into long branches before register allocation. However, the number of instructions in the program are not known until after register allocation since the spill instructions change the number of instructions in the flow graph.

I propose the following approach. The compiler generates all branches to positions in the flow graph as short branches. Subroutine calls and unconditional branches outside the procedure are generated as long jump operations. Typically, all branches will be to nearby locations, so there will be no need for translation of short branches to long branches. If long branches are necessary, translate the short branches here in the object module generator. How is this done? The algorithm for identifying short branches that must be translated into long branches is an optimistic one:

1. Assume that all branch instructions are short ones. Scan through the flow graph performing the first pass of the assembler. Whenever a branch instruction is found that must be long, translate it into the appropriate long instruction sequence. If there are no branch instructions translated to long instructions (the common case), then the first pass is completed and the compiler can proceed to the second pass of the assembler.

2. If there are branch instructions translated into long instruction sequences on this scan through the flow graph, repeat pass one of the assembler. The instructions that have already been translated into long instructions are no longer considered—their fate has already been determined.

In the worst case, this is an inefficient algorithm. It can take as many passes through the flow graph as the number of branch instructions. It can never take more passes, using the same kind of arguments we used to prove that optimization algorithms take no more passes than the number of blocks. It is typically an efficient algorithm since usually all of the branches will remain short. This is the algorithm used in the Bliss compiler by Wulf et. al. (1975).

When must a branch instruction be translated into a long jump sequence? The compiler is making a pass through the instructions in a flow graph in sequential order and comes upon a branch instruction. If the instruction branches to an earlier instruction and it is too far away to be implemented as a short branch, then replace the instruction by a long branch. If the branch instruction branches forward and the address specified by the previous pass through the flow graph is too far away, then translate the instruction into a long jump sequence.

This procedure obviously is the correct check for backward branches. For forward branches, the previous pass will have computed an address both for the branch instruction itself and the forward destination to which it is branching. The address of the branch instruction on this pass is greater than or equal to its address on the previous pass. Since the compiler is replacing small instructions by larger ones, the distance between the destination and the location of the branch is increasing. Whenever the distance is greater than that represented by a short branch, change it to a long branch.

Repeat the process until there are no changes. At that point, leave all branches short that have not already been changed.

14.5 Generating the Assembly File and Additions to the Listing File

The assembly file is an optional text file that attempts to create input to the assembler so that the result of assembly will be an object file identical to the original object file.[3] This goal is not always achievable. The compiler may generate object modules that are not directly expressible in the available assembly language. Of course, the assembly language can be extended to

---

3. Let me go on record with all other writers of optimizing compilers: Attempts to edit the assembly file to improve performance are misguided. The results will frequently be less efficient, if it works at all. It is much more likely that an edit will generate an incorrect program because the editor could not follow all of the assumptions made by the compiler. However, advanced users find these files useful, so they should be generated.

support all of these features, but frequently the assembler is a less important piece of software, so its support is limited.

This file can be generated during the second assembler pass, at the same time that the object module is being generated. The compiler has a representation of the flow graph that mimics the instructions to be generated. All that the assembly listing needs to do is translate the internal representation of the instructions into an external representation matching the instruction in the flow graph. Since the internal representation mirrors the external representation, this is a clerical process.

At times, a similar representation of the program is desired in the listing file. This too can be performed at the same time as the assembly file is generated. In fact, columns can be added to indicate the address of the instruction in the segment and the binary representation of the instruction.

14.6 Generating the Error File

The error file records all errors and warnings that have been identified by the compiler. It is one of the most important user interfaces since it communicates to the user about the errors that have occurred within the program being compiled. Most of these error messages are associated with parsing or semantic analysis. The front end is assumed to generate an abstract syntax tree that represents a program with legal static semantics (that is, it obeys all of the language rules having to do with form). The optimizer and code generator should generate few messages.

14.7 References

Wulf, W., et al. 1975. *The design of an optimizing compiler*. New York: American Elsevier.

15 COMPLETION AND FUTURES

We have reached the end of all of the technology. The proof of piecing this technology together will come in building a compiler using it. Together with teams I have worked with, I have used most of these techniques. I myself (with anyone interested in participating) will implement the design. Of course, I invite you to do the same.

How will I build a compiler? I will build it out of technology that is freely available. I have no desire to rebuild something that has a reasonable implementation already. This section will discuss what I plan to build and how I will build it.

15.1 Target Machine

First, for what processor should I build a compiler? The INTEL-based processors have a host of reasonable compilers, and each of the UNIX vendors have built reasonable compilers for their RISC chips. As you probably noted, I have a fondness for the Alpha processor, but there are a number of good compilers for it. I will build a compiler with two targets: a fake RISC processor useful for testing and verification of the compiler, and the ARM or StrongARM processor used in real-time systems.

The fake RISC processor will be used for initial testing. It is based on an idea that I have seen used by both Rice University and Bill Waite at University of Colorado. The idea is to define a RISC processor where each instruction can be described as a C macro. Consider the iADD instruction for integer add operations. It can be defined by the macro

```
#define iADD(S1,S2,T) T=S1+S2
```

where there are global variables defined to represent each of the registers in the register set. All of the characteristics of the machine can be simulated in C. What is the advantage? The compiler can run and generate assembly language for the program. The program can be executed on any reasonable processor. Each instruction in the assembly language can be simulated in this way.

In fact, additional expressions can be added to the definitions to measure the characteristics of the program. For example, a counter can be incremented in the macro simulating a branch operation. Thus we can know how many times all of the branches are executed or, even more specially, how often a particular branch is executed.

The StrongARM processor was chosen as the real machine to compile for because there are inadequate optimizing compilers for that processor. I find no joy in building a compiler that will always be worse than a compiler that already exists, so I am choosing a processor with less support. Thus I have a chance of building a compiler that might be useful.

15.2 Host Machine

What machine should I use to host this project? I prefer a good-size PC with one of the excellent C/C++ program environments: Visual C/C++, Borland C/C++, or Symantec C/C++. These environments make it easy to write small sections of code and check-debug them. The support for UNIX facilities like *make* are less adequate; however, there are some facilities for configuration and project management.

UNIX would be a second choice. In that case, I would use an editor such as GNU EMACS as a programming environment in which to embed all other activity.

15.3 Source Language

I want to write a compiler for a full language, not a toy, and I do not want to write a front end. Thus I will compile for the C language and use one of the freely available C front ends as the starting point. In this case, I will use LCC, created by Frazer and Hanson. This is a well-written and well-documented C front end that can be adapted to generate the intermediate representation that is needed for the optimizing compiler.

Some modifications will need to be made to the front end to increase the information passed to the optimization phases. LCC assumes that it is directly generating assembly language or object modules. Thus information is used and lost. This information must be preserved. In particular, the alias information concerning load and store operations must be preserved for use within the optimizer. Also, arrays should not be directly changed into pointer expressions, but kept as array references instead.

15.4 Using Other Technology

There are other pieces of software I will use in the project. The intermediate representation in this book is based on the intermediate representation used in the Rice Massive Scalar Compiler Project. I will use the code that they have written to manipulate the intermediate representation.

There are other tools for drawing graphs and pretty-printing trees available on the Internet that can be used for generating dumps of data structures. Remember the earlier discussion about each phase of the compiler needing an interpreter. Actually, we only need four interpreters. The first one interprets the abstract syntax tree output by the front end. That can be interpreted by using any of the available LCC compilers. The second is an interpretation of the flow graph when it is in normal form. The third is an interpretation of the flow graph in static single assignment form, and the final one is an interpreter or executor for the object file output.

15.5 The Spike Approach

The team at COMPASS, Inc. developed a useful approach to building big compilers that I will use on this project. It is called the spike approach. First the team develops a medium-level design for the compiler. This book fits the bill for that design. With the medium-level design, one knows all of the data structures that are necessary and all of the big problems that might occur.

Then the team develops a minimum implementation of each phase of the compiler. In other words, the team builds a spike through the compiler where a little of each phase works. Do a sufficient amount so that some application program will work. The obvious first spike is to build enough of the compiler to compile and execute the null program.

Then the team widens the spike, implementing more of each phase. Widen the spike to compile some arithmetic statements. Then widen it further to compile "Hello World." Keep widening the spike until complete functionality is provided in the compiler.

This works when the design is available in advance. What the team is really doing is choosing an order in which to implement algorithms and data structures that are already known to be needed so that the team works together to get results through the compiler. This is gratifying to the team: They see some results early. It is also gratifying to the clients or management because there is visual verification of progress. There is little more distressing than a programmer informing you that all of his module will work, but it won't be available until one month before delivery.

This approach does not work if the design is insufficient or not done. In that case, part of the compiler will be implemented before the team realizes that one or more of the modules is inadequate for the quality of compiler needed. The only solution is to go back and rewrite. Do the design first—don't fall into this trap.

APPENDIX A: PROOF OF THE ANTICIPATION EQUATIONS

The anticipation equations were constructed to match the definition of anticipation. I do not know of a book or article that proves the direct correspondence. In fact, the largest solution to the anticipation equations is the solution that matches the definition. This appendix provides a proof of this correspondence and in the process shows why the largest solution is necessary. Recall that the anticipation equation is being applied for a single temporary T.

OBSERVATION Assume that *ANTIN* and *ANTOUT* is the maximum solution to the anticipation equation. Assume that $B_0, B_1, B_2, \ldots, B_n = B_0$ is a cycle in the flow graph such that the temporary T is not killed or locally anticipated in any of the blocks in the cycle. If there is a block B_i in the cycle such that $ANTIN(B_i)$ is false, then there is a block B_j in the cycle with a successor S such that $ANTIN(S)$ is false.

PROOF Note that $ANTIN(B_i)$ being false means that $ANTIN(B_k)$ is false for each block B_k in the cycle. Why? *ANTOUT* for each block is the intersection of the *ANTIN* information for each of its successors. Walk around the cycle backward starting at block B_i. Combining the information that none of the blocks kills T or makes T locally anticipated with $ANTIN(B_i)$ means that *ANTIN* is false for the predecessor block. Continue the walk; each block in turn will have *ANTIN* being false.

To prove the observation, I will assume the negative and show that there is a contradiction. Assume that each successor S of the blocks in the cycle has $ANTIN(S)$ equal to true. The proof consists of showing that all of the values of *ANTIN* for the blocks in the cycle can be changed to true. This change can then be propagated through the rest of the flow graph, changing some of the other values of *ANTIN* to true but never changing a value that was already true. The larger solution demonstrates a contradiction since the solution was assumed to be the largest.

First note that the values of *ANTIN* (together with the corresponding values of *ANTOUT*) can be changed to true for each block in the cycle without violating the equations for the blocks in the cycle. Each successor already has the value true, so the *ANTOUT* values will satisfy the equation. The *ANTIN* values for the blocks in the cycles are required to be the same as the *ANTOUT* values. Thus they can all be changed to true.

Having made this change, the predecessors of the blocks in the cycle may no longer satisfy the equations. Some of the predecessors that initially had false values for *ANTOUT* now have true values. This can change the value of *ANTIN* for these predecessors from false to true. Note that it can never change the value from true to false, so continue this process of updating the predecessors (and the indirect predecessors) until all blocks again satisfy the equations. Since the values can only change from false to true and there is only a finite number of blocks, this update process must end and provide a new larger solution. This demonstrates the contradiction.

OBSERVATION Consider a flow graph in which there is a path from each block to *Exit*. Let *ANTIN* and *ANTOUT* be the maximum solution to the anticipation equations for the temporary T. If *ANTOUT(B)* is false, then T is not anticipated at the end of B. If *ANTIN(B)* is false, then T is not anticipated at the beginning of B.

PROOF Consider the case in which *ANTOUT(B)* is false. The proof consists of showing that there is a path from B to *Exit* that either contains an instruction that kills T before an evaluation of T or contains no evaluations of T at all.

By assumption, *ANTOUT(B)* is false, so there is some successor B_1 with *ANTIN(B_1)* equal to false. *ANTIN(B_1)* being false means that T is not locally anticipated in B_1. If B_1 kills T, then we are done because the path can be extended with any path from B_1 to *Exit* giving a path violating the definition of anticipation at B.

Now continue to add blocks $B = B_0, B_1, \ldots, B_n$ to the path such that B_i is a predecessor of B_{i+1} and T is not locally anticipated or killed in any of the blocks after B and *ANTOUT(B_i)* is false for each of these blocks. The problem is to add another block to the path in such a way that a path to *Exit* can be constructed. There are three possibilities:

- If B_n has no successors, then B_n is equal to *Exit* since this is the only block with no successors. When this situation occurs, a path from B to *Exit* has been constructed containing no instructions that kill or evaluate T. The path thus violates the definition of anticipation, and T is not anticipated at the end of B.

- B_n has a successor B_{n+1} such that *ANTIN(B_{n+1})* is false and B_{n+1} is not on the path. Since *ANTIN(B_{n+1})* is false, T is not locally anticipated in the block. If T is killed in the block, then the path can be extended from B_{n+1} to *Exit* by any path, giving a path that violates the definition of anticipation.

- B_n has no successor with *ANTIN* equal to false that is not already on the path. A way to continue expanding the path must be found. If I can show that there is always a way to continue the path, then the proof is completed since the two previous possibilities lead to a path violating the definition of anticipation.

Appendix A: Proof of the Anticipation Equations

If B_n has no successors that have *ANTIN* equal to false and are not in the path, choose one of the successors S that is already in the path. We have a cycle starting with S and continuing through the other blocks on the path until B_n is reached. All of the blocks on this cycle satisfy the conditions of the previous observation, so there is a successor Q of one of the blocks B_k that is not in the cycle and has the value *ANTIN*(Q) equal to false.

Now add the blocks $S, \ldots, B_k, Q$ to the path after B_n. Although some blocks have been added to the path multiple times, the path has been extended by at least one new block Q. This shows that the third case always leads to the addition of at least one block and completes the proof of the observation.

APPENDIX B: SUPERBLOCK FORMATION

When the body of a loop is a nest of simple condition statements, it can be reformed to aid instruction scheduling. In this case, the body of the loop performs conditional branching to create multiple paths through the loop which branch back together at the end of the loop body. The merging of these paths makes instruction scheduling more difficult. The inner loop of the running example demonstrates this problem.

The superblock transformation alleviates this problem. It transforms a directed acyclic subgraph of the flow graph containing a single entry block into an extended block which can be easily scheduled.

The transformation is simple. If there is a block B in the directed acyclic subgraph with two predecessors, then make a separate copy of B and the subgraph with entry B for each of the predecessors. Repeat this until no block has multiple predecessors in the block.

When should superblock formation be applied? It should be applied to inner loops containing branches that are frequently executed. There is a useful side effect of superblock formation. A single loop is changed into a nested set of loops. This gives new opportunities for optimization.

BIBLIOGRAPHY

Aho, A. V., and J. D. Ullman. 1977. *Principles of compiler design.* Reading, MA: Addison-Wesley.

Aho, A. V., J. E. Hopcroft, and J. D. Ullman. 1974. *The design and analysis of computer algorithms.* Reading, MA: Addison-Wesley.

Aho, A. V., J. E. Hopcroft, and J. D. Ullman. 1983. *Data structures and algorithms.* Reading, MA: Addison-Wesley.

Aho, A. V., R. Sethi, and J. D. Ullman. 1986. *Compilers: Principles, techniques, and tools.* Reading, MA: Addison-Wesley.

Allen, F. E., J. Cocke, and K. Kennedy. 1981. Reduction of operator strength. In *Program flow analysis: Theory and application,* edited by S. Muchnick and N. D. Jones. New York: Prentice-Hall.

Allen, R., and K. Kennedy. "Advanced compilation for vector and parallel computers." San Mateo, CA: Morgan Kaufmann.

Alpern, B., M. N. Wegman, and F. K. Zadeck. 1988. Detecting equality of variables in programs. *Proceedings of the Conference on Principles of Programming Languages, POPL88,* San Diego, CA. 1-11.

Auslander, M., and M. Hopkins. 1982. An overview of the PL.8 compiler. *Proceedings of the ACN SIGPLAN '82 Conference on Programming Language Design and Implementation,* Boston, MA.

Backus, J. W., et al. 1957. The Fortran automatic coding system. *Proceedings of AFIPS 1957 Western Joint Computing Conference (WJCC),* 188-198.

Bagwell, J. T. Jr. 1970. *Local Optimization, SIGPLAN Notices,* Association for Computing Machinery 5(7): 52-66.

Bala, V., and N. Rubin. 1996. Efficient instruction scheduling using finite state automata. Unpublished memo, available from authors. (Rubin is with Digital Equipment Corp.)

Ball, T., and J. R. Larus. 1992. Optimally profiling and tracing programs. *Proceedings of the Nineteenth Annual ACM SIGPLAN-SIGACT Symposium on Principles of Programming Languages, POPL92,* Albuquerque, NM. 59-70.

Ball, T., and J. R. Larus. 1993. Branch prediction for free. *Proceedings of the SIGPLAN '93 Symposium on Programming Language Design and Implementation, PLDI93,* Albuquerque, NM. Published as *SIGPLAN Notices* 28(7): 300-313.

Barrett, W. A., et al. 1986. *Compiler construction: Theory and practice*. Science Research Associates, Inc.

Bauer, F. L., et al. 1974. Compiler construction: An advanced course. In *Lecture notes in computer science,* vol. 21. Berlin, Germany: Springer-Verlag.

Beaty, S. J. 1991. Instruction scheduling using genetic algorithms. Ph.D. diss., Colorado State University.

Briggs, P., and L. Torczon. 1993. An efficient representation for sparse sets. *ACM Letters on Programming Languages and Systems* 2(1-4): 59-69.

Briggs, P., K. D. Cooper, and L. Torczon. 1992. Coloring register pairs. *ACM Letters on Programming Languages and Systems* 1(1): 3-13.

Briggs, P., K. D. Cooper, and L. Torczon. 1992. Rematerialization. *Proceedings of the Fifth ACM SIGPLAN Conference on Programming Language Design and Implementation,* San Francisco, CA. Published as *SIGPLAN Notices* 27(7): 311-321.

Briggs, P., K. D. Cooper, and L. Torczon. 1994. Improvements to graph coloring register allocation. *ACM Transactions on Programming Languages and Systems* 16(3): 428-455.

Callahan, D., K. D. Cooper, K. Kennedy, and L. Torczon. 1986. Interprocedural constant propagation. *Proceedings of the SIGPLAN Symposium on Compiler Construction,* Palo Alto, CA. Published as *SIGPLAN Notices* 21(7): 152-161.

Chaitin, G. J. 1982. Register allocation and spilling via graph coloring. *Proceedings of the SIGPLAN '82 Symposium on Compiler Construction,* Boston, MA. Published as *SIGPLAN Notices* 17(6): 98-105.

Chaitin, G. J., et al. 1981. Register allocation via coloring. *Computer Languages* 6(1): 47-57.

Chase, D. R., M. Wegman, and F. K. Zadeck. 1990. Analysis of pointers and structures. *Proceedings of the Conference on Programming Language Design and Implementation, PLDI90,* White Plains, NY. 296-310.

Chow, F. 1983. A portable machine independent optimizer—Design and measurements. Ph.D. diss., Stanford University.

Cooper, K. D., M. W. Hall, and L. Torczon. 1992. Unexpected side effects of inline substitution: A case study. *ACM Letters on Programming Languages and Systems* 1(1): 22-32.

Cooper, K., and K. Kennedy. 1988. Interprocedural side-effect analysis in linear time. *Proceedings of the SIGPLAN 88 Symposium on Programming Language Design and Implementation,* Altanta, GA. Published as *SIGPLAN Notices* 23(7).

Cooper, K., and K. Kennedy. 1989. Fast interprocedural alias analysis. *Conference Record of the Sixteenth Annual Symposium on Principles of Programming Languages,* Austin, TX.

Cormen, T. H., C. E. Leiserson, and R. L. Rivest. 1990. *Introduction to Algorithms*. New York: McGraw-Hill.

Coutant, D. S. 1986. Retargetable high-level alias analysis. *Conference Record of the 13th SIGACT/SIGPLAN Symposium on Principles of Programming Languages*, St. Petersburg Beach, FL.

Cytron, R., and J. Ferrante. 1987. An improved control dependence algorithm. (Technical Report RC 13291.) White Plains, NY: International Business Machines, Thomas J. Watson Research Center.

Cytron, R., et al. 1989. An efficient method of computing static single assignment form. *Conference Record of the 16th ACM SIGACT/SIGPLAN Symposium on Programming Languages,* Austin, TX. 25-35.

Cytron, R., J. Ferrante, and V. Sarkar. 1990. Compact representations for control dependence. *Proceedings of the SIGPLAN '90 Symposium on Programming Language Design and Implementation,* White Plains, NY. 241-255. In *SIGPLAN Notices* 25(6).

Cytron, R., J. Ferrante, B. Rosen, M. Wegman, and F. Zadeck. 1991. Efficiently computing static single assignment form and the control dependence graph. *ACM Transactions on Programming Languages and Systems* 13(4): 451-490.

Dhamdhere, D. M., B. Rosen, and F. K. Zadeck. 1992. How to analyze large programs efficiently and informatively. *Proceedings of the SIGPLAN '92 Symposium of Programming Language Design and Implementation.* San Fransisco, CA. Published in *SIGPLAN Notices* 27(7): 212-223.

Drechsler, K.-H., and M. P. Stadel. 1988. A solution to a problem with Morel's and Renvoise's "Global optimization by suppression of partial redundancies." *ACM Transactions on Programming Languages and Systems* 10(4): 635-640.

Drechsler, K.-H., and M. P. Stadel. 1993. A variation of Knoop, Ruthing, and Steffen's lazy code motion. *ACM SIGPLAN Notices* 28(5): 29-38.

Ferrante, J., K. J. Ottenstein, and J. D. Warren. 1987. The program dependence graph and its use in optimization. *ACM Transactions on Programming Languages and Systems* 9(3): 319-349.

Fischer, C. N., and R. J. LeBlanc, Jr. 1988. *Crafting a compiler.* Redwood City, CA: Benjamin/Cummings.

Fischer, C. N., and R. J. LeBlanc, Jr. 1991. *Crafting a compiler with C.* Redwood City, CA: Benjamin/Cummings.

Fisher, J. A. 1981. Trace scheduling: A technique for global microcode compaction. *IEEE Transactions on Computers* C-30(7): 478-490.

Frailey, D. J. 1970. *Expression Optimization Using Unary Complement Operators, SIGPLAN Notices,* Association for Computing Machinery 5(7): 67-85.

Frazer, C. W., and D. R. Hanson. 1995. *A retargetable C compiler: Design and implementation.* Redwood City, CA: Benjamin/Cummings.

Freudenberger, S. M., T. R. Gross, and P. G. Lowney. 1994. Avoidance and suppression of compensation code in a trace scheduling compiler. *ACM Transactions on Programming Languages and Systems* 16(4): 1156-1214.

Golumbic, M. C., and V. Rainish. 1990. Instruction scheduling beyond basic blocks. *IBM Journal of Research and Development* 37(4).

Gross, T. 1983. Code optimization of pipeline constraints. (Stanford Technical Report CS 83-255.) Stanford University.

Hall, M. W. 1991. Managing interprocedural optimization. Ph.D. Thesis, Computer Science Department, Rice University.

Hall, M. W., and K. Kennedy. 1992. Efficient call graph analysis. *ACM Letters on Programming Languages and Systems* 1(3): 227-242.

Hall, M. W., K. Kennedy, and K. S. McKinley. 1991. Interprocedural transformations for parallel code generation. *Proceedings of the 1991 Conference on Supercomputing*, 424-434.

Hendron, L. J., G. R. Gao, E. Altman, and C. Mukerji. 1993. A register allocation framework based on hierarchical cyclic interval graphs. (Technical report.) McGill University.

Hendron, L. J., G. R. Gao, E. Altman, and C. Mukerji. 1993. Register allocation using cyclic interval graphs: A new approach to an old problem. (Technical report.) McGill University.

Howland, M. A., R. A. Mueller, and P. H. Sweany. 1987. Trace scheduling optimization in a retargetable microcode compiler. *Proceedings of the Twentieth Annual Workshop on Microprogramming (MICRO-20)*, 106-114.

Huber, B. L. 1995. Path-selection heuristics for dominator-path scheduling. Master of Science thesis, Michigan Technical University.

Joshi, S. M., and D. M. Dhamdhere. 1982. A composite hoisting-strength reduction transformation for global program optimization, parts I and II. *International Journal of Computer Mathematics* 11: 21-41, 111-126.

Karr, M. 1975. P-graphs. (Report CA-7501-1511.) Wakefield, MA: Massachusetts Computer Associates.

Kerns, D. R., and S. J. Eggers. 1993. Balanced scheduling: Instruction scheduling when memory latency is uncertain. *Proceedings of Conference on Programming Language Design and Implementation (PLDI93)*, Albuquerque, NM. 278-298.

Kildall, G. A. 1973. A unified approach to global program optimization. *Conference Proceedings of Principles of Programming Languages I*, 194-206.

Knoop, J., O. Ruthing, and B. Steffen. 1992. Lazy code motion. *Proceedings of the ACM SIGPLAN Conference on Programming Language Design and Implementation PLDI92*, 224-234.

Knoop, J., O. Ruthing, and B. Steffen. 1993. Lazy strength reduction. *Journal of Programming Languages* 1(1): 71-91.

Knoop, J., O. Ruthing, and B. Steffen. 1994. Optimal code motion: Theory and practice. *ACM Transactions on Programming Languages and Systems*, New York, NY. 16(4): 1117-1155.

Lam, M. S. 1990. Instruction scheduling for superscalar architectures. *Annual Review of Computer Sciences.*

Lengauer, T., and R. E. Tarjan. 1979. A fast algorithm for finding dominators in a flow graph. *Transactions on Programming Languages and Systems* 1(1): 121-141.

Leverett, B. W., et al. 1979. An overview of the Production-Quality Compiler-Compiler project. (Technical Report CMU-CS-79-105.) Pittsburgh, PA: Carnegie Mellon University.

Lewis II, P. M., D. J. Rosenkrantz, and R. E. Stearns. 1978. *Compiler design theory.* Reading, MA: Addison-Wesley.

Lorho, B. 1984. *Methods and tools for compiler construction: An advanced course.* Cambridge University Press.

Markstein, P. Forthcoming. Strength reduction. In unpublished book on optimization, edited by M. N. Wegman et al. Association of Computing Machinery.

Markstein, P., V. Markstein, and F. K. Zadeck. Forthcoming. In unpublished book on optimization, edited by M. N. Wegman et al. Association of Computing Machinery.

McKeeman, W. M. 1974. Symbol table access. In *Compiler construction: An advanced course,* edited by F. L. Bauer et al. Berlin, Germany: Springer-Verlag.

Morel, E., and C. Renvoise. 1979. Global optimization by suppression of partial redundancies. *Communications of the ACM* 22(2): 96-103.

New York University Computer Science Department. 1970-1976. *SETL Newsletters.*

O'Brien, et al. 1985. *XIL and YIL: The Intermediate Language of TOBEY, ACM SIGPLAN Workshop on Intermediate Representations,* San Fransisco, CA. Published as *SIGPLAN Notices,* 30(3): 71-82.

Pittman, T., and J. Peters. 1992. *The art of compiler design: Theory and practice.* New York: Prentice-Hall.

Pugh, W. 1992. The omega test: A fast and practical integer programming algorithm for dependence analysis. *Communications of the ACM* 8: 102-114.

Purdom, P. W., and E. F. Moore. 1972. Immediate predominators in a directed graph. *Communications of the ACM* 8(1): 777-778.

Reif, J. H., and H. R. Lewis. 1978. Symbolic program analysis in almost linear time. *Conference Proceedings of Principles of Programming Languages V, Association of Computing Machinery.*

Rosen, B. K., M. N. Wegman, and F. K. Zadeck. 1988. Global value numbers and redundant computations. *Conference Record of the 15th ACM SIGACT/SIGPLAN Symposium on Principles of Programming Languages, POPL88,* Austin, TX, pp. 12-27.

Ryder, B. G. 1979. Constructing the call graph of a program. *IEEE Transactions on Software Engineering* SE-5(3).

Scarborough, R. G., and H. G. Kolsky. 1980. Improved optimization of Fortran programs. *IBM Journal of Research and Development* 24: 660-676.

Sheridan, P. B. 1959. The arithmetic translation compiler of the IBM Fortran automatic coding system. *Communications of the ACM* 2(3): 9–21.

Simpson, L. T. 1996. Value-driven redundancy elimination. Ph.D. thesis, Computer Science Department, Rice University.

Sites, R. 1978. Instruction ordering for the CRAY-1 computer. (Technical Report 78-CS-023.) University of California at San Diego.

Steensgaard, B. 1996. Points-to analysis by type inference of programs with structures and unions. In *International Conference on Compiler Construction,* number 1060. In *Lecture Notes in Computer Science,* 136–150.

Sweany, P. H., and S. Beaty. 1992. Dominator-path scheduling: A global scheduling method. *Proceedings of the 25th International Symposium on Microarchitecture (MICRO-25),* 260–263.

Tarjan, R. E. 1972. Depth-first search and linear graph algorithms. *SIAM Journal of Computing* 1(2): 146–160.

Tarjan, R. E. 1975. Efficiency of a good but not linear set of union algorithm. *Journal of ACM* 22(2): 215–225.

Torczon, L., 1985. Compilation dependencies in an ambitious optimizing compiler. Ph.D. thesis, Computer Science Department, Rice University, Houston, TX.

Waite, W. M., and G. Goos. 1984. *Compiler construction.* Berlin, Germany: Springer-Verlag.

Warren, H. S. 1990. Instruction scheduling for the IBM RISC System/6000 processor. *IBM Journal of Research and Development* 34(1).

Wegman, M. N., and F. K. Zadeck. 1985. Constant propagation with conditional branches. *Conference Proceedings of Principles of Programming Languages XII,* 291–299.

Wilhelm, R., and D. Maurer. 1995. *Compiler Design.* Reading, MA: Addison-Wesley.

Wilson, R. P., and M. Lam. 1995. Efficient context-sensitive pointer analysis for C programs. *Proceedings of the SIGPLAN '95 Conference on Programming Language Design and Implementation,* La Jolla, CA. Published as *SIGPLAN Notices* 30(6): 1–12.

Wolfe, M. 1996. *High performance compilers for parallel computing.* Reading, MA: Addison-Wesley.

Wulf, W., et al. 1975. *The design of an optimizing compiler.* New York: American Elsevier.

Zadeck, F. K. 1984. Incremental data flow analysis in a structured program editor. *Proceedings of the ACM SIGPLAN '84 Symposium on Compiler Construction,* Montreal, Quebec. Published as *SIGPLAN Notices* 19(6).

INDEX

A

Abnormal edges, 114-115, 167, 234
  critical edges, 178
  definition, 277
  LIMIT phase, 299-300, 302, 304, 313
  partial redundancy elimination, 277-278
  store operations, optimization of, 331
Abstract syntax tree, 18, 21-24, 94, 98. *See also* Tree, walk of
  for A = B + C * (B+A), 100-101
  fetch of local variable in, 105
  translation into flow graph of, 24-29
Addition, 100, 101, 205, 214-215
Address graph, 160-161
Addresses, 20
  absolute, 413, 414
  computation, 159-161
  differentiation, 21, 23
  flow-sensitive information, 162-163
  invariant expressions, 207
  modification of, 162
  relocation, 413
  variables whose addresses are taken, computing set of, 157-158
Addressing arithmetic, and instruction elimination, 139
Aho, A. V., 91
Algebraic identities, 28-29, 31, 94, 189-190
  list of, 137-140, 145
  simplification of, 139, 140
Algebraic simplifications, 190-192, 227, 230
Alias analysis, 34, 139, 147-164
  constant propagation and, 203-204
  dependence analysis, 151
  direct modification, 155-156
  dominator-based optimization, precise modification information for, 159-161
  flow graph, modification information used to build, 157-158
  flow-insensitive analysis, 150
  flow-sensitive information improved by optimization, 162-164
  Fortran EQUIVALENCE statement, use of, 157
  heap allocation operations, tags for, 158-159
  indirect modification, 156
  interprocedural analysis, 151
  level of, 150-151
  local expressions, including effects of, 161-162
  modifies relation, 120, 151-153
  tag table, building, 154-155
Allen, Fran, 3
Allocation instructions, 163
Alpha processors, 47-48, 99, 301, 421
  335-336
  caches, 336
  multiply instruction on, 362
  scheduling, 338, 372, 376
Ancestor nodes, 205-206
Anchor, trace, 346, 348
AND operator, 108-109, 149, 301, 364
ANSI C language, 149, 158-159
Anticipated set, 120
Anticipation
  computing, 122-124, 131-132
  definition, 121
  moving store operations, 284, 286
  operands, 270
  proof of equations, 425-427
  temporaries, 255, 270 (*See also* ANTIN; ANTLOC)
Antidependence, 241, 242, 358
ANTIN, 258, 276, 277, 425-427
ANTLOC, 256, 264, 273-274, 280, 292
ANTOUT, 425-426
Arrays
  analysis of expressions, 20
  flow-sensitive information, 163

435

Arrays (*continued*)
   initialization, 112
   interprocedural analysis, 35
   pointers for indexing, 12-13
   subscripted, 98-99, 242-244
   symbolic references, 20
   tags, 154, 155
Assembly file, generation of, 419-420
Assembly language, 16, 95
Assignment nodes, 21
Assignment statements, 101, 112
Atomic tags, 155
Availability
   computing, 131-132
   definition, 126
   moving store operations, 284, 286
   temporaries, 255
Available set, 120, 375-377
Available-expression table, 189-190, 192
AVLOC, 280, 281
AVOUT, 256-257

B

Back edges, 68, 81
BackwardState attribute, 370-371, 383
Bala, V., 366, 367
Ball, T., 346
Beaty, S., 345
Benchmarks (code samples), 6, 7
Bin packing, 58, 388-389
Binary_Instruct procedure, 107
Bit vectors, 91, 128, 130
Block scheduling, 339-340
   definition, 337
   limited to single block, 55
   multiple blocks, 344 (*See also* Traces)
   operations performed, 339-340
   superscalar processors, 337
Block_End nodes, 358, 360-361, 378
BlockList work list, 199
Blocks, 95-96
   boundaries of, 360-361, 378, 389, 390
   building flow graph with, 103
   control dependence, 77-80
   creating, 103, 111
   deleting empty, 47
   destination pairs replaced with fall-through values, 48
   dominance, 70-74
   elimination, 202
   extended, 339-340, 344-345
   insertion, 102-103
   IR, 16-18
   multiple, 350
   peephole optimization, 302-303
   register pressure in, 317-319, 323-324, 326-329
   reordering and combining, 112
   simulating execution of, 119, 200
   starting, 103
   structure of, 112
   subscripted array reference, 98
Block_Start nodes, 358, 360-361, 378
Boolean equations, 262
Boolean matrix, 66, 363-366
Boolean values, 108, 195
Boolean variables, 122-126
Bottom value, 141
Branches
   between blocks, 16-17
   in extended blocks, 345
   out-of-order execution and, 386-387
   into traces, 344
   useless, 57
Branching instructions, 16, 57, 95, 97-98, 102, 112, 194, 251
   conditional, 200, 202, 417-418
   unconditional, 104, 417-418
Branching operations, 102, 336
Branching statements, 98, 107, 345
BREAK statement, 108, 247
Briggs, Preston, 91, 389, 391, 393

C

C language, 6, 114, 118, 193, 422
   characteristics of, 12-13
   data repetition in, 112
   formal parameters, rules for, 148
   function variables, 234
   in-line expansion, 238
   integer overflow, 143
   modification information, 158-159, 163
   switch statement, 65
   varying value, 197
C++ language, 159, 422
Cache
   Alpha processor, 336
   flushing, 128

Index

referenced values in, 35-36
  usage, 246
Call graphs, 64, 233-234
Called procedures, 238, 239-240
CalleeSave/CallerSave registers, 398
Calling procedures, 239-240, 397-398
Case statement, 65, 106-108, 195, 236, 237
Chain-linked hash table, 190, 307-309
Chaitin, G. J., 4, 310, 313, 314, 391-393, 399
Chow, F., 290
Cloning procedures, 239
Coalescing. *See* Register coalescing
Code generation, 5-6, 13, 24, 47
  for flow graph operation, 139-141, 143
  lowering, 99
  pipeline architecture and, 54
  standard single-pass technique, 18
Code lowering, 16, 98-100, 145
  global optimization phase, 37
  instructions prior to instruction scheduling and register allocation, 47-49
Code motion, 20, 32, 55-56, 187, 188
  out of loops, 193
  techniques for, 42-46
Code samples, 6, 7
COLLAPSE procedure, 356
COMBINE_PRED function, 368
COMMON blocks, 112, 154-157
COMPASS compilers, 3, 104, 115
Compile time, 412
Compiler structure, 12-63
  back end, 5-6, 297
  dependence optimization, 35-37
  dominator optimizations (*See* Dominator optimizations)
  flow graph, building (*See* Flow graphs)
  front end, 18, 21-23, 422-423
  global optimization (*See* Global optimization)
  instruction scheduling (*See* Scheduling)
  interprocedural analysis (*See* Interprocedural analysis)
  limiting resources (*See* Limiting resources)
  object module, forming of, 21, 63
  outline of, 13-21
  register allocation (*See* Register allocation)
  rescheduling, 62-63
Computational instructions, 118
  insertion on impossible edge, 277
  moving, 251, 278

COMPUTE_THROUGH procedures, 321-322
Conditional branching, 10, 59, 198
  destination pairs replaced with fall-through values, 48
  edges, 114
  expressions, 108-109
  instructions, 97, 103-104
  replacement by unconditional branches, 190-192
  simulating, 197-198
  superblock formation, 248
Conditional branching instructions, 200, 202, 417-418
Conditional branching statements, 220-222
Conditional expressions, 102, 109-111, 192-193
Conditional jump instructions, 417-418
Conditional move instructions, 335
Conflict graphs, 298, 389, 391-392
  computing, 306-312, 314
  conflict matrix, 307-309, 394
  construction, 309-312
  definition, 306
  local, 403-404
  nodes removed from, 394
  partial, 310-311
Constant folding, 29, 31, 46, 139, 192, 227, 301. *See also* Constant propagation
Constant propagation, 31, 39, 163, 188, 189, 193-204, 236
  alias analysis information, 203-204
  arithmetic, representing, 194-195
  arithmetic, simulating, 195-197
  conditional branches, simulating, 197-198
  flow graph, simulating, 198-202
  global, 139
  induction variables, identification of, 202
  initialization of, 200-201
  null pointer checks, elimination of, 202-203
  zero-iteration, modification of test for, 193
Constants, 35, 95, 141, 192, 196
  equivalence of, 141
  loading into temporaries, 137
  for load/store operations, 100
  multiple loads of, 193 (*See also* Constant propagation)
  multiplication by, 99, 290-293
  offsets, 155
  operands, 16, 107
  subscripts, 155

Control dependence, 77-80, 220, 221
Control flow, 98, 100, 234, 390-391
Converging paths, 167-170
Cooper, Keith, 4, 232, 238, 395
Copy operations, 374
    on abnormal edges, 299-300, 304
    elimination, 279-280
    for expression temporaries, 116-117
    flow graph computations, 121
    formal temporary table, 152
    global optimization, 252-269
    inserting, 238
    killing, 288-289
    limiting resources and, 296
    loop invariance, 205
    modification, 162
    moving, 250-251, 288-289
    moving store operations and, 284, 285
    peephole optimization, 304-306
    replacing by equivalent, 176-186
    tags for, 153
    temporaries as destinations of, 116
Copy propagation, 29
Critical edges, 113-114, 178
Critical instructions, 361, 370
Critical path information, 344
Cross compiler, 138
Cross edges, 69
Cytron, R., 168

D

Data structures, 64, 94, 112. *See also* Conflict graphs; Flow graphs; Formal temporary table; Interference graphs; UNION/FIND
    of branches taken, 188
    C language pointers, 163
    call graphs, 64, 233-234
    creation of, 413
    dependence graph, 242
    DEPENDS, 162
    dumps of, 423
    elimination of unneeded instructions, 140-141
    local information, computation of, 120
    pointers and, 203
    store operations, 284
    tags, 154, 203-204
    for value-numbering, 141-142

Dead-code elimination, 20, 44, 137, 141, 173, 188, 197, 214, 219-222, 237, 291, 299
Debugging, 415, 417
Definition command, 414-415
Definition(T) attribute, 176, 215, 227
DEFS set, 352-355
DELETE. *See* INSERT/DELETE transformation
Deletion
    computations from flow graph, 121
    linked lists, 91
DEPEND, 187
Dependence analysis, 148, 151, 240-244
Dependence graph, 55, 56, 242
Dependence optimization, 20, 29, 35-37, 82
Dependence-based transformations, 187-188, 244-246
DEPENDS data structure, 162
Depth-first search, 67-70
    dominator tree, 71-74, 339
    infinite loops, identification of, 82-83
    lifetime analysis of temporaries, 135
    loops, computing, 88
    multiple-entry loop identification, 83-85
    points-to set computation, 161
    single-entry loop, 81
    translating SSA to normal form, 183-184
Dhamdhere, D. M., 288, 290
Direct modification, 155-156
Directed edges, 16-17
Directed graphs, 64, 65-67, 98. *See also* specific types of graphs
Dominance frontier, 75-77, 168-172
Domination
    multiple-entry loops and, 84, 85
    temporaries, evaluations of, 128
Dominator optimizations, 18-19, 29-34, 187-231
    constant propagation (*See* Constant propagation)
    dead-code elimination, 219-222
    expression reshaping, 39
    flow-sensitive information, 163
    global optimization and, 37, 39
    global value numbering, 222-230
    induction variables, computing, 208-212
    local transformations used in, 137
    loop-invariant temporaries, computing, 204-208
    renaming temporaries, 189-192, 218-219

reshaping expressions, 212-216
storing information with optimizations, 192-193
strength reduction, 39, 216-218
Dominator relation, 70-74
Dominator tree
   peephole optimization, 302, 303
   reassociation, 214-215
   redundant expression elimination, 189, 190
   scheduling, 372-373
   scheduling and, 339, 345
Double-precision numbers, 279
   addition operation, 107
   constants, 195
   instructions for manipulation of, 95
   strength reduction and, 291
   tag size, 155
Dreschsler, K. H., 255
Dynamic programming, 10
Dynamic semantics, 101, 106-107
Dynamic storage, 13

E

EARLIEST transformation, 255-261, 263-269, 321, 330-331
   abnormal edges, 277
   LATER computed from, 273
   LATERIN computed from, 273-275
   operands evaluated prior to related instructions, 271-273
   pseudo-code for, 273
Edges, 96, 103, 234. *See also* Abnormal edges
   attributes describing, 112
   as Boolean matrix bits, 66
   classification in flow graph, 114-115
   conflict graph, 307-309
   control dependence and, 79
   depth-first walk algorithm, 67-70
   directed, 16-17
   directed graphs, 65-66
   dominance frontier, 76
   eliminating, 202
   executable attribute, 199-200
   impossible, 115, 277, 313
   infinite loops, elimination of, 83
   insertion of T evaluations on, 255, 276
   in interference graph, 358-361
   tail,head, dependence of, 358-360
   undirected graphs, 66-67

Elimination. *see* Redundant expressions, elimination of
Entry block, 80, 86, 96, 113
Entry node, 17-18, 65, 67
   dominator computation, 73-74
   moving copies toward, 288, 289
   moving STORE instructions toward, 281-284
Epilogue instruction
   flow graph, 96-97
   loop, 385-386
Equivalence relations, 64
EQUIVALENCE statement, Fortran, 148, 157
Error file, generation of, 420
EVAL operation, 354-356
Excess_Pressure set, 323-324, 326
Executable attribute, 199-200
Exit block, 80, 96, 113
   anticipation, computation of, 131-132
   infinite loops and, 82-83, 115
   loops and, 86
Exit node, 17-18, 65
   moving copies toward, 288
   moving STORE instructions toward, 281-282, 284-288
   postdominators, 74
Exit operations, 234
Expression temporaries, 105, 110, 116-117
   instructions killing, 117, 120
   instructions modifying, 117-118, 120
   modification of, 147
   renaming, 219
Expression tree, 95, 115-117, 120, 147
   instructions in, 249-251, 278
   reshaping expressions in, 215-216
Expressions, 21, 94
   addition and subtraction of, 160
   branching operations, to determine, 102
   conditional, 109-111
   conditional branching, 108-109
   conditional expression as operand of, 110
   elimination of redundant, 249 (*See also* Partial redundancy elimination (PRE))
   generated by compiler, 145
   global optimization, 252
   independent optimization of, 117
   moving out of loops, 251
   operands of, 101-102, 270-273
   reshaping, 37, 39, 187, 212-216
   simplification, 189

Expressions (*continued*)
  tree-walking procedure for, 106–107
  used as statement, 102
Extended blocks, 339–340, 344–345

F

FARTHEST transformation, 286
FAT algorithm, 389, 404–410
Fetch, 2
  computation, 100
  of local variable in abstract syntax tree, 105
  node, 21, 23
  subscripted variables, 24
FIND. *See* UNION/FIND
Fischer, C. N., 64
Fisher, J. A., 344
Floating point, 335–336
  addition functional unit, 364–366
  addition operation, 107
  algebraic simplification, 138
  computation, 9–10
  divide instructions, 57, 335, 362
  manipulation instructions, 95
  multiplication functional unit, 364–366
  operations, 55, 56, 240
  registers, 51, 60, 316
  rounding mode, 138
  temporaries, 209
Flow graphs, 17, 94–136, 162. *See also* Static single assignment (SSA) form
  accumulation for each procedure, 34
  building, 18, 24–29, 100–111, 137–144, 157–158 (*See also* Intermediate representation (IR))
  critical edges, 113–114
  as directed graphs, 64, 65
  edges, classification of, 114–115
  global anticipated information, 121–124
  global available temporary information, 126–132
  global optimization of, 29
  global partial redundancy information, 124–126
  higher level operations classes in, 24–25
  instruction structure, 113, 251
  lifetime analysis, 132–136
  local optimization information, 117–120
  lowering of, 20, 98–100
  modifies relation, representation of, 151–152
  procedure storage method, 94–98
  simplifications, 25, 28–29
  simulation, 198–202
  structure, 112–115
  support procedures to manipulate, 102–105
  temporaries, classification of, 115–117
Flow Value context, 102
Flow-insensitive analysis, 150
Flow-sensitive information, 162–164
Flow_walk procedure, 108–109
Formal temporary table, 25, 104–105, 107, 142, 152, 219
Fortran, 6, 36, 65, 98, 114, 118
  characteristics of, 13
  COMMON blocks, 112, 154–157
  EQUIVALENCE statement, 148, 157
  function arguments, 234
  in-line expansion, 238–239
  modification information, 148, 149, 151, 156–157
  subroutine, 12–13
Fortran/Level H compilers, 3, 5
Forward edges, 69
ForwardState attribute, 370–371, 383
FreeRegisters set, 406
Freudenberger, S. M., 344
Front end, compiler, 18, 21–23, 422–423
Function calls, 98, 220, 234, 236
  lowering, 99
Function units, for instructions, 361–366, 378

G

Generators attribute, 84–86, 88
Global anticipated information, 121–124
Global available temporary information, 126–132
Global constant propagation, 138, 188
Global information
  definition, 117
  live temporaries, 133
  partial redundancy, 124–126
Global optimization, 20, 29, 37–46, 249–295. *See also* Dominator optimizations
  abnormal edges, processing, 276–278
  components, 187–189
  copy instructions, moving, 288–289
  expression and its operands, relation between, 270–273

Index

impossible edges, processing, 276-277
infinite loops and, 82
lazy code motion, temporaries, 273-276
list of, 20
load instructions, moving, 278-281
lowering, 37
main structure, 252-253
redundant expression elimination, 38, 39
reshaping, 37, 39
store instructions, moving, 281-288
strength reduction, 38-42, 290-295
theory and algorithms, 253-269
Global register allocation, 60, 311, 390-400
    assigning registers to temporaries on stack, 395-397
    building stack of temporaries to color, 394-395, 407
    heuristic, description of, 391-392
    overall algorithm, 394
    physical register, choice of, 397-398
    spilling, implementation of, 399-400
    when heuristic does not work, 392-394
Global scheduling, 339
Global temporaries, 174
    register allocation, 297-298, 389-390, 406-407
    in SpillRegisters, 400-401
Global value numbering, 222-230
Global variables, modification of, 235
Goto statements, 111
Graph coloring, 58-60, 388-389, 391-392, 406, 407
Gross, T., 4, 344

H

Hall, M. W., 232, 234, 245
Hardware bypasses, 57
Hardware simulation, 363-372
Heap tags, 154, 155, 158-159
Hendron, Laurie, 4, 389
High_Pressure set, 323-324, 326
Host machine, 422
Huber, B. L., 345

I

IDEFS set, 339, 361, 372-373
    computing, 351-356
    definition, 350

IDOM set, 71, 73, 350-352, 361
If statement, 103, 345
Immediate dominator, 71, 72
Impossible edges, 115, 276-277, 277, 313
Indirect modification, 156
Induction candidates, 208
Induction sets, 210-212
Induction temporaries, 208-212, 217-218, 252
Induction variables, 202, 208-213, 291
Infinite loops, 65, 82-83, 115
Initiation interval, 379, 381-386
Inlining procedures, 236-239
Input dependence, 241, 359
Input operands, set of, 95
Input/output (I/O), 2, 114, 220
INSERT/DELETE transformations, 266-269, 272
    abnormal edges, 277
    computation of, 273
    moving load operations, 278
    store operation, 286-287
Instruction dependence graph. *See* Dependence graph
Instruction interference graph. *See* Interference graph
Instruction sequence, 94-95, 112
Instructions
    adding to flow graph, 103
    algebraic identities applied to, 140
    algebraic transformation to decrease, 137-138
    blocks as lists of, 112
    components, 16, 95
    constants, operands as, 194
    critical, 370, 3612
    dead, 188
    elimination of, 137, 139-141, 208
    equivalence of, 139-141
    evaluating, 201, 284-286
    fetching, 2
    folding constants into (*See* Constant folding)
    insertion, 102, 107
    issued, 334-335
    killing copy operations, 288-289
    killing store operations, 282-283, 284-285
    killing temporaries, 117-120
    latency, 337
    moving, 55-56, 249, 345
    operands of, 299, 302

Instructions (*continued*)
  out-of-order execution, 335
  peephole optimizations, 46
  priority of, 361-363
  representing procedures as, 94
  scheduling (*See* Scheduling)
  simple, 24
  simulating, 199-200
  structure of, 113
  value numbering, 137, 140
Integer add operations, 107, 421-422
Integer arithmetic, algebraic simplifications of, 139
Integer constants, 195
Integer instructions, 56, 95, 240
Integer multiply instructions, 57, 304, 362
Integer operations, 55
  copy operation, peephole optimization, 304-306
  distributive and associative laws applied to, 187, 189, 213-216
Integer overflow, 143
Integer registers, 51, 60, 316
Integer temporaries, 96
Integer units, 335-336, 364-366
Integers
  array of, 141
  implementing sets of, 90-92
  tag size, 155
Interference graphs, 343, 356-362, 374, 378. *See also* Conflict graphs
Intermediate representation (IR), 13-18, 98, 142
Interprocedural analysis, 4, 19, 29, 34-35, 113, 151, 201, 232-235
Invariant-code identification, 207
Irreducible loops, 81, 83-86, 88-89
IUSE set, 339, 351-356, 361, 372

J
Join sets, 168-170
Jump-table instructions, 198

K
Kennedy, K., 4, 37, 232, 234, 240, 245
Killdall, G. A., 5
Kind field, 154, 195
Knoop, J., 255, 290

L
Labels
  goto statements, 111, 112
  program, 16
Language semantics, rules of, 101, 280-281
Language standards, 5-6, 101
Larus, J. R., 346
LATER transformation, 273-275
LATERIN, 262-269, 273-276, 292
LATEST transformation, 261-269, 273
Lazy code motion, 251, 255
  implementation for temporaries, 273-276
  moving copy operations, 289
  moving store operation, 283-284, 286
  strength reduction and, 290-295
LeBlanc, R. J., Jr., 64
Lewis, H. R., 350
Lifetime analysis. *See* Live/dead analysis
Limiting resources, 20, 46-54, 59, 219, 296-300, 296-333
  combined register renaming and register coalescing, 296, 298, 299-300, 312-316
  conflict graph, computing of, 298, 306-312
  peephole optimization, 296, 298-306
  register pressure, computing of, 316-319
  register pressure, reducing, 297, 298, 319-322
  scheduling and, 340, 341
  spilling, 322-332, 394
Linked lists, 66, 91, 112, 176, 307
Linker, commands to, 413, 414
Live temporaries, 132-136, 174, 321-323, 326-328. *See also* Register pressure
  across block boundaries, 389
  in blocks, allocation of, 400
  classification of, 401-403
  in conflict graph, 309-311
  definition, 133
Live/dead analysis, 132-136, 309-311, 318-319, 327
Load constant instructions, 139, 140, 160, 194, 202
LOAD instructions, 56-57, 279, 329-330, 335
  edges, dependencies of, 359-360
  equivalence of, 141
  instructions for, 100
  IR, 15
  killed, 250, 332

Index   443

loop invariance, 205
modifies relation and, 150-151
out-of-order execution and, 386-387
representation in expression tree, 147
tags, 207
Load integer constant (iLDC), 96
Load integer value from static memory (iSLD), 96
Load operations, 10, 21, 55
  address computation, 160
  Alpha processors, 99, 336
  array, 99
  avoiding, 245
  Compute Priority subroutine, 399-400
  constants, 137
  formal temporary table, 152
  global optimization, 253
  killed by store operations, 278, 280
  modification, 148-150, 162
  moving, 42, 187, 249-250, 252, 278-281, 284, 320, 321, 329, 331-332, 341
  normal, information on, 24
  optimizing placement of spilled LOADs, 331-332
  optimizing time to perform, 20
  peephole optimizations and, 301
  register allocator, insertion by, 298, 299
  register pressure reduction and, 319-321, 323-332
  scheduling, 338
  spilling and, 53-54, 59, 63, 370, 392-393, 401
  tags for, 153-154
  temporaries as destinations of, 116
  values of variables, 96
Load time, 412
Local expressions, 161-162
Local information, 117-120, 133
Local optimizations, 137-146
Local register, redefinition of, 60
Local register allocation, 399, 411
Local register register allocation, 59, 61
Local temporaries, allocation of, 105, 120, 389-390
Local variables, 105, 116
Logical AND/OR/NOT operators, 108-109, 149, 196, 301, 364, 366, 367
Longjmp operations, 114, 234, 277
Loop distribution, 246

Loop tree, 86-90, 317-318
Loop unrolling, 55, 246-248, 338, 341-343, 378, 384
Loop-invariant temporaries, 204-208
Loops, 80-90
  blocks in, algorithm for computing, 81
  computing, 88-90
  definition, 80
  disjoint, 82, 86
  generators attribute, 84-86, 88
  infinite, 82-83
  instructions, order of generation of, 101
  moving code out of, 7, 126
  moving inside procedure, 239-240
  multiple-entry, 81, 86, 88-89
  nested (See Nested loops)
  reducing pressure in, 323-324
  restructuring, 187
  scheduling, 341-344
  single-entry, 80-81, 83, 86, 88-89
Lortho, B., 64
Lowering. See Code lowering
Lowney, P. G., 344, 345

M

Machine state, 363-370, 378
Massive Scalar Compiler Project, 4, 96, 162, 277, 423
McKeeman, W. M., 190
McKinley, K. S., 245
Memory
  improving pattern of references to, 35-37
  reducing references to, 35
Memory allocation operations, 163-164
Memory loads, 115-116
Memory location (MEMORY(T)), 329-330, 393
  modification, 147
  register pressure reduction and, 319-320
  tags for, 153
MOD (modified variables), 34
Modification, temporaries, 120, 148-156, 161-162, 278. See also Alias analysis
Morel, Etienne, 5, 42, 255
MOTION, 187
Multiple entry points, for procedures, 65
Multiple-entry loops, 81, 83-86, 88-89
Multiple-instruction sequence, 99

Multiplication, 55, 57, 196, 214-215, 335
   loop invariance, 205
   modifying to repeated additions, 187, 189, 208
   strength reduction, 213

N
NaN (Not a Number), 138
Nested loops, 81-82, 89, 95
   constant propagation algorithm, 202
   dominator-based optimization, 192-193
   multiple-entry, 85-86
   unroll and jam transformation, 35
   varying, computation of, 206-207
Nodes
   abstract syntax tree, 21
   depth-first search, 70
   directed graphs, 65-66
   dominator computation, 73-74
   integers assigned to, 66
   predecessor, 66
   successor, 66
   that return a value, 106-107
   undirected graphs, 66-67
Normal edges, 114, 277
NoValue context, 102
NoValue_Walk procedure, 107-108
Null pointer checks, 193, 202-203

O
Object module, 21, 63, 412-420
Offset tag field, 155
Operands, 16, 101
   address expressions and, 20
   of branching instructions, 98
   computing, 64
   conditional expressions, 109
   constants, 95
   definitions of, 299
   evaluation, effect on expression of, 117
   evaluation prior to related instructions, 270-273, 302
   expression, 101-102, 270-273
   expression, relationship with, 270-273
   induction candidates, 208
   of instruction, 140
   of language construct, 101
   moving, 115-116, 117
   NaN (Not a Number), 139
   renaming, 180
   tags treated as, 153
   temporaries, 25, 95
   undefined value, 168
   use of, 57, 143
   variant, value for, 207
Operands(I), 113
Operation codes (opcodes), 16-17, 95, 96, 105, 249, 372-373
Optimizing compilers
   definition, 1-2
   history of, 2-4
   recent developments, 4-5
OR operator, 108-109, 364, 366, 367
OUT set, 350, 356
Out-of-order execution, 335
Output dependence, 241, 358-359, 2242
Output operands, set of, 95

P
Packets, 54-55, 57, 112, 334-335, 372
Partial anticipation
   definition, 124
   solving for, 128-130
Partial availability
   definition, 126
   solving for, 128, 130-131
Partial ordering relations on sets, 64
Partial redundancies
   global information, 124-126
   store motion and, 44
Partial redundancy elimination (PRE), 42, 117, 188, 189, 219, 251, 252, 254-255, 277-278, 282-286
   strength reduction by, 290-295
Partition, temporaries, 178-180, 218, 223, 311-316
Partition sets, 64
Pascal language, 65, 234
Pattern matching, encoding of, 144-145
Peephole optimization, 31, 46, 56, 189, 227
   copy operations, 304-306
   LIMIT phase, 296, 298-306, 312
   local transformations used in, 137
   rescheduling due to, 62
   scheduling and, 340, 341
Phases, 13, 18-21. *See also* specific phases
   abnormal edges, 299-300, 302
   arithmetic of, 197

Index

constants, operands as, 194
definition, 165
determining value of, 199-201
eliminating, 173-174, 179, 192
eliminating copies from, 312-315
evaluation of, 167
global value numbering, 224-230
induction candidates, 208-212
insertion points, 167-168, 171, 172-174
loop invariance, 205
modification, 202
peephole optimization, 302-305
replacing by equivalent copy operations, 176-186
temporaries used in, 174-175
Physical registers, 60
available, 296, 297, 319, 340-341
choosing, in register allocation, 397-398
multiple temporaries packed in single, 222-223
temporaries replaced with, 58-61
Pipeline architecture, defined, 54
Pipelined processors, 334, 335
Pointers, 6, 12-13, 24, 101, 118
alias analysis, 20, 24, 203
heap allocation operation, handling from, 163-164
modification information, 163
modifies relation, effect on, 149
Points-to set (PT(x)), 159-161, 162
definition, 159
Postdominance, 74-75
control dependence and, 77, 78
definition, 74
Postdominator block, branches redirected to, 222
PQCC project, 4
Predecessor (PRED) attributes of blocks, 113-114
Predecessors, 66
availability, equations for, 127
dominators, 71
multiple-entry loops and, 84
partial anticipatability, computation of, 128-129
PredLeft attribute, 374-376
Pressure attribute, 326
Priority attributes, 362-363, 376-377, 400

Procedure calls, 19, 34, 107-108, 141, 201, 220, 233, 234-235, 251
interprocedural analysis, 151
LOAD instructions killed by, 250
lowering, 99
modification of tag or temporary, 160
tags as Attributes of, 154
Procedures. *See also* Interprocedural analysis
components of, 94
storage of, 94-98
Profitability (temporary insertion), 254, 258-260, 265-268
Program flow graph, 70
Program labels, 16
Prologue pseudo-instruction, 96-97

R

Range checks, simplification of, 193
Ready set, 375-376
Reassociation, 214, 219
Reduced instruction set computer (RISC) systems, 2, 4, 47, 95, 240, 421
branches in, 417
condition codes, 359
dependence optimization, purpose of, 35-37
high-performance compilers for, 4
instruction initiation, 54-55
multiple instruction-issue character of, 55
out-of-order execution, 386
pipeline architecture, 54
processing by, 334-335
Reducible loops. *See* Single-entry loops
Redundant branches, 16
Redundant computations, 7, 18, 32
Redundant expressions. *See also* Partial redundancy elimination (PRE)
elimination of, 29, 38, 39, 96, 187-188, 214
increasing number of, 42
scheduling, resulting from, 373
Redundant temporary evaluations, 128
REF (referenced variables), 34
Register allocation, 4, 13, 20-21, 46-47, 58-62, 279, 298, 370, 388-411
bin packing, 388-389
constraints, 388
direct graph implementation, 66
FAT algorithm, 389, 404-410

Register allocation (*continued*)
　global (*See* Global register allocation)
　graph coloring, 388-389, 391-392, 396, 406, 407
　interference relationship, 64
　lifetime analysis of temporaries, 135
　LIMIT phase preparation for, 48-54
　local, 399, 411
　loop nests used during, 82
　optimal allocation, 390
　scheduling and, 46, 338, 340-341, 370, 375
　single-pass, 389, 408-409
Register coalescing, 48, 296, 298, 299-300, 312-316
　conflict graph and, 311-312
　implied, 316
　local form of, 301, 316
　scheduling and, 375
Register copy operations, and value numbers, 142
REGISTER phase, 297-298
Register pressure, 323
　in block, 317-319
　computing, 50-51, 316-319
　definition, 49-50, 317
　maximum, 317, 401
　multiple register sets, 316, 319
　reducing, 297, 298, 319-322, 323-324
　scheduling and, 341, 376, 377
　transformation, 49-54
　updating, 326
Register renaming, 296, 298, 299-300, 311-316
Register set, 51
Register spilling. *See* Spilling
Register stack, temporaries on, 392-397, 399
Registers
　input to instructions, 16
　for load/store operations, 100
　modification of, 113
　physical, 20
　reduction of number needed, 20, 296, 298
　target, 16, 110
　temporary, 397
　using as few as possible, 388
Register-to-register copy operations, 278
　address computation, 160
　removing, 47, 48
Reif, J. H., 3, 350

Relational tests, 188
Relocation, addresses, 413
Renaming. *See also* Register renaming
　adding optimizations to process, 189-192
　algorithm, 174
　operands, 180
　temporaries, 48, 174-176, 179-180, 218-219, 237-238, 384, 401
Repeat nodes, 112
Rescheduling, 62-63, 298, 340, 341
RESHAPE, 187, 213
Resource information, precomputing of, 350-356
　definition and use information, 350-351
Rosen, B., 288
Rubin, N., 366, 367
Run time, 412-413
　computation, 161-162
　stack, tags for, 154, 155
Ruthing, O., 255, 290
Ryder, B. G., 234

S

Safety (temporary insertion), 254-255, 258-260, 265-268
Scalar optimization, 4
Scalar replacement, 35, 245-246
Scalar variables, 158
Schedule_Importance procedure, 376-378
Schedule_Packet procedure, 375
SchedulePackets, 373-374
Scheduling, 4, 20, 46-47, 54-58, 62-63, 297, 334-387. *See also* Packets; Traces
　algorithm, 372-378
　example, 341-344
　hardware simulation, 363-372
　interference graph, 356-361
　LIMIT phase preparation for, 48-54
　multiple blocks, 344 (*See also* Traces)
　in nonsequential order, 370
　out-of-order execution, 386-387
　priority of instructions, computing, 361-363
　register allocation, effect on, 338, 340-341
　register allocation and (*See* Register allocation)
　resource information, precomputing of, 350-356
　sequence of phases involving, 340-341
　simultaneous initiation of instructions, 54-55

in single block, 55
software pipelining (*See* Software pipelining)
structure of instruction-scheduling phase, 339-340
  superblock formation, 248
  techniques, 55-56
  types of schedulers, 337
Schwartz, Jack, 3
Scratch registers, 60
Scratch_table, 226, 230
Semi-dominator, 72
Sethi-Ullman register numbering, 94
Setjmp/longjmp operations, 114
SETL newsletters, 3
Shift operations, 335-336
Shortjmp operations, 277
Simple procedure-level optimization, 239-240
Simpson, L. Taylor, 224
Single-entry loops, 80-81, 83, 86, 88-89
Sites, Richard, 4
Size context, 102
Size tag field, 155
Small-constant immediate operands, 47
Software pipelining, 37, 56, 240, 334, 335, 339, 365, 378-386
  definition, 337
  dependence test, 243
  dependence-based transformations, 244
  epilogue, formation of, 385-386
  execution of program, effect on, 336-337
  initiation interval, estimating, 381-382
  limiting conditions, 381-382
  loop scheduling, 341-344
  loop unrolling and, 247, 384
  nonsequential scheduling, 370
  prologue, formation of, 384-385
  renaming temporaries, 384
  reverse scanning of instruction schedule, 368-370
  single iteration, schedule for, 382-383
Source language, 422-423
  modifies relation, effect on, 149, 151, 158-159
  semantics, 151
  trace, effect on, 348
Source languages, 6, 7
  characteristics of, 12-13
  front ends for, 18, 422-423

Source program, 13
  execution of, 18
  representation, 14-18
  representation of, 5-6
  storage methods, 15
  translation into abstract syntax tree, 18, 21
Spike approach, 423-424
Spill code, 47, 62-63
Spill instructions, optimizing placement of, 329-332
Spill points, 393
  choosing temporary to spill, 324
  computing, 322-329
Spilling, 50, 51-54, 59, 63, 320, 392, 394, 396, 399-400, 401, 410-411
  avoiding in register allocation, 388
  instructions, 370
  pipelining and, 384
SpillRegisters, 393, 396, 399, 400-401
Stack, 190, 394-395, 407-408
  moving store operations, 285-286
  register stack, temporaries on, 392-397, 399
  tags, 154, 155
  translating SSA to normal form, 182-183, 185-186
  uninitialized variable or data structure on, 280-281
Stadel, M. P., 255
Stalls, processor, 334, 337-338
Start_block procedure, 103, 111, 190
StartTime(T) attribute, 405-406
State, machine, 363-370, 378
Static single assignment (SSA) form, 3, 5, 95, 165-186. *See also* Dead-code elimination
  creating, 167-174
  definition, 165
  global value numbering, 222-230
  LIMIT phase, 298-300, 312-313
  modification, 163
  modifies relation, representation of, 151, 152-153
  redundant computations elimination, 32
  redundant expression elimination, 189
  register renaming/coalescing, 312-313
  renaming temporaries, 174-176
  translating to normal form, 176-186
  VALUE transformations, 187-189
Steensgaard, B., 161
Steffen, B., 255, 290

Storage
  data, 112
  flow graph, 139
  procedures, 94-98
  reference, modification of, 161-162
  subscripted variables, 24
STORE instructions, 56-57, 329, 331
  edges, dependencies of, 359-360
  LOAD instructions killed by, 250
  modifies relation and, 150-151
  moving, 251, 278, 281-288, 320-321, 329
  multiple outputs of, 207
  spilling and, 370, 401
Store operations, 10, 21, 55, 278
  address computation, 160
  array, 99
  avoiding, 245
  Compute Priority subroutine, 399-400
  formal temporary table, 152
  global information, 286-287
  global optimization, 252-253
  instructions for, 100, 279
  killing, 282-283, 284
  load operations killed by, 278, 280
  load optimization and, 280
  loop invariance, 205
  modification, 148-150, 155-156, 158, 162-164
  moving, 42-46, 187, 280, 341
  normal, information on, 24
  optimizing, for spills, 330-331
  optimizing time to perform, 20
  peephole optimizations and, 301
  register allocator, insertion by, 298, 299
  register pressure reduction and, 319-321, 323-326, 328-332
  spilling and, 53-54, 59, 63, 392-393
  tags, 153-154, 207
  temporaries as destinations of, 116
  value numbers and, 142
STORE_ANTIN, 330
STORE_ANTLOC, 284, 286, 330
STORE_ANTOUT, 330
STORE_AVIN, 330
STORE_AVLOC, 284, 286, 330
STORE_AVOUT, 330
STORE_EARLIEST, 331
STORE_IN(T), 329, 330
Store_modifies(T) attribute, 147

STORE_OUT(T), 329, 330
STORE_TRANSP, 284, 286, 330
Strength reduction (SR), 6, 20, 32, 187, 188-189, 211, 216-218, 219, 249, 252
  in code motion, 42
  global optimization phase, 38-42
  integer multiplication, 213
  loop nests used during, 82
  by partial redundancy elimination, 290-295
StrongARM processor, 421-422
Strongly connected regions, 180-186, 211-212, 224-230
Structure tags, 155, 156
Structured statements, processing, 107-108
Subroutine calls, 24-25, 114, 145
Subroutines, 6
  expanding at subroutine call point, 145
  to test IR, 15
Subscripted array reference, 98-99, 242-244
Subscripted constants, 155
Subscripted variables, 24
Successor (SUCC) attributes of blocks, 113-114
Successors, 66, 70, 115
  anticipation, equations for, 122, 125
  control dependence and, 77, 78
  partial availability, computation of, 130
  postdominators, 74
  trace, 346, 349-350, 376
Superblock, 55, 60, 341
  formation, 248, 428
  traces, 349
Supercomputers, 4
Superscalar processors, 335, 337
Sweaney, P. H., 345
Switch statement, 65, 114, 195, 236, 237
Switches, and control dependence, 77-78
Symbol node, 21, 101
Symbol table, 18, 101, 190

T

Tags, 153-162, 203-204, 207, 359
Target machine, 100, 421-422
  instructions, 46, 47, 98
Target register, 16, 110
Target(I), 113
Targets, tags treated as, 153
Tarjan, R. J., 72, 179

Index

Temporaries, 24, 55, 95, 116. *See also* Expression temporaries; Formal temporary table; Live temporaries; Partition, temporaries; Variable temporaries
  anticipation of, 121-124
  assigning to registers, 20-21, 51, 297-298, 316, 391
  available, 126-132
  classifying, 115-117, 401-403
  conditional expressions, 109-111
  constants, 137, 194
  constant_temporary(temporary) data structure, 141
  conventions for use of, 104-105
  defining instruction(temporary) data structure, 142
  definitions of, 174-176, 194, 339
  evaluation of, 132, 137, 165, 174, 208, 249-269, 298
  expression operand, value of, 101-102
  induction, 208-212
  instructions modifying, 113
  killing, 117-120, 135
  local variables, 105, 116
  loop-invariant, 204-208
  modifies(T) set, 120, 147
  mutually dependent, 180-186
  nonconstant values, 194
  NumNeighbors attribute, 309
  partial anticipation, 124-126
  queried during evaluation of instruction, 113
  redundant evaluations, 128
  renaming (*See* Renaming)
  replacing with physical registers, 58-61
  as resources, 359
  size of data, value of, 102
  spilling, 50, 320
  splitting, 59
  in static single assignment form, 152-153
  store_modifies(T) set, 147
  subroutines, expansion of, 145
  support procedures for, 104
  tags, 204
  transparent, computing of, 321
  undefined evaluation at Entry, 168
  undefined values, 194-195
  use of, 298, 327, 339, 350
  use points, 132
  uses of, 165, 174-176

value_number(temporary) data structure, 142
values of variables, 96
variable, 105, 110
Temporaries, evaluations of
  elimination (deletion) of, 263-269, 276 (*See also* INSERT/DELETE transformation)
Temporary tag field, 154
Then statement, 103
Through(L) attribute, 321-323
Top operation, 176
Top values, 141
Topological sort, 180-184, 224, 374
Torczon, L., 232
Trace attribute, 348
Traces, 56, 339-340, 343, 372-374
  anchor, 346, 348
  computing, algorithm for, 347-348
  criteria for choosing blocks in, 346
  definition, 337, 345
  disjoint, 346
  dominators, 346, 348-350
  interference graph nodes, 357
  resource information, precomputing of, 350-356
  scheduling backwards, 377
  size of, 346
  successors, 346, 349-350
Transformations. *See also* Phases
  decreasing references to memory, 35
  local, 137-146
  order of, 18-21
TRANSFORM_COPIES, 289
Translation process, 14, 24. *See also* Intermediate representation (IR)
TRANSP, 278. *See also* STORE_TRANSP
Tree. *See also* Abstract syntax tree
  dominator information, 72-73
  loop tree, 86-90, 317-318
  procedures, representation of, 94-95
Tree, walk of, 67
  bottom-up, 101
  to build flow graph, 101-102
  dominance frontier, computing, 76-77
  flow graph, structure of, 105-111
  register pressure, determination of, 317-318
Tree edges, 67-68, 70, 72
Tree-oriented algorithms, 95

True dependence, 241, 242, 358
Two-pass assembler, simulation of, 416-417

U

Ullman, J. D., 91
Unary operations, optimization based on, 143
Unconditional branches, 198, 220
    conditional branches replaced by, 190-192
    goto statement translated into, 111
Unconditional branching instructions, 104, 417-418
Unconditional jump instructions, 418
Undefined values, 194-197
Undirected graphs, 64, 66-67. *See also* Depth-first search
Union tags, 155, 156
UNION/FIND, 161, 179, 312-313, 314, 316, 352-355
Unroll. *See* Loop unrolling
Unroll and jam, 35-37, 246
Use command, 415
USE-DEF chains, 165
Uses(T) attribute, 176, 227

V

VALUE, 187-189
Value context, of flow graph tree, 101-102
Value numbering, 137-138, 140-142, 189-190
    global, 313-314
    modification, effect of, 157-158
    scheduling and, 372-373
Value propagation, 29
Value table, 372-374
Value-numbering algorithm, 193
Value_number(temporary) data structure, 142
Value_representative attribute, 223-230
Values
    bottom, 141
    concept of, 15
    constant, 18, 141
    differentiation, 21, 23
    expressions computing, 109-111
    latency, 337
    linked list of, 112
    nonconstant, 194
    in temporaries, tracing of, 137-139
    top, 141
    undefined, 168, 194-195
Value(T) attribute, 194-195
Value_table, 224-226, 230
Value_Walk procedure, 108-109, 110
Variable, address of, 96
Variable temporaries, 105, 110, 116-120, 147, 162
Variant(T) attribute, 205, 207
Varying value, 195-197
Vectorization techniques, 4

W

Waite, Bill, 421
Warren, H. S., 376
Wegman, M. N., 5
WHILE loop, 107-108, 247
Wolfe, M., 37, 232, 240
Work-list algorithms, 132
    dead-code elimination, 220-222
    dominance frontier, computing, 171-172
    flow graph simulation, 198-202
    global optimization, 252-253
    induction candidate temporaries, finding, 209-210
    LATERIN computation, 274-275
    Live, computation of, 174
    partial anticipatability, computation of, 129
    points-to set computation, 161
    strength reduction, 293
Wulf, William, 3, 419

Z

Zadeck, F. K., 5, 288